FAIR TRIAL

FAIR TRIAL

RICHARD B. MORRIS

Fourteen
Who Stood Accused
from ANNE HUTCHINSON
to ALGER HISS

1952
ALFRED · A · KNOPF
NEW YORK

L. C. CATALOG CARD NUMBER: 52–6423

THIS IS A BORZOI BOOK,
PUBLISHED BY ALFRED A. KNOPF, INC.

FIRST EDITION

TO

Harry J. Carman

A N D

Edward Mead Earle

CONTENTS

Introduction

The fourteen notable criminal cases reviewed in this book
span the history of American law from the founding of the
colonies to the age of the A-bomb. In six cases juries returned acquittal verdicts; in the remainder the accused were
convicted. I do not suggest that the verdicts were necessarily
wrong in any specific cases. The reader is invited, after reviewing the facts in each case, to answer for himself a crucial question: *Did the accused receive a fair trial?*

One cannot answer that question without keeping in mind
the radical revision Anglo-American concepts of fair trial
procedure have undergone since the trial of Anne Hutchinson in 1637. In the interval between the outbreak of the
American Revolution and the ratification of the Federal
Constitution it came to be recognized as a fundamental right
in the United States that no person be "deprived of life,
liberty, or property without due process of law." The es-
sence of due process is fair trial procedure. The Fifth and
Sixth Amendments to the Federal Constitution itemized
such trial safeguards as the presentment or indictment by a
grand jury in capital and other infamous crimes; the prohibition against double jeopardy and against compelling a
person in a criminal case to be a witness against himself;
the right to a speedy and public trial by an impartial jury
of the district wherein the crime shall have been committed;
the right of the accused to be informed of the nature and
cause of the accusation, to be confronted with the witnesses
against him, to have compulsory process for obtaining witnesses in his favor, and to have the assistance of counsel for
his defense. The Eighth Amendment prohibited excessive
bail and fines as well as the infliction of cruel and unusual
punishments.

By these later standards the accused in the early colonial

cases were not afforded fair trials. Virtually all of the safeguards now recognized as basic to the preservation of individual liberty were then violated. On the other hand,
trials conducted since 1789 have, in form if not in substance,
conformed more closely to modern notions of fair trial procedure. This means that the chances of an innocent person's
being acquitted when accused are immeasurably greater today than in Captain Kidd's generation. Nevertheless, the
safeguards written into the Federal and state constitutions
and the codes of criminal procedure offer no positive assurance in fact. All three of the twentieth-century trials treated
in this book expose glaring deficiencies in the conduct and
procedure of American criminal trials which have not been
eradicated.

In the first place, trials too often assume the character of
a sporting event or a circus performance. For this situation
the press, by its sensational and undisciplined coverage of
trials, must shoulder responsibility with the courts. The
Hall-Mills trial is a gruesome case in point. The courts have
been notoriously unsuccessful in eliminating from the courtroom outside pressures that preclude a dispassionate administration of justice. Trials for political offenses, labor
cases, and, in some regions of the country, criminal trials
where the defendant is a Negro are often conducted in an
emotional atmosphere. Take the shockingly unfair trial of
Leo Franks, for instance. In that case the clothes of the
murdered girl were handed to her mother to identify. The
witness screamed and burst into tears. Immediately almost
every man in the audience reached for his gun. After such
overt threats one could hardly expect a jury to consider the
evidence rationally.

There was a time when an indictment by a grand jury
and a trial by a petit jury were considered as safeguarding
the rights of the accused to a fair trial. That was the case
in the days of John Peter Zenger, when grand juries had a
lot more backbone than at the present day. Nowadays the
grand jury invariably acts as a rubber stamp for the prose-

cutor. Since it may, and often does, accuse a man of an atrocious crime upon the mere ex parte statements of malicious witnesses, it is doubtful if this archaic institution provides any substantial measure of protection against unfair prosecutions.

Much the same criticism might be made of the petit jury. That body began as a group who were both witnesses and triers and who based their verdict on *their own* information. By colonial times the jury had come to make its findings upon evidence supplied by *others*, the jurors having ceased to be witnesses and having become judges of the facts. Long before the colonial period ended, jurors could no longer be subjected to severe penalties for bringing in a verdict contrary to the evidence. This transition dates the supremacy of the jury in criminal trials. It was now necessary to protect the accused from these biased judges of fact. To this end, the right to challenge jurors was introduced, along with improved methods of impaneling the jury. In the course of time prospective jurors were subjected to tedious and prolix examinations. Weeks of brawling came to be devoted to the selection of a jury. The trials of Aaron Burr and the Haymarket prisoners are notorious examples. In America this vexatious system remains substantially unreformed while the British have moved ahead of us. In Great Britain the judge fills the box, and the attorneys are silent spectators. Juries are often chosen inside half an hour. We might well take a leaf from English practice.

Regardless of the method of selection, it is doubtful if any system can be humanly devised which will assure a jury free of deep-seated prejudices and possessed of that measure of emotional stability and intellectual discipline essential for a rational and critical examination of the evidence. Once hailed as a palladium of personal liberty, the jury is now feared as an irresponsible group who give no reasons for their verdict. Significantly, in those states where waiver of jury trial is permitted, the accused eagerly grasp at the opportunity of not being tried by their peers.

The development and perpetuation of archaic rules of evidence are defended on the ground that jurors are admittedly incompetent. But these rules often obstruct the quest for truth. Only after the most involved and tortuous legal moves was the defense in the Dan Sickles case permitted to bring out facts absolutely vital to its side. Unreasonable restrictions are still imposed on opinion testimony and on hearsay evidence. The examination of witnesses leaves much to be desired. Too often witnesses are forced to make categorical answers and not permitted to qualify their replies. Too often do witnesses find themselves unshielded against gratuitous insults. In anticipation of the dreadful prospect of being subjected to the ordeal of cross-examination, most of us, like Mr. Winkle after his encounter with Serjeant Buzfuz, would rush with delirious haste to the George and Vulture and order something a good deal more potent than soda water. The partisan character of expert testimony constitutes one of the most glaring deficiencies of present trial procedure. The Carlyle Harris case is a classic illustration. As a result, juries invariably regard the experts as paid perjurers for the side that called them to the stand. To rid such testimony of the ring of partisanship and to give it a more objective character, it has been proposed that the court be permitted to bring in its own testimonial experts. Where the veracity of a witness is crucial, as in the trial of Alger Hiss, it is proposed that the court should be empowered to appoint its own psychologists or psychiatrists to testify to the mental state of the witness and his propensity to pathological lying, for example. Admittedly, the functions of a veracity expert would overlap those long assigned to the jury; but the jury still would have the power to reject such opinion testimony.

No aspect of American trial procedure is subject to more flagrant abuse than the practice of finessing or deceiving one's adversary. In Great Britain the prosecutor must disclose to the accused before trial all the evidence he intends to offer. Only in this way can the accused be given a reasonable opportunity to prepare his defense and to guard against surprise witnesses sprung by way of rebuttal at the very closing moments of a trial. The failure to institute this reform in American trial practice imperils the innocently accused. At the time of Bacon's Rebellion in Virginia in 1676, Edward Bland, on trial for treason, pleaded that a pardon sent over from England was at that moment lodged in the Governor's pocket. The trial commissioner ruled "that he pleaded his pardon at sword's point," and he was condemned and executed. Even at this late date we experience a sense of shock at the unfairness of the government in withholding the French pass that Captain Kidd sought to introduce as evidence to clear himself of the charge of piracy. Unfortunately, along with the unfair use of surprise testimony, prosecutors even today see nothing unethical in concealing evidence that might be helpful to the accused.

Some critics of our present trial procedure feel that its deficiencies resulted from the so-called judicial reforms associated with Jacksonian democracy. During that period many states, bowing to widespread animus against the bench and bar, stripped the trial judge of the right to put questions to a witness even where it might be necessary to bring out the truth and denied him the right to sum up evidence or in his charge to comment on the testimony of witnesses. Were we to abandon the notion that the judge is a tongue-tied moderator and restore to him his old common-law powers, it is argued, many of the unfair elements in present trial practice would be rectified. Others find that the judge even at the present day holds too exalted a position and regard the "cult of the robe" as impairing sensible trial procedure. Experience scarcely justifies such an opinion. The American judge is likely to be a conventional man, sharing the conventional prejudices of his community, his independence of judgment curbed by his necessity of seeking election. Generally underpaid, the bench in America, with certain conspicuous exceptions, does not attract the most distinguished members of the bar. Again the contrast with

England is lamentable. To substitute the prejudice of a judge for the prejudices of a jury may in fact result in little gain in the quest for fair and efficient trial procedure.

The bullying conduct of Sir Edward Ward in the Kidd case or of De Lancey at the Zenger trial would not for a moment be tolerated today. There are sufficient lawyers of backbone to stand up to such characters. Judge Roy Bean, one of the old frontier justices, used to charge in cattle-rustling cases: "The jury will now deliberate, and if it brings a verdict short of hangin' it'll be declared in contempt. Gentlemen, is yore verdict ready?" Judges seldom behave with that candor any more. But the printed record on appeal fails utterly to disclose the tone of the voice or the stage effects of a judge's charge or his manner toward the witnesses of the side he dislikes. One could deal today with Judge Bean, but the insidious bias of present-day trial judges is most difficult to bring out into the open. As long as judges may openly justify their rulings on plausible grounds while secretly resolving to help one side, the paper safeguards of a fair trial may be rendered completely ineffectual.

Sensitive as we should continue to be to any infringement of the rights of the accused, we must always keep in mind that in a criminal trial the people, too, have their rights. Highly formal and technical rules should not be permitted to defeat the ends of justice. As Benjamin N. Cardozo so eloquently expressed it, "justice, though due to the accused, is due to the accuser also. The concept of fairness must not be strained till it is narrowed to a filament. *We are to keep the balance true.*"

While some appellate courts have been noteworthy in guarding against prejudicial error, others have been accused of lacking in vigilance in enforcing proper trial procedure. Trial judges who fail to keep that true balance between the opposing interests are too often not held to strict accountability. Substantial improprieties in conduct on the part of prosecutor and defense counsel remain unredressed. Openings and summations are customarily charged with emotive words. The accused, contrary to established rulings, is habitually stigmatized as a "cold-blooded murderer" or a "traitor," and loose and libelous epithets are freely bandied about. As recently as May 1947 a group of taxi-drivers were tried in Greenville, South Carolina, for the lynching and mutilation of a young Negro named Willie Earle. Making the customary regional obeisance to the bloody shirt, the defense attorney went on to observe: "Willie Earle is dead, and I wish more like him were dead. . . . You might shoot a mad dog and be prosecuted, but if a mad dog were loose in my community I'd shoot the dog and let them prosecute me." This extract is not an unrepresentative sampling of the intellectual level to which summations have descended in present-day criminal trials.

Forensic utterance today contrasts strikingly with that of the era of William Wirt and Daniel Webster. Those days of great rhetorical efforts have gone forever. The conversational style of public address attributed to Wendell Phillips now prevails in the courtroom. Where that leads to a more efficient administration of justice the change is to be applauded; but too often informality has become synonymous with carelessness, with indifference to language, to manners, and to the facts in the case. Perhaps the fault lies as much with the times as with the men. But it is scarcely a matter of dispute that the quality of the criminal bar has in fact seriously deteriorated in recent generations.

In the belief that the right to a fair trial is the keystone of our system of personal liberties, these fourteen cases are submitted to the rigorous scrutiny of the reader. The summations are now completed, the judge has given his charge, and the jury has the case. As Brutus asks the crowd when Cæsar's body is brought in:

> *I do entreat you, not a man depart,*
> *Save I alone, till Antony have spoke.*

RICHARD B. MORRIS

FAIR TRIAL

I

Jezebel before the Judges
Anne Hutchinson tried for sedition

It could have been today instead of 1637. Allowing for differences in political climate, the sedition trial of Anne Hutchinson before her judges at Cambridge could have been staged at Foley Square, New York, any time during the last few years. But Anne Hutchinson would have had a different sort of trial. The accused would still have no guarantee that her judges would judge her dispassionately, or that the jury would be uninfluenced by the inflammatory outpourings of the press. She could still not be certain that her prosecutor would not seek political advantage from her conviction. Nonetheless, she would be shielded against prejudice and hysteria to a degree unknown among the Puritan theocrats. She would be presumed innocent up to the moment when by the unanimous verdict of a trial jury she might be convicted on evidence establishing her guilt beyond a reasonable doubt. The bulwarks constructed over the course of the past three hundred years for the protection of the innocently accused would safeguard her rights.

By our standards, Anne Hutchinson did not get a fair trial in 1637. She might today.

During times of acute political tension orthodoxy becomes a test of loyalty. People who have heterodox ideas and try to do something about them find themselves in jeopardy. People like Anne Hutchinson. It is then that the courts rouse themselves to determine the point at which ideas translated into action become an imminent danger to the state. In totalitarian states people who openly attack the leaders and foment a political opposition are liquidated out of hand or accorded the kind of trial designed to serve as a sounding-board for the state's propaganda machine.

Anne Hutchinson's trial much more closely resembled a typical political trial conducted behind the iron curtain than the sort of judicial proceeding we now have a right to expect in our own country.

To understand why Anne Hutchinson became the greatest political issue in the history of early Massachusetts, we must find out how this emigrant to the New World was able to win so many followers to her camp in so brief a time. That she was a woman of rare intelligence, superabundant physical energy, and great personal magnetism even her enemies grudgingly conceded. From her father, who had been imprisoned for rebellion against church laxity, she had inherited a stubborn pride and an integrity of mind. A strong streak of mysticism, which colored both her personality and her views, explained her unbridled enthusiasms. In the mother country she had come under the spell of the learned John Cotton, who preached at the fashionable St. Botolph's Church at Boston, in Lincolnshire. Renowned as one who "loved to sweeten his mouth with a piece of Calvin before he went to sleep," Cotton was conspicuous among the Cambridge-trained Puritans for his scholarship and eloquence. Like other leading Puritans of his day he had dedicated himself to the task of cutting out what they termed the gangrene of impure doctrine from the body of the Church of England. He would have dropped many of the doctrines and practices the church had taken over from Roman Catholicism. But the English ecclesiastical authorities deemed Cotton's theological surgery to border on malpractice. Denounced to the Court of High Commission in 1632, Cotton fled to Massachusetts, that haven for discontented religious rebels.

Cotton's most devoted follower was disconsolate at his going. Before long a revelation from Isaiah came to Anne Hutchinson: "Thine eyes shall see thy teachers." She interpreted this as an order to leave her comfortable world and share the fate of her pastor in that little Utopian commonwealth which was being builded on the shores of New Eng-

land. At the time of her exodus she had been married twenty
years and had a sizable family. Her husband, William, was
characterized by Winthrop, her enemy, as "a man of very
mild temper and weak parts, and wholly guided by his
wife." He seems to have followed unquestioningly the leadership of his spouse, whom he cherished as "a dear saint
servant and of God."

Anne and her family settled in Boston, a tight little frontier town of a thousand souls. But if she expected peace she
was soon disabused, for the populace was jittery and suspicious. And with good reason. They were well aware that
enemies from without the colony, seeking to annul the
charter, seemed to be on the verge of success. Horror stories
filtering in from outlying settlements told how the savage
Pequots were scalping saints and sinners indiscriminately.
Despite the expulsion from the colony, some years before,
of that unreconstructed pagan Thomas Morton of Merrymount, discordant elements were not discouraged from settling. Take the learned Roger Williams, for example. From
his pulpit at Salem he "divulged new and dangerous opinions against the authorities of magistrates." Recognized in
our day as a liberal and a democrat, Williams's contem-
poraries were wont to think of him as a "wild Ishmael, his
hand against every man." In 1636, in the dead of winter,
Williams was expelled and forced to make his way through
the wilderness to Rhode Island.

Scarcely had the colony had time to recover from the
Williams affair when a far greater peril threatened its internal security. Anne Hutchinson was too active a mind to
sit back and succumb to the ordinary routine of household
drudgery. She began to have meetings in her front parlor,
to which the women of Boston flocked. Starting out with
discussions of child care and nursing problems, she soon
moved into the realm of theology, where she was tempera-
mentally most at home. Now, one would hardly expect a
bluestocking in Boston to be looked upon with favor in
those pioneer days. John Winthrop, a founding father,

summed up the feeling of the more conventional when he observed that this "godly young woman of special parts" had gone astray "by occasion of her giving herself wholly to reading and writing." Had she "attended her household affairs and such things as belong to women, and not gone out of her way and calling to meddle in such things as are proper for men, whose minds are stronger," that antifeminist magistrate continued, "she had kept her wits and might have improved them usefully and honorably in the place God had sent her." But Winthrop never succumbed to Anne's charm.

People soon crowded into her meetings to hear her capsule version of the long Sabbath sermons, which seldom escaped the sharp barbs of her wit. Save for her hero, John Cotton, the ministers failed to rise to the impeccable standard she set. She was particularly scathing in her criticism of the Reverend Mr. Wilson, pastor of the First Church of Boston, who shared that congregation with John Cotton, its teacher. When Wilson rose to preach, Mistress Hutchinson walked out of the meetinghouse, and other members of the congregation contemptuously turned their backs on him. From sneering silence the congregation soon turned to open defiance. In every meetinghouse the pastors were shocked to find their interpretations openly challenged. The Reverend Thomas Weld complained: "Now, after our sermons were ended at our public lectures you might have seen half a dozen pistols discharged at the face of the preacher," so numerous were the objections "made by the opinionists in the open assembly against our doctrine delivered. Now the faithful ministers of Christ must have dung cast on their faces," he continued in Biblical vein, "and be no better than legal preachers, Baal's priests, Popish factors, Scribes, Pharisees, and opposers of Christ himself!"

Meantime Mistress Hutchinson's following grew. "It was strange to see how the common people were led" to condemn the Reverend Mr. Wilson, Winthrop caustically commented, for matters that "divers of them did not understand." Another hostile critic, Edward Johnson, satirized in his *Won-der-Working Providence* the spell she cast over her admirers. "Come along with me," one of them is quoted as declaring, "and I'll bring you to a woman who preaches better Gospel than any of your blackcoats that have been at the Ninnyversity. I had rather hear such a one that speaks from a mere motion of the spirit, without any study at all, than any of your learned scholars, although they may be fuller of the Scripture." But to the thrill-starved females of Boston no one was "fuller of the Scripture" than Anne Hutchinson, and so they continued to drink at her spiritual fountain, with the result, according to Winthrop, that "many families were neglected and much time lost."

But Anne Hutchinson was not only spreading disrespect for the clergy. She was fashioning theological views that bordered close on heresy. "It was not long," Cotton Mather tells us, "before 'twas found that most of the errors then crawling like vipers about the country were hatched at these meetings" held at the home of this "virago." The Boston ministers, Cotton excepted, not only were lacking in ability, Anne charged, but labored under a "covenant of works." They were formalists, sticking to the letter of the Mosaic law and neglecting its spirit, "a company of legal professors" who "lie poring on the law which Christ hath abolished." As a result of this preoccupation with the written word, she contended, they misled the people about the most important of all issues—salvation. Sound Calvinist doctrine held that the Lord's elect alone could be saved from everlasting damnation, and in no other way than through the covenant of grace, manifested by the spirit of the Lord within them. Giving this doctrine an extremely literal interpretation, Anne Hutchinson insisted that the indwelling of the Lord's spirit was evidenced by a serenity of soul. To obtain so blissful a state, mere pietism, fasting, prayers, and outward religious observance would not suffice. In fact, even a minister of the gospel might not possess such a heaven-directed heart, and, if he did not, would be damned. The effect of her views was to subordinate the role of the formal church and to dramatize the part the individual played in his own salvation.

These were fighting words. If unopposed, they would have undermined the theocracy based upon the prestige of the ministry. How seriously Anne's followers took her charges was dramatically demonstrated at this time when the men of Boston refused to go off to the Pequot War because their chaplain, the Reverend John Wilson, was under a "covenant of works." The targets of Anne's criticism came to feel that she was hatching a dangerous heresy, known in Europe as Antinomianism and associated with the disciples of Johannes Agricola, a German tailor. Some feared that her views would bring about a reign of terror such as swept Münster when the demagogic Anabaptist John of Leyden seized the reins of power. To the conservative theocrats her doctrines were not only heretical but actually subversive.

Had Mistress Hutchinson's orbit been restricted to women, the perils probably could have been minimized. In those days women could not vote nor hold office, nor did they directly share in formulating church policy. But the spell she cast brought many members of the opposite sex under her intellectual sway, and among them some of the colony's most notable personages. Only a short time before, young Sir Harry Vane, whose father had been a privy councilor, had found it expedient to migrate to Boston because of his defiance of the church authorities. Almost immediately upon arrival he was elected Governor. Vane soon became one of Anne Hutchinson's most ardent supporters. Twenty years her junior, Sir Harry was a quick captive to her charm and learning. Ugly rumors, for which there is not the slightest supporting evidence, were spread concerning this friendship. Some thirty years later, and five years after Vane had paid with his head because Charles II considered him "too dangerous a man to let live, if we can honestly put him out of the way," the Secretary of State recorded in his official papers the canard "from Major Scott's mouth" to the effect that "Sir Harry Vane in 1637 went over as Governor to New England with two women, Mrs. Dyer and Mrs. Hutchinson, and he debauched both, and both were delivered of monsters." This political calumny is wrong in every detail except for the curious references to the miscarriages suffered during the days of their persecution by Anne and the handsome Mary Dyer, her devoted follower (later martyred as a Quaker). While even the Cavalier historian Clarendon grudgingly admitted that the "unbeautiful" Vane made "men think there was somewhat in him of extraordinary," John Winthrop soon had good reason to feel toward him much as Cromwell did at a later day when he prayed "that the Lord would deliver him from Sir Harry Vane!"

Anne's spell over the opposite sex brought her the firm allegiance of her brother-in-law, the Reverend John Wheelwright, who had come over from England in the late spring of 1636. She schemed to have Wheelright selected as a third pastor of the First Church of Boston, alongside Wilson and Cotton, but Winthrop rudely scotched the proposal. Instead Wheelwright was invited to Mount Wollaston, the site where Morton's house stood before the incensed Puritans burned it to the ground. This snub was not soon forgotten by the Hutchinsonians. On January 20, 1637, a fast day set aside because of "the dissensions in our churches," Wheelwright delivered a forthright sermon in Boston which was calculated to destroy any possibility of conciliation. Pulling no punches, he excoriated those who made broad their phylacteries, enlarged the borders of their garments, loved the chief seats in the synagogues, and wanted to be called of men "Rabbi, Rabbi." His allusions were too obvious to be lost on his critics.

The authorities now felt that any further delay would be fatal. In March the General Court brought Wheelwright to trial for sedition and contempt. The opposing forces, led by Vane and Winthrop, were evenly balanced, but the clergy tipped the scales against the prisoner, who was duly convicted. Still clinging to the hope that the opposition might be pacified, the court postponed sentencing Wheelwright.

With Boston hotly pro-Wheelwright and pro-Hutchinson, the conservatives realized that in any election conducted in the capital they could never unseat Vane and his following. A motion was carried at the General Court to hold the next meeting of that body at Cambridge, then called Newtowne, a small community far less infected with the Hutchinsonian virus. The main business of that court was to be the election of the governor and magistrates. While the voters were now permitted to vote for their candidates by proxy, all parliamentary questions were decided by a viva voce vote of those present. This placed at a considerable disadvantage busy Bostonians who could not attend in person. Winthrop and Vane were the opposing candidates on election day, May 27, 1637. "There was great danger of a tumult that day," reported Winthrop, "and some laid hands on others." At the height of the fracas the Reverend Mr. Wilson, stout and fiftyish, clambered up a spreading oak and, in what was literally the first stump speech in American history, vehemently harangued the crowd to vote for Winthrop. Vane and his entire slate went down to defeat. Winthrop won the governorship, Dudley was elected Deputy Governor, and Endecott, a lion among the anti-Hutchinsonians, was chosen an assistant for life. In a rebellion against the new leadership, the town of Boston sent Vane, Coddington, and Hough to sit in the General Court as deputies.

One of the very first acts of the newly constituted General Court was the passage of an immigration law that imposed heavy penalties on strangers harbored without permission of the magistrates. At the time the law was passed it was known that a party of Anne Hutchinson's followers were on their way from England. This inhospitable measure, a flagrant violation of the charter, was scathingly attacked by Vane, and the arguments waxed hot and heavy in the early summer months. Finally, exasperated at the futility of further resistance, Vane sailed for England in August. At

a political demonstration by the Hutchinsonians, Vane
made a forthright plea for religious toleration and expressed
the hope that "Ishmael shall dwell in the presence of his
brethren."

But the expulsion of Wheelwright and the departure of
Vane failed to stifle "the breeder and nourisher of all these
distempers." Moved by a burning fanaticism, the elders
were as determined as was the self-righteous Elijah to see
that dogs should eat the flesh of this forthright female and
that "the carcase of Jezebel shall be as dung upon the face
of the field." When Anne Hutchinson's partisans now
urged that the government had gone far enough in crushing
the opposition, they were told off in language such as Jehu
used to Joram. "What peace," that man of the Old Testament cried out, "so long as the whoredoms of thy mother
Jezebel and her witchcrafts are so many?"

The government party now had Anne Hutchinson arrested and brought to trial. Hers was a political trial and
must be judged by the standards of that day. Whether it
was the royal government trying Raleigh, or the Puritans
when in power bringing the royalists to justice, the political
trials of that era were partisan affairs that would outrage
our sense of fair play. Furthermore, it must be remembered
that in seventeenth-century England the rules of criminal
procedure and evidence were still in formation. In Massachusetts, a frontier colony less than a decade old, these rules
were still more elementary. Moreover, the Massachusetts
Puritans, never too cordial toward the technicalities of the
English common law, looked toward the Bible for instruction in criminal matters. Even John Cotton, considered a
Hutchinsonian at this time, had declared: "The more any
law smells of man the more unprofitable" it is. Such theo-
cratic views could be handy weapons for leaders engaged in
a fight to maintain their arbitrary power undiminished.

From the start of Anne Hutchinson's trial certain procedural safeguards were ignored which we now consider fundamental. The prisoner was brought to trial without indict-

ment or information, without being informed of the precise charges against her, and without even knowing what the penalty was. Since no lawyer was as yet practicing in the colony, the denial of counsel to the accused was less prejudicial in fact than it seemed on its face. But the denial of jury trial seems far more shocking. Only a year before, John Cotton had drafted a code of laws in which he did not provide for trial by jury because it was unknown in the Bible; but the authorities, regardless of their conservatism, felt this was going too far, and failed to adopt his draft. Within four years after the Hutchinson trial the colony's first written code of laws impliedly recognized jury trial and allowed the accused in criminal cases the right to elect to be tried by bench or jury.

In the absence of an indictment, the crime for which Anne Hutchinson was put on trial must be inferred from the remarks of her judges. From the record it is clear that she was tried for sedition and contempt. In a theocracy like Massachusetts, traducing the ministers constituted subversive behavior. Since only a short time before this trial the Court of King's Bench in England had declared the charter vacated, the Bay Colony rulers deemed a united front necessary to defend the commonwealth's independence. This objective, in their minds, justifiably transcended all issues of free speech and toleration. Hence, while the judges refrained from imposing the death penalty in this case, they would have felt perfectly justified in so doing. They kept this in mind when, in 1641, they adopted the Body of Liberties, the Bay Colony's first written code. Therein the death penalty was provided for any person who "shall treacherously or perfidiously attempt the alteration and subversion of our frame of polity or government fundamentally."

The scene of Anne Hutchinson's trial is now known as Cambridge. The trial was held in the meetinghouse, a rough-hewn board building, its crevices sealed with mud. Winter had descended unusually early that November. Ice was

piled up along the river's banks, and in the unheated meetinghouse the temperature was appropriately frigid, considering the work that had to be done. The governor and
magistrates occupied a table and chairs, while the deputies
sat on rude wooden benches.

By present-day standards of judicial propriety, John
Winthrop, who presided over the tribunal, should have disqualified himself, as he was the prisoner's bitterest foe
among the laity. Curiously, Winthrop was generally mag-
nanimous, but in the Hutchinson affair he assumed the dual
role of judge and prosecutor with unaccustomed relish.
While normally poised and dignified on other occasions, at
this time he treated the spectators to frequent unjudicial
outbursts of rancor and exasperation. Had Winthrop needed
a model for his behavior, he might well have chosen that
Puritan hero Sir Edward Coke, who went to untoward
lengths in badgering and reviling Sir Walter Raleigh when
that talented Elizabethan was tried for treason. The fact is
that Winthrop's conduct conformed to the accepted behavior of judges and prosecutors in English state trials. A
man who believed that democracy was "the meanest and
worst of all forms of government" and that the only liberty
which should be tolerated was that "exercised in a way of
subjection to authority" could be counted on to bring the
full power of the oligarchy to bear upon dissenters, whether
political or religious. "The eyes of all people are upon us,"
Winthrop had once counseled the settlers. "If we shall deal
falsely with our God in this work we have undertaken, we
shall be made a story and a byword through the world."
This was a major test, and Winthrop had no intention of
letting the Lord down.

Had Anne Hutchinson nurtured any hope of receiving
charitable treatment at the hands of her judges, it must
have been quickly dissipated when she saw Winthrop
flanked by his old political rival, Thomas Dudley, the
Deputy Governor, on one side, and by John Endecott on
the other. When Dudley died, some verses were found in his

pocket which revealed that his bigotry remained pure and uncorrupted.

> *Let me of God and churches watch*
> *O'er such as do a toleration hatch,*

the Deputy Governor warned, and for his epitaph chose: "I died no libertine." The grim-visaged Endecott appeared even more fanatical in his black skullcap. His tight mouth and massive jaw, only partly concealed by a gracefully pointed beard, were double assurance that these proceedings would be carried out to a suitable conclusion. The man who cut down Morton's maypole would never brook defiance of the Bible Commonwealth.

Before her judges stood the prisoner, a woman in her late forties, bereft of counsel, as was the fashion of the time. Although she was in an advanced state of pregnancy, she was forced to remain standing. Only when "her countenance discovered some bodily infirmity" was she finally permitted to sit down.

WINTHROP: Mrs. Hutchinson, you are called here as one of those that have troubled the peace of the commonwealth and the churches here; you are known to be a woman that hath had a great share in the promoting and divulging of those opinions that are causes of this trouble, and to be nearly joined not only in affinity and affection with some of those the court had taken notice of and passed censure upon, but you have spoken divers things as we have been informed very prejudicial to the honor of the churches and ministers thereof, and you have maintained a meeting and an assembly in your house that hath been condemned by the general assembly as a thing not tolerable nor comely in the sight of God nor fitting for your sex, and notwithstanding that was cried down you have continued the same. Therefore, we have thought good to send for you to understand how things are, that if you be in an erroneous way we may reduce you so you may become a profitable member here among us; otherwise, if you be obstinate in your course, then the court may take such course that you may trouble us no further. Therefore, I would intreat you to express whether you do not assent and hold in practice to those opinions and factions that have been handled in court already, that is to say, whether you do not justify Mr. Wheelwright's sermon and the petition.

MRS. HUTCHINSON: I am called here to answer before you but I hear no things laid to my charge.

WINTHROP: I have told you some already and more I can tell you.

MRS. H.: Name one, Sir.

WINTHROP: Have I not named some already?

MRS. H.: What have I said or done?

WINTHROP: Why for your doings, this you did harbor and countenance those that are parties in this faction that you have heard of.

MRS. H.: That's matter of conscience, Sir.

WINTHROP: Your conscience you must keep or it must be kept for you.

MRS. H.: Must not I then entertain the saints because I must keep my conscience?

WINTHROP: Say that one brother should commit felony or treason and come to his brother's house. If he knows him guilty and conceals him, he is guilty of the same. It is his conscience to entertain him, but if his conscience comes into act in giving countenance and entertainment to him that hath broken the law he is guilty too. So if you do countenance those that are transgressors of the law you are in the same fact.

MRS. H.: What law do they transgress?

WINTHROP: The law of God and of the state.

MRS. H.: In what particular?

WINTHROP: Why in this among the rest, whereas the Lord doth say, "Honor thy father and thy mother."

MRS. H.: Aye, Sir, in the Lord.

WINTHROP: This honor you have broke in giving countenance to them.

MRS. H.: In entertaining those did I entertain them

against any act (for here is the thing) or what God hath appointed?

WINTHROP: You knew that Mr. Wheelwright did preach this sermon and those that countenance him in this do break a law.

MRS. H.: What law have I broken?

WINTHROP: Why the fifth commandment.

MRS. H.: I deny that, for he saith in the Lord.

WINTHROP: You have joined with them in the faction.

MRS. H.: In what faction have I joined with them?

WINTHROP: In presenting the petition.

MRS. H.: Suppose I had set my hand to the petition, what then?

WINTHROP: You saw that case tried before.

MRS. H.: But I had not my hand to the petition.

WINTHROP: You have counseled them.

MRS. H.: Wherein?

WINTHROP: Why in entertaining them.

MRS. H.: What breach of law is that, Sir?

WINTHROP: Why dishonoring of parents.

MRS. H.: But put the case, Sir, that I do fear the Lord and my parents, may I not entertain them that fear the Lord because my parents will not give me leave?

WINTHROP: If they be the fathers of the commonwealth, and they of another religion, if you entertain them then you dishonor your parents and are justly punishable.

MRS. H.: If I entertain them, as they have dishonored their parents, I do.

WINTHROP: No, but you by countenancing them above others put honor upon them.

MRS. H.: I may put honor upon them as the children of God and as they do honor the Lord.

WINTHROP: We do not mean to discourse with those of your sex but only this; you do adhere unto them and do endeavor to set forward this faction and so you do dishonor us.

MRS. H.: I do acknowledge no such thing. Neither do I think that I ever put any dishonor upon you.

WINTHROP: Why do you keep such a meeting at your house as you do every week upon a set day?

MRS. H.: It is lawful for me so to do, as it is all your practices, and can you find a warrant for yourself and condemn me for the same thing?

WINTHROP: There was no meeting of women alone, but your meeting is of another sort for there are sometimes men among you.

MRS. H.: There was never any man with us.

WINTHROP: Well, admit there was no man at your meeting and that you was sorry for it, there is no warrant for your doings, and by what warrant do you continue such a course?

MRS. H.: I conceive there lies a clear rule in Titus, that the elder women should instruct the younger, and then I must have a time wherein I must do it.

WINTHROP: All this I grant you, I grant you a time for it, but what is this to the purpose that you, Mrs. Hutchinson, must call a company together from their callings to come to be taught of you?

MRS. H.: Will it please you to answer me this and to give me a rule for them I will willingly submit to any truth. If any come to my house to be instructed in the ways of God what rule have I to put them away?

WINTHROP: But suppose that a hundred men come unto you to be instructed will you forbear to instruct them?

MRS. H.: As far as I conceive I cross a rule in it.

WINTHROP: Very well and do you not so here?

MRS. H.: No, Sir, for my ground is they are men.

WINTHROP: Men and women, all is one for that, but suppose that a man should come and say, "Mrs. Hutchinson, I hear that you are a woman that God hath given his grace unto and you have knowledge in the word of God. I pray instruct me a little." Ought you not to instruct this man?

MRS. H.: I think I may.—Do you think it not lawful

for me to teach women and why do you call me to teach the court?

WINTHROP: We do not call you to teach the court but to lay open yourself.

MRS. H.: I desire you that you would then set me down a rule by which I may put them away that come unto me and so have peace in so doing.

WINTHROP: We are your judges and not you ours, and we must compel you to it.

MRS. H.: If it please you by authority to put it down, I will freely let you, for I am subject to your authority.

Winthrop's unjudicial counterblast would have exploded more appropriately from the parapets of the Court of High Commission, at that very time engaged in stifling the Puritan clergy at home. The Governor up to this point had come off a poor second in his duel with an expert intellectual fencer. Dudley felt called upon to take up the attack.

DUDLEY: I would go a little higher with Mrs. Hutchinson. About three years ago we were all in peace. Mrs. Hutchinson from that time she came hath made a disturbance, and some that came over with her in the ship did inform me what she was as soon as she was landed. Now it appears by this woman's meeting that Mrs. Hutchinson hath so forestalled the minds of many by their resort to her meeting that now she hath a potent party in the country. Now, if she in particular hath disparaged all our ministers in the land that they have preached a covenant of works, and only Mr. Cotton a covenant of grace, why this is not to be suffered.

MRS. H.: I pray, Sir, prove it that I said they preached nothing but a covenant of works.

DUDLEY: Nothing but a covenant of works, why a Jesuit may preach truth sometimes!

MRS. H.: Did I ever say they preached a covenant of works then?

DUDLEY: If they do not preach a covenant of grace clearly, then they preach a covenant of works.

MRS. H.: No, Sir, one may preach a covenant of grace more clearly than another, so I said.

MR. ENDECOTT: I desire to speak, seeing Mrs. Hutchinson seems to lay something against them that are to witness against her.

WINTHROP: Only I would add this. It is well discerned to the court that Mrs. Hutchinson can tell when to speak and when to hold her tongue.

MRS. H.: It is one thing for me to come before a public magistracy and there to speak what they would have me to speak and another when a man comes to me in a way of friendship privately. There is difference in that.

Mistress Hutchinson had now worked herself up to a pitch of righteous anger. In the words of one observer, "she vented her impatience with so fierce speech and countenance, as one would hardly have guessed her to have been an antitype of Daniel, but rather of the lions, after they were loose." The clergy who were there in force to bear witness against Anne could scarcely conceal their dismay at the way the trial was going. The fanatical Reverend Hugh Peters, who had come from Salem to further the prosecution, now broke in, declaring: "That which concerns us to speak unto you, as yet we are sparing in, unless the court command us to speak, then we shall answer to Mrs. Hutchinson, notwithstanding our brethren are very unwilling to answer." The situation was embarrassing, but Winthrop's casuistry reassured him. "This speech was not spoken in a corner but in a public assembly, and though things were spoken in private yet now coming to us, we are to deal as public."

Without further coaxing, Peters proceeded to relate how the prisoner had charged the ministry with teaching a covenant of works, going so far as to maintain that there "was a broad difference between our brother Mr. Cotton and ourselves."

"What difference do you conceive to be between your teacher and us?" Peters had insistently demanded. Cotton, she informed the elders, "preaches the covenant of grace and you the covenant of works."

Then the Reverend Mr. Wilson, who, of all the ministers, bore the greatest grudge against Anne Hutchinson, proceeded to corroborate Peters. One after another, Thomas Weld and John Eliot of Roxbury, George Phillips of Watertown, and Zechariah Symmes of Charlestown—all as unrelenting in their hostility as Peters and Wilson—rose in their turn to back up Peters's accusations. Even the gentle Thomas Shepard, minister of Cambridge, while extremely "loath to speak in this assembly concerning this gentlewoman in question," felt impelled to assert what "my conscience speaks unto me." But he added that perhaps her heretical remarks were "but a slip of her tongue." "I hope she will be sorry for it, and then we shall be glad of it."

Dusk had descended upon the meetinghouse. But the magistrates were unwilling to adjourn on the charitable note that Shepard had struck. Summing up the day's evidence against the prisoner, the Deputy Governor turned to Anne Hutchinson and declared:

DUDLEY: I called these witnesses and you deny them. You see they have proved this and you deny this, but it is clear. You said they preached a covenant of works and that they were not able ministers of the New Testament. Now there are two other things that you did affirm which were that the Scriptures in the letter of them held forth nothing but a covenant of works and likewise that those that were under a covenant of works cannot be saved.

MRS. H.: Prove that I said so.

WINTHROP: Did you say so?

MRS. H.: No, Sir, it is your conclusion.

. . .

The wrangling was at last interrupted by the lateness of the hour. "Mrs. Hutchinson," Winthrop declared, his patience fast ebbing, "the court you see hath labored to bring you to acknowledge the error of your way that so you might be reduced. The time now grows late. We shall therefore give you a little more time to consider of it and therefore desire that you attend the court again in the morning."

The first day had gone very well for the prisoner. She had outfenced the magistrates in a battle of wits and forced the ministers into the unchristianlike stand of having publicly revealed a private and confidential conversation. Had she had the benefit of counsel learned in the law, a nice legal question might have been raised in her behalf. Although the common-law decisions of the period were indecisive, a clever lawyer might have made a good case for the position that in English law confessions to ecclesiastics were privileged communications. Of course, Mistress Hutchinson's statements to the ministers had been more in the nature of a confidential communication than a confession according to church law, and in view of the temper of the bench it is obvious that her objection would most certainly have been dismissed on technical grounds, if no others were ready to hand. But on the moral issue Mistress Hutchinson had come off with flying colors.

The Boston bluestocking's resourcefulness had not yet been fully tested. Hardly had Winthrop convened the court the next morning when Mistress Hutchinson dropped a bombshell. During the night, she declared, she had looked over certain notes of the conference that had been taken by the Reverend Mr. Wilson. This was Vane's copy, which that disappointed young statesman had turned over to his friend before sailing for home. "I find things not to be as hath been alleged," she charged. As "the ministers came in their own cause," they should be forced to take an oath. While Winthrop insisted that since this was not a jury trial the court had full discretion in the matter of the oaths of witnesses, Bradstreet piously implored Mistress Hutchinson that, had the ministers been in error in reporting her remarks, "you would make them to sin if you urge them to swear." But the prisoner was unmoved by this plea, and many members of the court supported her.

"An oath, sir," she exclaimed to Stoughton, "is an end of all strife, and it is God's ordinance."

Sneeringly Endecott broke in: "You lifted up your eyes as if you took God to witness you came to entrap none—and yet you will have them swear!"

A hurried conference took place on the bench. Finally, in a face-saving concession, Winthrop ruled: "I see no necessity of an oath in this thing, seeing it is true and the substance of the matter confirmed by divers, yet that all may be satisfied, if the elders will take an oath they shall have it given them." Even now the court hesitated to humiliate the ministers by refusing to admit their unsworn word. "Mark what a flourish Mrs. Hutchinson puts upon the business that she had witnesses to disprove what was said, and here is no man to bear witness," the Deputy Governor broke in sarcastically.

She replied with dignity: "If you will not call them in that is nothing to me."

Before that issue was finally disposed of, three defense witnesses were heard—Coggeshall, Leverett, and the Reverend John Cotton. Coggeshall, a Boston deputy, had, only a moment before, annoyed the magistrates by requesting that the ministers consult with Cotton on the propriety of their taking such an oath and had earned Endecott's sharp rebuke. "I think that this carriage of yours tends to further casting dirt upon the face of the judges." Another magistrate, Roger Harlakenden, had then exclaimed: "Her carriage doth the same!"

As a witness for the defense Coggeshall was roughly handled. Winthrop pointed out that "Mr. Coggeshall was not present" at the conference.

"Yes, but I was," Coggeshall insisted, "only I desired to be silent till I should be called."

"Will you, Mr. Coggeshall, say that she did not say so?"
the Governor asked.

"Yes," was the categorical reply. "I dare say that she did
not say all that which lay against her."

Coggeshall's contradiction of the ministers' unsworn version of the conference so infuriated the Reverend Mr. Peters
that he shouted at the witness: "How dare you look into the
court and say such a word?"

Coggeshall folded up like a spent bellows. "Mr. Peters
takes upon him to forbid me. I shall be silent."

The magistrates and divines now primed their muskets for
the next defense witness. Leverett, a ruling elder in the Boston church, asserted that Mistress Hutchinson charged the
ministers with failing to preach a covenant of grace with
Cotton's clarity. But his remarks compounded the confusion.

Both sides now readied themselves for the defense's star
witness, the Reverend John Cotton, who in a way was as
much on trial as the prisoner. In answer to Winthrop's summons he rose from a seat beside the prisoner. As he proceeded to give his own version of the conference, he must
have seemed to the spectators like a tightrope walker crossing a yawning chasm on a swaying wire—a thrill which, like
the theater, their Puritan piety forbade them from enjoying. A forthright refutation of the ministers' accusation
would have earned him the lasting enmity of his envious
and less gifted colleagues. But should he repudiate Mistress
Hutchinson's touching advocacy and devotion, he would destroy his reputation for loyalty and integrity. The course he
pursued was a blend of courage and tact.

In recalling the disputed passages between Mistress
Hutchinson and the pastors, Cotton admitted that he was
exceedingly uncomfortable that "any comparison should be
between me and my brethren." When pressed to describe the
differences as the prisoner had analyzed them, he testified
that she had pointed out that he "preaches the seal of the
spirit upon free grace and you upon a work." These points,
to Cotton's way of thinking, did not seem "so ill taken" as

they are now represented. "I must say," he added, "that I did not find her saying they were under a covenant of works, nor that she said they did preach a covenant of works."

As to the issue of their competence, the Deputy Governor asked the witness: "They affirm that Mrs. Hutchinson did say they were not able ministers of the New Testament."

"I do not remember it," Cotton replied.

The learned divine's soft answers and his conciliatory but firm testimony added up to a serious modification of the black-and-white version of the conference insisted on by the elders. Everyone present felt that a turning-point had been reached at the trial. Had the defense now rested, the Governer and his supporters would have been in an extremely awkward position.

But Mistress Hutchinson's impulsiveness was to take a great load off the consciences of the magistrates. Like other women before her, she insisted on having the last word, and her rashness proved a fatal error. When Cotton took his seat, she asked the court for "leave" to "give you the ground of what I know to be true." Recklessly she plunged ahead. "The Lord knows that I could not open Scripture," she asserted. "He must by his prophetical office open it unto me." Then, more boldly, she added: "Now if you do condemn me for speaking what in my conscience I know to be truth, I must commit myself unto the Lord."

MR. NOWELL: How do you know that that was the spirit?

MRS. H.: How did Abraham know that it was God that bid him offer his son, being a breach of the sixth commandment?

DUDLEY: By an immediate voice.

MRS. H.: *So to me by an immediate revelation.*

At this point the Deputy Governor sneered: "How! An immediate revelation!" Patiently Anne Hutchinson insisted that the Lord, through the medium of the Bible, had shown her the way; Isaiah and Daniel were cited in her support. Fortified by her faith, she shouted defiantly:

"Therefore I desire you to look to it, for you see this Scripture fulfilled this day and therefore I desire you that as you tender the Lord and the church and commonwealth to consider and look what you do. You have power over my body, but the Lord Jesus hath power over my body and soul, and assure yourselves thus much, you do as much as in you lies to put the Lord Jesus Christ from you, and, if you go on in this course you begin, you will bring a curse upon you and your posterity, and the mouth of the Lord hath spoken it."

Another version of the trial has Mistress Hutchinson warning the magistrates and elders: "Take heed how you proceed against me, for I know that for this you go about to do to me, God will ruin you and your posterity, and this whole state!"

For a moment the courtroom was stunned. So the ancient Hebrews in the synagogue of Nazareth must have reacted when they heard from the mouth of young Jesus doctrines that seemed blasphemous to their ears. No man standing on the soil of Massachusetts Bay had ever gone that far. Neither the ribald and profane Morton of Merrymount nor the eloquent and forthright Roger Williams had ever dared to invoke a curse upon the elders of the New Zion. Mistress Hutchinson's few rash words had entirely undone the effect of her own witnesses' testimony. Her judges had successfully baited her, and now they sought to spring the trap.

WINTHROP: Daniel was delivered by a miracle. Do you think to be delivered so, too?

MRS. H.: I do here speak it before the court. I look that the Lord should deliver me by his providence.

MR. HARKALENDEN: I may read Scripture and the most glorious hypocrite may read them and yet go down to hell.

MRS. H.: It may be so.

.   .   .

Would Cotton dare stand by her now? Everyone in the courtroom wondered. Endecott lost no time in pinning him down. Turning to the Boston divine, he asked whether he approved of her revelations "as she hath laid them down."

"I do not know whether I do understand her," Cotton answered. "But this I say, if she doth expect a deliverance in a way of providence—then I cannot deny it."

The Deputy Governor wanted a more categorical answer. "Good Sir, I do ask whether this revelation be of God or no."

MR. COTTON: I should desire to know whether the sentence of the court will bring her to any calamity, and then I would know of her whether she expects to be delivered from that calamity by a miracle or a providence of God.

MRS. H.: By a providence of God I say I expect to be delivered from some calamity that shall come to me.

WINTHROP: The case is altered and will not stand with us now, but I see a marvellous providence of God to bring things to this pass that they are. We have been harkening about the trial of this thing, and now the mercy of God by a providence hath answered our desires and made her lay open herself and the ground of all these disturbances to be by revelations.

With indecent haste Winthrop sought to keep Cotton from extricating his chief disciple.

"We all consent with you," the other judges added. Resuming the attack against the prisoner, Winthrop stigmatized Anne Hutchinson's views as "desperate enthusiasm." Endecott resented Winthrop's obvious effort to shift the attack back to Jezebel.

"Do you witness for her or against her?" he demanded of Cotton, whose answer was worthy of a medieval Schoolman.

MR. COTTON: This is what I said, Sir, and my answer is plain that if she doth look for deliverance from the hand of God by his providence, and the revelation be in a word or according to a word, that I cannot deny.

Mr. Endecott: You give me satisfaction.

Dudley: No, no, he gives me none at all.

Mr. Cotton: But if it be in a way of miracle or a revelation without the word, that I do not assent to, but look at it as a delusion, and I think so doth she, too, as I understand her.

Dudley: Sir, you weary me and do not satisfy me.

Mr. Cotton: I pray, Sir, give me leave to express myself. In that sense that she speaks I dare not bear witness against it.

Mr. Nowell: I think it is a devilish delusion.

Winthrop: Of all the revelations that ever I read of I never read the like grounds laid as is for this. The Enthusiasts and Anabaptists had never the like.

Mr. Cotton: You know, Sir, that their revelations broach new matters of faith and doctrine.

Winthrop: So do these, and what may they breed more if they be let alone? I do acknowledge that there are such revelations as do concur with the word, but there hath not been any of this nature.

Dudley: I never saw such revelations as these among the Anabaptists; therefore I am sorry that Mr. Cotton should stand to justify her.

Hugh Peters burst out: "I think it is very disputable which our brother Cotton hath spoken." "It overthrows all," Winthrop solemnly added.

Dudley: These disturbances that have come among the Germans have been all grounded upon revelations, and so they that have vented them have stirred up their hearers to take up arms against their prince and to cut the throats of one another, and these have been the fruits of them, and whether the devil may inspire the same into their hearts here I know not, for I am fully persuaded that Mrs. Hutchinson is deluded by the devil, because the spirit of God speaks truth in all her servants.

WINTHROP: I am persuaded that the revelation she brings forth is delusion.

Then, according to the record, "all the court but some two or three ministers" cried out, 'We all believe it! We all believe it!'"

The court was ready to proceed to sentencing when Deputy Brown urged that a more severe punishment be meted out to the prisoner than that which had already been imposed on her disciples, "for this is the foundation of all mischief and of all those bastardly things which have been overthrowing by that great meeting. They have all come out from this cursed fountain." Winthrop was about to put the motion for sentence when Coddington rose to his feet and made a last effort in behalf of the prisoner.

"I do not see any clear witness against her," he pointed out, "and you know it is a rule of the court that no man may be a judge and an accuser too. I would entreat you to consider whether those things which you have alleged against her deserve such censure as you are about to pass, be it to banishment or imprisonment," he continued. "I beseech you do not speak so as to force things along, for I do not for my own part see any equity in the court in all your proceedings. Here is no law of God that she hath broken nor any law of the country that she hath broke, and therefore deserves no censure."

Coddington had courageously raised fundamental issues only to be rudely handled by the Deputy Governor, who observed: "We shall be all sick with fasting." But the opposition would not be stampeded by their stomachs. Colburn openly dissented "from censure of banishment," and even the Deputy Governor refused formally to condemn Anne Hutchinson on the technical ground that the witnesses against her had not testified under oath. To "end all scruples," Winthrop ordered the elders to be sworn. There was a whispered consultation among the divines. The Reverend Messrs. Weld, Eliot, and Peters held up their hands. The Governor turned to them and put the oath: "You shall swear to the truth and nothing but the truth as far as you know. So help you God."

Anne Hutchinson's strategy had now badly backfired, for her insistence that the ministers be put to the oath merely gave them the opportunity of repeating their testimony in court for a second time and impressing it on the spectators all the more vividly. The Reverend John Eliot, some day to be renowned as the Apostle to the Indians, was most explicit in his testimony, while the other two pastors hedged somewhat.

Now the court saw no reason to delay sentence longer. The last few moments as preserved in the trial record are characteristic of the whole proceedings:

MR. STOUGHTON: I say now this testimony doth convince me in the thing, and I am fully satisfied the words were pernicious, and the frame of her spirit doth hold forth the same.

WINTHROP: The court hath already declared themselves satisfied concerning the things you hear, and concerning the troublesomeness of her spirit and the danger of her course amongst us, which is not to be suffered. Therefore if it be the mind of the court that Mrs. Hutchinson for these things that appear before us is unfit for our society, and if it be the mind of the court that she shall be banished out of our liberties and imprisoned till she be sent away, let them hold up their hands.

All but three raised their hands. Coddington and Colborn were the lone dissenters, and one deputy declared that he could not hold up his hand "one way or the other."

WINTHROP: Mrs. Hutchinson, the sentence of the court you hear is that you are banished from out of our jurisdiction as being a woman not fit for our society, and are to be imprisoned till the court shall send you away.

MRS. H.: I desire to know wherefore I am banished.

Winthrop: Say no more, the court knows wherefore
and is satisfied.

Winthrop had the last word. In all, the trial consumed
but two days as contrasted with major criminal trials today,
which are seldom terminated under six weeks and not infrequently run on for many months. In sentencing Anne
Hutchinson to deportation the authorities were invoking a
penalty employed promiscuously against serious offenders as
well as paupers and vagrants. Even strangers who were so
indiscreet as to come to the Bay Colony leaving their wives
behind in the old country would be summarily expelled.

The condemnation of Anne Hutchinson spurred the decision to liquidate the entire opposition party. At the time of
Wheelwright's conviction some sixty leading Bostonians had
signed a petition denying that Wheelwright had "stirred
up sedition in us." Though the tone of their remonstrance
was temperate, the signers were neither forgiven nor forgotten. Leading Hutchinsonians—including Coddington and
Coggeshall, who had dared to speak up for the accused at
the trial—were given three months to leave the colony; others were disfranchised. Charging that "there is just cause
of suspicion" that the Hutchinsonians, "as others in Germany, in former times, may, upon some revelation, make
sudden eruption upon those that differ from them in judgment," the court ordered some fifty-eight citizens of Boston
and seventeen from adjacent towns to be disarmed unless
they repudiated the "seditious libel," by which term their
petition was now stigmatized. Winthrop recounts that some
of the "chief military officers" whose loyalties were suspect
were now forced into line, but Captain John Underhill, the
bawdy military stalwart, remained obdurate and had to be
banished. If any plot had sprouted, it was nipped in the
bud. As Winthrop felicitously puts it, "when they saw no
remedy, they obeyed."

With calculated cruelty Anne Hutchinson was separated
from her family and committed to the home of Joseph Weld,

brother of her archenemy, the Roxbury divine. Throughout
the winter the elders labored with her, but in vain. Finally,
in March 1638, they gave her an ecclesiastical trial. Momentarily yielding to the buzzing of her tormentors, she signed
a retraction of her views. Then, with characteristic impulsiveness, she recanted. "My judgment is not altered, although my expression alters!" she exclaimed. It must have
been a peculiarly agreeable task for the Reverend Mr. Wilson to pronounce her excommunication and order her "as a
leper to withdraw yourself out of this congregation." As she
passed Winthrop on leaving the trial, that worthy muttered:
"The Lord sanctify this unto you." She answered defiantly:
"The Lord judgeth not as man judgeth. Better to be cast out
of the church than to deny Christ!"

How Cotton, of all the Hutchinsonians, escaped the fate
of the rest is a story in itself. But as a realist he saw no
prospect of holding out against the wolf pack. Publicly declaring that he had been made use of as a "stalking horse,"
he turned against his friend and disciple at the church trial.
He now savagely charged her with "all promiscuous and
filthy coming together of men and women," and predicted
that if she continued in her course she must inevitably become unfaithful to her husband. By such smear tactics, un-
worthy of a great churchman, Cotton recovered "his former
splendor" in the eyes of the orthodox.

Even when she was banished from the commonwealth and
had made her new home in Rhode Island, Anne's enemies
still pursued her. With amazing impudence the Bay Colony
authorities sent four laymen down to Anne's settlement to
convince her of her errors. She made short shrift of them. As
soon as they announced that they had come from Boston,
she shouted bitterly: "What from the Church at Boston? I
know no such church, neither will I own it. Call it the whore
and strumpet of Boston, no Church of Christ!" Sprayed by
this picturesque Biblical buckshot, her visitors scampered
for cover.

But Anne and her brood continued to be wanderers. After

her husband's death she settled at Pelham Bay, then in Dutch New Netherland, where in 1643 she and most of her family were treacherously murdered by Indians. A divine judgment, the Puritan elders called it, scarcely able to conceal their jubilation at the news that this Jezebel, their greatest foe, could no longer oppose them, at least on this earth.

II

The Politicians and the Pirate
the ordeal of Captain Kidd

The extent to which the state provides procedural safeguards for the accused may be considered a barometer of its
own security. When a government is shaky and needs a
scapegoat, it will not scruple to exploit every legal techni-
cality to obtain a conviction. It will even withhold evidence
vital to the defendant's case. The Kidd case constitutes a
classic example of how arbitrarily a government can behave
when unchecked by more modern rules of due process. In
addition, the conviction of the accused in that case established a precedent for the inglorious practice, by no means
moribund, of trying a man on a technical charge because it
may prove impossible to bring him to justice for the pri-
mary offense. Kidd was really framed on a murder charge
by a government that recognized the precarious character of
its piracy case against him. In this respect his trial captures
contemporary overtones. It is not dissimilar to the spectacle
offered by a powerful democracy in railroading to prison a
notorious public enemy for failing to declare all his income,
or by a totalitarian state in convicting a cardinal of violating currency regulations because more serious acts against
the state might be more difficult to establish.

The Kidd affair was the greatest scandal of its generation.
It involved the highest figures in English and colonial life,
from the King down. But it began as a thoroughly respectable, even commonplace business scheme worked out by
three principals who had very much in common. All three
were fired by ambition. All three had married heiresses as a
conventional step toward acquiring wealth. All three cen-
tered their operations in the province of New York.

The initiator of the project was Robert Livingston, son of

a Scottish political refugee, who had astonished the slower-paced Dutchmen of the province by his amazing dynamism. "Beginning as a little bookkeeper," an unfriendly critic pithily summed up his career, "he had screwed himself into one of the most considerable estates in the province." His courtly manners and mastery of both Dutch and French soon won for him the secretaryship of Indian affairs in the frontier trading post of Albany. Exploiting inside information about deals and Indian trade, he acquired affluence with astonishing rapidity. His marriage to Alida Schuyler, widow of a Van Rensselaer, brought him aristocratic connections of the first magnitude. The acquisition of Livingston Manor, a huge tract in the present Dutchess and Columbia Counties, gave him an established position among the landed gentry.

Livingston was a political opportunist who switched sides whenever expedient. First he opposed Jacob Leisler, a German emigrant who illegally took over the government of New York at a time when James II fled from England. Then he fought Governor Fletcher, a thoroughly corrupt adventurer, who withheld accounts Livingston claimed were due him for moneys advanced the colony at healthy interest. He "never disbursed six pence," Fletcher charged, "but with the expectation of twelve pence in return." When Fletcher would not yield, Livingston took ship for London to fight for his rights.

Livingston reached London in the winter of 1695. News had already leaked out that William III, in a move to consolidate imperial authority in America, planned to appoint the Earl of Bellomont as governor of New York, Massachusetts, and New Hampshire. Livingston made a point of cultivating Bellomont and offered to slice a treasure-hunting melon with him. Bellomont did not need much coaxing.

This gout-ridden peer, baptized Richard Coote, was in desperate financial straits. Although one of Ireland's largest landowners, he had failed to squeeze a shilling from his impoverished tenantry through either of the timeworn devices of rackrenting or evictions. For a time his fortunes received a temporary lift by his marriage to a Worcestershire heiress named Catherine Nanfan, and through a crown grant of a huge leasehold of a forfeited estate. The pay-off for his services to the house of Orange kept him from toppling into bankruptcy. But in those days there were limits to deficit financing. Bellomont needed a job, and the King had every confidence in him. "I send you, my Lord, to New York," he told him, "because an honest and intrepid man is wanted to put these abuses down, and because I believe you are such a man."

The abuses to which the King referred were piratical depredations that could no longer be ignored. Blackbeard, Bradish, Bellamy, and other raiders had now moved beyond legalized privateering (authorized attacks on and seizures of enemy ships in wartime) to the equally lucrative, if riskier, work of piracy (robbery committed upon ships of friendly nations). Since it was notorious that many of the ships that flew the Jolly Roger were fitted out in New York, Bellomont promptly castigated that colonial port as a "nest of pirates." His predecessor, the crooked Fletcher, was known to have commissioned pirates and connived with such prominent families as the De Lanceys to help them dispose of their plunder. Bellomont planned to end such dealings, but when he approached the Admiralty for help, he found that branch of the government frigid toward official intervention.

Here is where Livingston came into the picture. He proposed to Bellomont a plan to outfit an armed privateer to clear the Arabian Gulf and the Bay of Bengal of piracy. Toward this project the Admiralty was cordial, though how even an armchair admiral could have expected to put down the formidable menace of piracy with one petty craft has never been satisfactorily explained. Livingston, as agent of the expedition, assumed responsibility for the outfitting of the ship and the selection of her commander. Fortuitously, there was in London at this very time a prosperous Scottish sea captain named William Kidd, then forty-one years of age (as was Livingston), and boasting a gallant naval record. Kidd was just the sort of person who would be picked today for the panel of a blue-ribbon grand jury in New York's Federal court. He had settled in New York in 1689 and married a wealthy widow, who had already outlived two husbands; and he had achieved sufficient station and respectability to be designated as foreman of a grand jury in a treason trial, and to be set down in the records as "William Kidd, Gentleman." On the same side of the political fence as Livingston in New York local politics, Kidd had attacked Fletcher's regime and only recently testified that Fletcher had used terrorist tactics to win an election in New York City for his candidate.

On October 10, 1695 Bellomont, Livingston, and Kidd drew up a contract whereby the peer agreed to secure government commissions to war upon enemy shipping or hostile privateers and to raise four fifths of the cost of the venture, Kidd and Livingston to put up the rest. Kidd specified that he would take any prizes to Bellomont at Boston, to engage seamen on a "no purchase (prize), no pay" arrangement, and to award them no more than a fourth part of such prizes. Together Livingston and Kidd agreed that if they took no prizes they would refund to Bellomont all the money invested by his friends on or before March 25, 1697, but that in such eventuality they themselves could keep the ship. After the crew had been paid off, Bellomont's investors were to receive four fifths of the proceeds, Livingston and Kidd to divide the remaining fifth. From this agreement it is clear that had Kidd come home empty-handed, both he and Livingston stood to lose heavily. As further security for Bellomont, Livingston was required to give a bond in the sum of £10,000 that Kidd would be faithful to his trust.

Never investing a florin himself, Bellomont induced other celebrities to underwrite the venture to the tune of £6,000, among them the Earl of Orford, First Lord of the Admiralty, Sir John Somers, Chancellor and lord keeper of the great seal, the Duke of Shrewsbury, Secretary of State, and the

Earl of Romney, that intriguing and licentious master-general of ordnance. According to Bishop Burnet, the King himself had agreed to invest £3,000, but though he reneged in the end, the crown was declared in to the extent of one tenth of whatever profits materialized. With Orford and Somers financially committed, it must have been child's play for Bellomont to procure for Kidd a privateering commission from the High Court of Admiralty and a special royal commission under the great seal, placed thereon by Somers himself. This parchment authorized Kidd to seize pirates, but cautioned him against molesting "our friends and allies" at his peril. In his sailing order to Kidd, dated London, February 25, 1696, Bellomont wrote: "I pray God grant you good success, and send us a good meeting again." There may very well be honest differences of opinion about the success of Kidd's voyage, but there should be unanimous agreement that the next meeting of these two business partners was one of the weirdest in financial history.

The ship selected for the cruise was the *Adventure Galley* of 287 tons and thirty-four guns, which Kidd fitted out in Plymouth, England. His start was delayed three weeks when his crew was pressed for the navy, and because of a shortage of hands in a wartime period he sailed to America to fill out his company. He arrived in New York with only 70 hands, and while at anchor in the Hudson increased his crew to 155 men, a motley collection of waterfront deserters, maritime riffraff, and rogues who had sailed under the black flag. Fletcher, who had commissioned some of the very pirates whom Kidd was authorized to destroy, piously warned that no good would come of it all.

In September of '96 the *Adventure Galley* weighed anchor and sailed for Madagascar, chief haunt of the pirates in Eastern waters and major center of illegal trade between the East Indies and America. A whole year went by without a single capture. Whether Kidd's discontented men finally forced his hand, as he subsequently asserted, or whether the hard terms of the contract and the remoteness from home encouraged Kidd to switch from fighting pirates to becoming one himself is a moot point, but by the summer of 1698 the dispatch pouches to London were bulging with complaints against him. In November of that year orders were sent to the governors of the American plantations to apprehend Kidd as a pirate.

In extenuation of Kidd it should be pointed out that in wartime merchant ships generally flew under false colors and carried several sets of papers, producing the one that would match the nationality of the ship making the search. In turn, captains of privateers customarily sailed under false colors as a decoy. In this contest of deception the privateer had the edge, as the merchantman had no opportunity for second guessing. This substitution of passes and confusion of nationalities served as Kidd's defense in the main charge against him, the seizure on the Malabar coast of his richest prize, the *Quedah Merchant*, a vessel belonging to the Great Mogul. Kidd claimed that the merchantman flew Armenian colors and that her English captain, when challenged, produced a French pass, whereupon Kidd had the English colors raised on the *Adventure Galley*. As Kidd later tried to explain to Bellomont, the astonished master then admitted that it was a "good prize." Actually, the *Quedah Merchant* was seized on January 30, 1698, some *five months* after the signing of a peace treaty between England and France. But the news of that signing did not reach the Indian Ocean until April 1698, and by the terms of the treaty captures beyond the equator were not illegal if made within *six months* after the signing of the document. Had Kidd been able to introduce this pass in evidence and prove its authenticity, he would have had a formidable defense against piracy, though he would still have had to do some tall explaining as to why he divided up the spoils before the vessel had been lawfully adjudged a prize.

Unfortunately for Kidd, his seizures in Eastern waters brought down upon his head the mortal antagonism of the East India Company, that great private monopoly exercising trading and governmental powers in India. Rightly concerned about piracy, the company was less justifiably, but perhaps equally, outraged by the activities of interlopers from America who sought to trade in an area it viewed as its own preserve. In short, the Kidd affair was the climax of a private war between the New York merchants and the East India Company.

Transferring his prizes or loot (whichever version we prefer) from his own galley, now leaking like a sieve, to the *Quedah Merchant,* Kidd headed homeward. He felt confident that both his papers and his backers would clear him. On arriving at the West Indies in April 1699, he learned that the King had proclaimed him a pirate, specifically excepting him from a general offer of amnesty to all pirates who gave themselves up. He was fast attaining the unenviable if unearned role of Public Enemy No. 1. Ships of the line were out searching for him. Leaving the East Indiaman at Santo Domingo in the custody of a Yankee sea captain whose sloop he purchased, Kidd sailed for New York, with a brief but sensational stop in Delaware Bay for stores. Since five of the colonists who ventured to trade with him were promptly jailed, Kidd became understandably cautious. He approached New York through Long Island Sound, anchoring off Oyster Bay. From there he got in contact with a New York attorney, James Emmot, whom he asked to intercede for him with Bellomont, then in Boston.

Now, the turn of events must have been a great shock to the Governor. In England the backers of the Kidd expedition were under an all-out attack, and Bellomont knew that he could not afford to temporize. But the tone of his correspondence betrayed that he was not above some double-dealing to save his own good name. Lacking confidence in the integrity of his own law-enforcement officials, the Governor had refused to publish the order for Kidd's arrest for fear that Kidd would be warned off by Livingston and James Graham, a fellow Scot and New York's Attorney General. In opening negotiations Kidd was most unfortunate in his choice of attorneys. Emmot was a Fletcherite and *persona non grata* to the Earl, who soon denounced him as a "Jacobite," a term of opprobrium like "Communist" today. While the Governor refused Kidd an outright pardon, his letter of June 19, 1688 to his partner evidenced no intention of extraditing him to England for trial. "Mr. Emmot," Bellomont wrote, "delivered me two French passes taken on board the two ships which your men rifled, which passes I have in my custody and I am apt to believe they will be a good article to justifie you if the peace were not, by the Treaty between England and France, to operate in that part of the world at the time the hostility was committed, as I am almost confident it was not to do!" Continuing in this deceptively friendly tone, Bellomont assured Kidd that it was his understanding that mutinous seamen had forced the accused's hand.

> I have advised with his Majesty's Council and showed them this letter this afternoon, and they are of opinion that if your case be so clear as you (or Mr. Emmot for you) have said, that you may safely come hither, and be equipped and fitted out to go and fetch the other ship, and I make no manner of doubt but to obtain the King's pardon for you and those few men you have left, who I understand have been faithful to you and refused as well as you to dishonor the commission you had from England.

Bellomont was desperately eager to lure Kidd and his accomplices into port, but not empty-handed. "I will not meddle with the least bit of your treasure," he treacherously promised, adding: *"I assure you on my word and on my honor I will performe nicely what I have now promised."*

Although Bellomont's word of honor rated high in the plantations, Kidd's suspicions were now aroused. He buried a chest of gold and four bales of goods on Gardiner's Island, reimbursing John Gardiner, the manorial proprietor, with some muslin and striped goods as a present for his wife (a piece of cloth of gold is still in the possession of Gardiner descendants). Other plunder was consigned to Thomas Clarke of Setauket, coroner of New York. This share may ultimately have found its way into the hands of Mistress Kidd. But Kidd, like a true Scotsman, was more cautious about his treasure than about his person. He finally came to Boston with his wife and family. For a short time they lodged at the home of Duncan Campbell, a fellow Scot, who, as intermediary between Bellomont and Kidd, gave Bellomont's wife "three or four small jewels." Bellomont, as he confessed later to the Lords of Trade, advised her to keep them "for the present," justifying his complicity in the bribe on the ground that "my shewing an over-nicety might do hurt, before I had made a full discovery what goods and treasure were in the sloop."

With that implacable zeal which he had displayed only a few years before when he had sought unsuccessfully in Parliament to have certain personal enemies impeached, Bellomont now hounded Kidd. On July 6 the Governor wrote the Board of Trade: "I have the misfortune to be ill of the gout at a time when I have a great deal of business to exercise both my head and my hand." Kidd had arrived at Boston the week before, he reported, adding righteously: "I would not so much as speak with him but before witnesses. I thought he looked very guilty." Now they could be reassured. Kidd and "five or six of his men" were in Boston jail. News of Kidd's arrest brought Livingston to Boston. He backed up his barefaced demand for the return of his bond by repeating a threat of Kidd's. He told the Governor that the prisoner was reputed to have sworn that unless the bond were turned back, he would never bring in the *Quedah Merchant* and cargo, but instead would satisfy Livingston privately. Bellomont did not dare call Livingston's bluff, and the bond was never forfeited. Instead the Governor's venom was henceforth directed solely against Kidd.

To the New York sea captain this startling reversal in his fortunes came as a stunning blow. He now acted like a man who had something to cover up. According to the Governor, he offered Lady Bellomont a £1,000 bribe. Commenting on July 26 on Kidd's examination before the Governor and council, Bellomont wrote: "I observed he seemed much disturbed, and the last time we examined him I fancied he looked as if he were upon the wing and resolved to run away." The Governor moved with celerity, searching out the hidden plunder at Kidd's quarters in Boston, on Gardiner's Island, and in the custody of Coroner Clarke, none of which, Kidd asserted, came from the *Quedah Merchant*. In all, the recovered loot amounted to £14,000, probably a small fraction of the total left behind in Santo Domingo. The cargo alone Kidd had valued at £30,000. While four fifths of the prize belonged to Bellomont's backers under the original agreement, he could not take a chance and let Kidd sail back to the West Indies. He was sure that Kidd would never return voluntarily to Boston, and that, even were he so foolhardy, the prize was too hot to be distributed. Sarah Orne Kidd was successful in persuading Bellomont to turn back to her some of the property she claimed to be her own, and very likely this alluring lady, who was resourceful enough to acquire a fourth husband after Kidd's demise, was able to secrete some of the less bulky treasure.

"I am forced to allow the sheriff forty shillings per week for keeping Kidd safe. Otherwise I should be in some doubt about him," Bellomont wrote. "He has without doubt a great deal of gold, which is apt to corrupt men that have not principles of honor. I have, therefore, to try the power of iron against gold, put him in irons that weigh sixteen pounds." Reminding the Lords of Trade that the notorious informer Titus Oates "had a hundred weight of iron on him while he was a prisoner in the late reign," Bellomont prided himself on his moderation. The pre-trial examination convinced him that "there never was a greater liar or thief in the world than this Kidd."

Although Kidd seemed securely anchored in jail, the Governor was nervous. On November 30 he wrote a London

official: "These pirates whom I have in jail make me very
uneasy for fear they shall escape. I would give £100 were
they all in Newgate." His prayer was soon granted. Since
the Massachusetts act of 1692 punishing piracy with death
had been disallowed by the crown, and under the colony's
laws piracy could not be punished as a capital felony, Bellomont asked the Lords of Trade for orders in this case.
Under a parliamentary statute, only just enacted, pirates
could be tried in the colonies by commissioners appointed
by the crown, but the King could not afford to trust Kidd
to the tender mercies of a colonial jury. Accordingly, he was
extradited to stand trial in England.

The twelve months that followed proved decisive for the
fortunes of most of the principals in the Kidd affair. Captain Kidd, some of his crew, and others charged with piracy
were transported in chains to London. Kidd's ship arrived
in the Downs on April 11, 1700. At that very moment King
William, by prorogation, had brought to an end an acutely
embarrassing session of Parliament, in the course of which
the Tories had made political capital of Somers's action in
affixing the great seal to Kidd's commission. A storm descended on the head of the Lord Chancellor, who for a
number of years, during the absence of the King on the Con-
tinent, had been head of the council of regency that ruled
England. Somers was forced off the bench. "Our rulers have
laid hold of our lands, our woods, our moneys," the Tories
charged. "And all this is not enough. We cannot send a
cargo to the farthest ends of the earth, but they must send
a gang of thieves after it." While Somers's enemies were unable to carry a resolution attacking Kidd's commission as
dishonorable to the King, they managed, before Parliament
was prorogued, to put through a resolve to the effect that
Kidd should not be tried, discharged, or pardoned until the
next session.

This resolve was shrewdly calculated, for in January of
the following year the Tories came into power. Now the
Kidd affair moved rapidly toward a climax. On March 27

Kidd was brought by the keeper of Newgate to the House
of Commons and examined. Four days later he was heard
again, this time at his own request. The very next day was
held one of the most turbulent sessions in parliamentary
history. At the end of that day it was announced that Kidd
would be proceeded against according to law and that impeachment proceedings would be instituted against Somers
and Orford. Only three weeks before, the Earl of Bellomont
had died in New York, but for Somers and Orford no such
peaceful severance of their ties to Kidd was in store. Tried
by the House of Lords in a session that began on May 14
and ended on the 17th of June, Somers, whose eloquence
matched his vast erudition, vigorously denied that he was
in any way responsible for Kidd's piratical exploits or that
he had given him encouragement or hope of protection.
Fifty-four peers voted to acquit the ex-Chancellor, but
thirty-two went on record as "not content." Six days later
the Lords unanimously acquitted the Earl of Orford. In
seeking the downfall of the ex-Chancellor and the First
Lord of the Admiralty the Tories were really aiming to discredit the monarchy. Somers managed to clear himself (ultimately to regain prestige as head of a Whig junto), but
the King could not let the charges against Kidd be dropped.
Kidd had to be the "fall guy." His conviction was the minimum needed to retrieve the Whig Party's fading fortunes.
Innocent or guilty, he must hang.

When, on May 8 and 9, 1701, a week before Somers faced
his peers in the House of Lords, Kidd went on trial in Old
Bailey, the atmosphere of that historic courthouse hung
heavy with prejudice and tension. Normally, admiralty
courts had jurisdiction over crimes committed on the high
seas, but since an admiralty court would not resort to tor-
ture to extort confessions and required eyewitness testimony
to convict, no pirate was ever hanged in a trial in admiralty.
To deal with such public malefactors who might easily intimidate or suborn witnesses, a statute of Henry VIII's
reign authorized a trial by special commission, such trial to

be conducted according to the less tender rules of the common law. Such trial by commission having proved far more efficacious in hanging pirates than had admiralty, it was only natural that it should be employed in the Kidd case.

By modern standards of due process the denial of counsel to Kidd seems outrageous, but from an early period persons accused of treason or felony were refused help of counsel and permitted no legal advice except where a point of law was directly involved. That palladium of constitutional liberties the great Coke had justified such denial on the amazing ground that the prosecutor should prove his case so clearly that no defense was possible. Furthermore, Coke argued, the court was really the prisoner's counsel. But such solicitude for prisoners was seldom exhibited in state trials, and Kidd's was no exception. Over his trial hovered the shadow of the late Chief Justice, the notorious George Lord Jeffreys, whom Charles II had once castigated as having more "impudence than ten carted whores." The memory of his Bloody Assizes had died hard. Although the judge who presided over the Kidd trial had himself successfully defied Jeffreys's bullying tactics, Sir Edward Ward, Chief Baron of the Exchequer and a staunch Whig, was not above some forthright browbeating on his own part. Like Jeffreys, he acted in this case as an agent of the prosecution, bullied Kidd's witnesses, hampered Kidd's shrewd attempts to impeach the witnesses for the crown, and delivered the kind of charge to the jury that made acquittal impossible. Finally, his observation to a defense witness in Kidd's piracy trial: "That was before he was turned pirate," would, under modern trial procedure, constitute a prejudicial error.

The Lord Chief Baron was only one of a cluster of titled bigwigs who confronted Kidd from the bench. With the baron sat Sir Henry Hatsell, Baron of the Exchequer, Sir Salathiel Lovell, Recorder of London, Sir John Turton and Sir Henry Gould, justices of the King's Bench, and Sir John Powell, a justice of Common Pleas. The last-named was the chuckling old gentleman described by Dean Swift in a letter to Stella. Folks had not yet forgotten his comment in a witchcraft trial over which he had presided. It was alleged that the prisoner could fly. Powell smiled benevolently at the accused and remarked: "You may—there is no law against flying." The chief counsel for the prosecution was the learned Dr. George Oxenden, a middle-aged specialist in admiralty law who had held the distinguished Regius Professorship of Civil Law at Cambridge. Associated with him were Knapp, Somers, and Campbell.

From the start it was flagrantly clear that the thoroughly frightened Whigs were out to convict Kidd by any means that came to hand. The authorities were so concerned about Kidd's French passes that they unscrupulously withheld them at the piracy trial, though Kidd repeatedly demanded them. These passes had been examined by the Commons on April 16 and then returned by the clerk of the House to the Admiralty. Although that department was specifically directed to turn over all records in the case, Orford could not afford to have the passes produced at the trial. In fact, the piracy case seemed so shaky that it was decided to try Kidd first on a murder charge. He was put on trial for the killing of an insubordinate seaman. In those days such an offense could hardly have been accounted more than manslaughter. So well recognized was the master's disciplinary authority over insubordinate seamen on the high seas that it was the rarest occasion when a sea captain would be put in the dock for the murder of a member of his crew. Just how much pressure was brought to bear on Bradenham, the ship's surgeon, to turn state's evidence will never be known. His testimony that Gunner Moore's death was directly caused by a blow Kidd inflicted with a bucket was decisive. And the price of his testimony was a pardon.

The bill of indictment against Kidd is best epitomized in a contemporary ballad sung to the tune of *Coming Down.*

Many long leagues from shore when I sail'd,
Many long leagues from shore when I sail'd,
Many long leagues from shore

> *I murdered William More,*
> *And I laid him in his gore, when I sail'd.*

> *Because a word he spoke when I sail'd,*
> *Because a word he spoke when I sail'd,*
>   *Because a word he spoke,*
>   *I with a bucket broke*
> *His scull at one sad stroke, while I sail'd.*

But to the actual trial itself:

CLERK OF ARRAIGNMENT: William Kidd, hold up thy hand.

KIDD: May it please your Lordships, I desire you to permit me to have counsel.

THE RECORDER: What would you have counsel for?

KIDD: My Lord, I have some matters of law relating to the indictment, and I desire I may have counsel to speak of it.

DR. OXENDEN: What matter of law can you have?

CLERK OF ARRAIGNMENT: How does he know what he is charged with? I have not told him.

THE RECORDER: You must let the Court know what these matters of law are before you can have counsel assigned you.

KIDD: They be matters of law, my Lord.

THE RECORDER: Mr. Kidd, do you know what you mean by matters of law?

KIDD: I know what I mean. I desire to put off my trial as long as I can, till I can get my evidence ready.

THE RECORDER: Mr. Kidd, you had best mention the matter of law you would insist on.

DR. OXENDEN: It cannot be matter of law to put off your trial, but matter of fact.

KIDD: I desire your Lordship's favor. I desire that Dr. Oldish and Mr. Lemmon here be heard as to my case.

CLERK OF ARRAIGNMENT: What can he have counsel for before he has pleaded?

THE RECORDER: Mr. Kidd, the Court tells you you shall

be heard what you have to say when you have pleaded to
your indictment. If you plead to it, if you will, you may assign matter of law, if you have any, but then you must let
the Court know what you would insist on.

Kidd was impaled on the horns of the same kind of dilemma that confronted Giles Corey of Salem Village, who a
few years earlier had been pressed to death for refusing to
plead to a witchcraft indictment. Should he plead, he knew
for certain that he would not receive a fair trial. But if he
stood mute he would suffer *peine forte et dure* (crushing to
death with weights). It was a hard choice, and it is understandable why Kidd, who had the instincts of a gambler,
should have chosen differently from the venerable Corey.
But before yielding, the accused put up a gallant battle.

KIDD: I beg your Lordship's patience, till I can procure
my papers. I had a couple of French passes which I must
make use of, in order to my justification.

THE RECORDER: That is not matter of law. You have
had long notice of your trial, and might have prepared for
it. How long have you had notice of your trial?

KIDD: A matter of a fortnight.

DR. OXENDEN: Can you tell the names of any persons
that you would make use of in your defense?

KIDD: I sent for them, but I could not have them.

DR. OXENDEN: Where were they then?

KIDD: I brought them to my Lord Bellomont in New
England.

THE RECORDER: What were their names? You cannot
tell without book. Mr. Kidd, the Court sees no reason to put
off your trial, therefore you must plead.

CLERK OF ARRAIGNMENT: William Kidd, hold up thy
hand.

KIDD: I beg your Lordship I may have counsel admitted, and that my trial may be put off. I am not really
prepared for it.

THE RECORDER: Nor never will, if you can help it.

DR. OXENDEN: Mr. Kidd, you have had reasonable notice, and you knew you must be tried, and therefore you cannot plead you are not ready.

KIDD: If your Lordships permit those papers to be read, they will justify me. I desire my counsel may be heard.

MR. CONIERS: We admit of no counsel for him.

THE RECORDER: There is no issue joined, and therefore there can be no counsel assigned. Mr. Kidd, you must plead.

KIDD: I cannot plead till I have those papers that I insisted upon.

MR. LEMMON: He ought to have his papers delivered to him, because they are very material for his defense. He has endeavored to have them, but could not get them.

MR. CONIERS: You are not to appear for anyone, till he pleads, and that the Court assigns you for his counsel.

THE RECORDER: They would only put off the trial.

MR. CONIERS: He must plead to the indictment.

CLERK OF ARRAIGNMENT: Make silence.

KIDD: My papers are all seized, and I cannot make my defense without them. I desire my trial may be put off till I can have them.

THE RECORDER: The Court is of opinion that they ought not to stay for all your evidence; it may be they will never come. You must plead; and then if you can satisfy the Court that there is a reason to put off the trial, you may.

KIDD: My Lord, I have business in law, and I desire counsel.

THE RECORDER: Mr. Kidd, the course of Courts is, when you have pleaded, the matter of trial is next; if you can then show there is cause to put off the trial, you may, but now the matter is to plead.

KIDD: It is a hard case when all those things shall be kept from me, and I am forced to plead.

THE RECORDER: If he will not plead, there must be judgment.

KIDD: My Lord, would you have me plead and not have my vindication by me?

CLERK OF ARRAIGNMENT: Will you plead to the indictment?

KIDD: I would beg that I may have my papers for my vindication.

CLERK OF ARRAIGNMENT: W. Kidd, you stand indicted by the name of William Kidd, etc. Art thou guilty or not guilty?

KIDD: I cannot plead to this indictment, till my French passes are delivered to me.

CLERK OF ARRAIGNMENT: Are you guilty or not guilty?

KIDD: My Lord, I insist upon my French papers. Pray let me have them.

THE RECORDER: That must not be now, till you have put yourself upon your trial.

KIDD: That must justify me.

MR. RECORDER: You may plead it then, if the Court see cause.

KIDD: My justification depends on them.

MR. RECORDER: Mr. Kidd, I must tell you, if you will not plead, you must have judgment against you, as standing mute.

KIDD: I cannot plead till I have these papers; and I have not my witnesses here.

MR. RECORDER: You do not know your own interest. If you will not plead, you must have judgment against you.

KIDD: If I plead, I shall be accessary to my own death, till I have persons to plead for me.

MR. RECORDER: You are accessary to your own death, if you do not plead. We cannot enter into the evidence, unless you plead.

CLERK OF ARRAIGNMENT: Are you guilty or not guilty?

MR. RECORDER: He does not understand the law. You must read the statute to him.

CLERK OF ARRAIGNMENT: Mr. Kidd, are you guilty of this piracy, or not guilty?

KIDD: If you will give me a little time to find my papers, I will plead.

CLERK OF ARRAIGNMENT: There is no reason to give you time. Will you plead or not?

MR. CONIERS: Be pleased to acquaint him with the danger he stands in by not pleading. Whatever he says, nothing can avail him till he pleads.

MR. RECORDER: He has been told so, but does not believe us.

MR. CONIERS: If there be any reason to put off his trial, it must be made appear after issue is joined.

MR. RECORDER: If you say guilty, there is an end of it; but if you say not guilty, the Court can examine into the fact.

OFFICER: He says he will plead.

CLERK OF ARRAIGNMENT: W. Kidd, art thou guilty, or not guilty?

KIDD: Not guilty.

CLERK OF ARRAIGNMENT: How wilt thou be tried?

KIDD: By God and my country.

CLERK OF ARRAIGNMENT: God send thee a good deliverance. (And so of all the rest.)

KIDD: My Lord, I beg I may have my trial put off for three or four days, till I have got my papers.

MR. RECORDER: The Judges will be here by-and-by, and you may move the Court then; we are only to prepare for your trial. We do not deny your motion, but when the Court is full, they will consider of the reasons you have to offer.

The trial of Kidd upon the indictment for murder proceeded at once.

CLERK OF ARRAIGNMENT: How say'st thou, William Kidd, art thou guilty of this murder whereof thou standest indicted, or not guilty?

KIDD: Not guilty.

CLERK OF ARRAIGNMENT: How wilt thou be tried?

KIDD: By God and my country.

DR. OLDISH: My Lord, it is very fit his trial should be delayed for some time because he wants some papers very necessary for his defense. It is very true he is charged with piracies in several ships, but they had French passes when the seizure was made. Now, if there were French passes, it was lawful seizure.

MR. JUSTICE POWELL: Have you those passes?

KIDD: They were taken from me by my Lord Bellomont, and these passes would be my defense.

DR. OLDISH: If those ships that he took had French passes, there was just cause of seizure, and it will excuse him from piracy.

KIDD: The passes were seized by my Lord Bellomont, that we will prove as clear as the day.

MR. JUSTICE POWELL: What ship was that which had the French passes?

MR. LEMMON: The same we were in, the same he is indicted for.

CLERK OF ARRAIGNMENT: Set all aside but Captain Kidd. William Kidd, you are now to be tried on the bill of murder; the jury is going to be sworn. If you have any cause of exception, you may speak to them as they come to the Book.

KIDD: I challenge none. I know nothing to the contrary but they are honest men.

The first witness for the crown was Joseph Palmer of the *Adventure Galley,* who, when captured by Bellomont in Rhode Island, informed of the circumstances surrounding the death of Moore, the gunner. He testified as follows:

JOSEPH PALMER: About a fortnight before this accident fell out, Captain Kidd met with a ship on that coast, that was called the *Loyal Captain.* And about a fortnight after this, the gunner was grinding a chisel aboard the *Adventure,* on the high seas, near the coast of Malabar in the East Indies.

MR. CONIERS: What was the gunner's name?

PALMER: William Moore. And Captain Kidd came and walked on the deck, and walked by this Moore, and when he came to him, says, "Which way could you have put me in a way to take this ship, and been clear?" "Sir," says William Moore, "I never spoke such a word, nor ever thought such a thing." Upon which Captain Kidd called him a lousy dog. And says William Moore, "If I am a lousy dog, you have made me so. You have brought me to ruin, and many more." Upon his saying this, says Captain Kidd, "Have I ruin'd you, ye dog?" and took a bucket bound with iron hoops and struck him on the right side of the head, of which he died the next day.

MR. CONIERS: You say he called him a lousy dog?

PALMER: Yes.

MR. CONIERS: What did William Moore say to him then?

PALMER: He said, "If I am a lousy dog, you have brought me to it. You have ruined me and many more." Upon this, says Captain Kidd, "Have I brought you to ruin, you dog?" Repeating it two or three times over, he took a turn or two upon the deck and then takes up the bucket, and strikes him on the head.

MR. COWPER: You say he made a turn or two on the deck, and then struck him.

PALMER: Yes.

MR. CONIERS: Tell my Lord what passed next after the blow.

PALMER: He was let down the gun-room, and the gunner said, "Farewell, farewell. Captain Kidd has given me my last." And Captain Kidd stood on the deck and said, "You're a villain!"

LORD CHIEF BARON WARD: Was this Moore in a good condition of health before this blow was given him?

PALMER: Yes, my Lord.

L. C. B. WARD: And afterwards he complained?

PALMER: Yes, my Lord.

L. C. B. WARD: When he was dead, what marks were on his head?

PALMER: On the right side of his head, on this place

(pointing to his own head) it was bruised a considerable breadth, and in one place I could feel the skull give
way.

MR. COWPER: How long after the blow did he die?

PALMER: The next day following.

MR. COWPER: And you say you saw him dead then?

PALMER: Yes, sir.

L. C. B. WARD: Captain Kidd, if you will ask him any
questions, you may.

Kidd, bereft of trial counsel, handled his own cross-
examination.

KIDD: My Lord, I would ask this man, what this Moore
was doing when this thing happened.

L. C. B. WARD: Mr. Palmer, you hear what he says.
What was Moore doing?

PALMER: He was grinding a chisel.

KIDD: What was the occasion that I struck him?

PALMER: The words that I told you before.

KIDD: Was there no other ship?

PALMER: Yes.

KIDD: What was that ship?

PALMER: A Dutch ship.

KIDD: What were you doing with the ship?

PALMER: She was becalmed.

KIDD: This ship was a league from us, and some of the
men would have taken her, and I would not consent to it.
And this Moore said, I always hindered them making their
fortunes. Was not that the reason I struck him? Was there
a mutiny on board?

PALMER: No. You chased this Dutchman, and on the
way took a Malabar boat, and chased this ship all the
whole night. And they showed their colors, and you put up
your colors.

KIDD: This is nothing to the point. Was there no mutiny aboard?

PALMER: There was no mutiny, all was quiet.

KIDD: Was there not a mutiny, because they would go and take that Dutchman?

PALMER: No, none at all.

MR. CONIERS: Call Robert Bradenham (who appeared). . . . Was you there when the blow was given?

BRADENHAM: No.

MR. CONIERS: Was you sent for when Captain Kidd had given the gunner the wound upon the head?

BRADENHAM: I was sent for to his assistance after he was wounded, and I came to him, and asked him how he did. He said, he was a dead man, Captain Kidd had given him his last blow. And I was by the gun-room, and Captain Kidd was walking there, and I heard Moore say, "Farewell, farewell, Captain Kidd has given me my last blow." And Captain Kidd, when he heard it, said, "Damn him, he is a villain!"

MR. CONIERS: Did you hear him say so?

BRADENHAM: I did hear it.

MR. COWPER: Was it in a way of answer to what he said?

BRADENHAM: Yes.

MR. COWPER: How long did he live after the blow?

BRADENHAM: He died the next day. The wound was but small, but the skull was fractured.

MR. COWPER: Do you believe he died of the wound?

BRADENHAM: Yes.

MR. COWPER: Had you any discourse with Captain Kidd after this about this man's death?

BRADENHAM: Some time after this, about two months, by the coast of Malabar, Captain Kidd said, "I do not care so much for the death of my gunner, as for other passages of my voyage, for I have good friends in England that will bring me off for that."

L. C. B. WARD: Then you may make your defense. You are charged with murder, and you have heard the evidence that has been given. What have you to say for yourself?"

KIDD: I have evidence to prove it is no such thing, if they may be admitted to come hither. My Lord, I will tell you what the case was. I was coming up within a league of the Dutchman, and some of my men were making a mutiny about taking her, and my gunner told the people he could put the captain in a way to take the ship and be safe. Says I, "How will you do that?" The gunner answered, "We will get the captain and men aboard." "And what then?" "We will go aboard the ship and plunder her and we will have it under their hands that we did not take her." Says I, "This is Judas-like. I dare not do such a thing." Says he, "We may do it. We are beggars already." "Why," says I, "we may take the ship because we are poor?" Upon this a mutiny arose, so I took up a bucket and just throwed it at him, and said, "You are a rogue to make such a notion." This I can prove, my Lord.

L. C. B. WARD: Call your evidence.

MR. COWPER: Mr. Palmer, was there any mutiny in the ship when this man was killed?

PALMER: There was none.

L. C. B. WARD: Captain Kidd, call what evidence you will.

KIDD: They are prisoners. I desire they may be called up.

L. C. B. WARD: Whatever other crimes they may be guilty of, they may be witnesses for him in this case.

MR. BARON HATSELL: Mr. Palmer, did he throw the bucket at him, or strike him with it?

PALMER: He held it by the strap in his hand.

KIDD: Call Abel Owens. (Who appeared.) Can you tell which way this bucket was thrown?

MR. JUSTICE POWELL: What was the provocation for throwing the bucket?

OWENS: I was in the cook-room, and hearing some difference on the deck, I came out, and the gunner was grinding a chisel on the grind-stone, and the captain and he had some words, and the gunner said to the captain, "You have brought us to ruin, and we are desolate." "And," says he, "have I brought you to ruin? I have not done an ill thing to ruin you. You are a saucy fellow to give me these words." And then he took up the bucket, and did give him the blow.

KIDD: Was there not a mutiny among the men?

OWENS: Yes, and the bigger part was for taking the ship, and the captain said, "You that will take the Dutchman, you are the strongest, you may do what you please. If you will take her, you may take her, but if you go from aboard, you shall never come aboard again."

L. C. B. WARD: When was this mutiny you speak of?

OWENS: When we were at sea.

L. C. B. WARD: How long was it before this man's death?

OWENS: About a month.

MR. JUSTICE POWELL: At this time when the blow was given, did Moore the gunner endeavor to make any mutiny?

OWENS: No.

MR. JUSTICE POWELL: Was there any mutiny then?

OWENS: None at all.

KIDD: Did not he say, "He could put me in a way to take the Dutchman, and be clear"?

OWENS: I know there were several of them would have done it, but you would not give consent to it.

KIDD: No, but this was the reason I threw the bucket at him.

L. C. B. WARD: Captain Kidd, he tells you this was a month before you struck him.

JURY: My Lord, we desire he may be asked, whether he did throw the bucket, or strike him with it.

L. C. B. WARD: Answer the jury to that question.

OWENS: He took it with the strap, and struck him with it.

KIDD: Did I not throw it at him?

OWENS: No, I was near you when you did it.

MR. CONIERS: Did you see the stroke given?

OWENS: I did see the stroke given.

L. C. B. WARD: Captain Kidd, will you call any more?

KIDD: Yes, my Lord. Call Richard Barlicorn.

MR. JUSTICE POWELL: What questions would you have him asked?

KIDD: Richard Barlicorn, what was the reason that blow was given to the gunner?

BARLICORN: At first, when you met with the ship there was a mutiny, and two or three of the Dutchmen came aboard, and some said she was a rich vessel, and they would take her. And the captain said, "No, I will not take her," and there was a mutiny in the ship, and the men said, "If you will not, we will." And he said, "If you have a mind, you may; but they that will not, come along with me."

KIDD: Do you think William Moore was one of those that was for taking her?

BARLICORN: Yes. William Moore lay sick a great while before this blow was given, and *the doctor said when he visited him that this blow was not the cause of his death.*

L. C. B. WARD: Then they must be confronted. Do you hear, Bradenham, what he says? He says you said, "That blow was not the cause of his death." Did you ever say so?

BRADENHAM: *My Lord, I never said so.*

L. C. B. WARD: Did you see that young man there?

BRADENHAM: Yes, he was aboard the ship.

L. C. B. WARD: Was Moore sick before that blow?

BRADENHAM: He was not sick at all before.

BARLICORN: He was sick sometime before, and this blow did but just touch him, and the doctor said he did not die on the occasion of this blow.

MR. JUSTICE GOLD: Did you ever say so, Mr. Bradenham?

BRADENHAM: No, my Lord.

MR. SOL. GEN.: You say he did but just touch him. Were you present when the blow was given?

BARLICORN: No, but I saw him after he was dead, and I was by when the doctor said he did not die of that blow.

MR. COWPER: What did he die of?

BARLICORN: I cannot tell. He had been sick before. We had many sick men aboard.

MR. SOL. GEN.: How long did he lie after this blow before he died?

BARLICORN: I cannot tell justly how long it was.

L. C. B. WARD: How long do you think? You took notice of the blow. How long did he live after that?

BARLICORN: I believe about a week.

L. C. B. WARD: And the two witnesses swore he died the next day.

BARLICORN: I cannot tell justly how long he lived afterwards.

JURY: We desire to know whether he knew what was the occasion of this blow.

BARLICORN: All the reason I can give is because it was thought he was going to breed a mutiny in the vessel.

L. C. B. WARD: Did you hear of that by anybody?

Kidd now made a desperate attempt to impeach the crown's star witness by a line of questioning that annoyed Baron Ward.

KIDD: Was Bradenham in the mutiny? Declare that.

L. C. B. WARD: Mr. Kidd, why do you ask that question?

KIDD: I ask him, whether Bradenham was not in any mutiny in the ship.

L. C. B. WARD: Why do you ask that?

BARLICORN: If anything was to be, he was as forward as anyone.

L. C. B. WARD: You say he was as forward as any, but it does not appear anyone made a mutiny at this time.

BARLICORN: I do not know, sir.

L. C. B. WARD: Have you any more to call?

KIDD: My Lord, here is another witness.

L. C. B. WARD: What is your name?

HUGH PARROT: Hugh Parrot.

L. C. B. WARD: Mr. Kidd, what do you ask him?

KIDD: I ask you whether Bradenham was in a mutiny on my ship.

HUGH PARROT: I cannot say whether he was or no.

L. C. B. WARD: Capt. Kidd, you are tried for the death of this Moore: now why do you ask this question? What do you infer from hence? You will not infer, that if he was a mutineer, it was lawful for you to kill Moore.

KIDD: Do you know the reason why I struck Moore?

HUGH PARROT: Yes, because you did not take the *Loyal Captain,* whereof Captain Hoar was commander.

L. C. B. WARD: Was that the reason he struck Moore, because the ship was not taken?

PARROT: I shall tell you how it happened, according to the best of my knowledge. My commander fortuned to come up with this Captain Hoar's ship and some were for taking her, and some not. And afterwards there was a little sort of mutiny, and some rose in arms, the greater part. And they said they would take the ship. And the commander was not for it, and so they resolved to go away in the boat and take her. Captain Kidd said, "If you desert my ship, you shall never come aboard again, and I will force you into Bombay, and I will carry you before some of the Council there." Insomuch that my commander stilled them again and they remained on board. And about a fortnight afterwards, there passed some words between this William Moore and my commander, and then, says he, "Captain, I could have put you in a way to have taken this ship and been never the worse for it." He says, "Would you have me take this ship? I cannot answer it. They are our friends." And my commander was in a passion, and with that I went off the deck, and I understood afterwards the blow was given, but how I cannot tell.

MR. JUSTICE POWELL: Capt. Kidd, have you any more to ask him, or have you any more witnesses to call?

KIDD: I could call all of them to testify the same thing, but I will not trouble you to call any more.

L. C. B. WARD: Have you any more to say for yourself?

KIDD: I have no more to say, but I had all the provocation in the world given me. I had no design to kill him. I had no malice or spleen against him.

L. C. B. WARD: That must be left to the jury to consider the evidence that has been given. You make out no such matter.

KIDD: It was not designedly done, but in my passion, for which I am heartily sorry.

Thereupon Ward charged the jury. His insistence that Kidd's wielding the bucket was an "unjustifiable act" virtually amounted to instructing the jury to find the prisoner guilty of murder.

KIDD: My Lord, I have witnesses to produce for my reputation.

L. C. B. WARD: Mr. Kidd, we gave you time to make your defense. Why did not you produce them? You were asked more than once, if you had any more to say, and you said, you would call no more witnesses.

KIDD: I can prove what service I have done for the King.

L. C. B. WARD: You should have spoken sooner. But what would that help in this case of murder? You said you had no more to say before I began.

Then an officer was sworn to lock up the jury. An hour later the jury returned.

CLERK OF ARRAIGNMENT: Gentlemen, answer to your names. Nathaniel Long.

NATH. LONG: Here, etc.

CLERK OF ARRAIGNMENT: Are you all agreed of your verdict?

OMNES: Yes.

CLERK OF ARRAIGNMENT: Who shall say for you?

OMNES: Foreman.

CLERK OF ARRAIGNMENT: William Kidd, hold up thy hand. (Which he did.) Look upon the prisoner. Is he guilty of the murder whereof he stands indicted, or not guilty?

FOREMAN: Guilty.

CLERK OF ARRAIGNMENT: Look to him, Keeper.

Immediately following this conviction, Kidd and his accomplices had to stand trial five successive times for piracy. The crown's case depended on proving that Kidd had captured ships belonging to nations in amity with England. The Prosecution counted heavily on the informer Palmer, and was not disappointed. Especially damaging was that witness's testimony as to Kidd's relations with the pirate Culliford. Typical of the crown's case was the evidence in the first and most important of these piracy trials, the prosecution for the illegal seizure of the *Quedah Merchant*.

PALMER: When we came to Madagascar, in the latter end of April, or beginning of May 1696, there was a ship called *The Resolution*, which was formerly called *The Mocca Frigate*. Several of the men came off to Captain Kidd, and told him they heard he came to take and hang them. He said that it was no such thing, and that he would do them all the good he could. And Captain Culliford came aboard of Captain Kidd, and Captain Kidd went aboard of Culliford.

MR. CONIERS: Who was that Culliford?

PALMER: The Captain of the ship. And on the quarterdeck they made some bomboo [1] and drank together. And Captain Kidd said, "Before I would do you any harm, I would have my soul fry in Hellfire," and wished damnation to himself several times, if he did. And he took the cup and wished that might be his last, if he did not do them all the good he could.

MR. POWELL: Did you take these men to be pirates?

PALMER: They were reckoned so.

DR. NEWTON: Did Captain Kidd make Culliford any presents?

PALMER: Yes, he had four guns of him.

DR. NEWTON: Of whom?

---

[1] Also *bumbo,* a rum or gin drink.

PALMER: Of Captain Kidd. He presented him with them.

MR. POWELL: Was there not a present on the other side?

PALMER: I believe there was. I heard Culliford say, "I have presented Captain Kidd to the value of four or five hundred pounds."

MR. COWPER: Were these kindnesses done to Culliford after Culliford's men said they heard Captain Kidd came to hang them?

PALMER: Yes.

MR. COWPER: What did Captain Kidd do after that?

PALMER: He went aboard the *Quedah Merchant.*

MR. COWPER: What did he do with his own ship?

PALMER: She was leaky, and he left her.

MR. COWPER: Did he carry, or attempt to carry, any of the ships he took, in order to condemn them, besides that French banker?

PALMER: He never did, nor talked of any such thing.

L. C. B. WARD: Mr. Kidd, will you ask this witness any questions?

KIDD: I ask him whether I had no French passes.

PALMER: Indeed, Captain Kidd, I cannot tell. I did hear him say that he had French passes, but I never saw them.

L. C. B. WARD: Those goods that were taken out of the *Quedah Merchant,* whose goods were they supposed to be?

PALMER: The Armenian merchants'. I have heard Captain Kidd say several times, he had French passes.

KIDD: And did you hear anybody else say so?

PALMER: No.

KIDD: It is in vain to ask any questions.

L. C. B. WARD: Then you may make your own defense. Come, Mr. Kidd, what have you to say in your own defense?

KIDD: I had a commission to take the French, and pirates. And in order to that, I came up with two ships that had French passes both of them. I called you all a-deck to

consult. And did not a great many of the men go aboard?
Did not you go? You know, Mr. Palmer, I would have given
these ships to them again, but you would not. You all voted
against it.

But Palmer would not be pinned down. He insisted that
the owners of the ship were Armenians, who came to Kidd
"crying and wringing their hands" to return her to them. As
far as he himself was concerned, he denied having ever seen
the French pass although he had "heard of it." Repeatedly
the Lord Chief Baron reminded Kidd that even if the ship
had a French pass, he should have condemned her as a
prize.

L. C. B. WARD: Out of the goods that were taken, some
were sold in the country there, and the produce of them was
so much money. It is proved that the money was divided,
and pursuant to the articles set up, you were to have forty
shares, and the rest of the men whole, or half shares, as they
deserved. Now this money, both these men swear it was
taken by you. And the first swears, that the goods not sold
then that remained in the ship were also divided, and that
you had forty shares of them. And the other says, he did
not see the goods divided, but two of the men acknowledged it.

KIDD: My Lord, this Frenchman was aboard five or six
days before I understood there was any Englishmen aboard.
"Well," said I, "what are you?" "An Englishman, I am
master." "What have you to show for it?" "Nothing," says
he. When they see a French pass, they will not let the
ship go.

MR. JUSTICE POWELL: You have produced Letters Patents that impowered you to take pirates. Why did you not
take Culliford?

KIDD: A great many of the men were gone ashore.

MR. JUSTICE POWELL: But you presented him with
great guns, and swore you would not meddle with them.

L. C. B. WARD: When the question was put, "Are you

come to take us and hang us?" you answered, "I will fry in Hell before I will do you any harm."

KIDD: That is only what these witnesses say.

L. C. B. WARD: Did you not go aboard Culliford?

KIDD: I was not aboard Culliford.

L. C. B. WARD: These things press very hard upon you. We ought to let you know what is observed, that you may make your defense as well as you can.

A passenger named Davis testified that Kidd had remarked that the passes were French. Bradenham also asserted that he had heard Kidd so describe them, but had never seen them himself. A reputation witness for Kidd, one Captain Humphrey, then took the stand to describe Kidd's heroism in a naval engagement in "the late war."

L. C. B. WARD: How long was this ago?

HUMPHREYS: Twelve years ago.

L. C. B. WARD: That was before he was turned pirate.

KIDD: I have many papers for my defense, if I could have had them.

L. C. B. WARD: What papers were they?

KIDD: My French passes. My Lord Bellomont had them.

L. C. B. WARD: If you had had the French passes, you should have condemned ships.

KIDD: I could not, because of the mutiny in my ship.

In his charge to the jury Ward stressed the point that where men commit acts not authorized by their commission, "it is as if there had been no commission at all." After a half-hour's deliberation the jury obliged the court with a guilty verdict.

Again Kidd had to stand trial immediately, this time for the piracy of a ship called *A Moorish Ketch*. Relenting somewhat, the court now permitted Kidd to introduce a few more character witnesses in his behalf. Colonel Hewson attested that Kidd "was a mighty man" in a naval engagement that took place in the West Indies some nine years before, and Thomas Cooper described a fight with Du Cass in which "Captain Kidd behaved himself very well in the face of his enemies." To the inquiry of a juror: "How many years ago was this?" Cooper replied: "About ten years ago." Unfortunately for the accused, his reputation witnesses all spoke of a time quite remote from the recent expedition.

Sir John Turton's charge was even more prejudicial to Kidd than Ward's had been. The justice declared that Kidd had wrongfully transgressed his commission by seizing ships and goods of nations at peace with the King of England. He commented on Kidd's reported exchange of presents with Culliford as indicative of a lack of aggressive intent toward a notorious pirate. *"The evidence seems strong against them which I leave you to consider of."* After a short space the jury brought in a verdict of guilty, and the same verdict was returned on the three remaining indictments. Then proclamation for silence was made while sentence was pronounced.

Dr. Oxenden: You the prisoners at the bar, William Kidd, Nicholas Churchill, James Howe, Gabriel Loffe, Hugh Parrot, Abel Owens, Darby Mullins, Robert Hickman, and John Eldridge, you have been severally indicted for several piracies and robberies, and you William Kidd for murder. You have been tried by the laws of the land, and convicted; and nothing now remains, but that sentence be passed according to the law. And the sentence of the law is this:

> You shall be taken from the place where you are, and be carried to the place from whence you came, and from thence to the place of execution, and there be severally hanged by your necks until you be dead. And the Lord have mercy on your souls.

Kidd: My Lord, it is a very hard sentence. For my part, I am the innocentest person of them all, only I have been sworn against by perjured persons.

.   .   .

Despite the exhortation of the Reverend Paul Lorrain, ordinary of Newgate, Kidd remained adamant in denying his piracy. Even in the speech at the execution attributed to him, but spiced up as a journalistic sensation of the day, he denied giving Gunner Moore the blow with premeditated malice. Kidd was hanged at Wapping on the shore of the Thames on May 23, 1701, between high-water mark and low-water mark (*infra fluxum et refluxum maris*), according to admiralty custom. But the gruesome operation had to be performed twice. The first time, the rope by which he was suspended broke and he fell to the ground, still conscious, with the halter around his neck. Again he was taken to the top of the ladder. He died game.

According to a minority view of the United States Supreme Court, such a happening at the present day would constitute double jeopardy and cruel and unusual punishment. Something very much like Kidd's painful experience occurred in Louisiana in 1946, when an attempted electrocution of Willie Francis failed, presumably because of some mechanical defect. But the majority of the highest court held that Francis, like Kidd, would have to die a second time.

Incurable romantics have searched the Highlands of the lower Hudson and dredged in coves and inlets of New England and Long Island to find Captain Kidd's buried treasure. The effects that Bellomont had seized, amounting to some £6,500, were shipped home and forfeited to the King as "droits of the Admiral." The proceeds later were turned over by Queen Anne to the seamen's hospital at Greenwich. But the rest of his property has never been completely accounted for, nor has the mystery of the *Quedah Merchant* and her cargo in Santo Domingo ever been cleared up. A legend persisted that Kidd's men sailed her into the Hudson and there scuttled the vessel, but there is some likelihood that the East Indiaman continued her career as the *Widdah*, first as a lawful merchantman, then as a pirate under the command of the notorious Bellamy, flying the black flag with

death's-head and bones across at her mizzenmast, finally
breaking up in a heavy gale on the sands of Cape Cod,
where her crew came to a miserable end.

What treasure Kidd buried was more than likely tracked
down by Lord Bellomont, that pedigreed bloodhound, or by
a charming widow who signed her name with a rude "S. K."
Nevertheless, the hoard of Captain Kidd still haunts the
dreams of every latter-day Billy Bones who may still see
Kidd's body, covered with tar and hung in chains, gibbeted
on the shore of the reach of the Thames, or awaken to the
shrill voice of Captain Flint ringing in his ears: "Pieces of
eight! Pieces of eight!"

III

The Case of the Palatine Printer

Zenger's fight for a free press

Until very recent years it was an acknowledged touchstone of American democracy that few, if any, limits were imposed on public criticism of the government or its officials. Whether such criticism was informed and responsible or foolish and immoderate, the right to make it was safeguarded. Freedom of speech, freedom of the press, and the toleration of an organized opposition had come to be accepted as bulwarks of the democratic way of life. Nor did political loyalty signify unqualified and blind allegiance to those in office at any one time. American Presidents, from Washington to Truman, have felt the sting of venomous attack. Save for the aberrations of John Adams's administration, however, and the occasional sedition scares since that time, Americans in the past felt free to criticize public officials and even to argue for changes of government so long as they did not resort to violence to attain their ends. This long-standing liberal tradition goes back to the courageous battle put up against the royal government in America by a New York printer named John Peter Zenger.

The Zenger case destroyed once and for all the notion that government officials were entitled to unqualified allegiance and support, that they were untouchables immune from criticism. Above loyalty to the government, the verdict placed loyalty to the people. Coming a generation before the preliminaries of the American Revolution, the trial helped create that climate of civil disobedience in which the idea of political independence was conceived and nurtured.

The Zenger trial served to highlight the technique the government employed back in the 1730's to curb political discussion. At that time neither Great Britain nor any other nation in the Western World recognized the right freely to communicate ideas and to criticize public officials. In England no work could be printed without a license. These licenses were first regulated by the Court of Star Chamber, a tribunal of odious memory to defenders of due process; then during the period of the Puritan Revolution by Parliament, and subsequently by the crown. For all Milton's heroic literary labors on behalf of free thought, speech, and printing, "this iron yoke of outward conformity" was not easily shattered. When Parliament saw that the licensing machinery had broken down, it dropped the requirement of a license, without relaxing the strict curbs imposed on the reporting of its own proceedings. The *Gentleman's Magazine* soon circumvented this prohibition by reporting the debates as emanating from a "Senate of Great Lilliput," but even then the editor lived in the shadow of arrest.

The dropping of the requirement that printers secure licenses before publishing did not in fact enhance the citizen's right to criticize the government. The crown now turned to the more dangerous weapon of criminal prosecutions for seditious libel. Since the government and a servile judiciary considered that any published reflections on the rulers would undermine their authority, they were not disposed to admit the truth in defense in an action for seditious libel nor were they willing to entrust to the jury the issue of whether the writing was in fact seditious. These rulings of the court made convictions a foregone conclusion until the Zenger case boldly challenged both propositions. Not until the jury in that trial assumed the right to decide the law as well as the fact could editors and publishers have any assurance of a fair trial.

To understand the predicament that faced John Peter Zenger, the provincial newspaper editor, it must be borne in mind that printers and editors in the American colonies operated under the same kind of restraints as in contemporary England. Sir William Berkeley, Virginia's reactionary Governor back in the seventeenth century, had occasion to "thank God that there were no free schools nor printing presses" in his colony and to express the hope that "we shall not have them these hundred years." His reasons were typical of the authoritarian, antidemocratic viewpoint of his day. "Learning," he maintained, "brought disobedience and heresy and sects into the world and printing has divulged them, and libels against the best of governments. God keep us from both!" Later royal governors would have applauded these forthright sentiments had not the assembly's control over their salaries instructed them in the virtues of discretion.

Actually, formal censorship in the colonies anticipated the appearance of newspapers. In 1686 James II instructed the Governor of New York, Thomas Dongan, to permit no person to keep a printing press nor allow any printed matter to be issued "without your especial leave and license be first obtained." Similar instructions were issued to the governors of other colonies. Hence nobody was particularly surprised when *Publick Occurrences*, the first newspaper in the English plantations, was suppressed, four days after its initial appearance in 1690, for presuming to report that the English armed forces had allied themselves with "miserable" savages. Later, James Franklin, the editor of the *New England Courant*, was jailed for attacking the provincial government. For a time he managed to evade the censors by the flimsy subterfuge of putting on the masthead the name of his half brother, Ben, then sixteen years old and destined to become the most formidable fighter for liberty among all colonial newspaper publishers.

But it was New York rather than Boston that was to be the scene of the crucial fight for the freedom of the press. The man who spearheaded this fight had come to New York in 1710, a young Palatine immigrant. Apprenticed to the elder William Bradford, New York's leading printer, John Peter Zenger was still in his employ in 1725 when the *Gazette*, New York's first newspaper, appeared. But Zenger soon came to recognize his employer's journal as filled with "dry, senseless stuff and fulsome panegyrics." Official printer to the province, Bradford had quickly learned that if you had to get along with the authorities, it was good business to be mouselike. But Zenger was not mouselike. Honest, courageous, and straightforward, he felt impelled to break with Bradford to keep his self-respect.

For a number of years after Zenger set up his own printing shop, he scraped together a meager existence by publishing dull theological tracts. He eked out an additional pittance by playing the organ at the Garden Street Church. Then suddenly, at a time when he was skating on the thin ice of solvency, Zenger unexpectedly found a couple of "angels" who gave him the financial backing necessary to launch the *Weekly Journal.*

No more propitious time for the establishment of an outspoken newspaper could have been chosen than the moment Zenger selected to bring out his paper. Only a few months before there had arrived in New York a new governor, the undiplomatic and avaricious William Cosby. Rumors, perhaps unfounded, had followed hard on his arrival. He was accused of having employed highhanded methods as chief of the British garrison at Minorca. These malicious stories scarcely prepared the colonists either for the "God damn ye" manners of Cosby or for the arbitrary tactics he was soon to introduce into his administration of the governorship of New York and the Jerseys. Cosby made one tactless move after another. He infuriated the assembly by demanding a sizable cash gift above and beyond his salary. Although nepotism and plural job-holding were commonplace at that time, the public was shocked when he appointed his son, Billy, as secretary of the Jerseys. But the issue that brought matters to a head was his insistence that the corpulent Rip Van Dam, a prominent merchant who had been Acting Governor since the death of Montgomerie, turn over to him half of his salary covering the period between Cosby's appointment in England and the time he actually assumed office in New York. With stolid Dutch courage and an understandable reluctance to part with perfectly good pounds sterling, Van Dam declined to comply.

Cosby then brought the kettle to a boil by instituting suit for his back salary. Since as Governor he was the judge in Chancery, he did not have quite the effrontery to bring the case before himself. But in order to avoid having the issue tried by a jury, which would most certainly find against him, he had the action brought on the exchequer side of the Supreme Court, where, since the matter was in equity, there would be no jury. Cosby's daring move was without precedent in the province. In seeking to have the court exercise a jurisdiction it had never assumed in New York in the past, Cosby was viewed as a trickster. But if he had counted on the court's being subservient to his will, he was rudely shocked. Chief Justice Lewis Morris, a powerful political figure in the colony and a landowner of baronial proportions, was impressed by the arguments of Van Dam's lawyers, James Alexander and William Smith. Although the two other Supreme Court justices supported Cosby, Morris left the bench and declared that he would refuse to sit in equity cases henceforth. Momentarily blocked, Cosby now displayed a reckless disregard of the independence of the judiciary by contemptuously supplanting Morris. In his place as Chief Justice, he designated a man who would take orders, the thirty-year-old James De Lancey, then an associate justice of the court. Court-packing moves on the part of the executive have never been popular in America, and this instance proved no exception. The Governor had grossly underestimated the courage, the pugnacity, and the prestige of his opponents. A stalwart in the politics of New York and New Jersey for a generation, the distinguished lord of Morrisania now set out to vindicate himself. Running for the assembly from the town of Eastchester, Lewis Morris beat a Cosbyite hands-down and administered to the Governor his second stinging rebuke.

As though Cosby had not made enemies enough by now, he began to investigate the land titles that had been granted to certain prominent patentees by previous administrations. Now, there had been more than a suspicion of fraud and collusion in some of the huge tracts obtained from Cosby's predecessors in office. On the surface, the chief executive's motives seemed impeccable, but the truth, as his enemies soon discovered, was that he was anxious to carve out for himself, his sons, and his brother-in-law certain choice parcels of Mohawk Valley lands. When he sought to go into equity to cancel some of these patents he brought down on his head the implacable enmity of New York's most influential lawyers and proprietors, notable among them James Alexander, William Smith, and Cadwallader Colden. It was correctly argued that the Governor, as Chancellor, would be judging titles to land in which he was an interested party. This impropriety convinced his enemies that Cosby "would stop at no injustice in order to fill his pockets."

Lewis Morris and his two lawyer friends, Alexander and Smith, recognized in Zenger a ready tool in their fight against the administration. The New York *Weekly Journal,* independent and truculent from its very first issue in 1733, unleashed a savage attack on Cosby. The second issue of the paper carried an article on the liberty of the press, with direct allusions to Governor Cosby. Master of *double-entendre,* Alexander is believed to have provided most of the satirical copy. Issue after issue contained mock advertisements of strayed animals recognizable as political foes. Francis Harison, recorder of the city and the most notorious of Cosby's henchmen, was by innuendo described as "a large spaniel, of about 5 foot 5 inches high," who "has lately strayed from his kennel with his mouth full of fulsome panegyricks." The high sheriff was clearly discernible as "a monkey of the larger sort, about 4 foot high," which had "lately broke his chain and run into the country." It was grim, Swiftian humor, but the Governor's party was not amused. When the St. Michael's Day election resulted in a victory for the anti-Cosbyite slate of aldermen, Zenger's press distributed song sheets praising the city's legislators

as standing for "liberty and law." It took a century more
before this municipal assembly came to be reviled as a gang
of boodlers. With studied insolence, Zenger's stanza cheered
those who would "boldly despise the haughty knave that
would keep us in awe." As if it were not enough for the moment to draw the Governor's fire, the song sheet went on to
assail the courts:

The pettyfogging knaves deny us rights of Englishmen;
We'll make the scoundrel raskals fly, and ne'er return
   again.

In order that there would be no doubt which particular
knaves were meant, the same ballad referred to "our judges,
they would chop and change for those that serve their turn."
By the standards of the day, these verses constituted a carefully calculated piece of contempt of court. The Rip Van
Dam case was then being litigated, and it would have taken
a far greater measure of self-control than the new Chief
Justice possessed to refrain from charging the grand jury on
the subject of these "scandalous songs" by "half-witted
men" with a "knack of rhyming." De Lancey himself had
a fine talent for slander. When a presentment was returned,
the Supreme Court, in October term 1734, ordered the songs
burned by the common hangman.

Cosby had disposed of the scurrilous ballads but had yet
to muzzle the hostile newspaper. That was the next target.
Without the support of the assembly, the Governor and
council, on November 2, 1734, ordered that four particularly slanderous issues of Zenger's paper be burned by the
common hangman. But the mayor and the judges of the
court of quarter sessions defied an order to attend the auto-
da-fé, set for four days later. Warned by the populace, the
public hangman refused to carry out the council's orders.
But the sheriff, the Governor's willing tool, had his own
Negro slave throw the defamatory numbers of the *Weekly
Journal* into the bonfire. Save for the officers of the garrison
and a bare handful of curious and idle, the lurid spectacle
was boycotted by the town's ten thousand inhabitants.

Cosby's next move was directed against Zenger himself. On November 17 the printer was arrested on order of the council and locked up in the common jail on the third floor of the City Hall. For three days he was held completely incommunicado. Then Alexander and Smith, acting as his attorneys, had Zenger brought before the court on a writ of habeas corpus. His lawyers submitted an affidavit that, except for tools and clothes, the prisoner was worth no more than £40, and insisted on their client's right to moderate bail on the basis of the Habeas Corpus Act and the English Bill of Rights. But De Lancey denied their pleas and set the exorbitant bail of £400 for Zenger and £200 each for two sureties. In fixing bail at this prohibitive figure, the court neatly circumvented the issue whether the colonists were entitled to the benefits of the Habeas Corpus Act, an issue unsettled at that time. As in more recent instances where the court has found it expedient to fix six-digit bail, he in effect denied the prisoner due process. Why Zenger's wealthy backers did not post this bail is not clear, but it is not unlikely that their failure to help him get out of jail was calculated to arouse public sympathy for the prisoner and animosity toward his persecutors. If this was their motive, they were abundantly successful.

This aspect of the Zenger case, among others, was taken to heart by the founders of our national government. To avoid such abuses of judicial discretion, the Eighth Amendment to the Federal Constitution provides that "excessive bail shall not be required." Its purpose is to prevent the effectual denial of bail by fixing the amount so unreasonably high that it cannot be given. As Justice Robert H. Jackson has so admirably expressed it, in political trials a judge must always be on guard against imprisoning persons because "he thinks their opinions are obnoxious, their motives evil, and that free society would be bettered by their absence." To guarantee equal treatment before the law for all persons regardless of their troublemaking propensities, we

must be continually on guard against budding De Lanceys
in judicial ermine.

Zenger was confined to the dungeon of the old City Hall.
The same edifice housed the courts and the mayor and aldermen. Even the attic was utilized by the thrifty public
officials, who provided therein accommodations for judgment debtors. The *Journal's* editor remained in jail until his
trial—in all, some ten months. Nevertheless, during this
time, save for one issue, the prisoner arranged to have his
paper appear every Monday. Commenting on his incarceration in the very next number following his arrest, Zenger
pointed out that the Chief Justice had seen fit to modify
the arrangements governing the first few days in jail, when
he was held incommunicado. Now, he told his readers, he
enjoyed "the liberty of speaking through the hole of the
door to my wife and servants." Through this circumscribed
means of communication he hoped to "entertain" the public
with his weekly, "as formerly."

When the prosecution sought to secure a compliant grand
jury, it ran into a stone wall. January 28, 1735, the last day
of the court's term, went by without the grand jury having
returned an indictment against Zenger. But Richard Bradley, the Attorney General, was not a man who was easily
thwarted. He proceeded at once to file an information
against the prisoner. Zenger was charged with having declared that the liberties and property of the people of New
York were in jeopardy, "men's deeds destroyed," judges arbitrarily displaced, new courts erected without consent of
the legislature, trial by jury "taken away when a governor
pleases," and men of property "denied the vote." At common law an information was a simple complaint by the officer exhibiting it. It could be utilized for such offenses as
batteries, cheats, perjuries, conspiracy, and libels. But this
method of hurdling the indictment procedure was most un-
popular in New York. Time after time grand juries had
shown themselves sympathetic with those accused and had

now come to be regarded as a bulwark of the citizen's rights. Bradley was accused of reviving the information procedure "to bring him business in a very mean and sordid manner" and of flouting the preference of the people for procedure by inquest. Such criticisms the Attorney General brushed aside as stemming from the "levelling" spirit of the colonies.

In April term 1735 Zenger was arraigned for seditious libel. In a preliminary move Smith and Alexander had the effrontery to attack the commission of Chief Justice De Lancey on the ground that it had been granted during pleasure and not during good behavior, as was the commission of the King's Bench. De Lancey, who held his post by virtue of the ability of the Governor to remove judges without cause, denied all their exceptions. In an outburst of irritation he finally shouted at Smith: "You have brought it to that point that either we must go from the bench or you from the bar and therefore we exclude you and Mr. Alexander from the bar!" This peremptory disbarment of the two prominent attorneys from the practice of their profession demonstrated how the rash use of the weapon of contempt of court constituted in its way as formidable a threat to freedom of expression as did resort to prosecutions for seditious libel. It is a source of some reassurance that the United States Supreme Court has recently confined the summary power in contempts to actual contempts in the presence of the court, and that the observation of Chief Justice Taft that "the judge must banish the slightest impulse to reprisal" when he himself is the object of criticism indicates that American courts today would no longer condone De Lancey's behavior. There are still some grievous exceptions, and Congress seems a law unto itself, but present-day judges have shown exemplary restraint under outrageous provocation.

The disbarment raised a new issue. Going over the head of the Governor and appealing directly to the assembly, Smith and Alexander protested their disbarment as being contrary to the provision of Magna Charta: "We will deny no man, we will delay no man, justice or right." Fortunately

for John Peter Zenger, progress had been made in the field
of criminal procedure since the days of Captain Kidd. By
this date the prisoner's right to counsel in a criminal trial
was fully recognized. Even De Lancey had to admit it. To
represent Zenger, in the place of the disbarred pair, the
Chief Justice designated John Chambers, a sound practitioner and a Middle Templar. Chambers was on the spot.
While he wanted to give the prisoner the benefit of a conscientious defense, he had no itch to wear the mantle of martyrdom. Accordingly, he trod softly. His first move was to
plead not guilty to the information. Then in order to avoid
further antagonizing the court he failed to move that the
exceptions of Zenger's previous attorneys be made part of
the record.

Some iron was injected into the defense when, on July
29, Chambers moved for a struck jury. The clerk, however, instead of producing the freeholders' book from which
jurors were chosen, came up with a list of forty-eight persons which he claimed came from that book. By a suspicious coincidence, some of the persons on that list were
officeholders appointed by Cosby, others were not qualified
because they did not possess freehold estates, and a third
group were tradesmen who had business dealings with the
Governor. Prodded by Zenger's friends, Chambers moved
that the forty-eight veniremen "should be struck out of the
freeholders' book as usual" in the presence of the parties,
and that the clerk should then hear objections and allow
such exceptions as were just. The court, reluctantly, so ordered. Even though Chambers permitted the Attorney General to challenge, without showing cause, "any person he
disliked," the jurors who were finally agreed upon were very
much to Zenger's liking. Seven of the twelve were of Dutch
ancestry. Cosby's conduct had doubtless kept alive in their
breasts a few remaining sparks of anti-British sentiment.

The Zenger trial started out as a routine performance.
Bradley opened for the crown by reading the information, which contained quotations from the *Journal* deemed

"false, malicious, seditious, and scandalous." The government expected a conventional defense. Despite his battle over the struck jury, Chambers gave every indication that he would not meet the issue squarely. Instead of insisting that the accusations against Cosby and his administration were true, he pleaded for latitude of expression. Challenging by innuendo the theory of libel that the crown had propounded, he argued that "in all libels there must be some particular persons so clearly pointed out, that no doubt must remain about who is meant." This was the kind of defense that the Cosbyites had anticipated. Bradley was thoroughly prepared to meet it.

At this crucial point in the trial an incident occurred that signalized the intention of the accused to choose his own ground and not to fight a battle on a site preferred by the crown. Just as Chambers was about to call his witnesses, an impressive personage rose from a seat among the spectators and informed the court that he spoke in behalf of the prisoner. As he moved down the aisle to take his place at the defense table, the courtroom seethed with excitement. The bewigged and red-robed judges sat up sharply. Court and spectators alike were surprised by a move that had been planned by Zenger's friends in complete secrecy.

Zenger's new counsel was quickly identified as Andrew Hamilton, a leading member of the Philadelphia bar and a foremost political figure in Pennsylvania. A Scotsman like Alexander and Colden, he had been educated at St. Andrews and enjoyed a reputation as a bencher of Gray's Inn. Then fifty-nine years old and in his prime as an advocate, Hamilton had not made the tedious three-day journey from the Quaker City only to be browbeaten by a poorly trained Chief Justice, whose bullying tactics attested to his insecurity in the role he had to perform. Zenger's friends had played their trump card. While Chambers was not supplanted, Hamilton ran the show from this point on, and the direction and pace of the trial perceptibly changed. Bradley now realized that a battle was impending which he had tried hard to forestall.

Hamilton now addressed the court:

> May it please your honor. I am concerned in this cause on the part of Mr. Zenger, the defendant. The information against my client was sent me a few days before I left home, with some instructions to let me know how far I might rely upon the truth of those parts of the papers set forth in the information, and which are said to be libellous. And though I am perfectly of the opinion with the gentleman who has just now spoke on the same side with me as to the common course of proceedings, I mean in putting Mr. Attorney upon proving that my client printed and published those papers mentioned in the information: yet I cannot think it proper for me (without doing violence to my own principles) to deny the publication of a complaint, which I think is the right of every free-born subject to make, when the matters so published can be supported with truth; and therefore I'll save Mr. Attorney the trouble of examining his witnesses to that point; and I do (for my client) confess, that he both printed and published the two newspapers set forth in the information, and I hope in so doing he has committed no crime.

Bradley sought to avoid the issue of truth at any cost. "Since Mr. Hamilton has confessed the fact," he told the court, "I think our witnesses may be discharged. We have no further occasion for them." Hamilton readily conceded that if the crown's witnesses were brought to court merely to prove the printing and publishing of the newspaper issues, "we have acknowledged that, and shall abide by it." Accordingly, Bradley's witnesses, including Zenger's journeyman printer and his two sons, were dismissed.

The Attorney General now maintained that, since Zenger

had confessed the publishing of the libels, "the jury must find a verdict for the King; for supposing they were true, the law says that they are not the less libellous for that. Nay, indeed, the law says their being true is an aggravation of the crime."

This was the nub of the case. In refutation, Hamilton argued that "bare printing and publishing" did not constitute a libel. The crown would have to prove something in addition. It would have to show that "the words themselves must be libellous, that is, *false, scandalous, and seditious,* or else we are not guilty." But the Attorney General was armed with British cases where severe sentences had been imposed for bringing the government into contempt by false and scurrilous libels. "If this is not a libel, I would not recognize one if I saw it," Bradley declared. Persons who took such liberties with governors and magistrates ought to be punished for sedition, he insisted. Since Bradley had been so inept as to choose all his examples from Star Chamber, Hamilton was quick to make political capital of such precedents. He stigmatized that court "as the most dangerous court to the liberties of the people of England that ever was known in that kingdom." Did the Attorney General wish to set up a Star Chamber in New York? Did he want the judgments of that discredited body to serve as "precedents to us"? Justification might be shown for giving the King immunity from attack, but the Governor, he cogently argued, was not the King. At most he was the head of a corporation, and as such had no right to claim "the sacred rights of Majesty." "Let us not," he warned, "make bold to transfer that allegiance to a subject which we owe to our King only." "What strange doctrine is it," he asked, "to press everything for law here which is so in England?"

Bradley insisted on the letter of the law. Once more he repeated: "If such papers are not libels, I think it may be said, there can be no such thing as a libel." His argument brought on a running debate with Hamilton that cut right across the central issue of the case: was truth a defense in seditious libel?

HAMILTON: May it please your Honor. I cannot agree with Mr. Attorney. For though I freely acknowledge that there are such things as libels, yet I must insist at the same time that what my client is charged with is not a libel; and I observed just now that Mr. Attorney in defining a libel made use of the words *"scandalous, seditious, and tend to disquiet the people";* but (whether with design or not I will not say) he omitted the word *"false."*

BRADLEY: I think I did not omit the word "false." [1] But it has been said already that it may be a libel, notwithstanding it may be true.

HAMILTON: In this I must still differ with Mr. Attorney; for I depend upon it, we are to be tried upon this information now before the court and jury, and to which we have pleaded *not guilty,* and by it we are charged with printing and publishing, a *certain false, malicious, seditious, and scandalous libel.* This word "false" must have some meaning, or else how came it there?

Now the last thing the Cosbyites had wanted was a public airing of the delinquencies of the royal administration of New York. But if the defense were permitted to reduce the issue to the factual basis of Zenger's charges, Cosby's actions would have to be reviewed. De Lancey, with ill-concealed partisanship, now interposed a ruling to thwart this design. "You cannot be admitted, Mr. Hamilton, to give the truth of a libel in evidence," he told the prisoner's counsel. "A libel is not to be justified; for it is nevertheless a libel that is true."

Any experienced trial practitioner is anxious to avoid repeated clashes with the judge. He appreciates the fact that the judge can exclude evidence in favor of his client and can charge the jury to the disadvantage of his side. De Lancey had shown that he would not hesitate to go so

[1] Zenger's own report of the trial supports Hamilton's contention.

far as to disbar attorneys who defied him. It took exemplary
courage for Hamilton to retort: "I am sorry the court has
so soon resolved upon that piece of law. I expected first to
have been heard to that point. I have not in all my reading
met with an authority that says we cannot be admitted to
give the truth in evidence upon an information for a libel."
But this was not the last instance of De Lancey's mischievous intervention. "The law is clear. You cannot justify a
libel," he curtly instructed Hamilton. Nonetheless, Zenger's
attorney insisted that the court consider precedents supporting the contention of the defense that the truth of a
libel is admissible in evidence. The courtroom was silent
while the judges perused the reports, but not a single person
in the room believed that De Lancey was in a frame of
mind to allow himself to be persuaded by cases. In the
clash that followed, the Chief Justice lost what little measure of self-control he had possessed up to now.

CHIEF JUSTICE: Mr. Hamilton, the court is of opinion,
you ought not to be permitted to prove the facts in the
papers. These are the words of the book: *"It is far from
being a justification of a libel that the contents thereof are
true, or that the person upon whom it is made had a bad
reputation, since the greater appearance there is of truth
in any malicious invective, so much the more provoking
it is."*

HAMILTON: These are Star Chamber cases, and I was
in hopes that practice had been dead with the court.

CHIEF JUSTICE: Mr. Hamilton, the court have delivered
their opinion, and we expect you will use us with good
manners; you are not to be permitted to argue against the
opinion of the court.

HAMILTON: With submission, I have seen the practice
in very great courts, and never heard it deemed unmannerly
to—

CHIEF JUSTICE: After the court have declared their
opinion, it is not good manners to insist upon a point in
which you are overruled.

HAMILTON: I will say no more at this time. The Court I see is against us in this point, and that I hope I may be allowed to say.

CHIEF JUSTICE: Use the court with good manners, and you shall be allowed all the liberty you can reasonably desire.

In the face of this outrageous bullying, Hamilton preserved his manner and his temper. "I thank your honor," was all he said in reply. There was no use wasting words with the bench. Turning to the jury, he proceeded to deliver a summation memorable in the annals of forensic utterance.

Then, gentlemen of the jury, it is to you we must now appeal, for witnesses to the truth of the facts we have offered and are denied the liberty to prove, and let it not seem strange that I apply myself to you in this manner. I am warranted so to do both by law and reason. The last supposes you to be summoned out of the neighborhood where the fact is alleged to be committed; and the reason of your being taken out of the neighborhood is, because you are supposed to have the best knowledge of the fact that is to be tried. And were you to find a verdict against my client, you must take upon you to say the papers referred to in the information, and which we acknowledge we printed and published, are *false, scandalous, and seditious;* but of this I can have no apprehension. You are citizens of New York. You are really what the law supposes you to be, honest and lawful men; and, according to my brief, the facts which we offer to prove were not committed in a corner. *They are notoriously known to be true;* and therefore in your justice lies our safety. And as we are denied the liberty of giving evidence, to prove the truth of what we have published, I will beg leave to lay it down as a standing rule in such cases, that *the sup-*

*pressing of evidence ought always to be taken for the
strongest evidence;* and I hope it will have that weight
with you.

Hamilton was ready to admit that attacks on the "private
and personal" affairs of public officials were "base and un-
worthy"; but the case was different, he contended, "when
a ruler of a people brings his personal failings, but much
more his vices, into his administration, and the people
find themselves affected by them." Such a circumstance
alters the case "mightily." In "a free government" the rulers
should "not be able to stop people's mouths when they feel
themselves oppressed." Hamilton now anticipated the momentous arguments of Tom Paine. He moved directly
against the monarchy.

"It is true in time past," he observed, "it was a crime to
speak truth, and in that terrible court of Star Chamber
many worthy and brave men suffered for so doing; and yet
even in that court, and in those bad times, a great and
good man durst say what I hope will not be taken amiss of
me to say in this place, to wit, the practice of informations
for libels is a sword in the hands of a wicked king, and an
arrant coward to cut down and destroy the innocent. The
one cannot, because of his high station, and the other dares
not, because of his want of courage, revenge himself in
another manner."

The two-pronged thrust was aimed both at the King and
at the Attorney General who had innovated the device of
informations. The King could not answer, but Bradley was
beside himself with wrath. "Pray, Mr. Hamilton," he
warned, "have a care what you say. Don't go too far neither.
I don't like those liberties!" Hamilton replied with a shrewd
mixture of bland diplomacy calculated to warn off the
Attorney General and political pyrotechnics aimed to sweep
the jury off its feet.

Sure, Mr. Attorney, you won't make any applica-
tions. All men agree that we are governed by the best

of kings, and I cannot see the meaning of Mr. Attorney's caution. My well-known principles and the sense I have of the blessings we enjoy under his present majesty makes it impossible for me to err, and, I hope, even to be suspected in that point of duty to my king. May it please Your Honor, I was saying, that notwithstanding all the duty and reverence claimed by Mr. Attorney to men in authority, they are not exempt from observing the rules of common justice, either in their private or public capacities. The laws of our mother country know no exemption.

When power is under control, it may serve a useful purpose, Hamilton contended, but when it is out of bounds it "brings destruction and desolation." Liberty, he argued, is the "only bulwark against lawless power." "It is an old and wise caution," he warned, "that when our neighbor's house is on fire, we ought to take care of our own. For though, blessed be God, I live in a government where liberty is well understood, and freely enjoyed. Yet experience has shown us all that a bad precedent in one government is soon set up for an authority in another. Therefore I cannot but think it mine, and every honest man's, duty that (while we pay all due obedience to men in authority) we ought at the same time to be upon our guard against power, wherever we apprehend that it may affect ourselves or our fellow subjects." As Hamilton reached his memorable peroration, not even a whisper could be heard in the courtroom.

I am truly very unequal to such an undertaking on many accounts. And you see I labor under the weight of many years, and am borne down with great infirmities of body; yet old and weak as I am, I should think it my duty, if required, to go to the utmost part of the land where my service could be of any use in assisting to quench the flame of persecutions upon informations set on foot by the government to deprive a people of the right of remonstrating of the arbitrary attempts of men

in power. Men who injure and oppress the people under
their administration provoke them to cry out and com-
plain; and then make that very complaint the foundation for new oppressions and prosecutions. I wish I
could say there were no instances of this kind.

But to conclude, the question before the court and
you, gentlemen of the jury, is not of small nor private
concern. It is not the cause of a poor printer, nor of New
York alone, which you are now trying. No! It may in
its consequences affect every freeman that lives under
a British government on the main of America. It is the
best cause. It is the cause of liberty; and I make no
doubt but your upright conduct this day will not only
entitle you to the love and esteem of your fellow citizens; but every man who prefers freedom to a life of
slavery will bless and honor you, as men who have
baffled the attempt of tyranny; and by an impartial
and uncorrupt verdict have laid a noble foundation for
securing to ourselves, our posterity, and our neighbors,
that to which nature and the laws of our country have
given us a right—the liberty both of exposing and opposing arbitrary power (in these parts of the world, at
least) by speaking and writing truth.

Hamilton had finished. Despite De Lancey's frantic efforts at preserving order, the courtroom seethed with excitement. Jury and spectators alike had followed Hamilton with
intense interest and were obviously carried away by the
burning sincerity of his appeal. His audacious argument anticipated by a whole generation James Otis's defiance of
royal authority in the Writs of Assistance case. It had
clinched the verdict. Even the bench and prosecution
seemed momentarily crushed. The Attorney General felt
that the only way to counteract the overwhelming impact
upon the jury of Hamilton's summing up was to point out
its complete irrelevance. "Mr. Hamilton had gone very
much out of the way," Bradley observed, "and had made

himself and the people very merry." But the fact, he asserted, was that the cases upon which the defense relied were to no purpose. Since Zenger had confessed the printing, the jury could have no doubt as to the scandalous character of the papers. Under the circumstances there could be only one verdict: guilty. That was the crown's case. That was the law. The jury should do its duty.

De Lancey, in his instructions to the jury, made a desperate effort to bring them back under direction and control. Hamilton had taken great pains, he told them, to show "how little regard juries are to pay to the opinion of the judges." But, despite the effort of the prisoner's counsel to get the jury to disregard instructions, the law was clear, the Chief Justice insisted. "The only thing that can come in question before you is, whether the words as set forth in the information make a libel. And that is a matter of law, no doubt, and which you may leave to the court." Then he read them a ruling of a British judge to the effect that an accusation that officials are "corrupt" is "a reflection on the government." No government can subsist if the people have an ill opinion of it. No government "can be safe" if those who "endeavor" to procure "animosities" remain unpunished.

But Hamilton was too wise to let the case go to the jury before he had made his peace with the court. After an incessant siege of wrangling between court and counsel, jurors had been well known to turn against the rebel whom they had once esteemed. Turning to the bench, Hamilton declared: "I humbly beg your honor's pardon. I am very much misapprehended if you suppose what I said was so designed." Apologizing for the "freedom" he found himself under the necessity of using, he asserted that "there was nothing personal designed." His contentions "arose from the nature" of the defense.

Zenger, too, had been prepared to make his own closing speech to the jury had the situation been sufficiently desperate. From notes among James Alexander's papers, it is apparent that he had intended to remind the jurors that he had lain in jail for twelve months while his family had been supported by charity, and that he and his parents had "fled from a country where oppression, tyranny, and arbitrary power had ruined almost all the people." Had his peers returned a verdict of guilty against him, Zenger proposed injecting a note of melodrama. He would have turned on them and asked them to make an end of his life, "for I can't bear the thought of having my family starve and my poor little babes crying for bread." Coming after Hamilton's magnificent effort, this tear-jerker would have been anticlimactic. Zenger forbore any demonstration on his own part, for neither he nor anyone else in the courtroom had any doubt about the verdict. The prisoner's own report of the trial ends appropriately on a personal note:

> The jury withdrew, and in a small time returned, and being asked by the clerk whether they were agreed of their verdict, and whether John Peter Zenger was guilty of printing and publishing the libels in the information mentioned, they answered by Thomas Hunt, their foreman: *Not Guilty.* Upon which there were three huzzas in the hall, which was crowded with people and the next day I was discharged from my imprisonment.

Since the funds to pay for Zenger's keep during the period he was confined in jail were not raised until the day following the trial, the printer did not participate in the gala victory banquet his friends and well-wishers held the night of the verdict at the Black Horse Tavern on Smith Street. It was only fitting that Andrew Hamilton should be the lion of that occasion.

The Zenger trial had almost immediate transatlantic repercussion. A London correspondent of Ben Franklin's *Pennsylvania Gazette* pithily reported the reaction in the mother country. "A Goliath in learning and politics," he observed, "gave his opinion of Mr. Hamilton's argument in these terms: 'If it is not law, it is better than law, it ought to be law, and will always be law wherever justice prevails.' " Perhaps Gouverneur Morris was a trifle overenthusiastic when, at a later time, he hailed the case as "the morning star of that liberty which subsequently revolutionized America." The fact was that neither in New York nor in Great Britain did the Zenger case gain ready acceptance as a binding legal precedent. Nobody was ever convicted in the province of New York for seditious libel, but most of the colony's printers continued to struggle with official censorship long after Zenger had successfully defied Cosby.

The issue of freedom of the press arose again in inflammatory form after the repeal of the Stamp Act and the passage of the Mutiny Act. A Tory-minded assembly branded as "false, seditious, and infamous" two broadsides which savagely attacked that body. Unwilling to suffer martyrdom, the printer accepted an offer of immunity and named Alexander McDougall as the author of the tracts. Seven years before the McDougall affair, John Wilkes had been committed to the Tower and expelled from the House of Commons for daring to assert in his newspaper, the *North Briton*, that the King, on the opening of Parliament, did not speak the truth. Now, like Wilkes, this radically minded New Yorker was confined to jail for some three months when he refused to post bail. In McDougall's case, unlike Zenger's, the criminal proceedings were instituted by a legislative body, and were dropped only because of the death of the chief witness for the prosecution.

Despite the Zenger and McDougall cases, the New York Constitution of 1777 failed to contain a provision safeguarding freedom of the press (nine other states as well as the Federal Bill of Rights did make such provisions, however). The issue in New York remained unsettled. Across the seas the British Parliament in 1792, in Fox's Libel Act, gave the jury power to render a general verdict on the whole matter put in issue and denied the right of the court to find the defendant guilty merely on proof of publication. Thus, fifty-seven years after the jurors in the Zenger case had boldly assumed the right to judge law as well as fact, Parliament gave legal sanction to their stand. While one half of the argument of Zenger's cohorts was now the law in England, the proposition that truth was a defense in criminal libel still remained to be firmly established on both sides of the ocean.

Curiously enough, the repressive Sedition Act of 1798, enacted during John Adams's troubled administration, allowed "the truth of the matter in the publication charged as libel" to be introduced by the defense and gave the jury the power to determine criminality. Despite these two technical safeguards, that statute, as Woodrow Wilson has pointed out, "cut perilously near the root of freedom of speech and of the press." After ten convictions under this Federal act, some on pretty frivolous grounds, seditious libel suits were halted by President Jefferson. A repentant government repaid the fines it had imposed.

In the states, on the other hand, criminal-libel suits continued to be prosecuted under the common law. When, in 1802, Harry Croswell, publisher of the Hudson *Wasp* and a violent Federalist, was prosecuted in New York by the Jeffersonian Republicans for a criminal libel on Jefferson, Chief Justice Lewis charged the jury to confine themselves to the fact of publication, and ruled that truth could not be given in evidence. In his argument for a new trial, Alexander Hamilton, Croswell's counsel, contended "for the liberty of publishing truth, *with good motives and justifiable ends,* even though it reflects on government, magistrates, or private persons." Assailing "the little, miserable conduct of the judge in Zenger's case," Hamilton went on to attack Lord Mansfield for his charge in the celebrated case of the Dean of St. Asaph, in which he declined to follow the Zenger jury. In that case the great Erskine had persuaded the jury to bring in a verdict of "guilty of publishing only." On the issue of the jury's role in criminal libel, Mansfield's views were dismissed by Hamilton as "not those fit for a republic."

In a brilliant peroration Hamilton denied that tyranny could ever be introduced in this country by arms. "These

can never get rid of a popular spirit of inquiry," he proph-
esied. "The only way is to crush it down by a servile tribunal. It is only by the abuse of the forms of justice that
we can be enslaved. An army never can do it." James Kent,
that erudite and conservative Federalist, then dominating
the state Supreme Court, supported Hamilton all along the
line, and studded his opinion with arguments culled from
the Zenger case. At long last two pre-eminent New Yorkers,
Hamilton and Kent, had fashioned a legal rubric for the
freedom of the press, a principle upheld by the legislature in
1805, and incorporated into the Constitutions of 1821 and
1846. These provisions served as models for the press guarantees of many of our present-day state constitutions. Following New York, a majority of states adopted the rule that
truth is justified provided the publication is made with good
motives and for a justifiable end. A number of states went
even farther and made truth a complete defense in criminal
proceedings even if told maliciously. In England, Lord
Campbell's Act, passed in 1843, vindicated in full the arguments of James Alexander, William Smith, Andrew Hamilton, and their Palatine printer client.

The increasing resort to prosecutions for sedition during
the past decade poses a legitimate question: how would
Zenger fare today before an American court? Would the
present climate of opinion assure so intemperate a critic of
the government as the *Journal's* editor a fair trial? There
are a number of straws in the wind indicating that an Andrew Hamilton could conceivably face a more bitter forensic
battle today in the Federal district court at Foley Square
than in the old New York Supreme Court, which convened
just a few blocks away, in the City Hall, then at the corner
of Nassau and Wall Streets.

Much has happened since the year 1919, when Justice
Holmes, in his notable dissent in the Abrams case, cautioned
that "only the emergency that makes it immediately dangerous to leave the correction of evil counsels to time warrants making any exception to the sweeping command, 'Con-

gress shall make no law . . . abridging the freedom of
speech.' " In the face of formidable threats to our national
security, Congress and the courts have seriously restricted
freedom of expression. The kind of emergency that Justice
Holmes considered as justifying such curtailment of expression was "a clear and present danger." But in sustaining
certain sections of the Smith Act as applied to the Red sedi-
tionists' trial of 1950, the Federal courts have substituted
for the test of "a clear and present danger" the less precise
formula: "a sufficient danger of a substantive evil." As the
two dissenting Supreme Court justices pointed out in that
decision, this doctrine "waters down the First Amendment
so that it amounts to little more than an admonition to Congress." Once we start making freedom of speech turn, not
on what is said, but on the intent with which it is said, "we
enter territory dangerous to the liberties of every citizen."

In one other respect the Red seditionist trial marked a
serious reversal of a trend begun in the Zenger case. The
Federal courts now hold that in sedition cases the degree of
danger to society is an issue to be determined by the judge
rather than the jury. The argument of Judge Learned Hand
that the conflict of momentous issues cannot be entrusted to
juries constitutes a sorry commentary on the low repute of
the jury system. Seditious libel is by its very nature of large
public interest. To apply this new doctrine to the broad
areas of communication of ideas would be to turn the clock
back to the year 1735 when Andrew Hamilton defied De
Lancey, and a courageous New York jury decided for themselves issues of both law and fact.

As freedom of expression, both of the printed word and in
other media of communication, is being circumscribed by
Federal and state legislation, as well as by the activities of
unofficial self-constituted censorship groups, it is not surprising that an attempt should be made to undermine the
proposition of the Zenger case that truth is a defense to a
criminal prosecution for libel. Recently the state of Louisiana has seen fit to enforce a revised defamation act passed

in 1942, which provided that truth is *not* a defense in defamation, but can be considered as a mitigating factor. Under this statute, criminal prosecutions were instituted in 1951 against a group of newspapermen who had the courage to speak out against several public officials and three admitted gamblers. In acquitting the accused, Judge Bernard Cocke of New Orleans upheld the right to criticize the public acts of officials. "Without that right," he warned, "we would have a dictatorial form of government."

To restore freedom of speech to its honored place in a free society, we must be on guard that we do not replace that Jeffersonian toleration of diverse views by a national quarantine of hostile doctrine, that we do not make conformity compulsory, that we do not limit our protection of free speech to none but safe views, which rarely need protection. The establishment of such curbs would be an admission that we had lost faith in the democratic process. Grounds exist for viewing present-day encroachments on the freedom of the human mind as constituting a more formidable threat than they did in 1735. Hence those who believe in freedom cannot afford to be one whit less vigilant in defending it than were the citizens of New York in the time of John Peter Zenger.

IV

The Spooner Triangle Love Slaying

when Eros saved his surprise for the very last

One of the weightiest criticisms foreign observers have leveled against the American legal system is that politics seasons justice. Too often have prosecutors sought advantage by tempering the force of the law for their political friends and vigorously executing it against their foes. When, as during a time of civil war, the flame of party passion burns brightest, an accused may well encounter insurmountable obstacles to obtaining a fair trial if he happens to owe allegiance to the wrong side. If, in addition, the crime is atrocious and shocking, the odds against the suspect lengthen appreciably.

The Spooner murder case was a test of Massachusetts justice. The crime was atrocious. The chief suspect was a Tory whose character and morals were not what they should have been. The prosecutor was a Patriot. The trial took place in the midst of the American Revolution. Such circumstances would almost certainly preclude a dispassionate administration of justice. Yet only eight years earlier another murder trial, conducted under conditions verging on civil war, revealed that a jury could rise above politics and return a just verdict. That was the Boston Massacre case, in which John Adams, in the teeth of bitter criticism from his own side, defended the British redcoats charged with murder, secured the acquittal of six of the accused, and persuaded the jury to find the remaining two guilty of manslaughter rather than murder.

The Spooner trial had two points of similarity with the Boston Massacre case. The charge was murder, and two of the accused were British redcoats. But it had several noteworthy points of departure. The evidence against the prisoners was far more conclusive. The sanity of one of the prin-

cipals was in question, and that principal happened to be a
woman. This last aspect made the task of the defense a
formidable one, for it served to confirm certain prevailing
notions about the criminality of women.

Today sociologists assure us that the female criminal is
deadlier than the male, that the intimate family circle has
more to fear from female members than from males, and
that married homemakers, eaten up with envy and revenge,
have a higher criminal potential than spinsters. But to an
Englishman or an American of the eighteenth century such
conclusions would scarcely be news. Moll Cutpurse and Moll
Flanders had their counterparts in many an accomplished
prostitute shipped to the colonies from Bridewell. Britishers
who, like Dr. Johnson, patronizingly regarded Americans as
a "race of convicts" and "the bastards of England" were
fond of quoting the remark of one member of "a jolly female crew" to another, in a favorite bit of doggerel, "The
Sot-Weed Factor":

You'd blush (if one cou'd blush) for shame,
Who from Bridewell or Newgate came.

Philadelphia society matrons must have blushed through
their rouge on learning that the "Princess Susanna Carolina
Matilda, Marchioness of Waldegrave," whom they had re-
gally entertained, was plain Sarah Wilson, transported for
the theft of some of the royal jewels. But this imposture was
matched by Mary Moder, a professional thief, who persuaded London ladies of quality that she was a German
princess, and by that elegant pickpocket Jane Webb, whose
career of impersonation and deception ended on the gallows
at Tyburn.

Even women with more respectable backgrounds could go
berserk. Lucy Byrd, the frustrated wife of Virginia's richest
planter and a character straight out of Juvenal, took her fits
of temper out on her servants and slaves, burning them with
a red-hot iron when the mood dictated. In fact, the court
records of the period are replete with accounts of cruelties
inflicted on servants by malevolent and degraded mistresses.

Husband-murderers were by no means unknown in that day and age. The accounts of the trial in the mother country of Elizabeth Jeffries and her lover for murdering her butcher husband in his bed were avidly read at the time. A half century before the bloody events of Worcester about to be recounted, Jemima Westerdon was arraigned in New Jersey for the fatal poisoning of her husband. Although the convicted murderess defiled the marriage bed by acts of "adultery and whoredom," and was properly sentenced "to be burnt till she be dead," she managed somehow to live out her natural life.

But the barbarous elimination of "Old Bogus" Spooner stands out as the greatest murder story of its generation. Indeed, the Boston *Independent Chronicle* went so far as to call this case "the most extraordinary crime ever perpetrated in New England." Today, with some eight thousand cases of murder and non-negligent manslaughter reported in the United States every year, we are less likely to be aroused by any but the most bizarre homicides; but the Spooner case had every element that would virtually monopolize the front pages of our newspapers for weeks at a time were it to occur today. It was a Revolutionary version of the sordid "dumbbell murder" case of Ruth Snyder and Judd Gray.

The feminine lead was played by a beautiful, oversexed, and discontented young matron. Her marriage, when barely eighteen, to Joshua Spooner, a prosperous but tightfisted businessman, much older than herself, was passionless. The dour, drab Joshua and his volatile, glamorous wife made an ill-mated pair. At thirty-two Bathsheba Spooner had reached a dangerous age. That she should have an affair with a handsome lad a dozen years her junior seemed almost inevitable. Puritan inhibitions notwithstanding, illicit sexual arrangements were by no means unknown in the backwater towns near Worcester, Massachusetts. Premarital chastity and conventional monogamy, judging from court records and church confessions, were about as exceptional in Revolutionary times as they seem to be in the Kinseyan era.

What distinguished this sordid triangle from the run-of-the-mill variety was that it ended fatally for all parties concerned.

Analysts would seek the roots of Bathsheba's emotional instability in her family background and would doubtless stress the fact that she was the child of an inharmonious but wealthy household. Her father was the imperious Timothy Ruggles, who held the office of Chief Justice of the Court of Common Pleas of Massachusetts until the Revolution. Popularly known as "the Brigadier," Ruggles, according to John Adams, hardly an impartial observer, was approached by people "with dread and terror." He was influential enough to defeat the formidable James Otis, of Writs of Assistance fame, in a contest to serve as delegate to the Stamp Act Congress, held in New York in 1765; but when that body took the liberty of stating colonial rights in forthright language, Ruggles, conservative by nature, refused to concur. From that time on, his popularity waned. When the Revolution broke out he became a Tory. To the patriots of Massachusetts Ruggles personified that species whose head was in England, whose body was in America, and whose neck ought to be stretched. Fearing that the patriots might carry out some such unwholesome notion, Ruggles left the country to start life anew in Nova Scotia. It is significant that he left behind his wife, Bathsheba Bourne Newcomb, and was never observed to have shed any tears at this separation. The feeling was mutual. Local Yankee tradition has it that she once served up her husband's favorite dog for his dinner. Thanks to the generosity of the rebel legislature, which proceeded to confiscate the bulk of Ruggles's property, his wife was permitted to retain one third of his estate.

The judge's daughter stayed on with her husband and children in Brookfield, near Worcester, where Tories and Toryism, though heartily detested, were never completely eradicated. But when it came to matters of the heart, Bathsheba did not let political considerations influence her. She was strictly neutral. When Ezra Ross, a well-set-up young veteran of the patriot army, was invalided home after campaigning since the start of the war, Bathsheba welcomed this interruption of the routine of household bickering and boredom. She did everything she could to aid his convalescence. The transition from nurse to mistress could have been foreseen.

Ezra could not long resist the irresistible, and, as his parents later described it, "tempted by long promises—and seduced both from virtue and prudence—by a lewd, artful woman, he too readily acceded to her measures black as they were." The attachment of the pair became a matter of some gossip. The handsome couple were frequently observed riding together, for Mrs. Spooner, with her surplus of physical energy, was an accomplished horsewoman. But Bathsheba soon discovered that her affair was not without consequences. Fearful that her husband's discovery of her pregnancy would bring her marital difficulties to a head, she confided in Ross. The two lovers frequently talked over various plans for doing away with Mr. Spooner. But when it came to converting these dreams into reality, Ezra stalled.

What Bathsheba needed to serve her cold-blooded purpose was a couple of desperadoes. Now, it so happened that there were then encamped at Cambridge, less than thirty miles away, a great number of redcoats who had fought with Burgoyne and were captured in the great capitulation at Saratoga in the fall of '77. Mrs. Spooner told Alexander Cumings, one of her servants, to be on the lookout for any deserters from that prison camp. The opportunity was soon vouchsafed. Spooner went off on a trip, and Ross, at Bathsheba's prompting, invited himself along. The coast was clear.

Fortuitously, two British soldiers, James Buchanan and William Brooks, came by and were hailed by Cumings and invited to accept the hospitality of the household. Buchanan, a Scot, was then thirty years of age, had been a sergeant under Burgoyne, and was trying to make his way to Canada to rejoin his wife and child. Brooks, a private, was an

Englishman three years his junior. Both had unsavory army
records: Buchanan had embezzled company funds, Brooks
was a known thief. They had walked out of the prison camp
and were on their way to Canada. Quite naturally they suspected a trap, but Cumings, according to their own subsequent confessions, reassured them that his mistress "had a
great regard" for the British army, "as her father was in it
and one of her brothers." Bathsheba invited the redcoats
into the sitting-room, where all three breakfasted together.
Since the weather was stormy, Bathsheba put them up for
the night. They could lodge with her, she told them, until
her husband's return. In the course of the next ten days
Bathsheba, that expert "seducer of souls," expatiated freely
on her marital unhappiness.

Spooner's return was a shock to Bathsheba. "I never was
so stumped in all my life," she frankly admitted to Jesse
Parker, a hired hand. According to her own account, she
never expected to see him alive again, as Ross had taken
with him an ounce of poison, which he promised he would
administer at the first opportunity. But to the queasy-
stomached Ross the chance never came. Spooner, who did
not share his wife's tolerance toward the British army, made
no bones about his feelings toward the redcoat guests. As
soon as he laid eyes on them, he turned suspiciously to
Bathsheba and asked who they were. Buchanan, she assured
him, was Alexander Cumings's cousin. Spooner stormed out
of the house and headed for the tavern. There another un-
pleasant surprise was in store for him. He was presented
with a bill for a substantial quantity of liquor consumed at
his household during his absence. By now he was beside
himself with wrath. Returning home, he curtly ordered the
soldiers to get out. They begged him to let them stay until
morning, and he grudgingly consented: "You may sit by
my fire till morning, but you must not let me see you afterwards." But he did not like their looks and asked a neighbor, Reuben Old, who had come to discuss business, to spend
the night with him. Spooner went upstairs, brought down

his money box, and lay down on the floor with it under his head. Meanwhile the impudent and unwanted guests were having a merry time by the kitchen fire. Every once in a while Old would look in. Buchanan, according to Old's later testimony, threatened that if Spooner turned him out he would "have his life before morning," a remark that was probably more authentic than another threat attributed to the sergeant, doubtless colored by subsequent events, that he "would put him in the well for two coppers." Buchanan later stoutly denied picking the well as the last resting-place of his host.

But the rogues managed to stay on the premises. The next night, after a pleasant day at the tavern, they returned to the house when Spooner was abed. Bathsheba hid them in the barn and sent out their breakfast the next morning. This arrangement continued for several nights. Whenever Spooner was away at the tavern, the skulking redcoats would come into the house and dine with his wife. If he returned unexpectedly early, they always managed to run into the cellar or get out by the back stairs without detection.

Bathsheba was now desperate. Her pregnant condition could hardly be concealed much longer. About a month before, when she realized that Ross could not be counted on, she had asked Cumings, her servant, to dispose of Spooner, and in return promised, according to his own testimony, to "make a man" of him. When he stalled, she naturally pounced on the two rogues who were enjoying her barn, her victuals, and her husband's liquor, and, from all evidence, making quite free with her person. In the last week of February, Buchanan and Brooks found accommodations at the home of Mary Walker, a widow living in Worcester. For three days Mistress Spooner spent most of her time visiting the soldiers, and their landlady was quite taken aback by her brazen behavior. "Brooks often laid his head upon Mrs. Spooner's neck, and oftentimes put his hand round her waist," Mary Walker later testified. Mrs. Spooner hastened to reassure her. "You must not wonder," she explained. "Billy [Brooks] has lived at my house and is as fond of me as he would be of a mother." By now the triangle had assumed the geometrical pattern of a pentagon.

As there appeared to be hands enough to accomplish the bloody deed, the time for action drew near. Various plans were considered. Brooks procured a dram of calomel, which he made into twenty papers. Now, for some reason, Mistress Spooner refused to administer the dose to her husband. Ross, still unable to screw up his courage beyond poisoning, actually dropped some aqua fortis (nitric acid) into Spooner's toddy, but without effect. Spooner must have noticed the taste, however, for he declared: "Somebody around here is trying to poison me!"

Now that Spooner's suspicions were aroused, it was necessary to move fast. On the very last day of February, Mistress Spooner was overheard remarking to Buchanan, on parting from him at the Walkers': "Tomorrow night at eleven o'clock. Remember, sergeant!"

He replied: "Tomorrow night at eleven o'clock."

The next day was the Sabbath. Ross, who had joined the redcoats, was restless and irritable and paced the floor constantly. When Mary Walker archly asked him "What made him so dull," he replied curtly: "Reason enough." The conspirators were having their difficulties. Ross, worried lest Spooner blame him for misusing a horse, had Bathsheba's maidservant conceal him in the buttery. When the two British prisoners of war approached the Spooner house on Sunday afternoon, they noted that company was calling. Mrs. Spooner came outside and told them that Ross was within, with a brace of loaded pistols, and that "he had promised her he would kill Mr. Spooner as he came from the tavern." When they went in, Ross showed them the pistols, and declared: "Spooner will die by this tonight!" But the redcoats dissuaded him on the ground that the noise of the shot would alarm the neighbors. Brooks then countered with the proposal that, if Ross would co-operate, they would knock Spooner down, since bludgeoning was a lot quieter than shooting. This agreed upon, they all sat down to a hearty supper, "with some flip before, topped off with rum." Each took turns as a lookout to warn against Spooner's return.

After supper Brooks went outside and stood concealed near the small gate leading into the kitchen. As the unsuspecting victim came past, he cracked him over the head with a log. Spooner's cries of "Murder! Murder!" were quickly stifled by his assailant, who proceeded to half strangle him. At this point Ross and Buchanan gave a hand. Before disposing of the body, Ross took Spooner's watch out of his pocket and handed it to Buchanan, who in turn pulled off the old man's shoes. Then Brooks and Ross lifted the helpless victim and dropped him, apparently still alive, in the well head-first.

After so cleverly dispatching their victim, they went into the parlor and told Bathsheba that the job had been accomplished. She rushed upstairs, opened a mahogany chest, and brought down Spooner's money box. Not having the key, she had Buchanan break the box open, and gave Ross two notes of $400 each to change and turn over to Brooks. But on further search she found $243 of paper money, which they preferred to the less easily negotiable notes. Ross, in turn, was given four ten-pound notes to purchase a riding-habit. In addition, Bathsheba gave her lover Spooner's jacket and breeches, which he was indiscreet enough to put on.

The smell of burning wool awakened the servant Cumings, whose alibi that he was in bed during the murder probably saved him from the gallows. He went into the parlor and found the four conspirators throwing clothes into the fire. Brooks's own breeches, covered with blood, were among the items consigned to the flames.

Then came one of those macabre moments which brought the brutal realities of the situation home in no uncertain terms to Cumings. Mistress Spooner asked him to fetch

some water to wash off Spooner's silver buckles. When he
went to the well, he found that he "could not dip the
bucket." He returned, shouting: "Mr. Spooner's in the well!"
A maidservant, Sarah Stratton, who had accompanied him,
rushed for her Bible. But there is no evidence that Cumings
made the slightest effort to recover his master's body. He
merely asked Mistress Spooner whether they had cut her
husband's throat. She replied: "No. They knocked him
down." This must have reassured him.

It was nearing midnight when the redcoats set off for
Worcester. They reached Mary Walker's home around
four a.m. and told the household "a parcel of lies" to explain the unconventional time of their arrival. When morning came, the three men started drinking "to drown the
thoughts of the horrid action we had been guilty of," according to their later confession. But instead of hitting the
trail for the north country, they went down to Brown's tavern for further refreshment. Apparently they got so roaring
drunk that they carelessly displayed Spooner's watch and
the pair of silver buckles, which his neighbors quickly recognized. Tongues began wagging very quickly.

But all the indiscretions were not committed by Brooks
and Buchanan. Mrs. Spooner spent a restless night. Her
hired girl, Sarah Stratton, later testified that she "sighed
and tumbled a good deal." When Sarah warned her that she
would have to tell the neighbors, Bathsheba offered to give
her "a good deal" if she would "keep it a secret." This secret was becoming too promiscuously shared for safety. The
morning after the murder Mrs. Spooner went out to the well
and with amazing sangfroid remarked to Cumings: "I hope
he is in heaven." Then she had the effrontery to order her
manservant to get a horse, ride to the local tavern, and in-
quire for her husband.

Cumings's inquiry at the tavern, which Spooner had
quitted at a respectable hour the night before, touched off
a searching party. Any detective-story addict would have
found their task a cinch. For a heavy blanket of snow that

had remained on the ground from the previous evening had preserved certain obvious clues. Ephraim Cooley kicked a heap of snow near the gate of the Spooner house and uncovered Mr. Spooner's hat. To simplify further searching, several sets of tracks leading to the well were found in the snow. Bloodstains spattered the well-curb. It did not require too much imagination, even for untrained rustics, to look into the well. An examination revealed Spooner's lifeless body, the face and temple badly battered and a wound in the scalp an inch and a half long.

By the time the coroner came, the corpse was laid out in the parlor. Mrs. Spooner, it was noted, "could not be persuaded to look at it." Then the local physician, Dr. Jonathan King, requested her to put her hand on the forehead. "Poor little man," she murmured hypocritically. This was the medieval ordeal by touch. If the flesh showed color under the finger of the suspected murderess, she was considered guilty. There is no record of the result of the "scientific" test in this case, but only a few years before, John Adams had had the battle of his life to secure an acquittal in a sensational murder case in Salem where the ordeal indicated the guilt of the accused.

The coroner's jury quickly returned a verdict that the deceased, "on the evening of the first of March about 9 o'clock, being returning home from his neighbors near by his own door, was feloniously assaulted by one or more ruffians, knocked down by a club, beat and bruised, and thrown into his well with water in it."

Brooks, Buchanan, and Ross were picked up at a neighboring farmhouse. On Brooks's shoes were found a pair of silver buckles, initialed "J. S.," which Spooner's nephew identified as belonging to his uncle. Spooner's watch was also located in Brooks's pocket. Other articles belonging to the deceased were found on Ross's person, as well as the four ten-pound notes Bathsheba had given him. All three realized that the game was up. Admitting that he had been an accessory, Ross denied that he "struck the first blow," and asked for a minister. When brought before William Young, local justice of the peace, the three men confessed their parts in the murder. For a brief time Mistress Spooner held out, but on being committed to jail she admitted "that she hired the people to concert the murder." Conscience-stricken at long last, she told the arresting constable: "If it was not for this thing I could meet my Judge," adding that "this happened by means of Ross's being sick at our house."

In April term, Brooks, Buchanan, and Ross were indicted for murder and a true bill was returned by the grand jury against Bathsheba, in which she was charged with "being seduced by the instigation of the devil" and with inciting and procuring the felony. But since the charge was murder, the accessory could be punished as though a principal. All four came to trial before the Supreme Court of Judicature held at Worcester later that same month in the old county courthouse. Presiding over the court was Chief Justice William Cushing, who held that post until his promotion to the Supreme Court of the United States in 1789. He was assisted by four associate justices. A signer of the Declaration, Robert Treat Paine, must have especially relished prosecuting the state's case against two followers of an enemy camp and the daughter of an unreconstructed Tory. To defend the prisoners the state assigned an exceptionally able Harvard-educated attorney, Levi Lincoln, then twenty-five years old and later to become a United States Attorney General in Jefferson's Cabinet. Hardly two years after the Spooner case he was to win a notable decision before the highest court of the commonwealth, declaring slavery illegal. Lincoln's chief reputation, however, was to be gained, not in criminal practice, but as a creditor's lawyer, and he later was a chief target for the anti-lawyer animus of the Shaysite forces in his part of the state.

Despite their pre-trial confessions, all four prisoners pleaded not guilty. But the prosecution came into court loaded with ammunition. The murderers had left a trail a mile long and had been amazingly indiscreet. It remains to be proved that any more recent addle-pated, sex-hungry spouse-killer has ever blabbed as freely and incriminatingly about her feelings toward her husband as Bathsheba had done. Witness followed witness on the stand to fill in, with damning circumstantial evidence, the outlines of the murder. Sarah Stratton accused Mistress Spooner of often having declared: "I hope Mr. Spooner is in heaven." Obadiah Rice put the quotation somewhat more picturesquely when he quoted Bathsheba some time before the murder as expressing the wish that "Old Bogus was in heaven." The justice of the peace took the stand to summarize the confessions of the three men. The constable then told how Mistress Spooner had admitted her complicity and cleared her two servants, Cumings and Sarah Stratton, of actual participation in the crime. "I bribed them to do and say what they had done," she had declared. The two employees proceeded to turn state's evidence to save their own necks.

In view of this mountain of uncontroverted evidence the formidable task that confronted the defense would have discouraged the most zealous advocate. Levi Lincoln offered no witnesses, but proceeded to sum up at once. He cautioned the jurors against allowing their political feelings toward Bathsheba's Tory father to color their verdict. He pointed out that the roles of the defendants must be carefully distinguished. True, there was a murder. Somebody must have done it. But it did not follow that A, B, and C were the murderers. That conclusion had to be proved beyond a reasonable doubt before the jury could convict them. Lincoln struggled valiantly to detach the fate of the youthful Ross from the more obvious doom that faced the two redcoats. Entering into a full discussion of the law of principal and accessory, he contended that the testimony was not sufficient to convict Ross of the offense charged in the indictment, though he might possibly be guilty of misprision of felony. The jury must be satisfied not only that he was present, but that he was present with a design to assist the murderers. Ross's failure to exploit numerous previous opportunities might well indicate that he had no such serious intention, his counsel argued.

Lincoln knew that Massachusetts juries had no compunctions whatsoever about convicting women of felony. Even though the witchcraft and Quaker episodes were exceptional, juries in less hysterical situations had shown not the slightest preference for the frailer sex when capital sentences were involved. In desperation, Lincoln distinguished the line of defense in Bathsheba's case from that in the case of the other prisoners. With considerable plausibility he argued that, even conceding her unhappy married life, conduct as irrational and indiscreet as Bathsheba's could only be prompted by an unsound mind. Since the plea of insanity was rare in early American murder trials, it is worth following Lincoln's arguments somewhat closely:

It was a well known principle, founded in nature, that the source of wickedness, the incentive to guilt, was the hope of impunity. But what hopes of being undetected, what presumption of impunity could she have? Was it possible to conceal the matter, considering the number of persons engaged, their character, their situation, and their profession, no plan formed to conceal it, no story agreed upon, no place to flee to—the matter entrusted to strangers, with no evidence of their fidelity? She is seen in company with them the night before, at Walker's—procures calomel—agrees on the time— reminds them of it before company, "at eleven o'clock." Why the calomel, if her husband was to be assassinated? She previously tells that Mr. Spooner is going on a long journey, and inquires if anybody wants to hire his farm. After the murder, she gives the murderers his watch, buckles, waistcoat, breeches, and shirts, and even puts them on, to be worn in the eye of the world, where they were well known to be Spooner's clothes, and from their goodness and fashion might be known not to belong to the persons wearing them, being low and vulgar. Was this the conduct of a person in the exercise of reason? Would it have been less rational to have written on their foreheads in capitals, "THE MURDERERS OF MR. SPOONER!"

Was it credible that it should ever enter into the head of a person of so much capacity and so much cunning, to entrust an affair so heinously criminal to strangers, deserters, and foreigners, who, had they escaped detection here, would probably have boasted of their feats, after they got off to the enemy; and if she was afraid they would not disclose it, to entrust it to other women and boys?

Must she not have had some chosen trusty confidant, or some reason to hope either to accomplish or conceal so detestable an action before she would have engaged in it, if she had been in her senses? It was perpetrated in the heart of a populous town, near neighbors where it must at farthest be discovered by the morning— liable to be heard in the time of it—by the people abroad, by the two travelers who lodged there that night, by the children, and others of the family.

Was it possible that she would commit so atrocious a crime, and run so great a hazard from no motive? It was said she was upon ill terms with her husband. This was to trump up one crime, that there may seem to have been a motive to have perpetrated another from. But to whom did she commit the execution of it? Whom did she make use of as her accomplices? Whom was her confidant? Whom did she trust with the management of a villainy, that so nearly affected her reputation, her safety, her life, her children, the lives of others, and the happiness of her friends? The answer was, to prostitutes, Tories, regulars, deserters, strangers, and foreigners. Was a woman that is admitted to have sense, so stupid, if in the exercise of her reason, as to trust all that was valuable to her and hers, in the hands of such persons? Could there be a doubt, in the minds of the jury, that this woman was not in a state of mind which

rendered her guilty in the eye of the law, of a most horrible crime, which would subject her to the last afflic-
tion of human power and vengeance?

In support of this defense it might be added that the record showed that Bathsheba Spooner was emotionally unstable. She was given to irrational outbursts. When, a few
days before the murder, Sergeant Buchanan offered her his
handkerchief, she shouted: "God damn the handkerchief! I
will not touch it." On being taken to jail in Obadiah Rice's
sleigh, she remarked: "This don't seem like Christmas day."
But since it was the month of March the reference seems
quite muddled. She also was quoted as saying that she had
"a great desire to see her Daddy," and that "if it had not
been for that this murder would never have been committed." An alienist might have made out a good case for insanity. Whether it was from the shock and disgrace of the
trial or a hereditary predisposition, it is nonetheless significant that Bathsheba's daughter became an incurable lunatic
and that her sister Mary's mind was temporarily unbalanced by the events of March and April 1778.

Were Bathsheba Spooner to stand trial today, her plea of
insanity would be supported by alienists of repute, and most
likely be sustained. But in those days insanity was an argument of last resort. It failed to budge the jury from their
duty. They returned verdicts of guilty, and sentence of
death was pronounced on all four prisoners by the Chief
Justice.

For Brooks and Buchanan no one had the slightest sympathy, but a good deal of irresponsible sentimentality was
worked up for Ross, the young war veteran, and Bathsheba,
the inscrutable widow. More tears were shed for them than
for their unfortunate victim. Ezra's aged parents petitioned
the Governor for a pardon, citing the lad's excellent war
record as well as the military achievements of four other
sons who had fought at Bunker Hill and marched south with
Washington. "A fourth mingled at the northward his bones

with the dust of the earth." Their son, they pathetically urged, had been the victim of "momentary impulses and alluring seducements." His pardon would console "his aged, drooping and distressed parents," laboring under the "weightiest afflictions, and turn the wormwood and the gall into something tolerable." But the Governor refused to intervene.

The greatest battle was reserved for Mrs. Spooner. Worcester's popular minister, the Reverend Thaddeus Maccarty, who enjoyed the widow's confidence, was shocked to learn that she was soon to become a mother. This fact he set forth in endorsing a petition for the respite of all the criminals, in which Mrs. Spooner herself joined. The council granted a four-week reprieve to the prisoners, setting their execution for July 2. But the condemned enjoyed little privacy or peace of mind. They were compelled to tell a reporter for Isaiah Thomas's Worcester *Spy* that they were annoyed by "the multitudes that crowd in upon them. They therefore induce that none may come to see them out of a vain curiosity, or merely to gaze at them, but leave them to enjoy their short time in as profitable a manner as may be."

Mrs. Spooner's plea was something special. Under the law of England, which was followed in Massachusetts with heavy reservations, a female convict pleading her belly was entitled to a writ *de ventre inspiciendo,* according to which a jury consisting of two men midwives and twelve matrons could be summoned to examine her. Hale, Hawkins, and other learned writers on English criminal law agreed that if the verdict were "quick with child"—that is, that the child was alive in the womb—execution should be stayed until the next session, or from session to session, until the child was delivered or time disproved the verdict. In both England and the colonies the plea had been successfully made. The execution of two of the Salem witches was respited because of their pregnancy, and in other colonies the plea not infrequently procured the condemned woman a reprieve, occasionally followed by a pardon. Indeed, as Misson, a French traveler, observed somewhat earlier in reporting English prison conditions, "the women or wenches that are condemned to death never fail to plead they are with child (if they are old enough) in order to stop execution till they are delivered." At times unfounded, this plea was much too often confirmed by medical examination. Misson had a facile explanation for the high incidence of pregnancy in condemned females. "Though they came never so good virgins into the prison," he points out, "there are a set of wags there that take care of these matters. No doubt they are diligent to inform them the very moment they come in, that if they are not with child already, they must go to work immediately to be so; that in case they have the misfortune to be condemned, they may get time, and so perhaps save their lives." "Who would not hearken to such wholesome advice?" he concludes.

The flavor of the old writ issued by the Massachusetts Council is worthy of preservation.

The Government and People of the Massachusetts Bay, in
  New England. To the Sheriff of Worcester: Greetings:
Whereas, Bathsheba Spooner, late wife of Joshua Spooner,
of Brookfield, in the said County of Worcester, stands attainted in due form of law before the superior court of judicature, etc., held at Worcester, within and for the county of Worcester, on the third Tuesday of April, being accessory before the fact to the murder of said Joshua Spooner, for which she has received sentence of death, and a warrant has issued in due form of law, to have the same sentence duly executed on the fourth day of June next; and whereas it has been represented to us in Council that the said Bathsheba Spooner, that she is quick with child, and we being desirous of knowing the truth of said representation, do command you therefore that taking with you two men midwives and twelve discreet lawful matrons of your community, to be first duly sworn, you in your proper person, come to the said Bathsheba Spooner, and cause her diligently to be searched

*by the said matrons in the presence of the said men mid-
wives by the breast and belly, and certify the truth whether
she be quick with child or not; and if she be quick with child,
how long she had been so, under your seal, and the seals of
the said men midwives, unto the Secretary's office of Massachusetts Bay aforesaid, at or before the said twenty-fifth
day of June next, together with the names of the matrons by
whom you shall cause the said search and inspection to be
made, hereof fail not, and make true return of the writ with
your doings hereon.*

*Witness: The major part of the Council of Massachusetts
Bay, in New England, at Boston, this twenty-eighth day of
May, A.D. 1778; by their Honors' Order.*

JOHN AVERY, *Deputy Secretary*

Two weeks later the sheriff of Worcester County made the
following return:

Worcester, ss.:   *In strict compliance with the within
directions and warrant, I have summoned two men midwives, and twelve lawful matrons, and caused the said matrons to be under oath, and in my proper person, with the
said men midwives and matrons attended on the said Bathsheba Spooner, they have made searches as required in the
within writ. The verdict of the above matrons is, That the
said Bathsheba Spooner is not quick with child.*

*Given under our hand and seal, this eleventh day of June,
A.D. 1778.*

WILLIAM GREENLEAF, *Sheriff* (Seal.)
JOSHUA WILDER, *Midwife* (Seal.)
ELIJAH DIX, *Midwife* (Seal.)

A list of matrons:

ELIZABETH RICE	MARY TODMAN
HANNAH PERRY	ZURBULCH STOWELL
CHRISTIAN WALKER	EZEBEL QUIGLEY
MARGARET BROWN	MARY BRIDGE
LIDIA BALL	HANNAH BROOKS
MARY STERNES	SARAH JONES

·   ·   ·

Bathsheba and the Reverend Mr. Maccarty kept up the battle. Their personal appeal to the male midwives, Joshua Wilder and Elijah Dix, led to another examination a few weeks later. The resultant conflicting opinions were forwarded to the council.

Worcester, June 27, 1778.

To the Honourable Board of Councillors,
for the State of Massachusetts Bay:

May it please your Honours, we, the subscribers have examined the body of Mrs. Bathsheba Spooner (by her desire), to find whether she is quick with child or not, and although it was our and the jury of matrons opinion on the examination of the eleventh instant, that she was not quick with child at that time, yet upon this further examination, we would inform your Honours that we must give it as our opinion that we have reason to think that she is now quick with child.

JOHN GREEN, ⎫
JOSHUA WILDER ⎬ *Midwives*
ELIJAH DIX ⎭
HANNAH MOWER, *Woman Midwife.*

Worcester, June 27, 1778.

To the Honourable Board of Councillors,
for the State of Massachusetts Bay:

Whereas, we, the subscribers matrons, on the examination of Mrs. Bathsheba Spooner, on the eleventh instant, did give it as our opinion on oath that she was not quick with child at that time, have again at this day on her request examined her present circumstances, and give it as our opinion that she is not now quick with child.

ELIZABETH RICE
MOLLY TATTMAN

As the names of only three matrons appear on the subsequent returns, it is clear that this second jury was purely informal and had no legal standing. Certainly the council did not feel itself bound by its verdict.

When Bathsheba learned that the first verdict would stand, she was stunned momentarily, but pulled herself together sufficiently to address this eloquent communication to the council:

May it please your honors:

With unfeigned gratitude I acknowledge the favor you lately granted me, of a reprieve. I must beg leave, once more, humbly to lie at your feet, and to represent to you that, though the jury of matrons that were appointed to examine into my case have not brought in my favor, yet that I am *absolutely certain* of being in a state, and above four months advanced in it; and that the infant I bear was lawfully begotten. I am earnestly desirous of being spared till I shall be delivered of it. I most humbly desire your honors, notwithstanding my great unworthiness, to take my deplorable case into your compassionate consideration. What I bear, and clearly perceive to be animated, is innocent of the faults of her who bears it, and has, I beg leave to say, a right to the existence which God hath begun to give it. Your honours' humane *Christian* principles, I am very certain, must lead you to desire to preserve life, even in its miniature state, rather than to destroy it. Suffer me, therefore, with all earnestness, to beseech your honors to grant me such a further length of time, at least, as that there may be the fairest and fullest opportunity to have the matter fully ascertained—and as in duty bound, shall, during my short continuance, pray.

But the bachelorless council remained inflexible in the face of the division of opinion among the jury and Bathsheba's perfectly reasonable request. Hatred of Tories stifled any normal humanitarian consideration. Execution was ordered for the appointed time. Mrs. Spooner took the bad news calmly, but requested that her body be examined after her death. As the mother of three children, she felt that she

was as competent an expert on her own pregnancy as anybody in the county.

For ten days prior to the execution crowds of people from
the surrounding countryside and even the seacoast towns
began flocking into Worcester. The town selectmen, alarmed
at this influx during a smallpox epidemic then raging, took
the occasion to insert an advertisement in the June 25 issue
of the *Massachusetts Spy* cautioning all physicians and
nurses who had recently been in attendance at local hospi-
tals that had been receiving smallpox patients, as well as all
persons "lately having had the smallpox not to appear in
the assembly of spectators unless sufficiently cleansed. Otherwise their attendance may prove fatal to many, and render the execution, which is intended for the warning and
benefit of all, a public detriment."

At half past two in the afternoon of July 2 the condemned
were brought from prison to the place of execution under
guard of a hundred men. The three soldiers who had so
recently fought on opposing sides walked together. Mrs.
Spooner, now exceedingly weak, was driven in the Reverend
Mr. Maccarty's chaise. Just as they reached the place of
execution a black cloud darkened the summer sky. The tension was soon punctured by a terrific clap of thunder, and
for thirty minutes a violent rainstorm pelted executioner,
prisoners, and the five thousand spectators, without discrimination. "Make way, make way!" shouted mounted officers trying to stem the panic-stricken multitude. Women
shrieked. Men cursed. As the prisoners were taken to the
tree of doom, preceded by four coffins, a bolt of lightning
struck near by. The reading of the death warrant to the
prisoners could scarcely be heard above the crescendo of
thunder.

Finally the storm abated, whereupon the Reverend Mr.
Maccarty read a passage from Deuteronomy xix, 13: "Thine
eye shall not pity him, but thou shalt put away the guilt of
innocent blood from Israel, that it may go well with thee."

When Mistress Spooner's turn came, she stepped out of the
chaise and ascended the ladder. The halters were fastened,
the malefactors pinioned, and their faces covered. Then the
sheriff notified all four that he would drop the stage immediately. Gallant in her last moments, according to eyewitnesses, Bathsheba exhibited none of the prudishness of the
notorious English parricide Mary Blandy, who, when climb-
ing the fatal ladder, covered with a black cloth, besought
her executioners: "Gentlemen, do not hang me high, for the
sake of decency!" Bathsheba took a tight grip on the sheriff's hand and remarked: "My dear sir, I am ready! In a
little time I expect to be in bliss, and a few years must
elapse when I hope I shall see you and my other friends
again."

One by one the bodies were cut down and carted away.
That evening an examination of Bathsheba Spooner's corpse
was made by surgeons in accordance with her request, and a
perfect male fetus of the growth of five months was taken
from her! Eros had saved his surprise for the very last.
Massachusetts never completely recovered from the shocking denouement. Bathsheba Spooner was the last female ever
to be executed in that commonwealth.

Present-day Worcester and Brookfield have not entirely
effaced the scars of the Spooner tragedy. Still extant today,
but in ruins, is the old well, Mr. Spooner's last mortal resting-place. The victim's gravestone stands in the old Brookfield cemetery. Its severe inscription can still be read: "HE
WAS MURDERED BY THREE SOLDIERS—AT THE INSTIGATION OF
HIS WIFE, BATHSHEBA." Bathsheba's family quickly buried
her body in an unmarked grave, now Green Hill Park, property of the city of Worcester. If her sardonic ghost still
haunts the spot, it has not been known to discourage spoon-
ing couples from following the dictates of their hearts.

V

The Trial of Aaron Burr

monomania or treason?

Since this nation was founded, more bulwarks have been erected to protect the accused against unfair trial procedure than to assure the government that it will be given a fair chance to present its case. But a dispassionate system of the administration of justice should provide safeguards for the people as well as for the accused. Perhaps no other political trial in American history has ever brought this double-pronged question into so sharp a focus as did the trial of Aaron Burr: can the accused get a fair trial when the President of the United States is personally behind his prosecution? Can the government get its full case before the jury when the court is presided over by a political enemy of that President? The Burr trial raised these questions without settling them, and even at this late date commentators have not agreed on the answers.

The difficulties that the government faced in the Burr trial stemmed not alone from the political complexion of the bench, but also from the constitutional definition of the crime of treason charged against the accused. Traditionally, prosecutions for treason had been a club wielded by authoritarian governments to crush opposition. The English courts had construed treason to embrace not only disloyal actions against the crown but disloyal intent as well. Through this interpretation treason could be nipped in the bud at the preliminary or conspiratorial stage before any overt act had been committed.

What the American colonists had seen of treason prosecutions hardly endeared them to the law. At the time of Bacon's Rebellion in 1676, opponents of Virginia's Governor were summarily executed for treason without trial. The leaders of Leisler's Rebellion in New York in 1689 and of the tenant uprising in that same province in the 1760's had been convicted of treason after regular trials, but, on sober second thought, almost everyone felt that the courts had gone too far in each case. Quite naturally, the founding fathers were sensitive to the broad construction the English courts had placed on the treason law. Every patriot who affixed his signature to the Declaration of Independence was, of course, guilty of treason against the crown. Accordingly, at the Constitutional Convention, after considerable debate, the framers defined treason against the United States as consisting "only in levying war against them, or, in adhering to their enemies, giving them aid and comfort." Article III, section 3, further provided that "no person shall be convicted of treason unless on the testimony of two witnesses to the same overt act, or on confession in open court." In this manner the framers demonstrated their conviction that it was far better that a few disloyal citizens escape punishment than that the crime of treason be used by the government as a weapon to muzzle the opposition.

In many respects it was most appropriate that the person who should provide the treason clause of the Constitution with its classic test should have been Aaron Burr. While Jefferson and Hamilton disagreed on most matters, they were in complete accord on one subject. Both regarded Aaron Burr as a scoundrel. Jefferson looked upon Burr "as a crooked gun, or other perverted machine, whose aim or shot you could never be sure of." Hamilton, who had felt it his "religious duty" to oppose Burr's career, criticized him as "an embryo Cæsar." In the bitter gubernatorial race in New York State in 1804 Hamilton went so far as to charge that Burr was a "dangerous man and one who ought not to be trusted with the reins of government." The duel with Hamilton that followed shortly upon the publication of these remarks wrote finis to Burr's local ambitions. His enforced exile opened broader horizons. Soon Burr was enmeshed in projects of a highly dubious, if not outright treasonable, nature.

Only recently Vice President of the United States, Aaron Burr could boast a splendid military record in the Revolution and an impeccable ancestry. His father had been president of Princeton and his maternal grandfather, Jonathan Edwards, was esteemed New England's greatest divine. In short, in any contest for the most glamorous American ever to stand trial for treason Aaron Burr would easily outrun the field. Fittingly, his trial has no counterpart in American history. While from beginning to end the opposing legal celebrities were incessantly skirmishing over intricate substantive and procedural issues, no one was allowed to forget for a moment that the stakes were political as well as legal. Across the stage paraded an amazing collection of colorful, weird, and even disreputable witnesses who never for long took the spotlight away from its central personage, an artful, unmoral, and desperate romantic. The much harassed prosecutor of Aaron Burr did not exaggerate when he exclaimed: "There never was such a trial from the beginning of the world to this day!" Those who packed the courtroom throughout the sweltering Richmond summer of 1807 would have emphatically added: "Amen." So, too, would the towering, roughhewn jurist who, by presiding over the trial, gained the eternal enmity of the President of the United States.

Despite an overwhelming mass of trial testimony and the equivocal evidence of Spanish and British archives not available at the Richmond trial, it is still impossible to define with precision Burr's ultimate objectives. That devious and serpentine character, fifty years of age at the time of his trial, had a well-equipped store of alternative plans, and probably could not even at this day clarify his exact intentions if psychical media successfully got in touch with him. He was prepared to seize Mexico and set himself up as Emperor, but he talked wildly about severing the Western part of the Union. While the British government might conceivably have regarded with equal favor a Mexican conquest or a separation of the Western states, it is incredible that Burr's contacts with the Spanish government, which actually gave him a small sum of money, could have been related to any but the latter project. For Spain to have financed an expedition against her own territory was fantastic. Whether Burr really planned to go through with his secession plan or was using it as a bait to get money from the coffers of Spain and Britain is highly debatable. To one investigator Burr's intrigues with foreign powers were "a consummate piece of imposture." Others are less positive.

The turning-point in the Burr "conspiracy" occurred on the night of October 8, 1806, which that arch double-dealer General James Wilkinson, himself secretly a pensioner of Spain, spent in decoding a cipher message from Burr. After a century and a half this letter still sizzles with untruths, half truths, and incriminating leads.

Your letter postmarked May 13th is received. I, Aaron Burr, have obtained funds and have actually commenced the enterprise. Detachments from different points and under various pretensions will rendezvous on the Ohio, first of November. Everything internal and external favors views. Naval protection of England is assured. Truxton is going to Jamaica to arrange with the admiral on that station. It will meet us at the Mississippi. England, a navy of the United States are ready to join, and final orders are given to my friends and followers. It will be a host of choice spirits. Wilkinson shall be second to Burr only; Wilkinson shall dictate the rank and promotions of his officers. Burr will proceed westward, first August, never to return. With him goes his daughter; her husband will follow in October with a corps of worthies.

The object is brought to the point so long desired. Burr guarantees the result with his life and honor, with

the lives and honor and the fortunes of hundreds of the
best blood of the country. Burr's plan of operations is
to move down rapidly from the Falls on the 15th of
November with the first five hundred or one thousand
men, in light boats now constructed for that purpose;
to be at Natchez between the 5th and 15th of December, there to meet you, there to determine whether it
will be expedient in the first instance to seize on or pass
by Baton Rouge. On receipt of this send Burr an answer. Draw on Burr for all expenses, etc.

The people of the country to which we are going are
prepared to receive us; their agents, now with Burr, say
that if we will protect their religion, and not subject
them to a foreign power, that in three weeks all will be
settled. The gods invite us to glory and fortune; it remains to be seen whether we deserve the boon.

Had Wilkinson done his agreed part, Burr might well
have been launched upon a career in America rivaling Na-
poleon's in Europe. But Wilkinson was as unscrupulous a
realist as Burr, and an even more calculating intriguer. He
pounced on this opportunity to cash in by denouncing the
man whose activities in the West were already beginning to
attract unfavorable notice. Accordingly he dispatched a letter to President Jefferson exposing the conspiracy. Immediately thereafter he offered to reveal information about the
plot against Spain to the Viceroy at Mexico City for the
nominal sum of $110,000. Like Burr, Wilkinson always
played for high stakes.

The general's message reached Jefferson on November 25.
Other warnings had already come to the President, but here
seemed proof positive of some illegal end. "For six or eight
months," Wilkinson asserted, "a numerous and powerful association, extending from New York to Louisiana . . . have
been engaged . . . for a descent on Mexico," with a revolt
of the Orleans Territory "an auxiliary step to the main design." Two days after receiving Wilkinson's evidence the

President issued a proclamation ordering that "all persons engaged" in the conspiracy be brought "to condign punishment." In Kentucky, District Attorney Joseph H. Daveiss, brother-in-law of John Marshall, had thrice in the period of three weeks brought Burr into court to answer charges of conduct injurious to the United States, and each time the crafty conspirator, defended by a rising young attorney named Henry Clay, walked out of court a free man.

Once the President's proclamation reached the West, however, Burr's disingenuous disavowals were to have less weight. Recognizing that he was in personal danger, Burr fled to Nashville. Here he completely hoodwinked Andrew Jackson, whose naïve faith in Burr was matched by his virulent anti-Jefferson bias. Securing a few boats, Burr now sailed down the Ohio with a handful of followers. The arch-conspirator was poised for the kill.

But Wilkinson was waiting. He declared a state of martial law in New Orleans and set himself up as a defender of the city "against revolution and pillage by a hand I have loved," going so far as to offer a reward of five thousand dollars to that man who would "cut off" the leader of the rebel band. To save his own neck and snatch a profit on the side, Wilkinson had no compunction whatever about liquidating his friends. When the Mississippi militia bottled up Burr's little fleet, the former Vice President took to his heels. Arrested at Bayou Pierre, Burr outtalked a grand jury, but was held without bail for military trial. This was obviously the one kind of trial that Burr, with his consummate skill as a jury lawyer, most emphatically did not want. But for Wilkinson, implicated up to his armpits in the conspiracy, a dead Burr was better than a live one. Burr fled, only to be captured in South Carolina.

On March 30, 1807 Burr was brought before Chief Justice Marshall, sitting in the United States Circuit Court of the district of Virginia. He was held for misdemeanor in organizing an expedition against Spanish territory—the very minimum that his operation could have added up to—but the question of treason was left for the grand jury to determine.

A dazzling battery of lawyers defended Burr—Edmund Randolph, Attorney General under Washington, and John Wickham, both of the Virginia bar; Benjamin Botts and Jack Baker, two younger but experienced jury lawyers; and Luther Martin, that mad volcanic genius from Maryland infatuated by Burr's daughter, Theodosia Allston. Later in the trial Charles Lee, formerly an Attorney General of the United States and only recently successful in his defense of Judge Samuel Chase in impeachment proceedings over which Aaron Burr had presided with dignity, also made an appearance in Burr's behalf. In comparison, the government's case was entrusted to a less glittering galaxy. It happened that the Attorney General of the United States at this juncture was Cæsar A. Rodney, whose father, Thomas Rodney, as judge in the Mississippi Territory, had ruled adversely to Burr's personal liberty. The younger Rodney now shrewdly forbore personally entering the case and turned the prosecution over to George Hay, the competent rather than brilliant U.S. district attorney for Virginia, who happened to be James Monroe's son-in-law. Associated with Hay were William Wirt, a rising young attorney, and a dour Scot named Alexander McRae, then Lieutenant Governor of the state, brought in for obvious political reasons. But Thomas Jefferson in Washington was the directing legal genius behind the prosecution at every stage, just as Aaron Burr himself was really chief counsel in command of his own defense.

The opening of court on May 22 was signalized by a shower of legal pyrotechnics. The barrage from both sides continued ceaselessly to the end. The first skirmish was fought over the composition of the grand jury. When the clerk proceeded to call those summoned on the grand jury, the defense demanded to see the panel. After perusing the list Burr rose to his feet, a Chesterfieldian figure, always poised and composed, frigidly logical, his inner fire glimpsed through snakelike eyes shining out of a white, poker face.

May it please the court. Before any further proceeding with regard to swearing the jury, I beg leave to remark some irregularity. If it can be made to appear that the marshal has struck off any part of the original panel and substituted other persons in their stead, the summons is illegal. Such is the law.

Marshall sustained the objection, ruling that a person substituted in place of one actually summoned "cannot be considered as being on the panel." Accordingly two persons were excluded from the grand jury. Burr then proceeded to exercise his privilege of challenging for favor, charging Senator William B. Giles with having publicly asserted that there was an insurrection or public danger. Giles conceded that he had voted to suspend the writ of habeas corpus under emergency conditions, but denied "personal resentments against the accused." Nonetheless, he withdrew. Burr then proceeded to challenge Wilson Cary Nicholas, charging him with bitter personal animosity. Nicholas followed Giles's example. In their places were substituted John Randolph (designated foreman) and William Foushee. Randolph then asked to be excused from serving on the grand jury on the ground that he had "formed an opinion" and that he "had a strong prepossession."

"Really," Burr declared, "I am afraid that we shall not be able to find any man without this prepossession." Marshall ruled "that a man must not only have formed but declared an opinion" and refused to exclude Randolph from service. Now Foushee admitted to having formed an opinion, and the district attorney interposed with righteous indignation that *"there was not a man in the United States who probably had not formed an opinion."* Were objections such as these to prevail, Hay argued, "Mr. Burr might as well be acquitted at once." Marshall refused to excuse Foushee and proceeded to have the grand jury sworn. The

dice were heavily loaded against Burr—fourteen Jeffersonian Republicans as against only two Federalists.

Burr's next battle was waged to limit the type of evidence
that could go to the grand jury. He requested the court for
an instruction on the admissibility of evidence. Hay sought
to block this move with a heated warning to the court not
to grant "particular indulgences to Colonel Burr, who stood
on the same footing with every other man charged with
crime." "Would to God that I did stand on the same
ground with every other man," Burr retorted. Instead, he
implied, he was being denied his civil rights. For the time
being, Marshall put off deciding this crucial issue.

Hay now moved to commit Burr on a charge of high treason. Botts urged lack of notice. When the district attorney
interrupted to signify his willingness to postpone the motion until the next day, Botts shouted: "Not a moment's
postponement! Colonel Burr appears in this court ready to
go on with his trial. He wishes no delay. His great object
is to satisfy his country, the minds of his fellow citizens,
and even the prosecutors, that he is innocent." Botts continued heatedly:

> We have, sir, made enough sacrifices. We have been
> deprived of our legal rights. Our person and papers have
> been seized. We have been subjected to a military per-
> secution unparalleled in this country, given into the
> custody of the satellites of military despotism, and
> guarded by a rigid form of military law. Surely our
> wrongs ought now to end. I sit down in anxious hope
> that the success of this motion may not add to the cata-
> logue of Col. Burr's grievances.

In view of the fierce resistance put up by the defense Hay
found it expedient to set forth the reasons for his motion to
commit Burr. "The fact is this," he declared, "Mr. Wilkinson is known to be a material witness in this prosecution.
His arrival in Virginia might be announced in this city before he reached it. I do not pretend to say what effect it

might produce upon Col. Burr's mind, but certainly Col. Burr would be able to effect his escape merely upon paying recognizance of his present bail."

Hay's imputation was hotly resented. Wickham retorted: "Here Col. Burr *is,* and always will be ready to meet every charge and to face every man who dares to say anything against him." As regards the essentiality of Wilkinson, Wickham queried: "Why is he not here? He is a military officer, bound implicitly to obey the head of the government. In the War of Europe a general has been known to march the same distance at the head of his army in a shorter time than General Wilkinson has had to pass from New Orleans to this place. Perhaps there are other reasons for his not coming."

Wirt argued the government's motion for commitment with irrefutable logic. For the prosecution to have waited until the star witness arrived before seeking to have the defendant committed would "in fact have been an invitation to the accused to make his escape." Continued Wirt:

Sir, if Aaron Burr be innocent, instead of resisting this motion, he ought to hail it with triumph and exultation. What is it that we propose to introduce? Not the rumors that are floating through the world, nor the *bulk* of the multitude, nor the speculations of newspapers; but the *evidence of facts*. Let the truth come out. Let us know how much of what we have heard is false, how much of it is true; how much of what we feel is prejudice, how much of it is justified by fact. Whoever before heard of such an apprehension as that which is professed on the other side? *Prejudice excited by evidence!* Evidence, sir, is the great corrector of prejudice. Why then does Aaron Burr shrink from it? It is strange to me that a man who complains so much of being, without cause, illegally seized and transported by a military officer should be afraid to confront this evidence.

The gentlemen would balance the account of popular prejudices. They would convert this judicial inquiry into a political question. They would make it a question between Thomas Jefferson and Aaron Burr. At present we have an acount to settle, not between Aaron Burr and Thomas Jefferson, but between Aaron Burr and the laws of his country. Let us finish his trial first. The administration, too, will be tried before their country, before the world. They, sir, I believe, will never shrink, either from the evidence or the verdict.

Never forgotten for a single moment of the entire trial was the bitter Jefferson-Burr feud. The prosecution counted on the prestige of the President to secure a conviction; the defense sought to portray the prisoner as a victim of personal persecution. Edmund Randolph castigated Jefferson for having expressed an opinion as to Burr's guilt "which was calculated to operate judicially upon the judges and the juries." Burr himself granted that the authority to commit "on probable cause" was necessary, but he urged that "this power ought to be controlled as much as possible." The state, he declared, had already had plenty of time to collect the evidence, but he himself must be ready to proceed to trial only in the government's "way" and not on equal terms. He charged the government with having publicized the affidavits collected against him, so that they were known to the grand jury. There was some justice in Burr's complaint, for the government had vast resources available for gathering evidence, resources not open to the ordinary citizen—and unlimited funds. "We have set on foot an inquiry through the whole country," Jefferson had stated. "Go into *any* expense necessary for this purpose," the President ordered Hay, "and meet it from the funds provided to the Attorney General for the other expenses." Elaborating on the government's advantages, Burr pointed out that the prosecution could have compulsory process to obtain affidavits, whereas he had "no such means as these, sir, and where then is the

equality between the government and myself?" He went on
to cite instances of harassment "contrary to the form of
law," charging that his friends "had been everywhere seized
by the military authority, a practice truly consonant with
European despotism," dragged into court, and compelled to
give testimony against him. His papers had been seized,
mails had been tampered with, and an order had been issued
to kill him, the maximum penalty that might have been imposed if he were formally convicted of treason. "The government," he observed, "may be tender, mild and humane
to everyone but me." With a masterly blending of satire and
logic he closed his argument:

> Our president is a lawyer, and a great one, too. He
> certainly ought to know what it is that constitutes a
> war. Six months ago he proclaimed that there was a civil
> war. And yet, for six months have they been hunting
> for it, and still cannot find one spot where it existed.
> There was, to be sure, a most terrible war in the news-
> papers; but nowhere else. When I appeared before the
> grand jury in Kentucky they had no charge to bring
> against me, and I was consequently dismissed. When I
> appeared for a second time, before a grand jury, in the
> Mississippi Territory, there was nothing to appear
> against me; and the judge even told the United States
> attorney that if he did not up his bill before the grand
> jury, he himself would proceed to name as many of the
> witnesses as he could, and bring it before the court.
> Still there was no proof of war. At length, however, the
> Spaniards invaded our territory, and yet there was no
> war. But, sir, if there was a war, certainly no man can
> pretend to say that the government is able to find it
> out. The scene to which they have now hunted it is only
> three hundred miles distant, and still there is no evi-
> dence to prove this war.

Marshall now made the first of a series of compromises.
While ruling against the commitment, he increased the pris-

oner's bail from the amount of $5,000 originally set to $15,000.

Meanwhile all Richmond awaited Wilkinson—in Edmund Randolph's words, "the alpha and omega of the present prosecution." "The funeral pile of the prosecutor is already prepared by the hands of the public attorney, and nothing is wanting to kindle the fatal blaze but the torch of James Wilkinson," who "is to officiate as the high priest of this human sacrifice," commented Randolph. Twice the grand jury was dismissed for a few days, as Washington Irving, who covered the trial for a New York pro-Burr paper, put it, "that they might go home, see their wives, get their clothes washed, and flog their Negroes." At long last, on June 15, James Wilkinson made an appearance. Washington Irving's hostile portrait is memorable:

> Wilkinson strutted into court and took his stand in a parallel line with Burr on his right hand. Here he stood for a moment swelling like a turkey-cock and bracing himself up for the encounter of Burr's eye. The latter did not take any notice of him until the judge directed the clerk to swear General Wilkinson. At the mention of the name Burr turned his head, looked him full in the face with one of his piercing regards, swept his eye over the whole person from head to foot, as if to scan its dimensions, and then coolly resumed his former position, and went on talking with his counsel as tranquilly as ever. The whole look was over in an instant, but it was an admirable one. There was no appearance of study or constraint in it; no affectation of disdain or defiance; a slight expression of contempt played over his countenance.

Two years later, in his *Knickerbocker's History of New York,* Irving burlesqued the brassy Wilkinson as the ludicrous General Jacobus von Poffenberg, "booted to the middle, sashed to the chin, collared to the ears, whiskered to the teeth." Wilkinson, who strangely enough enjoyed Jeffer-

son's complete confidence, gave the President quite a different version of the confrontation:

> I was introduced to a position within the bar very
> near my adversary. I saluted the bench and in spite of
> myself my eyes darted a flash of indignation at the little
> traitor, on whom they continued fixed until I was called
> to the book. Here, sir, I found my expectations verified
> —this lion-hearted, eagle-eyed Hero, jerking under the
> weight of conscious guilt, with haggard eye, made an
> effort to meet the indignant salutation of outraged
> honor; but it was in vain, his audacity failed him. He
> averted his face, grew pale, and affected passion to con-
> ceal his perturbation.

Even before Wilkinson's appearance, however, a new
issue, injected by Burr, threw Jefferson into a towering passion and caused Marshall acute embarrassment. On June 9
Burr called the attention of the court to the reference in the
President's communication to Congress of a letter and other
papers he had received from Wilkinson. "Circumstances had
now rendered it material," he argued, "that the *whole* of this
letter should be produced in court. Hence, I felt it necessary
to resort to the authority of this court to call upon them to
issue a subpœna to the President of the United States to
produce certain papers; or, in other words, to issue a subpœna duces tecum." Dumbfounded by the move, Hay asked
to what purpose. To confront Wilkinson with his own letter,
Wickham replied. Since Hay disputed Marshall's right to
grant the motion, the court had no alternative but to call
for arguments on both sides. In support of Burr's motion
Luther Martin, that "federal bulldog," bared all his fangs.

> This is a peculiar case, sir. The president has under-
> taken to prejudge my client by declaring that, "of his
> guilt there can be no doubt." He has assumed to him-
> self the knowledge of the Supreme Being himself, and
> pretended to search the heart of my highly respected

friend. And would this president of the United States, who has raised all this absurd clamor, pretend to keep back the papers which are wanted for this trial, where life itself is at stake? It is a sacred principle that in all such cases the accused has a right to all the evidence which is necessary for his defense. And whoever withholds, wilfully, information that would save the life of a person charged with a capital offense is substantially a murderer, and so recorded in the register of heaven.

Comments Beveridge: "Never since the days of Patrick Henry, had Richmond heard such a defiance of power." The tide of local opinion now began to inch toward Burr.

Jefferson reacted violently to Martin's defiant, even insolent attack. "Shall we move to commit L. M. as *particeps criminis* with Burr?" he suggested to Hay. "Fix upon him misprision of treason . . . and add another proof that the most clamorous defenders of Burr are all his accomplices." Fortunately Hay did not see fit to follow this emotionally rooted piece of advice.

In opposing Burr's motion, Wirt argued that the production of the papers requested could not conceivably remove the evidence of the accused's guilt. He did, however, make the significant concession that the President was not above the law, that a man does not "become a god even by becoming a king or an emperor." Getting down to the letter in issue, he argued that "a copy of this letter will answer every purpose of the original." This would be true provided one could be sure that it was a correct copy. But could one be sure? The fact was that Jefferson in his communication to Congress had left out the first incriminating sentence: *"Your letter postmarked May 13th is received."* Since this sentence showed that Burr was *replying* to a communication from Wilkinson, its inclusion might have had the effect of discrediting the informer! Wirt ducked this question. *"We will keep our eyes on Aaron Burr,"* he warned, in conclusion, *"until he satisfies our utmost scruples! . . .* On our part, we wish only a fair trial of this case. If the man be innocent in the name of God let him go!"

A man of Marshall's backbone could not let this challenge go unanswered, and the jurist promptly rebuked both sides for "the style and spirit of their remarks " and for seeking to excite public prejudice. But taking full advantage of Jefferson's vulnerable position, the defense ignored Marshall's admonition and continued their frontal attack on the chief executive. "The President testifies that Wilkinson has testified to him fully against Burr; *then let that letter be produced*," shouted Randolph. For the President "to give opinions concerning the guilt or innocence of any person" was unconstitutional, Martin outshouted Randolph. "Shall the cabinet of the United States be converted into a lion's mouth of Venice; or into a *reportorium* of the inquisition?" he asked.

At no point in the trial was Marshall's partisanship more evident than in his ruling on this motion. Any person under the law, he held, had a right to the process of the court to compel the attendance of his witnesses. Standing on solid Jeffersonian ground, Marshall contended that all men are equal in the eyes of the law. Even presidents are not exempt from testifying in court. The President was entitled to "guarded respect," but he was not to be invested with a halo. In ruling that a *subpœna duces tecum* could be directed to the President, Marshall concluded his remarks with a statement widely viewed in government circles as extremely prejudicial:

It is not for the court to anticipate the event of the present prosecution. Should it terminate as is expected on the part of the United States, all those who are concerned in it, should certainly regret, that a paper, which the accused believed to be essential to his defense, which may, for aught that now appears, be essential, had been withheld from him. I will not say that this circumstance would, in any degree, tarnish the reputation

of the government; but I will say, that it would justly
tarnish the reputation of the court which had given its
sanction to its being withheld. Might I be permitted to
utter one sentiment with respect to myself, it would be
to deplore most earnestly the occasion which should
compel me to look back on any part of my official conduct with so much self-reproach as I should feel could
I declare, on the information now possessed, that the
accused is not entitled to the letter in question, if it
should be really important to him.

McRae was on his feet at once to rebut "the impression
which has been thus conveyed by the court that we not only
wished to have Aaron Burr accused, but that we wished to
convict him." Such an impression, he charged, "is completely
abhorrent to our feelings." Marshall now sought to placate
the government by denying that it was "his intention to in-
sinuate that the attorneys for the prosecution, or that the
administration, had ever wished the conviction of Col. Burr,
whether he was guilty or innocent," but he restated his position in a way that was hardly calculated to heal the
wound. "Gentlemen had so often," he pointed out, "and so
uniformly asserted that Col. Burr was guilty," and "had so
often repeated it before the testimony was perceived on
which that guilt could alone be substantiated," that it appeared to the court "probable that they were not indifferent
on the subject."

As Hay wrote to Jefferson, Marshall's judicial slip produced a "sensation," and "the judge actually blushed." Indeed, Jefferson's own refutation of Marshall's arguments
was withering. "The Constitution," he wrote to Hay, "enjoyed [the President's] constant agency in the concerns of
six millions of people. Is the law paramount to this, which
calls on him on behalf of a single one?" Where would be
that vaunted independence of the three branches of the government, he cogently argued, if the President "were subject
to the *commands*" of the judiciary, and to imprisonment for

disobedience? This argument was, and remains, unanswerable, though in recent years House and Senate committees have revealed on occasion a total unawareness of Jefferson's classic stand in the Burr trial. The President disdained to comply with the court order, and there the matter rested.

After hearing the state's case the grand jury on June 24 found true bills for treason and misdemeanor against Burr and Blennerhassett. As Randolph commented, Wilkinson, that "mammoth of iniquity," narrowly escaped being indicted himself. The one-time Attorney General, who, not so many years before, had had to defend himself against the false accusations of having solicited money from France to influence our foreign policy toward England, remarked on Wilkinson's cross-examination: "All was confusion of language and looks. Such a countenance never did I behold; there was scarcely a variance of opinion among us as to his guilt." But how Wilkinson, Burr's deputy, could be guilty and Burr, the prime mover in the conspiracy, innocent was never cleared up by the defense.

Henceforth Wilkinson assumed the role of outraged innocence. Spurning to fight a duel when challenged by one of Burr's aides, he was publicly ridiculed as a traitor, coward, perjurer, and forger. Later he challenged Wickham for having made in court a slurring reference to his deposition. Wickham defended his right to comment on testimony in the interest of his client and insisted that any crimes imputed to the general should be decided by the courts and not by the code duello. Despite the contemptible figure he cut at Richmond, Wilkinson raised a question that still remains unanswered: are there any limits to the degree of vilification to which a witness may be subjected by an attorney?

The Burr case came up for trial on August 3. Two weeks were spent attempting to select from the panel twelve jurors who had not formed and expressed an opinion on Burr's guilt. Burr personally examined the jury, and this exchange between the prisoner and Hamilton Morrison was typical of the latent prejudice among the veniremen:

BURR: Have not these rumors excited a prejudice in your mind against me?

MORRISON: I have no prejudice for or against you.

BOTTS: Are you a freeholder?

MORRISON: I have two patents for land.

BOTTS: Are you worth three hundred dollars?

MORRISON: Yes, I have a horse here that is worth the half of it.

BOTTS: Have you another at home to make up the other half?

MORRISON: Yes, four of them.

Hardly had the titter that rippled across the courtroom subsided when Morrison, turning to the spectators, boldly retorted: "I am surprised that they should be in such terror of me. Perhaps my *name* may be a terror, for my first name is HAMILTON!" Outwardly unruffled by this low blow, Burr was on his feet at once. "*That* remark," he declared with reason, "is a sufficient cause for objecting to him. I challenge him peremptorily."

Owing to the difficulty in securing an unbiased jury, it was anticipated that sharp wrangling would take place over the kind of opinions formed which would exclude a man from the jury. Here Luther Martin was superlative. In one of those characteristically excursive arguments through which the court sat patiently during Richmond's torrid season, he declared that "it was one of the soundest principles of law that every man had a right to be tried by an impartial jury." The Constitution was emphatic, he declared, that "jurors would be free from all bias and prejudice," but in this case one prospective juror after another had "come with minds already prepossessed against the prisoner." While jurors should be free from impressions both as to the *intention* of the accused and as to the *act*, he contended, the inflammatory press made it difficult, if not impossible, to secure a single unprejudiced juror. In fact, unless a man were "some solitary hermit shut up in the hollow of a tree or in an inaccessible cave," he could not possibly have been without knowledge of the reports of the conspiracy. But that kind of jury could not be procured, Wirt retorted, "unless it had fallen from heaven."

Marshall's opinion on what constituted fairness and impartiality stands to this day as the classic utterance on that subject. It is not to be expected that a man who has prejudged the case, the jurist reasoned, would weigh evidence or argument as fairly as a man whose judgment is not made up. He conceded that "light impressions which may fairly be supposed to yield to the testimony" constituted no sufficient objection to a juror, but "strong and deep impressions which will close the mind against the testimony that may be offered in opposition to them" would constitute sufficient objection. This would not rule out a person who had formed an opinion on *any* fact, but on an "essential" point. Hence, concluded Marshall, a person who had declared that the prisoner "entertained treasonable designs for which he is charged, and was prosecuting them when the act charged in the indictment is alleged to have been committed is good cause of challenge." Accordingly, all of the suspended jurors were rejected for cause. To meet the contention of the defense that the first panel had numbered "too many members of assembly and candidates for public favor and office," the court called for a new venire of forty-eight talesmen. Having scored this victory, the defense now adopted less obstructive tactics. Picking men virtually at random and accepting even Miles Box, who had publicly stated that "Col. Burr ought to be hanged," Burr allowed a jury to be sworn. Perhaps he was convinced that the safest jurors would be those whose hostility had been exposed. More likely this disarming move was an act of desperate calculation on the part of the accused. He now recognized that if he won, it would be only on the law, not on the evidence. At length, on August 15, agreement on a jury was reached.

In opening for the government, Hay announced his intention to prove that on December 10, 1806 Burr had congre-

gated at Blennerhassett's Island thirty or so armed persons
for the purpose of levying war against the United States,
and that he then descended the Ohio and the Mississippi
with force and arms to take possession of New Orleans. "If
either charge be supported by evidence," Hay told the jury,
"it will be your duty to find a verdict against him." Denying the doctrine that to commit treason "actual hostility or
force must be employed," Hay found such a definition perfectly acceptable to "traitors themselves, assembled together
for the purpose of devising laws for their own security."
Calling on the jury "to do justice and to decide the cause
according to the evidence which will be produced before
you," Hay proceeded to an examination of the government's
witnesses.

First to take the stand was a fabulous adventurer, General William Eaton, wearing a huge sombrero and a red
Turkish sash, and bearing himself like an Oriental poten-
tate third class. As soon as Eaton was sworn, Martin called
on the government to prove an overt act before presenting
any testimony of treasonable intention. The court's ruling
sustaining the defense constituted a bitter blow to the government's case. Marshall asserted that the only evidence
which would be admitted at this stage of the proceedings
was of "the intention which compares a part of the crime,
the intention with which the overt act itself was committed,
not a general evil disposition, or an intention to commit a
distinct fact." Just how would this ruling affect Eaton's testimony? The court was willing to admit evidence relating
to the levying of war on Blennerhassett's Island or to the
seizing of New Orleans or to the separation of the Western
states from the Union by force. The court had indicated,
however, that it would exclude references to plans to be executed in the city of Washington or elsewhere relating to a
different act of treason, on the ground that they were not
pertinent to the present indictment. As a result the jury was
not permitted to hear the charge Eaton had previously made
in a public deposition that Burr had talked wildly about

seizing the capital and assassinating Jefferson. In short, the
rulings took the bite out of his testimony. As the case proceeded, the Marshall ruling barring evidence of *general*
treasonable designs was to have a profound impact. The
government reeled under the blow and never quite recovered its equilibrium.

Eaton began his testimony with an admission: "Concerning any *overt* act which goes to prove Aaron Burr guilty of
treason, I know nothing." But then he proceeded to give an
incriminating account of Burr's attempt during the winter
of 1805–6 to induce him to join an expedition against Mexico. "At length, from certain indistinct expressions and innuendoes, I admitted a suspicion that Col. Burr had other
projects." Burr needled Eaton by reminding him how Congress had criticized his conduct in Tripoli and had delayed
adjusting his claims outstanding against the government.
Eaton admitted that he had been seriously disaffected by
the government's shabby treatment and that he had given
Burr some measure of encouragement. Then, according to
the witness's story, Burr plunged ahead and "laid open his
project of revolutionizing the territory west of the Alle-
gheny," offering Eaton the military post of second in command to Wilkinson. "Mr. Burr," continued Eaton, "talked
of his revolution as a matter of right, inherent in the people,
and constitutional." Realizing at last that Burr was dangerous, Eaton called on the President. He warned that a revolt
in the West was imminent, and advised him to get the plotter out of the country. In keeping with his bizarre character
he advised Jefferson to buy Burr's future good behavior by
offering him a high diplomatic post. The President "expressed something like a doubt about the integrity of Burr,"
and the matter was dropped.

The defense pounced on Eaton at once. This smoothly
rehearsed story could not be allowed to stand unchallenged.
Did you conduct yourself in such a way as to put an end to
Burr's importunities? Martin demanded. Yes, Eaton replied,

at one of his last interviews with Burr he laid on the table a copy of a toast he had given to the public: "The United States, palsy to the brain that should plot to dismember, and leprosy to the hand that will not draw to defend our union!" But, when pressed, Eaton could not remember when or where that colorful toast was drunk nor could he produce a copy of the newspaper that he claimed had printed it. Then Burr, cold, reserved, collected, struck like an adder:

BURR: You spoke of accounts with the government. Did you, or the government, demand money?

EATON: They had no demand on me. I demanded money of them. I expended money for the service of the United States when employed as counsel at Tunis. It has been since settled and paid.

MARTIN: What balance did you receive?

EATON: That is *my* concern, sir.

BURR: What was the balance against you?

EATON (to the court): Is that a proper question?

BURR: My object is manifest. I wish to show the bias which has existed on the mind of the witness.

MARSHALL: No objections to the question.

EATON: About ten thousand dollars.

BURR: When was the money received?

EATON: About March last.

Since March was the very month of Burr's arraignment, it was clear that the government's witness had been bought and paid for. But Eaton insisted that Burr had planned to revolutionize the Western states.

"Did you understand that you had given me a definite answer?" Burr asked.

Eaton brazenly replied: "No. After you had developed yourself, I determined to use you until I got everything out of you, and on the principle that 'when innocence is in danger, to break faith with a bad man is not fraud, but virtue.'"

Commenting on Burr's cross-examination of Eaton, one

student of criminal trials has remarked: "If any informer ever left the stand more thoroughly impeached, his testimony has mercifully been omitted from the records."

Following in Eaton's wake was Commodore Truxton. He declared on direct examination that he knew "nothing of overt acts, treasonable designs, or conversations on the part of Col. Burr." His account was confined to Burr's efforts to get him to join the Mexican expedition "in the event of war with Spain which he felt inevitable." If that did not materialize, Burr had planned to settle a sizable following on the Washita. With that alternative in mind, Burr had arranged a substantial land transaction. Truxton, according to his own story, had declined to associate himself with the Burr enterprise. Here again Burr outscored the prosecution in his handling of witnesses.

BURR: Did you ever hear me express any intention or sentiment respecting a division of the union?

TRUXTON: I never heard you.

BURR: Did I not state to you that the Mexican expedition would be very beneficial to the country?

TRUXTON: You did.

BURR: Would you not have joined in the expedition if sanctioned by the government?

TRUXTON: I would most readily get out of my bed at twelve o'clock at night to go in defense of my country at her call against *England, France, Spain, or any other country.*

JUROR PARKER: Was this expedition only to be in the event of a war with Spain?

TRUXTON: Yes.

As it turned out, Hay had committed a colossal blunder in calling Truxton to testify for the government. He now tried feverishly to bolster his shaky case with a more dependable witness. He counted heavily upon Peter Taylor, an unworldly gardener, whom he put on the stand to testify to the direct link between Burr, Blennerhassett, and the assemblage on the latter's island. According to Taylor, Burr had told him: "I am the very man involved in this piece of business; and you ought to tell me all you know." Burr then informed him that he would give any young man who would go down the river with him a hundred acres, grog, and victuals, a rifle and blanket. "I will tell you what, Peter," Burr was quoted as having declared, "we are going to take Mexico, one of the finest and richest places in the whole world." Burr would set himself up as king, with his daughter, Theodosia, queen upon his death. When Taylor told Burr that "the people had got it into their heads that he wanted to divide the union," the romantic plotter replied that the two of them "could not do it themselves. All they could do was to tell the people the consequence of it." About two weeks later, Taylor testified, Burr sent him to a Dr. Bennett with a letter offering to buy arms belonging to the United States, or, if he did not choose to sell them, to "send him word *where* they were kept, and he could come and steal them away in the night." Taylor babbled on in an incriminating way: "I delivered the letter. He gave me directions to get it back and burn it, for it contained high treason. I did burn it. The doctor was present." Did the expedition have any guns, Taylor was asked. "Some of them had." "What kind of guns—rifles or muskets?" a juror named Sheppard pressed the witness. Taylor's answer disqualified him further as a weapons expert. "I can't tell whether rifles or muskets."

Colonel George Morgan, baron of Morganza, made a far more impressive witness on the stand. He recounted a dinner conversation with Burr during the course of which he had remarked that "we should have Congress sitting in this neighborhood or at Pittsburgh." "No, never," Burr was reported to have replied, "for in less than five years you will be totally divided from the Atlantic states." After dinner Morgan, according to his story, let Burr know that in his opinion any attempt to divide the states was "nefarious." The colonel retired at once, and left the next morning be-

fore breakfast. Morgan's testimony, inspired by neither hope
of gain nor fear of punishment, was the most damaging in
the entire trial. Broadly construed, it described Burr's intentions in a manner that served to corroborate Eaton's
charges. But the defense was alert to the danger of allowing
it to go unchallenged. As a rebuttal witness Morgan's son
John was called to the stand by Burr.

BURR: In what state of mind was your father?

JOHN MORGAN: He had lately had a fall which had
done him considerable injury.

BURR: I mean as to his capacity.

JOHN MORGAN: My father was old and infirm, and like
other old men, told long stories and was apt to forget his
repetitions.

So far nothing save talk had been elicited which might
shed light on Burr's treasonable intentions. The state now
moved to connect Burr *directly* with the *overt* act alleged to
have been committed on Blennerhassett's Island. The key
witness was a Dutch laborer named Jacob Allbright, who
proceeded to relate the crucial incident:

> I was hired on the island to help to build a kiln for
> drying corn. After working some time, Mrs. Blenner-
> hassett told me that Mr. Blennerhassett and Col. Burr
> were going to lay in provisions for an army for a year.
> When the night [of December 10] came on, I was among
> the men and also in the kitchen, and saw the boatmen
> running bullets. One of them spoke out to the others,
> "Boys, let's mold as many bullets as we can fire twelve
> rounds." After that a man by the name of Tupper laid
> his hands on Blennerhassett and said, "Your body is in
> my hands in the name of the Commonwealth." When
> Tupper made that motion, *there were seven or eight
> muskets leveled at him.* Tupper looked about him and
> said, "Gentlemen, I hope you will not do the like." One
> of the gentlemen who was nearest, about two yards off,

said, "I'd as lief as not." Tupper then changed his speech.

HAY: How many men were there in all?

ALLBRIGHT: About twenty or thirty. Every man belonging to the boats that I took notice of had arms.

WIRT: Had you seen Col. Burr on the island?

ALLBRIGHT: Yes.

Burr's cross-examination of this dangerous witness was as brilliant and devastating a performance as the entire trial afforded.

BURR: Was that Mr. Tupper called General Tupper?

ALLBRIGHT: Yes.

BURR: Did you know General Tupper?

ALLBRIGHT: Yes.

BURR: Is that the gentleman? (pointing to General Tupper, who was present in court).

ALLBRIGHT: Yes.

At the appropriate time Burr called the attention of the jury to the government's conspicuous failure to call Tupper to the stand though he was in attendance throughout the trial. The implication was clear that the government avoided this move for fear Tupper would controvert Allbright. In fact, a subsequent deposition by Tupper gave ground for the government's trepidation. Tupper asserted that he had gone to the island without intending to apprehend anyone, that he had been in no way molested, and that no one had leveled any muskets at him.

BURR: How long did you work with Blennerhassett?

ALLBRIGHT: Six weeks.

BURR: At what time was it that you saw me there?

ALLBRIGHT: I do not recollect.

BURR: The counsel for the United States know, I presume, this circumstance, and might have testimony to ascertain it.

HAY: We have not, as far as I am informed.

BURR: If they have no objection, I will state *when* I was on the island.

Hay said he had not, and Burr asserted that it was on the last day of August and the first of September. If Burr was telling the truth, then Allbright was either badly rattled or a downright perjurer. Before Burr sat down he elicited another damaging admission from the Dutchman. "Where does General Tupper live?" he asked. "In Marietta." "Does he not belong to the state of Ohio?" Allbright's affirmative answer placed the general's action in an entirely different light. Since Blennerhassett's Island was technically Virginia, Tupper's *opéra bouffe* invasion was illegal, and to resist an illegal arrest scarcely constitutes an overt act of treason.

Having produced one, slightly tarnished, witness to the overt act, the government needed but one more to satisfy the constitutional requirement. It took no chances: it produced three. William Love, Israel Miller, and Morris Belknap, each in turn, took the stand to swear that they had seen men assembled on the island, armed with guns, dirks, rifles, and pistols. But, aside from Allbright, no witness placed Burr himself on the island at the time of the military preparations. Burr now seized the opportunity to pour ridicule on the idea that a man like Blennerhassett could have been involved in an aggressive sortie. After Dudley Woodbridge had testified for the government that boats had been delivered to Blennerhassett and that, from the romantic Irishman's own description of the enterprise, he had inferred that "his object was Mexico," Burr took over.

BURR: You know Mr. Blennerhassett well. Was it not ridiculous for him to be engaged in a military enterprise? How far can he distinguish a man from a horse? Ten steps?

WOODBRIDGE: He is very nearsighted. He cannot know you from any of us at the distance we are now from one another. He knows nothing of military affairs.

* * *

Wirt was on his feet at once to rebut any inference that the myopic bungler was incapable of participating in a dangerous conspiracy. "Is he esteemed a man of vigorous talents?" he asked Woodbridge. "He is," the boat builder replied, adding the damaging characterization that "it was mentioned among the people in the country that he had every kind of sense but common sense."

Resting on insubstantial testimony, riddled by the merciless irony of the defense, the government's case was tottering. Although forced to concede that Burr was not at Blennerhassett's Island when the overt act was alleged to have taken place, the government now insisted that the question was not *where* the accused was when the treason was committed but "whether he *procured* it or had a part in it." Hay now made a last desperate effort to prove that the prisoner had not only instigated the treason but actively participated in it. He proposed to put General Wilkinson, the original informer, on the stand. Of course, everybody present knew that Wilkinson could not testify to the events on Blennerhassett's Island as he had openly broken with Burr two months before the alleged overt act. His evidence at best would provide corroboration of Burr's broad conspiratorial designs. Hence the announcement of Hay's purpose touched off a memorable ten-day debate, as both sides recognized that the introduction of such evidence was crucial.

The defense moved at once to bar such collateral testimony on the ground that no overt act was proved as charged. Arguing on the motion in masterly fashion, Wickman opened the debate. Only by the doctrine of constructive treason could Burr be said to be at Blennerhassett's Island, the prisoner's counsel contended, but this doctrine was prohibited by the Constitution. "No person can be convicted of treason in levying war," he instructed the court, "who was not personally present at the commission of the act which is charged in the indictment as constituting the offense." Then Randolph felicitated Marshall "on having the opportunity of fixing the law relative to this particular crime on grounds which will not deceive and with such regard for human rights that we shall bless the day on which the sentence was given to prevent the fate of Stafford."

McRae's reply was suitably blistering. "Let all who are in any manner concerned in treason be principals," he urged, "and it will tend more than anything to prevent and suppress treason!" In supporting McRae's argument, Wirt unleashed a forensic classic that schoolboys studied for generations. "We do not stand here to pronounce a panegyric on the prisoner," he pointed out, "but to urge on him the crime of treason against his country. When we speak of treason, we must call it treason. When we speak of a traitor, we must call him a traitor." The government, Wirt explained, was endeavoring to make the accused "*a traitor by connection,*" and for this purpose it was hardly necessary to insist that Burr be present on the island. It would be infamous were a man to be accounted innocent who devised and set in motion "the whole mechanism" of treason, by going "a hundred miles" away and arranging for the operation to be carried on by his agents, while "those whom he has deluded are to suffer the death of traitors."

Wirt contrasted the restless ambition of Burr, the archseducer, with the naïve simplicity of the man over whom he gained a strange ascendancy. That man was Harman Blennerhassett, "the Monte Cristo of Ohio." "Who is Blennerhassett?" Wirt asked. "A native of Ireland, a man of letters, who fled from the storms of his own country to find quiet in ours." Seeking the solitude of the frontier, he had acquired a beautiful island in the Ohio River. Here he built his estate and pursued his interest in music, literature, and science. Surrounded by a devoted wife and children, he enjoyed a life of peace and "innocent simplicity." But this tranquillity was fated not to last. The destroyer comes.

He comes to change this paradise into hell. Yet the flowers do not wither at his approach. No monitory shuddering through the bosom of their unfortunate possessor warns him of the ruin that is coming upon him. A stranger presents himself. Introduced to their civilities by the high rank which he had lately held in his country, he soon finds his way to their hearts by the dignity and elegance of his demeanor, the light and beauty of his conversation, and the seductive and fascinating power of his address. The conquest was not difficult. Innocence is ever simple and credulous. Conscious of no design itself, it suspects none in others. It wears no guard before its breast. Every door and portal and avenue of the heart is thrown open, and all who choose it enter.

Such was the state of Eden when the serpent entered its bowers. The prisoner, in a more engaging form, winding himself into the open and unpracticed heart of the unfortunate Blennerhassett, found but little difficulty in changing the native character of that heart and the objects of its affection. By degrees he infuses into it the poison of his own ambition. He breathes into it the fire of his own courage; a daring and desperate thirst for glory, an ardor panting for great enterprises, for all the storm and bustle and hurricane of life. In a short time the whole man is changed; and every object of his former delight is relinquished. No more he enjoys the tranquil scene. It has become flat and insipid to his taste. His ear no longer drinks the rich melody of music. It longs for the trumpet's clangor and the cannon's roar.

Yet, argued Wirt, the defense would have us believe that this deluded creature, who played at best a subordinate part in the drama of treason, was "the principal offender, while *he* by whom he was thus plunged in misery is comparatively innocent, a mere accessory!" "Is this reason? Is it law? Is it humanity?" Wirt asked. He climaxed his excoriation of Burr with these words: "Let Aaron Burr, then, not shrink from the high destination which he courted. Having already

ruined Blennerhassett in fortune, character, and happi-
néss forever, let him not attempt to finish the tragedy by
thrusting that ill-fated man between himself and punishment."

The only way to counteract the effect of this flight of
Ciceronian eloquence was by a shrewd mixture of ridicule
and logic. So Botts reasoned. "I cannot promise you, sir,"
he told the court, "a speech manufactured out of tropes and
figures." He would stick to the law and the facts in the case.
Taylor and Allbright were treated as ridiculous characters.
The whole notion that an act of war had been committed
should be laughed right out of court, Botts contended. "The
Mississippi Territory and Kentucky, so we are informed,
were the seat of war. But the simpletons of that state and
territory hunted but could not find war. It remained for us,
the members of the Virginia bar, to come out and astonish
the world with the profundity of our learning in matters
of war." Actually, nothing happened on Blennerhassett's
Island which could conceivably be regarded as warlike, he
concluded.

Were the court to rule now on the law, Hay's star witness would most likely be prevented from telling his story.
The government wanted Marshall to dodge the legal issue
and let all the evidence get before the jury. Then the jury
could decide both the law and the fact. Not many years
before, in the treason trial of John Fries, who had organized
a few hundred Pennsylvania farmers to resist taxes, Justice
Samuel Chase had ruled on the law in such a manner as to
make a guilty verdict inescapable. Chase was subsequently
impeached by the House of Representatives for misconduct
on the bench, but the Senate failed to sustain the charge.
At this point Hay's allusion to Chase's ruling constituted a
thinly disguised warning to Marshall: don't act the way
Chase did if you want to avoid trouble. The government's
veiled threat was grossly improper, and Charles Lee was
quick to point it out. Realizing his blunder, Hay backtracked at once. Marshall adopted a conciliatory tone: "I

did not consider you as making any personal allusion, but as merely referring to the law."

Considering the emotional undercurrents through the course of this historic debate, it seems fitting that it should be closed by one who was hardly sober at any stage of the trial. Inebriety now loosed the tongue of Luther Martin, and his intense hatred of Jefferson kept him upright and on his feet for two whole days. Broadcasting to the world his infatuation for Theodosia Burr Allston, wife of the Governor of South Carolina, he talked of "filial pity" and "the envenomed shafts of hatred and malice hurled at the heart of the father." That was a personal tribute he could not withhold. But in his closing appeal, addressed as much to the jury as to the bench, he shrewdly argued that the prejudice against Burr was so deep-rooted that he could not secure a fair trial:

> I have with pain heard it said that such are the prejudices against Col. Burr that a jury, even should they be satisfied of his innocence, must have considerable firmness of mind to pronounce him *not guilty*. I have heard it not without horror, God of heaven! Have we already under our form of government (which we have so often been told is best calculated of all governments to secure all our rights) arrived at a period when a trial in a court of justice, where life is at stake, shall be but a solemn mockery, a mere idle form and ceremony to transfer innocence from the gaol to the gibbet, to gratify popular indignation excited by bloodthirsty enemies! May that God who now looks down upon us, who has in his infinite wisdom called you into existence and placed you in that seat to dispense justice to your fellow citizens, to preserve and protect innocence against persecution—may that God so illuminate your understandings that you may *know* what is right; and may he serve your souls with firmness and fortitude to *act* according to that knowledge.

The oratory had ended. The fate of Aaron Burr was now in the hands of John Marshall, whose opinion was to become the authoritative exposition of the American law of treason. Sitting in the very same city only six months before, he had ruled in the Bollman case (involving one of Burr's accomplices) that a person who took even a remote part in a treasonable assembly was a traitor. Now he proceeded flatly to repudiate his previous pronouncement. To advise or procure a treason is not treason itself, Marshall ruled. To prove treason the government would have to establish that there had been an act of war and that Burr had participated therein. Addressing himself to the question of what constituted levying war, he asserted: "War could not be levied without the employment and exhibition of force. War is an appeal from reason to the sword; and he who makes the appeal evidences the fact by the use of the means. His intention to go to war may be proved by words; but the actual going to war is a fact which is proved by open deed." It was necessary, he ruled, for the government to prove an overt act of levying war. In this case the government had claimed that, though Burr was in fact absent at the time of the assemblage at Blennerhassett's Island, he was "yet legally present." While "the doctrine that in treason all are principals" was settled English law, under the American Constitution the traitor must *"truly and in fact levy war."* He must "perform a part in the prosecution of the war." Marshall demolished the argument for constructive treason. "The mind is not to be led to the conclusion that the individual was present by a train of conjectures, of inferences, of reasoning; *the fact must be proved by two witnesses,"* as required by the Constitution. Hence the testimony that the government now proposed to offer, since it concerned *subsequent* transactions "at a different place and in a different state," must be barred as irrelevant. The court's ruling brought the government's faulty case to an abrupt termination.

Marshall's closing remarks constitute a memorable enunciation of the independence of the judiciary:

> Much has been said in the course of the arguments on points on which the court feels no inclination to comment particularly; but which may, perhaps not improperly, receive some notice.
>
> That this court dares not usurp power is most true.
>
> That this court dares not shrink from its duty is not less true.
>
> No man is desirous of placing himself in a disagreeable situation. No man is desirous of becoming the peculiar subject of calumny. No man, might he let the bitter cup pass from him without self reproach, would drain it to the bottom. But if he have no choice in the case, if there be no alternative presented to him but a dereliction of duty or the opprobrium of those who are denominated the world, he merits the contempt as well as the indignation of his country who can hesitate which to embrace.
>
> The jury have now heard the opinion of the court on the law of the case. They will apply that law to the facts, and will find a verdict of guilty or not guilty as their own consciences may direct.

The very next morning, the 1st of September, the jury, after retiring briefly, returned with a verdict, which was read by Colonel Carrington, their foreman: *"We of the jury say that Aaron Burr is not proved to be guilty under this indictment by any evidence submitted to us. We therefore find him not guilty."*

Although not in accord with Anglo-American trial practice, there was much to be said for this Scotch verdict of "not proven." The Burr camp piously protested, but when one of the jurors, Richard E. Parker, a Jeffersonian partisan, declared that "he would not agree" to alter the verdict, the court accepted it and ordered that an entry should be made on the record of "not guilty."

The ordeal of Burr had not ended, nor had the ordeal of Hay. Jefferson prodded the district attorney to prosecute the high misdemeanor—the attempted filibustering expedition against Spanish territory. But even these minimal facts Hay could not prove because of rulings by Marshall excluding the bulk of his testimony. The jury, faced with no alternative but to accept Burr's highly improbable defense that the invasion was contingent upon a declaration of war by the United States, returned a "not guilty" verdict after a half-hour's deliberation. Finally, on a motion to commit the defendants on charges of treason and misdemeanor executed in Ohio after Blennerhasset and Burr had joined forces, Marshall fixed bail at five thousand dollars, and took off for a vacation.

The mood of the country was ugly. People agreed with Jefferson that it was Marshall, not the jury, that had freed Burr. When the story leaked out that during a court recess Marshall had attended a private dinner party at which Burr was also a guest, an unfortunate indiscretion, the tide of anti-Marshall feeling rose ominously. Marshall narrowly escaped impeachment when Jefferson sent on a copy of the Burr proceedings to Congress with the suggestion that that body determine whether the prosecution had failed because of the law, defective testimony, or the manner in which the law was administered. In Baltimore a hysterical crowd hanged in effigy Burr, Marshall, "Lawyer Brandy-Bottle" Martin, and Harman Blennerhassett while a fife band played *The Rogues' March*.

Burr's acquittal neither provided him with a vindication nor left him a free man. In Ohio, Kentucky, Mississippi, and Louisiana he was wanted for treason; in New York and New Jersey for murder. Everywhere creditors were restless to pounce upon him. His alternatives were suicide and exile, and Burr was not the suicidal type. In Europe, after the French government had turned down a treasonable and harebrained proposal he made against the United States, he abandoned political intrigue and lived the life of an idler and a roué, taking his pleasures from any harlot that the streets or boudoirs of Europe's capitals could offer and compiling a record for sexual activity that was unchallenged in American life until Professor Kinsey began assembling his statistical data. The deaths of his grandson and his daughter, Theodosia, who had an Œdipus complex, were far more crushing blows than his political debacle. After his return to New York he resumed the practice of law, aided in the Jackson-for-President movement, and gained the crowning masculine tribute of being divorced for adultery at the age of eighty.

Burr's trial settled the American law of treason. It remains today exactly as it was in the time of Jefferson and Marshall. But that does not mean, as some critics have pointed out, that it is as appropriate to the garrison state that has evolved since World War II as it was to the formative years of the republic. Marshall's strict construction of the treason provision of the Constitution was enunciated long before the appearance of fifth columns. At that time no political party in America had shown its subserviency to a foreign government hostile to our interests but not, technically, at war with us. Some of these deficiencies in the treason law have doubtless been met by recent Congressional legislation. Times of crisis like the present hold alternative risks. How can we enforce the treason and sedition laws so as to maintain the security of the nation without sacrificing the right of Americans to criticize, assemble, and form a political opposition? In the years ahead the answer to this question may well provide a decisive test for creative statesmanship.

VI

Grand Guignol at Harvard Medical School
Professor Webster and the missing corpus delicti

The Parkman murder case stands as a classic example of
how a jury can reach a sound verdict despite an unfair trial.
In this case the judge's charge violated a cherished tradition of Anglo-American criminal justice: every man is presumed to be innocent until he is proved guilty. In line with
this tenet, every essential allegation made by the prosecution must be proved beyond a reasonable doubt in order to
entitle the state to a verdict. But in the Parkman case the
burden of proof in one essential matter was thrown on the
accused. In the light of revelations after the trial was over,
no one will quarrel with the results. But the accused, regardless of his apparent guilt or of the atrocious nature of
the crime with which he is charged, is entitled to every
safeguard that the law provides.

The case first came to the attention of the public in an
unusual way. Today avid readers of the latest fabrication
of Erle Stanley Gardner or Dorothy Sayers would no doubt
pounce on the following item if it appeared in the morning
paper:

SPECIAL NOTICE

George Parkman, M.D., a well-known and highly respectable citizen of Boston, left his house in Walnut
Street, to meet an engagement of business, on Friday
last, November 23rd, between twelve and one o'clock,
P.M., and was seen in the southerly part of the city,
in and near Washington Street, in conversation with
some persons, at about five o'clock of the afternoon of
the same day.

Any person who can give information relative to him,

that may lead up to his discovery, is earnestly requested to communicate the same immediately to the City Marshal, for which he shall be liberally rewarded.

Unfortunately for the current crop of amateur detectives, the notice appeared in the Boston newspapers of November 25, 1849, long before any but a gallant remnant of wheelchair sleuths were born. At that primitive period of detecting one could not even have turned for help to the master of Baker Street, as he had not yet been conceived.

The first statement was followed up the very next day by a more specific announcement inserted by Dr. Parkman's brother-in-law, who happened to be Boston's wealthiest merchant:

$3,000 REWARD!

Dr. George Parkman, a well-known citizen of Boston, left his residence, No. 8, Walnut Street, on Friday last. He is 60 years of age, about 5 feet 9 inches high; grey hair, thin face, with a scar under the chin; light complexion, and usually walks very fast. He was dressed in a dark frock coat, dark pantaloons, purple silk vest, with dark figured black stock, and black hat.

As he may have wandered from home in consequence of some sudden aberration of mind, being perfectly well when he left his house; or, as he had with him a large sum of money, he may have been foully dealt with. The above reward will be paid for information which will lead to his discovery, if alive; or for the detection and conviction of the perpetrators, if any injury may have been done to him.

A suitable reward will be paid for the discovery of his body.

ROBERT G. SHAW

Information may be given to the City Marshall.

His impatient relatives, not getting results from the previous announcements, followed through with a last notice on November 28:

$1,000 REWARD!

Whereas, no satisfactory information has been obtained respecting Dr. George Parkman, since the afternoon of Friday last, and fears are entertained that he has been murdered, the above Reward will be paid for information which leads to the recovery of his body.

ROBERT G. SHAW

This much was known about the itinerary of the missing man. On Friday, November 23, Dr. George Parkman had left his Beacon Hill residence at 8 Walnut Street and walked to the Holland grocery store on the corner of Vine and Blossom Streets, where he spent about a dollar on sugar, butter, and sundries. Leaving the store, he was seen striding briskly in the direction of the Harvard Medical College. At North Grove he bowed to Elias Fuller, a prominent businessman who happened to be standing outside his counting-house. It was 1.40 in the afternoon. At that moment Dr. Parkman vanished into thin air.

The Boston Brahmin's disappearance was not the first instance in American history when the populace was thrown into frenzied excitement by the report of a missing person. Back in the troubled years of the War of 1812 Russell Colvin disappeared from his Vermont home. Folks began to wonder after his brother-in-law indiscreetly remarked: "We have put him where potatoes will not freeze." In fact, had Colvin not fortuitously turned up in the end, an innocent man would have been executed for his murder. Again in the next generation the sudden disappearance of William Morgan, following threats he had made to expose the secrets of the Freemasons, had severe repercussions and led to the founding of a national political party. The victim, it was later disclosed, was abducted from his Batavia, New York, home, murdered, and the corpse sent cascading over Niagara Falls. But his murder was never judicially established. A century later, in the gaudy era of Volstead, Judge

Crater, a New York jurist, strangely disappeared without the slightest trace, taking his secret along with him.

But the Parkman mystery stirred the imagination of the citizenry as did no other vanishing-act in the annals of American crime. Had Parkman been a neutral or average personality, he might have been able to bury himself in anonymity. But he happened to be Boston's leading eccentric, a queer combination of notable philanthropist and tightfisted miser. His spare frame, accentuated by tall silk hat and black frock coat, gave him a curiously elongated appearance, which belied his actual height. His long, angular face and sharp, protruding chin made him a perfect subject for caricature, and during the next few weeks a good many staff artists worked overtime to make the Parkman silhouette familiar to every American. About sixty years of age, Parkman was one of Harvard's most active alumni and had financed the building of the new medical college. Only three weeks previously he had taken a prominent part at the dedication of the structure. But unlike some modern donors to educational institutions, he was also concerned about the quality of the faculty. He established the Parkman chair in anatomy and physiology, which at that time happened to be filled by another Harvard man, that Back Bay wit Oliver Wendell Holmes, whose medical fame rested securely upon his report on the contagiousness of childbed fever. It was unthinkable that anything foul or disreputable should be associated with the great-uncle of the late George Apley.

Parkman's mysterious disappearance provoked the usual crop of wild rumors. He was reported as having been seen in a dozen different parts of Boston. An unknown female mesmerist declared that Parkman was taken in a hansom cab to East Cambridge by a gang of thugs, and, coincidentally, blood was found inside one cab. Even the Charles River was dragged. But the frantic family of the missing man clung to one slender clue. Parkman was the quintes-

sence of punctuality. When he left his Beacon Hill residence on Friday he told a servant that he had a one-thirty
engagement. With whom, he did not divulge. But this point
was cleared up quite unexpectedly on Sunday afternoon
when John White Webster, professor of chemistry and min-
eralogy at the Harvard Medical College, called at the home
of the Reverend Francis Parkman, brother of the missing
philanthropist. Abruptly upon entering the room, in which
the entire Parkman clan were forgathered, Webster stated:
"I came to tell you that at half past one on Friday I saw
your brother, and paid him some money." "Then you are
the gentleman that called at George's house at half past
nine on Friday morning, and made the appointment."
"Yes," said Webster, adding that he should have come before to inform the family, but had not seen the notice until
the previous evening.

The Reverend Dr. Parkman then remarked: "Dr. Webster, we are glad to see you, and to learn that you are the
person who called upon him; for we feared that he had been
lured by someone to East Cambridge, to do him some
harm."

"He did come to the college on Friday," Webster volunteered, "and I then paid him $483, and some odd cents."

Was he perfectly sure of the hour? "I am quite certain.
My lecture ended at one, and I waited twenty minutes or
half an hour."

Did he notice any papers or bundles in Parkman's hand?
"Yes, he had some papers," the professor informed Parkman's brother, "and he took out one and dashed his pen
across the paper." Webster made a sudden motion to suggest the mark, and added that, on paying the money, he
pointed out that the mortgage was not canceled. With his
characteristic impetuosity Parkman had replied: "I will
see to that, I will see to that," and scurried away from the
college.

That was Webster's story—the first solid clue. Aside
from the professor's evident nervousness, his auditors were

struck by his rude failure to express even a perfunctory word of sympathy.

Following this break, clues began to mount. During the course of the following week three letters were sent to Mr. Tukey, the city marshal. The first was crudely written:

> Dear sir,
>
> you will find Dr. Parkman
> Murdered on brooklynt heights
>
> yours truly,
>
> M_____, Capt. of the Darts

The second, scrawled on ragged paper in a hand similar to that of the first, was even more helpful:

> Dr. Parkman was took on bord the ship herculum and this is al I dare to say as I shal be kiled
>
> Est Cambridge one of the men give me his watch but I was feard to keep it and throwd it in the water right-side the road to Long brige to Boston.

The person who wrote the third note seemed to be some-what better educated. The leads he threw out were even more helpful than those of the previous two missives:

> Boston, Nov'r 31, '49
>
> Mr. Tukey,
> Dear Sir,
>
> I have been considerably interested in the recent affair of Dr. Parkman, and I think I can recommend means, the adoption of which might result in bringing to light some of the mysteries connected with the dis-appearance of the aforementioned gentleman.
>
> In the first place, with regard to the searching of houses, etc., I would recommend that particular atten-tion be paid to the appearance of cellar floors. Do they present the appearance of having been recently dug into and covered up again; or might not the part of the cel-lar where he was buried have been covered by the piling of wood? Secondly, have the outhouses and necessaries

been carefully examined? Have they been raked sufficiently?

Probably his body was cut up and placed in a stout bag, containing heavy weights, and thrown off one of the bridges—perhaps Cragie's. And I would recommend the firing of cannon from some of these bridges, and from various parts of the harbor and river in order to cause the body to rise to the surface of the water. This, I think, will be the last resort, and it should be done effectually.

And I recommend that the cellars of the houses in East Cambridge be examined.

Yours respectfully,
CIVIS

While the police moved off in all directions at the same time, following down every clue in uninspired fashion, the janitor of the Harvard Medical College did some sleuthing on his own. In Ephraim Littlefield the bump of curiosity and small-town snoopiness was generously developed. Indefatigable in attending to other people's business, Harvard's most famous janitor was exceptionally acute at drawing inferences from fragmentary clues. He had overheard enough of a conversation between Webster and Parkman on the evening of November 19 to whet his inquisitiveness. On the following day Webster had inquired about a basement vault used by Oliver Wendell Holmes's anatomy students to discard remnants of corpses and had plied him with a number of questions about ways of getting into it. Shortly after, Webster had sent the janitor to procure a pint of blood for him from the hospital. On the morning of the day that Parkman disappeared, Littlefield noticed a sledgehammer behind the door of Webster's room. Previously this had been in the laboratory, and the janitor returned it to its accustomed location, but never saw the object again. About 1.45 on Friday afternoon he saw Parkman approaching the college, "walking very fast." Later that afternoon he tried the door to Dr. Webster's small room adjoining his laboratory, only to find it bolted from the inside. The same was true of the door of his lecture room. To Littlefield, slave of custom, this was an extraordinary incident and excited his liveliest suspicions. On Saturday, Webster made a point of asking the janitor whether he had seen Parkman on the previous afternoon. On learning that he had, the professor had remarked: "That is the very time when I paid him $483.60," adding further gratuitous details that seemed unnecessarily labored.

Then, to top it all, Webster on the following Tuesday gave Littlefield an order for a Thanksgiving turkey, remarking with what seemed like studied casualness: "I am in the habit of giving away two or three every year, and perhaps I shall want you to do some odd job for me." Since the professor was a tightwad and head over heels in debt to boot, the janitor felt that he was either slightly "teched" or being rather subtle about a bribe.

Meantime Parkman, dead or alive, had still not been located, and as every significant clue seemed to point to the Medical School, the police on that same Tuesday descended en masse on the building and searched the premises, but found nothing. Naturally, Littlefield kept at the elbows of the officers in charge, and observed that when a question was asked about a private lavatory in Dr. Webster's laboratory, the professor diverted their attention to something else. Had Littlefield resorted to the analytical techniques of parlor detectives, he might have inventoried the clues up through Tuesday somewhat in the following fashion:

C1—Webster admitted seeing Parkman on Friday afternoon.

C2—Webster had owed Parkman money, but insisted that he paid him off that Friday.

C3—Anonymous notes stated that Parkman was killed in East Cambridge, and even less reputable locations.

C4—Responsible witnesses asserted that they saw
    Parkman after 1.30, the critical time, on the Fri-
    day afternoon of his disappearance.

C5—Webster's insistent inquiries about the vault.

C6—Webster's request for human blood.

C7—Webster's suddenly acquired habit of bolting his
    laboratory door.

C8—The Thanksgiving turkey.

C9—Webster's seeming anxiety about keeping the po-
    lice from searching his lavatory.

Despite a few red herrings, and very smelly ones, the
chain of inferences led right to the professor's lavatory, and
Littlefield, as thoroughly aroused as the hound that picks
up the scent of the fox, was determined to get the clinching
proof. Now, the only way to examine the locked lavatory
without Webster's knowledge was to dig through the wall of
the vault beneath, a substantial demolition job. Nothing
daunted, Littlefield grabbed hatchet, hammer, and chisel
and slowly removed the bricks. When he finally broke
through, he was able to make out, by holding a lantern
through the hole, what seemed like a human pelvis and two
fragments of legs. Then a search of the furnace in Dr. Webster's laboratory revealed a large number of bones and a set
of dentures, all fused indiscriminately with the slag, cinders,
and residuum of the coal.

The police now closed in. Making a hurried call on Webster at his Cambridge residence, they requested him to drive
back with them to the medical school. But instead they took
him to the Boston jail. This ruse proved a ghastly shock to
the professor. "What does all this mean?" he demanded
with righteous indignation. The police wasted no words:
*"We have done looking for the body of Dr. Parkman. You
are now in custody on the charge of the murder of Dr. Parkman."*

Like Lot's wife, curiosity got the better of the prisoner's
discretion, and he blurted out: "Where did they find him?

Did they find the *whole* of the body? Oh, my children!"
Asked if anyone had access to his private room, Webster
replied: "Nobody but the porter who makes the fires. Oh,
that villain! I am a ruined man!" Then, reaching into his
vest pocket and before anyone could stop him, Webster
clapped a pellet of strychnine into his mouth. But the suicide attempt did not come off. The professor was weak and
jittery for the rest of the evening. After he had calmed down
sufficiently, he was taken to the medical school and shown
the gruesome remains as they were passed up from the
vault. When it was evident that only fragments were located, Webster rapidly recovered some of his customary
sangfroid.

Reviewing the prisoner's behavior on the night of his arrest, we must bear in mind the note of caution injected by
Chief Justice Shaw in his classic charge to the jury. Not
overly much can be drawn from the conduct of a criminal
defendant at the time of his arrest, he observed. "Such are
the various temperaments of people, such is the rare occurrence of an arrest for this crime, who can say how a man
ought to behave?" For current faddists who are quick to
put implicit faith in lie-detecting apparatus or "truth
serum," Shaw's questions to the jury might well be taken
to heart. "Have *you* had any experience how *you* would behave in such a position? Judge you according to that."

In the run-of-the-mill homicide the prosecutor is handed
a mass of evidence tending to show (1) that A was killed;
and (2) that B killed A. But in the Webster case the state
was in jeopardy of seeking to prove that the prisoner had
killed a man who could not in fact be shown to be dead.
That is why Webster's inquiry about "the *whole* of the
body" was perhaps more artful than impulsive, for in order
to sustain a prosecution there must be clear proof of the
corpus delicti—that is, of the fact that the crime has been
committed. This fact must be proved beyond reasonable
doubt.

Fortunately for the prosecution, another cache of human

bones was uncovered the very day after Webster's arrest, this time in a tea-chest in the professor's laboratory. Embedded in a quantity of tanbark and covered with minerals was the entire trunk of a human body, the left thigh from hip to knee, and a hunting-knife. A piece of twine tied around the thighbone was to prove another significant clue, and still another was the discovery in Webster's bedroom closet of a pair of bloodstained slippers and a pair of stained trousers.

The professor's blunders did nothing to offset the powerful circumstantial case that was being constructed against him. In a letter to his daughter, Marianne, dated December 3 and intercepted by prison officials, he cautioned: "Tell mama *not to open* the little bundle I gave her the other day, but to keep it just as she receives it." This was sufficient to arouse the curiosity of the police. An examination of the bundle disclosed papers bearing on the state of Webster's personal indebtedness. Ten days later an indictment was returned against the prisoner.

Even before court convened, everybody was convinced that the Webster case would prove the most sensational murder trial in American history up to that time. The public, having voraciously devoured every macabre morsel fed to it by the press, descended on the courthouse in force and virtually invested that stronghold. To satisfy the clamor for admission, the police effected a change of audience every ten minutes, and it is estimated that some sixty thousand persons had at least a glimpse of the proceedings in the eleven-day period over which they extended.

Dominating the trial was the illustrious Chief Justice of the Massachusetts Supreme Judicial Court. No jurist in the land outranked in eminence Lemuel Shaw, that unreconstructed Whig. Formidable-looking, with a head that might have come from the Sistine Chapel, a shaggy mane of hair, and piercing eyes under heavy brows, Shaw lent a note of austerity to every trial over which he presided. There was not a member of the state bar who did not have occasion to fear his barbed tongue. The story was relished in legal circles that Benjamin Butler, when asked where he was taking his huge mastiff, replied that he was going down to the courthouse to show him the Chief Justice "so as to teach him to growl." Shaw was reinforced by Associate Justices Samuel Wilde, Charles A. Dewey, and Thomas Metcalf. The case for the commonwealth was in the hands of the Attorney General, John H. Clifford, later Governor of the state, assisted by George Bemis, a Harvard Law School product, better known for his achievements in the field of international law.

When Webster pleaded not guilty to the indictment, the court assigned Pliny Merrick, formerly a Common Pleas judge, and Edward D. Sohier, an accomplished jury lawyer, to defend him. Some of Webster's socialite friends approached Rufus Choate, the ranking trial lawyer of the day. Fresh from his great victory in the Tirrell murder case, Choate had secured an acquittal, on evidence nearly as strong as that in the Webster case, first on a charge of murder and then of arson. The jury had apparently been persuaded by the seemingly preposterous theory of somnambulism which Choate advanced, accepting his implausible contention that the homicide had been committed by the prisoner while he was asleep! Obviously, anyone who could perform that miracle might get Webster acquitted. But Choate was canny. He talked the case over with Daniel Webster, who suggested that there was no alternative but to admit the homicide and plead self-defense in extenuation. But when the prisoner continued to insist on his complete innocence, Choate declined to enter the case. It was not enough that Daniel Webster's "Constitution and Union" speech on the 7th of March, less than two weeks before the trial, had earned him the opprobrium of being called Benedict Arnold from the diehard abolitionists of his own state. Some folks actually were under the impression that the renowned statesman was being tried for the murder of Dr. Parkman! One British newspaper contributed to that misconception. With characteristic vagueness about American affairs, it stated: "Mr. Webster, the great American statesman, is to be tried in New York on the 10th of March for the murder of Judge Parker."

From the start of the trial on March 19, 1850, it was clear that Shaw planned to keep the reins in his hand. The fact that it took less than two days to agree on a jury bespoke the Chief Justice's desire to avoid the marathon of challenges that has characterized most *causes célèbres*. Only three out of the twelve jurors belonged to what is now spoken of condescendingly as the white-collar class. The rest were locksmiths, printers, slaters, painters, and carpenters. It was a bookseller, Benjamin H. Greene, whose conscience seemed most troubled. On examination he stated that he was opposed to capital punishment, but did not think that his opinion would interfere with his doing his duty as a juror. Shaw held that he was not disqualified. After some hesitation Greene took the oath and became the ninth juror, but when called to take his seat on the panel, he asked to be let off. The Chief Justice put it up to the juror to decide for himself whether his opinions would prevent him from giving an unbiased verdict. Greene protested that he felt he could be unbiased, but that he sympathized with both the prisoner and his family, and feared that his opinions on capital punishment might influence the rest of the jurors. Shaw refused to excuse him.

The Attorney General in his opening stated that the commonwealth would prove (1) that Dr. Parkman was murdered; and (2) that the deed was done by Webster. He then moved that the jury be permitted to go to the scene where the murder was alleged to have been committed. Sohier denied the necessity for this excursion on the ground that plans of the medical college were available, but Shaw, recalling a precedent in an arson trial a few years earlier, granted the motion, and the jury was taken to Webster's laboratory on the following morning.

To establish the corpus delicti, the state called to the

stand an imposing array of medical experts, who proceeded to demonstrate the enormous strides their science had already taken. A special medical committee appointed to investigate made ingenius calculations on the basis of the surviving bones in the skeleton and estimated that they belonged to a person of five feet ten and one-half inches, between fifty and sixty years of age, with "very little adipose matter." But on cross-examination Dr. Lewis, one of the committee, admitted that, though he had known Dr. Parkman about thirty years, "it would not spontaneously have occurred" to him that it was Parkman had he not known he was missing. Testifying that the remains corresponded to the physical details of Parkman when alive, Dr. Woodbridge Strong added some interesting advice on how to burn a body. Had the murderer been as well informed it is quite probable that the perfect crime might have been executed.

In early days in Cornhill, I had poor accommodations for dissecting, and it was frequently necessary to burn up the remains. Once I had a pirate given me by the United States marshal for dissection and, it being warm weather, I wanted to get rid of the flesh and only preserve the bones. He was a muscular, stout man, and I began upon it one night with a wood fire in a large old-fashioned fireplace. I built a rousing fire and sat up all night piling on the wood and flesh and had not got it consumed by morning. I was afraid of a visit from the police and by 11 o'clock they gave me a call to know what made such a smell in the street, but I finished it up that forenoon. However, I consider it no small operation to burn up a body. It needs the right sort of fuel. Wood is better than coal, and the lighter the kind of wood the better; you need frequently to stir the fire up; and you must have something that the flesh will not quench or put out. There is always a difficulty in getting rid of human remains by fire, on account of attracting suspicion by the smell. I have been

called upon by my neighbors or the police several times
on this account.

On cross-examination Dr. Strong admitted that, though he
had never used a furnace to burn a body, in his opinion the
particular furnace in Webster's laboratory was "the most
inconvenient place for such a purpose." A stove in the same
room would have answered better.

Then New England's most famous talker took the stand,
but what he had to talk about was hardly subject matter
for the breakfast table even for an autocrat. Dr. Holmes
testified that Parkman "never had any need of anatomical
subjects," adding the dubious compliment that "the remains indicate that the person who separated them knew
where to cut. There was no botching about the business."
But Holmes refused to be pinned down to an unequivocal
identification of the remains. He did not see "any particular
similarity between the parts and Dr. Parkman or anything
dissimilar."

Up to this point all that the state had demonstrated was
that the skeletal remains found in Webster's laboratory
were similar to the bone structure of Dr. Parkman's body.
But the corpus delicti had clearly not been established beyond dispute. The prosecution now dared an innovation
in criminal evidence by seeking the conclusive identification
of a corpse by mineral matter not innately part of the
body—in this case by false teeth. To this end the commonwealth called to the stand Dr. Nathan C. Keep, who had
been employed as Dr. Parkman's dentist for almost a quarter
of a century. When shown the dentures, he stated that he
recognized them *as the teeth I had made for Dr. Parkman
in 1846.*" Spectators followed with bated breath every detail
of his precedent-smashing testimony.

Dr. Parkman's mouth was a very peculiar mouth, in
many respects; differing in the relation that existed
between the upper and lower jaw so peculiarly, that the
impression left upon my mind was very distinct. I re-

member the peculiarity of the lower jaw with great
exactness.

The circumstances connected with the teeth being
ordered were somewhat peculiar. The first question
asked by Dr. Parkman, when the teeth were ordered,
was, "How long will it take to make them?" I took the
liberty to ask why he was so particular to know. He
told me that the Medical College was to be opened, and
that it was necessary for him to be there, and perhaps
to speak; and he wanted them by that time, or else he
did not want them at all. The time was short; the peculiarity of the mouth made it a case requiring as much
skill as could be used. I began to do it as soon as possible, giving a large part of my attention to it. In consequence of these circumstances, I remember very distinctly what was done, more than in ordinary cases. I
proceeded, in my usual mode to take the impression.
The first step was to take an exact facsimile of each
jaw with wax, metal, liquid plaster, etc. A plate was
made from that; and the next step was, of course, to
ascertain the relation between the upper and the lower
jaw. A model of the lower jaw was made from an impression taken with wax, while in a plastic state, and
by means of this the lower plate was fitted. The upper
plate was fitted in the same manner.

Dr. Keep at this point exhibited the original plates and
demonstrated to the jury that they fitted to the models of
Dr. Parkman's jaws. He then explained:

These plates were made before the gold plates, to
ascertain if there were any defect in the models. When
the plates were fitted to his mouth, I requested him to
close it until I satisfied myself as to the suitable distance.

A great irregularity on the left side of the lower jaw
of Dr. Parkman gave me great trouble in setting this
up. Each set of teeth was made in three blocks, and

then joined to the gold plate. There were spiral springs that connected the two sets of teeth to enable the patient to open his mouth and close it with less danger of the teeth being displaced, as they would have been without the springs. There was an accident which injured one of the teeth in the front block, and delayed the finishing of them until near the end of the night before the opening of the Medical College. They were finally finished, by setting my assistant at work on them, at just thirty minutes before the opening of the Medical College.

A further adjustment had to be made in the plates to make room for Dr. Parkman's tongue, Keep stated. Since then, have you seen much of Dr. Parkman? the dentist was asked. "Yes, I saw him frequently," he replied, and went on to elaborate:

> The last time I saw him was, as near as I can remember, about two weeks previous to his disappearance. He called late in the evening, about ten o'clock. He told me his trouble. I took his teeth, both upper and lower, examined them, and put on a new spring. He stayed about half an hour. . . . I had no more professional intercourse with him at all. I went into the country to pass Thanksgiving, and returned on the Monday morning. I was told that Dr. Lewis wanted to see me, and he presented me with these remains of mineral teeth. On looking at them, I recognized them to be the teeth I had made for Dr. Parkman. The most of the upper portion that remained was the block belonging to the left side of the lower jaw. Several other parts had been very much injured by fire. I proceeded to look for the mold upon which these teeth were made, put the metal upon its proper place, and it fitted exactly. There is sufficient left of these blocks to identify the place where they belonged. *There is no mistake.*

When asked on cross-examination just how he happened to have preserved Dr. Parkman's mold, Keep replied: "For future use, in case of accident to the teeth."

The establishment of the corpus delicti served to heighten the tension in the courtroom and provided a necessary foundation for the introduction of the state's star witness, Ephraim Littlefield. His appearance on the stand was breathlessly awaited. When, on the fourth morning of the trial, he began his incredible tale, the courtroom bulged with an overflow of spectators. As a result, the newspaper reporters found themselves consigned to the gallery. Littlefield began with a statement that he had served as janitor of the medical college for seven years and had known Dr. Parkman over twenty years. When questioned about a meeting between Webster and Parkman on Monday evening, November 19, he admitted being present. His story on direct examination follows:

> I was in Dr. Webster's back private room, assisting him, towards evening. Dr. Webster had three candles burning. He was looking at a chemical book. I stood at the stove stirring some water, in which something was to be dissolved. I heard no footstep, but saw Dr. Parkman enter the room from the lecture-room.
>
> Dr. Webster looked around, surprised to see him enter without being heard. He said, "Dr. Webster, are you ready for me?" He spoke loud and quick.
>
> Dr. Webster answered, "No, I am not ready tonight, doctor."
>
> Dr. Parkman said something else, I do not remember what. He either spoke of Dr. Webster's selling something mortgaged, or mortgaging something sold. Dr. Parkman took out papers from his pocket, and Dr. Webster said, "I was not aware it was so." Dr. Parkman said, "It is so, and you know it." Dr. Webster replied, "I will see you to-morrow."

Dr. Parkman stood near the threshold of the door, raised his hand, and said, "Something must be done to-morrow." He went out, and it was the last time I ever saw him in the building.

But that was only the beginning of Littlefield's tale. What happened after that? the witness was asked.

When I was standing in front of the College, about half past one o'clock, the next day, Tuesday, Dr. Webster came and asked me if I could carry a note to Dr. Parkman. I got a boy to carry it up. I had an interview with Dr. Webster about noon, the same day Dr. Parkman was there—Monday—before Dr. Parkman was there in the evening. I am very positive it was the same day. Dr. Webster asked if the vault had ever been fixed, where we used to put the remains of subjects from the dissecting-room, and from the Demonstrator of Anatomy's room. He added, that there had been something said about having it repaired, or a new one built. He asked what the matter was with it. He asked where it was built. I told him it was built right under his coal-bin, which was between his laboratory and the dissecting-room. I told him the weight of this coal sprang the wall, so as to make it leak, and caused an offensive odor to be sent to all parts of the building. I told him it had been fixed. He asked me how it was fixed. I told him the vault had been all "kivered" up with dirt, and there had been no smell since. He asked me how I got down under the building to "kiver" it up, or how anyone could get down. I told him we took up the brick floor in the dissecting-room entry, and then took up the board floor, about six feet long. He asked me if that was the only way to get down under the building. I told him it was under his laboratory or the front room, and told him how the walls run. He asked me if we could get a light into that vault; and I told him "No." He asked if I was sure of it. I told him I was, for I had tried, a few days before, to get a light into the vault. He said he wanted to get some gas out of the vault. I had tried to get a light in, to find something which Dr. Ainsworth had lost, and the foul air put it out. Dr. Ainsworth had let down an African skull, to macerate in the vault, and the rope had rotted off. I attempted to put a light down, and it went out. Dr. Webster told me he wanted to get some gas to try an experiment. I told him then would be a good time, as it was high tide and the water would press the gas up. I asked him how he was going to get the gas into any vessel. He said he had an apparatus that he could do it with. He told me that when he wanted to get the gas he would let me know. And that is the last I ever heard of it.

Did you have any other conversations with Professor Webster? Littlefield was asked.

I do not recollect any other interview with Dr. Webster, before the day of the disappearance. But now I do recollect a message to the Hospital. He said he wanted me to get him some blood for his next day's lecture. He said he wanted as much as a pint. I took a glass jar off from his shelf, holding nearly a quart, and asked if that would do to get it in. He said, "Yes. Get it full, if you can, over at the Hospital." At Dr. Holmes' lecture-room I saw the student who attends the apothecary's shop in the Hospital. I told him Dr. Webster wished to get a pint of blood. He replied: "I think we shall bleed someone tomorrow, and I will save the blood." Friday morning, I went to the apothecary's shop, and the student said he had no blood, as they had bled nobody. I told Dr. Webster, about eleven and a half o'clock, Friday. He said he was sorry, as he wanted to use it in his lecture.

In the morning, Friday, November 23rd, after I made his fire, swept the room, and went to set the broom behind the door leading from his back room to the laboratory, I saw the sledge-hammer behind the door. It was usually in the laboratory. The handle was about two feet long, of white oak, and would weigh six or seven pounds. I never saw it before anywhere else except in the laboratory. One side of the hammer was about as large around as half an orange, and it was rounded on both sides. I carried it downstairs into the laboratory. I have never seen anything of it since, though I have hunted the building all over.

The prosecutor now asked Littlefield to tell the jury what happened on Friday afternoon.

I do not remember anything particular till quarter before two, when I was standing looking out at the front door. I thought, before the Coroner's Inquest, that it was about half-past one; but, reflecting upon it, I remembered that that day I had examined the tickets at Dr. Holmes' door, which would make it quarter of an hour later. I saw Dr. Parkman approaching the College, walking very fast. I entered Dr. Ware's lecture-room, and lay on the settee nearest the register and nearest the door, waiting for Dr. Holmes' lecture to finish, to help and clear away his things. I did not hear anyone enter Dr. Webster's lecture-room.

After putting away Dr. Holmes' things, I came down and locked the front door. About quarter past two o'clock, Dr. Holmes went out. He is generally the last one to go out of the building. Then I went downstairs to prepare the furnaces for the next day. I then went down to Dr. Webster's laboratory door, to clear up his room—the door that leads to my cellar—the door under the stairs leading from Dr. Webster's small room to his laboratory stairs. I found that door bolted on the inside. I then went round to the next door that led to his laboratory, and found that fast. When I put in my key, I found I could not get in, and that it was bolted. I heard him in there walking. I heard the water run-

ning. I went upstairs, and tried the door that led into
the lecture-room from the front entry. I found the door
locked; it was bolted on the inside.

In the evening, about half-past five o'clock, I was
called out of my kitchen, and heard someone coming
down the stairs that led from the front entry. It was
Dr. Webster. He had a candlestick in his hand, and a
candle burning—he never did use a lamp. He blew it
out in my entry, and left it on the settee. He passed out
through the shed; and I saw nothing more of him that
night.

After Dr. Webster went, I fixed myself and went to a
party, getting home about ten o'clock, or a few minutes
after. The party was at Mr. Grant's.

What did you notice when you returned home? the witness was asked.

The first door I went to was the laboratory door. I
found it fast. Then I started to go to the dissecting-
room door. I unlocked the dissecting-room door, to put
out the lights. The students there used to dissect till
nine or ten o'clock. I found the lights out; bolted the
outside door of the dissecting-room, and went to bed.
*I never knew Dr. Webster's door locked before, on the
night of a lecture-day, since I have been in the college.*
On Saturday, there were but two lectures; and I had
but two fires to make. I made a fire in the dissecting-
room, but forget whether I went to unbolt the door of
the dissecting-room before or after I made the fire.
When I did go, I found it unbolted and ajar. I thought
I had fastened some student in, the night before. I
never knew anyone had a key of the outside door, except Dr. Leigh, the librarian, who has been there three
years.

I unlocked the lecture-room door—the one Dr. Webster came out the day before—and went in. I went
through but could not get through the private room

into the lower laboratory. The door was locked, and I
never had the key. He had the lock put on it to lock up
his laboratory when out of use, in the summer time. I
then went back to my room. Soon after I went back
Dr. Webster came, with a bundle under his arm,
through the east shed. I met him in the entry. He told
me to make him a fire. I made a fire in the stove in the
laboratory. I did no more work for Dr. Webster that
day.

Then Littlefield proceeded to tell what took place on
Saturday. While sweeping up around the building, he heard
Dr. Webster moving around the lower laboratory. He could
hear the water running in Webster's sink. This struck him
as unusual. That afternoon he first learned of Dr. Parkman's disappearance. On Sunday night he encountered
Dr. Webster on North Grove Street. When Webster saw
him, he came right up and asked: "Mr. Littlefield, did you
see Dr. Parkman during the latter part of last week?"
"Yes," the janitor replied. "Just when did you see him?"
Webster demanded. "On Friday about half past one." Webster persisted. "Where did you see him?" "About this very
spot," Littlefield answered. "Which way was he going?"
"Toward the college," Webster was told. Littlefield again
revealed his ability to recall small but significant details:

> Dr. Webster had his cane in his hand, struck it down
> upon the ground, and said, *"That is the very time when
> I paid him $483.60."* I remember he put the odd cents
> on. I told him I did not see Dr. Parkman come in or
> go out of the College, for I went directly into Dr.
> Ware's lecture-room and lay down on a settee. He said
> he counted the money down to Dr. Parkman in his
> lecture-room; and that Dr. Parkman grabbed the
> money from the table without counting it, and ran as
> fast as he could go, up two or three steps at a time. Dr.
> Webster said Dr. Parkman told him he would go with
> him to Cambridge and discharge a mortgage; and

added, "I suppose he did, but I have not been over to the Register of Deeds' Office to see."

The professor then went on to tell Littlefield that he had not known of Parkman's disappearance until he read it in the *Transcript*. Now he realized that he was the "unknown gentleman" with whom Parkman had the engagement. To Littlefield, Webster's behavior seemed very odd.

"When Dr. Webster spoke to me," the janitor explained, "he used to look me in the face, with his head up. He did not then, but looked down, and seemed confused and agitated. I never saw him look so before. His face was thoughtful; he looked pale."

The witness continued:

> On Monday I could not get into his room to make up the fire. The first I knew of his being in the College was when my wife told me that Dr. Samuel Parkman had been there to see Dr. Webster. I asked him how he got in, seeing all the doors were kept locked. I went up the laboratory stairs, and saw Dr. Samuel Parkman and Dr. Webster in the back room. They were talking about old Dr. George Parkman. I overheard conversation about some money; Dr. Parkman said the old doctor was very angry. I stayed there but a minute; did not see Dr. Samuel Parkman go away. The front doorbell rang, and I went to the door, and found there Mr. Parkman Blake. I had my key in the lecture-room, but it was bolted. I went down and came up the other way to Dr. Webster. He hesitated somewhat, and then said, "Let him in." I unbolted the door, but do not know how long Mr. Blake was there.
>
> When I again went to the laboratory door, it was twelve o'clock. I found the door locked. I don't know whether the door-bell rang or not. I went to the door, and found Kingsley, and they said they could trace Dr. Parkman nowhere but to the Medical College, and they had come to look. I told them I would show them

all the rooms that I could get into myself. I met Dr. Holmes on the stairs. He asked if they wanted to haul all the subjects out of their chests. They said no; they merely wanted to see if he had stowed himself away in the attic. Dr. Holmes told me to show them all around. I went to Dr. Webster's room first; it was locked. We knocked two or three times, with loud raps. Dr. Webster did not come at first. Finally he came. I told him what the officers had come for, but did not hear him say anything. We looked through the room, and went down into the laboratory. I showed them all over the rest of the building, and they went away.

Tuesday morning, I could not get in to make the fires, further than the lecture-room. I went about half-past nine o'clock, unlocked the lecture-room door, and found Dr. Webster in a sort of smoking-cap. I asked him if I should make a fire in his furnace. He said, "No." The things for his lecture that day would not stand much heat. Tuesday evening, I told my wife I guessed Dr. Webster had got his room open. I went up into Dr. Webster's back room. He was reading a paper. He asked me if I knew where Mr. Foster, a provision dealer, lived. I said that I knew him. He asked me if I had bought my Thanksgiving turkey. I said "No." I had thought of going out to Thanksgiving. He added, "Take that order, and get you a nice turkey. I am in the habit of giving away two or three every year, and perhaps I shall want you to do some odd job for me." I thanked him, and told him I should be most happy to do anything for him I could. He then gave me another order to Foster, to send him, to Cambridge, some sweet potatoes. I went to Foster's; he took the order, and told me to pick out a turkey. I came home, and stayed till half-past six. It was the first time Dr. Webster ever gave me anything. The idea of his giving a cent's worth was remarkable. Wednesday morning, Prof. Webster came to the College early. He went into the laboratory, and I heard him moving things around there. I went to the door and tried to listen, but the catch over the key-hole was down. I was picking a hole through the partition when my wife saw me. I cracked off a small piece, and thought Dr. Webster heard me. I went into the kitchen afterward; then came out and lay down on my face, and looked under the door. I thought I heard the moving of a coal-hod on the floor from near the door. I could see him, as high as his knees, going toward the furnace where the bones were found. Cannel coal and bark were kept near the laboratory stairs in a bin; hard coal was kept near the furnace. I could see no more of him. I lay there about five minutes. I went out with my wife about nine o'clock, and did not get back till one o'clock. About three o'clock I passed through the dissecting-room. In passing upstairs to the Demonstrator's room, I first felt heat in the wall from Dr. Webster's laboratory. The staircase brought me in contact with the wall. I put my hand upon it, and it was so hot I could not hold my hand on it long. *I knew it proceeded from a furnace, where I had never known any fire, and never made any fire.* I went into the store-room, of which I had a key. I put my key into the door of Dr. Webster's laboratory; it was not locked, but was bolted. I found the other cellar-door of the laboratory locked. I unlocked the lecture-room door, and went in, but found the door of the back room locked. I then went down into my cellar, and back of the building, to see if I could look in the window and see any fire. I climbed up the wall to the double window and got in. The first place I went to was the furnace. Now there was a fire, but not much of one. It was covered up by a soapstone cover, and the whole top of the range was covered over with pots of minerals, and an iron cylinder was lying on it. I did not move anything.

I then took up a broom, and went to where there

were two hogsheads full of water. I tried one of them
with the broom handle, and found the water was two-
thirds out; the other had a gasometer in it. I did not try
the water with the broom, but it was low; a spout was
lying in one hogshead, leading up to the sink. They
were full on Friday; there were also two barrels of
pitch pine kindlings, one of which, on Friday, had been
full and the other two-thirds full. The kindlings were
two-thirds gone. I could not think what he had done
with them. On the stairs I saw spots such as I had not
seen before; they were much spattered. I reached down
and tasted of one of the spatters; it tasted like acid.
The water was running. I noticed the running of the
water that week, because I had set it running before,
and he had stopped it. He said the noise disturbed him,
and it spattered the floor. I did not see Dr. Webster
that day. There were grape-cuttings, an empty box, and
a bag of tan, left by the laboratory door on Monday.
They stood there till Friday. I do not remember when
the tan went in, but he took in the grapevines and the
box himself on Friday. I tried to carry them into his
room several times during the week, but could not get
into his room.

Thursday I did not see Dr. Webster all day.

Tuesday morning, November 26th, after I left Dr.
Webster's room and went out, I saw Messrs. Clapp,
Kingsley, Fuller, and Rice come in by the shed. Mr.
Clapp said, "We are going to search every foot of land
in this neighborhood, and wish to search the College,
so that people around may not object to having their
houses searched." I told him I would show him all parts
of the College to which I had access. We then saw Dr.
Jacob Bigelow in the entry. Dr. Bigelow said, "Show
them everything." Someone said, "Let us begin with
Dr. Webster's rooms."

I went to the door leading to my cellar, and it was
fast. I went up to the lecture-room door, and, finding

it locked, rapped as loud as I could. Dr. Webster unbolted the door. I told him what the officers were there
for. We passed in, and down into his lower room. Mr.
Clapp went toward the small private room. Dr. Webster said that was the room where he kept valuable and
dangerous things. I hardly ever went into that room.
Mr. Clapp did not search it. We went down the laboratory stairs. *Mr. Clapp looked into a pane of glass in the
lavatory door, and asked, "What place is this?" I told
him, "That is Dr. Webster's lavatory; no one has access
to it but himself." Dr. Webster seemed to me to withdraw their attention to another part of the room, and
unbolted another door, that led to the store-room.* We
all went out.

Someone wanted to search the vault where the remains of subjects are thrown. We unlocked the access
to the vault, and lowered a lantern into it. All seemed
satisfied that there was nothing there which did not belong there.

We searched the whole building. Then someone asked
if there was any way of getting under it. I told of the
trap door; we got lights, and went down. Fuller and I
crawled across to the back side of the building; there
was nothing there. Then they searched my room.

But the failure of the police only spurred Littlefield
on to greater efforts. There was still one place the police
had not searched, and the janitor was determined to have a
look.

I was in the cellar in the forenoon, Thursday, and
went to work on the wall about three o'clock, to get
under Dr. Webster's laboratory near the lavatory, to
satisfy myself and the public. I could not go outside of
the building without everybody being at me, saying
that Dr. Parkman would be found in the Medical College if he was ever found anywhere. That was the only
place not searched. All the tools I used were a hatchet

and mortising chisel. All I did was to get out two layers of brick.

I was gone that night till about four o'clock at a ball of the Shakespeare Division of the Sons of Temperance. My wife called me about nine o'clock, and wanted me to go to work on the wall. After breakfast, Dr. Webster came into my kitchen and asked me if I had heard anything from Dr. Parkman. He said he had just come from Dr. Henchman's apothecary shop, where he heard of a woman having put a large bundle into a cab, which drove off. They took the number of the cab and afterward found it all covered with blood. I said there were so many flying reports now about Dr. Parkman that one did not know what to believe. He went upstairs; there were men there carrying up busts to place in the anatomical lecture-room. Dr. Henry J. Bigelow was there. I asked him if he knew there were reports and suspicions against Dr. Webster. He said he knew there were. I informed him what I was doing on the wall. He told me to go ahead.

In a few minutes, I went into the Demonstrator's room, and there I saw Dr. J. B. S. Jackson alone. I told him what I was doing in the wall. He replied, "Mr. Littlefield, I feel dreadfully about this." He added, "Do you go through that wall before you sleep?" He asked me what I would do, if I found anything. I told him I should go to Dr. Holmes. He said, "No, go to old Dr. Bigelow's, in Summer Street; then call at my house, and if I am not in, write your name on my slate there, and when I return I shall understand it."

About three o'clock, I went to Mr. Fuller's, and borrowed a crowbar. I went home and locked all the doors, leaving the keys inside. I told my wife not to let anyone in; but, if Dr. Webster came, to be sure and let him in—but not till she had given four raps on the floor. I blistered my hands in working through the wall and had to come up and put gloves on. Then I went and borrowed a cold chisel and hammer of Mr. Fuller, who seemed very ready to lend them. I got out three courses and a half of brick, the thickness of the wall.

Working feverishly against the time of Webster's return, Littlefield heard four raps on the floor. It was the signal, and he scrambled out from under the building just as quickly as he could. His wife met him in the entry. "I have made a fool of you this time," she told him. "Two gentlemen called here, and I thought that one was Dr. Webster, but they are Mr. Kingsley and Mr. Starkweather. They are at the door now." Littlefield then told the investigators just what he was doing. Curiously enough, instead of staying there with the janitor and giving him a hand, they seemed quite willing to let him get full credit for the discovery. Just after they left, his wife called over to him: "You have just saved your bacon, as Dr. Webster has just passed in." Webster then came out and engaged Littlefield and a police officer in conversation. He related to them the story that an Irishman had offered a twenty-dollar bill on the Cambridge side of the bridge to pay his toll of one cent. According to Webster, the marshal had called on him to find out to whom he had paid a bill of that denomination, but the professor had no clear recollection. As soon as he was alone, Littlefield went back to his work.

I went under the building again, requesting my wife to keep a close watch on the door. I took the crowbar and knocked the bigness of a hole right through. I did not use the chisel and hammer. I had drilled a hole with a crowbar before I went up, when Mr. Kingsley called. There are five courses of brick in the wall. I had trouble with my light, as the air drew strongly through the hole. I managed to get the light and my head into the hole, and then I was not disturbed with the draft. I held my light forward. The first thing which I saw was the pelvis of a man and two parts of a leg. The water was running down on these remains from the sink. I knew

that it was no place for these things. I went up and told
my wife that I was going down to Dr. Bigelow's; and I
told her what I had discovered. I locked the cellar door
and put the key in my pocket so that no one could get
down until I returned.

Then, when the police officials were notified and broke
into the lavatory, Professor Webster, according to Littlefield, was "much agitated." He asked for water, but could
not drink. "His hand trembled, and he snapped at the tum-
bler like a dog or a mad person."

Before Littlefield left the stand he was asked to identify
a bunch of skeleton keys that were found in one of Dr. Webster's drawers. The Attorney General answered a defense
objection by pointing out that they were tied to a piece of
twine similar to that found on the leg of the remains. As
the prisoner's counsel continued to object, the state withdrew the exhibit.

Littlefield had talked for eight hours, virtually without
interruption save for a luncheon recess. His damning story
was so detailed and circumstantial that Webster was hard
put to it to maintain his customary composure. The defense's only chance was to crack Littlefield on cross-examination. The very next morning Sohier began a rapid-fire,
staccato attack on the janitor, calculated to shake a person
of even less mercurial temperament than the witness.

SOHIER: You stated, Mr. Littlefield, in your direct examination yesterday, that "on Monday, the 19th of November, you saw Dr. Parkman with Dr. Webster at his
rooms in the college." *I want to know about what time.*

LITTLEFIELD: I can't tell the hour. It was dark, and they
had to have lights.

Q.: In what room did you see them?

A.: In the laboratory; I mean the back one.

Q.: In what position did you see Dr. Webster?

A.: He was standing by the stove.

Q.: Did you see Dr. Parkman come in?

A.: I did. I can't say if he saw me.

Q.: Did you hear anything pass between them?

A.: I did. When Dr. Parkman came in, I heard him say to Dr. Webster, "Dr. Webster, are you ready for me to-night?" "No," said Dr. Webster. He then put his hand in his pockets for some papers, which he took out, and accused Dr. Webster of selling something which he said "he had sold before."

Q.: Well, what else?

A.: Dr. Parkman then raised his hand.

Q.: You say that Dr. Parkman raised his hand. When did he do so and how?

A.: When he went out. He was near the door at the time. He stood at the door and made a motion with his hand. He then turned round and said to Dr. Webster: "Something must be done tomorrow."

Q.: He was excited?

A.: Yes.

Q.: Where were you on Thursday night previous to Dr. Parkman's disappearance? What time were you home?

A.: I was home at one o'clock.

Q.: What time did you go to the ball?

A.: I went there and remained till 12.30.

Q.: On the last occasion, until after you left home that last night, and on the 23rd of November, were you there?

A.: I don't know as I was.

Q.: Had you not made use of the Doctor's room that night to play cards?

A.: I decline answering that question (roars of laughter).

Q.: Had you not been there gambling?

A.: I decline answering that question (renewed laughter).

Q.: Do you know that the Doctor found out you were gambling?

A.: I don't know. He never said anything to me about it.

. . .

Aside from revealing the witness to be something of a playboy, Sohier's attempts to show that Littlefield might have had a motive for framing Webster failed to come off. Since the janitor had documented his story with a wealth of details, the defense now sought to discredit him by rattling him on dates. Littlefield was confused about whether he had got the turkey before or after he had undertaken the search, but Sohier failed to shake his story materially. Merrick now took over the cross-examination and sought to discredit the witness by establishing that he had been motivated by a desire to collect the reward.

Q.: How early did you begin to take a memorandum of the facts?

A.: I began it on Sunday night.

Q.: What hour on Sunday night?

A.: As soon as I went into my room—I told my wife about it.

Q.: It was on that Sunday night you began to watch Dr. Webster?

A.: It was.

Q.: Were you hunting round the neighborhood?

A.: Yes. I hunted round and went into an adjoining building and to an old cellar that was near.

Q.: Did you tell anyone where to get the reward?

A.: No, I did not.

Q.: Did you tell Dr. Webster you went?

A.: No, I did not.

Merrick then showed Littlefield the announcement of a reward, and the witness admitted having seen it on Monday and shown it to Dr. Holmes. But, on redirect by Clifford, Littlefield stoutly affirmed: "I never have made any claim to any reward. I say now that I never shall claim it."

Caroline Littlefield followed her husband on the stand. The janitor's wife made an amusing witness. When her spouse first told her that he believed Webster had murdered

Parkman, she had declared: "For mercy's sake! What makes you think so? Don't you ever mention such a thing again! If the Professor should hear of it, it will make trouble for you!" A typical struggling housewife, she was anxious to avoid trouble with her husband's superiors and to keep free of any grimy contact with the law. Her conventional mind closed tightly at the very idea of a Harvard professor descending to homicide.

Neatly and systematically Clifford nailed down all loose boards before closing his case. A hardware dealer identified Dr. Webster as the purchaser on November 27 of a half-dozen large fishhooks, which he recognized by a private mark and their unusual size. A twine-manufacturer gave evidence that certain pieces of twine found wrapped around parts of the corpse had unusual and identical characteristics. Finally the state introduced a penmanship expert, Nathaniel D. Gould, who flatly stated that the anonymous letters to City Marshal Tukey, which had the effect of diverting for a time attention from the medical college, were written by the prisoner.

Having failed to shake Littlefield's story in any material way, the defense counted, first, on character witnesses to establish the good reputation of the prisoner; and, secondly, on undermining the state's positive identification of the body. No man standing trial for murder had ever summoned to his defense a more imposing array of character witnesses than did John W. Webster. Boston Brahmins did their duty. The historian Jared Sparks, President of Harvard, spoke of the prisoner as "a kind man," while the New England filiopietist John G. Palfrey referred to him as "a man subject to harmless movements of passion, but they are soon exhausted." Peleg W. Chandler, famous as an editor of state trials, went down the line for the prisoner, as did the city marshal of Cambridge and an ex-mayor of that town.

To disprove the corpus delicti the defense put on the stand Boston's celebrated dentist Dr. William T. G. Mor-

ton, discoverer of anesthesia, himself a former student of
Dr. Keep's. Morton proceeded to show the jury how some
old plates from his office also seemed to fit the model of
Dr. Parkman's jaw. He further declared that in his opinion
there were no peculiarities by which the teeth found in the
furnace could be identified as those of Dr. Parkman. Like
that host of medical experts who were to follow him on the
stand in later criminal cases, Morton proved that it is not
generally too difficult to find reputable experts who will take
either side of a technical issue.

The defense counted heavily on testimony now adduced
that Parkman was seen on the streets of Boston on Friday
afternoon considerably after the time when the state contended he had been murdered. In rebuttal the state sought
to introduce four or five witnesses to show that a person
strongly resembling the missing man was seen on the
streets of Boston around the time of his death. The press
later identified Parkman's double as a resident of Springfield. But the Chief Justice sustained Merrick's objection to
such testimony on the ground that, were the person himself
present, there would, perhaps, be no objection, as the jury
might then draw their own conclusions. In his absence, the
testimony was held too remote.

Sohier's opening for the defense was an indifferent performance at best, but Merrick's summation was an ingenious effort. He denied that the commonwealth had shown
that the remains were Parkman's, and that, if they were,
just how the eccentric doctor was done away with. There
was no homicide without malice aforethought, the defense
lawyer argued. At most, contended Merrick, it was a killing
while the prisoner's "blood was hot, and passion high."
Turning on Littlefield, he savagely denounced the credibility of the state's star witness. "He went to the party and
danced eighteen or twenty times," thundered Merrick, "with
the conviction that a dead man's bones were almost under
his apartments at home, laid there by the hand of the wick-
edest criminal that had ever lived since Cain!" No person

with a conscience could do that, he implied. No self-respect-
ing person would accept a gift from a man he knew to be a
murderer.

In a powerful closing, the Attorney General demolished
the series of weak and implausible hypotheses offered by
the defense and staunchly defended Littlefield's integrity.
Merrick's "pathos and poetry" about the janitor's eating
"that consecrated meal received from a murderer" was
turned against him amidst the laughter of the courtroom.
"Why should he refuse it?" Clifford asked. "Should he refuse the only present ever given him by Dr. Webster, and
thus tell him his suspicions?" As it turned out, Littlefield
did not dine at home on Thanksgiving Day, and there was
no evidence to show if and when he ate the turkey. The
courtroom reverberated with Clifford's rendition of Webster's incautious query to the police officer after arrest: "Did
they find the *whole* of the body?" The Attorney General dismissed the argument of the defense that a man as intelligent
as Professor Webster would not be fool enough to have
acted so indiscreetly. "Crime is foolish," he insisted. "It has
always been so, from the beginning. It will always be so, in
the end. . . . Have you any doubt from all this evidence
that Dr. Webster had an agency in the death of Dr. Parkman? Can you doubt it for a moment?" On this note the
state concluded its devastating summation.

When Clifford took his seat the Chief Justice asked the
prisoner if he had anything to say. At that time defendants
in criminal cases were not permitted to testify, and Shaw
was careful to caution Webster "that this is a privilege
granted to you which you may use or not at your discretion." With an air of injured innocence and a reckless disregard for the consequences of his remarks, the professor
proceeded to assail his counsel, charging them with failing
to produce in court evidence available to them which would
have "firmly established" his innocence. After defending
himself on a few minor, peripheral points, he ended on a
melodramatic note:

If the Court will allow me to say one word more—
I have felt more distressed by the production of these
various anonymous letters, I had almost said, than by
anything else. And I call my God to witness, while I
positively declare, *I never wrote them!* Since my trial
my counsel has received on this day a letter from this
very "Civis"; and if he is present, and has a spark of
humanity, I CALL UPON HIM TO COME FORWARD, AND AC-
KNOWLEDGE IT!

A deathlike stillness followed this amazing show of effrontery. When, after an appropriate interval, it was clear
that "Civis" had no intention of revealing himself, Chief
Justice Shaw proceeded to charge the jury in a voice, according to one observer, "greatly disturbed by emotion."
In the main his exposition of the law has been followed re-
ligiously down to the present day, but at one crucial point
it was destined to raise a storm of controversy and to be
subsequently repudiated. With a lucidity characteristic of
every Lemuel Shaw utterance, the Chief Justice expounded
the law relating to circumstantial evidence. "Circumstantial
evidence may be of such a nature," he stated, "as to warrant a conclusive belief that somebody did it; and it would
be injurious to the best interests of society to have it so
ordered that circumstantial proof cannot avail."

Then Shaw addressed himself to the vital question: "Was
the body of Dr. Parkman found?" "It has sometimes been
said by judges," he observed, "that a jury never ought to convict in a capital case unless the dead body is found. That, as a
general proposition, is true. It sometimes happens, however,
that it cannot be found, where the proof of death is clear.
Sometimes, in a case of murder at sea, the body is thrown
overboard on a stormy night. Because the body is not
found, can anybody deny that the author of that crime is
a murderer?" While carefully refraining from expressing
an opinion on the weight of the evidence, Shaw pointed out

that if it could be shown that the teeth found in the furnace were the identical teeth belonging to Dr. Parkman, this would go far to prove that he was the person. Other evidence of a less conclusive nature, such as the shape, size, and height of the various bone fragments uncovered, would serve to corroborate the first evidence. On the other hand, Shaw charged the jury, the witnesses supporting the alibi of Professor Webster appeared to have suffered from a case of mistaken identity.

Shaw now reached that point in his charge for which he was to be sharply criticized. Did the facts show malice? In his exposition of the law the Chief Justice was at least consistent with the rule he had himself laid down five years earlier in the case of *Commonwealth* v. *York*, involving a murder charge against a Negro seaman. In that case Richard H. Dana had argued for the instruction that the burden of proof of malice in homicide rested upon the state, but Shaw, following a dubious line of rather remote English precedents, ruled that in case of an intentional killing where no circumstances appear to justify, excuse, or palliate the act, the law presumes malice, and it rests upon the accused to show circumstances to refute that malice by a preponderance of the evidence. At that time Associate Justice Samuel Sumner Wilde, an old Hartford Convention stalwart, entered a vigorous dissent, but there is no record of his having taken exception to Shaw's ruling in the Webster case. Since Shaw's charge had the effect of throwing on the defendant the burden of proof of a fact, while all that is necessary to entitle him to acquittal is a reasonable doubt of *any* of the essential elements of the crime, including, in the case of murder, the element of malice, it was a target for much criticism. Joel Parker, then a Harvard Law School professor, correctly pointed out that the case ran counter to a basic maxim of the criminal law: every man is presumed to be innocent until he is proved guilty—innocent of the malice as well as the homicide. More recent authorities have repudiated Shaw. The law today does not presume the worst of several possible solutions against the prisoner, but instead the one which would be most favorable to him.

In conclusion Shaw dissected character evidence that had been brought out at the trial. In some crimes, such as larceny, he instructed, a good character might be very important to a defendant, but "where it is a question of a great and atrocious crime, it is so unusual, so out of the ordinary course of things, he must have been influenced by such facts and circumstances as to create effects which have infrequently been produced upon a human mind, so that the evidence of character may be considered as far inferior to what it is in the case of smaller crimes." *"Against facts strongly proved,"* Shaw charged, *"character cannot avail. . . .* I commend this cause to your consideration. Take sufficient time, weigh the evidence, and give such a verdict as will satisfy your own judgment, and your own sound conscience, and I am sure it will be a true one." This was a hanging charge if ever there was one.

The jury retired at eight p.m. A short time later the prisoner was conducted to a private room in the building, where he remained until summoned to learn his fate. About two hundred persons remained in the courtroom, gathering in groups of ten or a dozen to speculate on the verdict. The jury's deliberations were marked by a complete absence of bickering. Out of deference to the court they abstained from taking a ballot for a half-hour or so. Then one of their number proposed that they "seek for divine wisdom and guidance." The proposal meeting with a cordial response, the foreman called on the mover to offer prayer. On the first ballot taken on whether the remains were those of Dr. Parkman the jury were unanimous. They were also unanimous that he came to his death at the hands of Webster. A few jurors shrank from the next logical step, the finding of Webster guilty as set forth in the indictment. Their reluctance sprang not from any doubt about the evidence, but from a humanitarian impulse. As one of the jurors later commented, the evidence pointed to the prisoner *"and to no one else."*

At 10.40 a movement was heard at the door of the court-room, and presently a number of gentlemen, including counsel on both sides and the clerk of court, entered. A whisper soon spread about the room that the jury had agreed on a verdict. Five minutes later the jury filed in and took their customary seats. Then Professor Webster followed, moving with his characteristically quick, nervous step, but looking the picture of dejection. After the judges had taken their places on the bench, the clerk of court addressed the jury: "Mr. Foreman and Gentlemen of the Jury. Have you agreed upon your verdict?" Mr. Byram, the foreman bowed assent.

The clerk then turned and addressed the prisoner: "John W. Webster, hold up your right hand!" The prisoner rose and stared straight at the foreman of the jury. The clerk then said: "Mr. Foreman, look upon the prisoner. Prisoner, look upon the jury.

"What do you say, Mr. Foreman, is the prisoner at the bar guilty or not guilty?"

"Guilty," was the solemn response.

Webster's head slumped downward. He had to sit down to prevent collapsing, and held his head in his hands. In a few moments he was removed to Leverett Street jail to await sentencing. On Monday, April 1, Shaw had the painful task of pronouncing sentence. Reviewing the verdict, he stated that the court could "perceive no just or legal ground of exception." Then, continuing his memorable pronouncement, he declared: "Guilty! How much does this single word import!" He reminded the accused "of the irreparable wrong done to the victim" of his cruelty. "If you consider your case a hard one or your punishment too severe, think, oh! think of him, instantly deprived of life by your guilty hand." Then, "if not lost to all sense of retributive justice, you may perhaps be ready to exclaim: 'I have sinned against Heaven and my own soul. My punishment is just.

God be merciful to me, a sinner!' . . . God grant that your
example may afford a solemn warning to all, especially to
the young!" Shaw continued. The present was no time for
words of advice, he observed sadly. On other occasions the
Chief Justice had been wont "to address the illiterate, the
degraded, the outcast, blessed with no means of moral and
religious culture," enjoying none of the benefits of cultivated
society. But in this case, with all the circumstances reversed,
"no word of ours could be more efficacious than the suggestions of your own better thoughts, to which we commend
you." And now nothing remained but the solemn duty of
pronouncing sentence:

> That you, John W. Webster, be removed from this
> place, and detained in close custody in the prison of this
> county, and thence taken, at such time as the Executive
> Government of this Commonwealth may, by their war-
> rant, appoint, to the place of execution, and there be
> hung by the neck until you are dead.
>
> And may God, of His infinite goodness, have mercy
> on your soul!

The prisoner sank back in his chair and wept, but his tears
were wasted. "Mr. Sheriff, the prisoner is in your custody,"
directed the Chief Justice, as though washing his hands of
the unsavory mess. Webster, manacled, was taken away.
"Mr. Crier, adjourn the court until tomorrow morning, at
9 o'clock."

A wave of irrational sympathy for the prisoner swept the
country, a hysterical symptom not infrequently associated
with celebrated murder trials. A Philadelphia paper compared Shaw's sentence to the "burning" of the witches and
the hanging of the Quakers in the Bay State, and ran this
objective headline: "JUDICIAL MURDER IN BOSTON." Another
typical comment: "If the jury had prayed less and deliber-
ated more, they could not in any event have gone beyond a
verdict of manslaughter."

Webster's appeal on several questions of procedure was

turned down, and his last recourse was to petition the Governor for a commutation of sentence. With crocodile tears he pleaded: "I ask to be permitted to declare in the most solemn manner that *I am entirely innocent* of this awful crime. I am the victim of circumstances," he whined, "or a foul conspiracy, or of the attempt of some individual to cause suspicion to fall upon me, influenced perhaps by the prospect of obtaining a large reward." But pro-Webster sentimentalists were to receive a paralyzing blow when the Reverend George Putnam on July 2 went before the council and read a confession that the professor had at last been induced to make. Admitting that he had asked Parkman to call to see him, Webster then proceeded to give his own version of the bloody turn of events:

Dr. Parkman agreed to call on me, as I proposed. He came, accordingly, between half past one and two. He came in at the lecture-room door. I was engaged in removing some glasses from my lecture-room table into the room in the rear, called the upper laboratory. He came rapidly down the steps and followed me into the laboratory. He immediately addressed me with great energy: "Are you ready for me, sir? Have you got the money?" I replied, "No, Dr. Parkman"; and was then beginning to state my condition, and make my appeal to him. He would not listen to me, but interrupted me with much vehemence. He called me "scoundrel" and "liar" and went on heaping upon me the most bitter taunts and opprobrious epithets. While he was talking, he drew a handful of papers from his pocket, and took from among them my two notes, and also an old letter from Dr. Hosack, written many years ago, and congratulating him [Parkman] on his success in getting me appointed professor of chemistry. "You see," he said, "I got you into your office, and now I will get you out of it." He put back into his pocket all the papers, except the letter and the notes.

I cannot tell how long the torrent of threats and in-
vectives continued, and I can now recall to memory but
a small portion of what he said. At first I kept interposing, trying to pacify him, so that I might obtain the
object for which I had sought the interview. But I could
not stop him, and soon my own temper was up. I forgot
everything. I felt nothing but the sting of his words.
I was excited to the highest degree of passion; and
while he was speaking and gesticulating in the violent
and menacing manner, thrusting the letter and his fist
into my face, in my fury I seized whatever was the
handiest,—it was a stick of wood,—and dealt him an
instantaneous blow with all the force that passion could
give it. I did not know, nor think, nor care where I
should hit him, nor how hard, nor what the effect would
be. It was on the side of his head, and there was nothing
to break the force of the blow. He fell instantly upon
the pavement. There was no second blow. He did not
move. I stooped down over him, and he seemed to be
lifeless. Blood flowed from his mouth, and I got a
sponge and wiped it away. I got some ammonia and
applied it to his nose; but without effect. Perhaps I
spent ten minutes in attempts to resuscitate him; but I
found that he was absolutely dead. In my horror and
consternation I ran instinctively to the doors and bolted
them,—the doors of the lecture-room, and of the laboratory below. And then, what was I to do?

It never occurred to me to go out and declare what
had been done, and obtain assistance. I saw nothing
but the alternative of a successful removal and concealment of the body, on the one hand, and of infamy and
destruction on the other. The first thing I did, as soon
as I could do anything, was to drag the body into the
private room adjoining. There I took off the clothing,
and began putting them into the fire which was burning
in the upper laboratory. They were all consumed there
that afternoon,—with papers, pocket book, or what-

ever else they may have contained. I did not examine the pockets, nor remove anything except the watch. I saw that, or the chain of it, hanging out; and I took it and threw it over the bridge as I went to Cambridge.

My next move was to get the body into the sink which stands in the small private room. By setting the body partially erect, against the corner, and getting up into the sink myself, I succeeded in drawing it up. There it was entirely dismembered. It was quickly done, as a work of terrible and desperate necessity. The only instrument used was the knife found by the officers in the tea chest, and which I kept for cutting corks. . . . While dismembering the body, a stream of cochituate was running through the sink, carrying off the blood in a pipe that passed down through the lower laboratory. There must have been a leak in the· pipe, for the ceiling below was stained immediately round it.

There was a fire burning in the furnace of the lower laboratory. Littlefield was mistaken in thinking there has never been a fire there. He had probably never kindled one, but I had done it myself several times. I had done it that day for the purpose of making oxygen gas. The head and viscera were put into that furnace that day, and the fuel heaped on. I did not examine at night to see to what degree they were consumed. Some of the extremities, I believe, were put in there on that day. The pelvis and some of the limbs, perhaps all, were put under the lid of the lecture-room table in what is called the well,—a deep sink lined with lead. A stream of cochituate was turned into it, and kept running through it all Friday night. The thorax was put into a similar well in the lower laboratory, which I filled with water, and threw in a quantity of potash which I found there. This disposition of the remains was not changed till after the visit of the officers on Monday.

When the body had been thus all disposed of, I cleared away all traces of what had been done. I took up the stick with which the fatal blow had been struck. It proved to be the stump of a large grape vine, say two inches in diameter, and two feet long. It was one of two or more pieces which I had carried in from Cambridge long before for the purpose of showing the effect of certain chemical fluids in coloring wood, by being absorbed into the pores. The grape vine, being a very porous wood, was well suited to this purpose. Another longer stick had been used as intended, and exhibited to the students. This one had not been used. I put it into the fire.

Why did the professor break down at long last and by his confession redden the face of every Webster fan throughout the country? Was his story impelled by conscience? Daniel Webster, prosecutor in the celebrated Knapp murder trial some twenty years before the Parkman murder, has left us a classic account of the psychology of confession:

The fatal blow is given! The deed is done. He has done the murder. No eye has seen him, no ear has heard him. The secret is his own, and it is safe!

Ah! gentlemen, that was a dreadful mistake. Such a secret can be safe *nowhere*. The whole creation of God has neither nook nor corner where the guilty can bestow it, and say, "It is safe." Especially, in a case exciting so much attention as this, discovery must come, and will come, sooner or later. A thousand eyes turn at once to explore every man, every thing, every circumstance, connected with the time and place; a thousand ears catch every whisper; a thousand excited minds intensely dwell on the scene, shedding all their light, and ready to kindle the slightest circumstance into a blaze of discovery.

Meantime the guilty soul cannot keep its secret. It is false to itself; or rather it feels an irresistible impulse of conscience to be true to itself. It labors under its guilty possession, and knows not what to do with it.

The human heart was not made for the residence of such an inhabitant. It finds itself preyed on by a torment, which it dares not acknowledge to God or man. A vulture is devouring it, and it can ask no sympathy or assistance, either from heaven or earth. The secret which the murderer possesses soon comes to possess him; and, like the evil spirits of which we read, it overcomes him, and leads him whithersoever it will. He feels it beating at his heart, rising to his throat, and DEMANDING disclosure. He thinks the whole world sees it in his face, reads it in his eyes, and almost hears its workings in the very silence of his thoughts. It has become his master. It betrays his discretion, it breaks down his courage, it conquers his prudence. When suspicions from without begin to embarrass him, and the net of circumstances to entangle him, the fatal secret struggles with still greater violence to burst forth. It *must* be confessed! It WILL be confessed! There is no refuge from confession, but suicide,—and suicide is confession.

But there was little justification for the charitable belief that Professor Webster was overwhelmed by a sense of guilt in the manner described by Daniel Webster or that he was telling the whole truth now any more than he had earlier. Instead, his confession smacked of a carefully calculated effort to rebut the inference of premeditation and malice. On order of the council the Governor refused to stay sentence, and Webster was hanged on Friday, August 30, on a scaffold in the prison yard.

While the country had been divided on the verdict, it now seemed reconciled to the execution. Even Horace Greeley, who was deeply disturbed at the idea of putting a man to death upon circumstantial evidence, drew a mead of satisfaction from the fact that "learning, talent, social position, cannot shield a culprit from the law's vigilance and penalties."

And so terminated what Greeley's paper categorized as
"a concatenation of horrors such as History has rarely recorded and Imagination has seldom transcended." But the
year was 1850, almost a hundred years before Auschwitz
and Buchenwald. Human butchery was still a retail com-
modity.

Webster's failure served to spur others with homicidal intent to carry out corpse-disposal with less chance of detection. But as though to demonstrate the adage that crime
does not pay, they always left dangling a telltale clue. A half
century after the Webster case the headless, armless, leg-
less torso of a man was found in the East River in New
York, wrapped in oilcloth. In the course of time other dismembered segments of the corpse turned up, each wrapped
in a piece of the same oilcloth. From color prints made of
the pattern, reporters for the *New York Journal* scoured the
city and eventually ran down the purchase. As the result,
"the Guldensuppe mystery" was solved, and a former mistress of the victim and her new lover were convicted.

But that was half a century ago. Murderers are still trying to execute the perfect crime that cannot be proved to
have taken place. Recently Donald Hume, a London sub-
urbanite, was charged with inviting one Stanley Setty, a
postwar black-marketeer, to his flat, stabbing him, cutting
him into segments, packaging him in felt and carpet, transferring these packages to a rented airplane, and dropping
the incriminating evidence into the sea off the east coast
of England. Unfortunately for Donald Hume, one parcel
was picked up on the mud flats by a fisherman. Other slips,
like having a stained carpet cleaned and dyed, asking a
mechanic to sharpen a carving-knife so that he could cut
the "joint on the table," and paying a taxi fare with a five-
pound note identified by its number as having been in the
possession of the victim, built up a nasty circumstantial
case against him. Still, the jury found it difficult to accept
the fact that he could have done the killing and dissecting
in his own flat, and disagreed. He was subsequently sen-

tenced to a twelve-year term after pleading guilty to being an accessory after the fact of murder.

Next to quicklime, Webster's furnace, suitably converted to oil, still seems like the best device for torso-disposers, provided that all false teeth are first removed.

VII

Armstrong's Acquittal by Almanac

Lincoln starts a legend

For the innocently accused to assume that the technical safeguards of the law may suffice to secure vindication would be dangerously unrealistic. When the cards seem perilously stacked against him, when the prosecutor goes into the courtroom with a strong prima-facie case, he had better be defended by an experienced trial lawyer, one sufficiently skillful to raise a doubt in the minds of the jurors. Otherwise he faces almost certain conviction. In British trial history a comparison of the fates of Adelaide Bartlett and Florence Maybrick would inevitably come to mind. Both were accused of fatally poisoning their husbands, but the former was acquitted, though the evidence against her was much stronger than against the latter, who was convicted. Edward Clarke, an eloquent Victorian period piece, who was Mrs. Bartlett's counsel, spelled the difference.

No cases in the annals of American criminal trials better illustrate the importance of that x-factor, the presence of a first-rate trial lawyer, than the murder trials of Duff Armstrong and James H. Norris. Both were tried for the murder of the same man. Both were accused by the same eyewitness. Norris went to prison; Armstrong went free. The wizardry of a great jury lawyer explained the different verdicts. Armstrong had been judicious enough to pick as his counsel a rising prairie politician and popular circuit rider named Abraham Lincoln. The tale of how Lincoln confronted the state's star witness with an almanac and knocked the props from under his testimony has become part of American folklore.

Since interest in that trial lawyer has burgeoned with the years, it is high time to set the record straight. The facts about the episode may recast the legend but they detract no whit from Lincoln's stature as a trial lawyer or from that broad humanity which marked his dealings with his fellow men. No stenographic record of the Armstrong trial was preserved. The newspapers gave the case no coverage. The sequence of trial steps must be reconstructed on the basis of the recollection of eyewitnesses—the judge, the prosecutor's staff, the jurors, the prisoner, and his family. Lincoln's erratic law partner, William H. Herndon, painstakingly assembled parts of the story after the President's death. But so many pieces were still missing from the jigsaw puzzle that he never did get it straight.

Here is what really happened. In November 1857 Lincoln was visited in Springfield by an old friend, Hannah Armstrong, who urged him to undertake the defense of her scapegrace son, William, nicknamed Duff, then in jail on a murder charge. Although Lincoln had an exacting law practice and heavy political commitments, Hannah counted on his ties to her family. These associations went back to the early thirties when Abe was trying to earn a miserable livelihood running a grocery business in the village of New Salem, along the Sangamon River, some twenty miles from Springfield, an unhappy venture that cost Lincoln all his worldly goods. Homeless and broke, he was put up for weeks at a time at the cabin of Jack and Hannah Armstrong at Clary's Grove, a few miles outside the village. At the end of a day's surveying, Lincoln shared a meal of milk, mush, and cornbread with the Armstrongs. The children flocked around Abe, who invariably brought them candy. After supper, while Hannah would patch his pants and darn his shirts, he would rock the cradle of her youngest born, Duff, and study his lawbooks.

The gaunt, ungainly surveyor had much in common with the farm folk of New Salem, but his consuming passion for learning and professional advancement set him quite apart from the bookless Armstrongs. It was here at New Salem that Lincoln prepared for the bar. Here he attended trials conducted by a local justice called Bowling Green. He observed an informal, frontier law in the making. He heard Green decide a hog case by declaring that the plaintiff's witnesses were "damned liars, the court being well acquainted with the shoat in question, and knowing it to belong to Jack Kelso." From New Salem Lincoln went on to wider frontiers. In two decades he had achieved fame at the state bar and eminence in politics. But if Hannah for a moment thought that Abe had forgotten his old friends, he was quick to reassure her. "You can count on me," Lincoln told her.

As soon as he began to dig into the case, Lincoln found that Duff was in serious trouble. His plight stemmed from an incident that had occurred in midsummer on the Salt Creek campground, not far from the Armstrong home. A camp meeting of three weeks' duration was in progress, and the listeners were duly admonished against drinking, gambling, swearing, and whoring. These admonitions had at best a temporary effect, for whenever there was a pause in the oratory, "breeze-shaken" sinners whose road to hell was floodlighted by the evangelists' rhetoric stampeded to the several bars set up at the edge of the grove.

August 29 was a Saturday night. Camp meeting was over for the day. Duff, according to his own story, told many years later, had been at the meeting for two or three days, spending most of the time drinking. Planning to sleep off the effects of liquor, he found a big drygoods box not far from the bars and stretched himself out on it for a night's sleep. Around ten o'clock a burly Petersburg farmer named James P. Metzker, nicknamed "Pres," came along. Pres, an acquaintance of Duff's, was in an ugly mood. He grabbed Duff by the legs, shouting: "Damn you, get up!" With that he yanked him off the drygoods box.

"Let me alone, Pres. I'm asleep," Duff expostulated.

But Duff's soporific mood seemed to bring out a perverse, bullying streak in the older man. Again Metzker dragged him off the box, grabbed his hat, and stamped on it. "You have no business hanging around here," he remonstrated. "You ought to be home picking up chips for your ma."

"What I do is none of your damn business," Duff answered. Defiantly he staggered over to one of the bars and called for a whisky. Barely had he lifted the glass to his lips when Metzker caught him by the throat, forcing him to spill the liquor. Duff's patience was now worn thin.

"Pres, if you do that again, I'll knock you down even if you are bigger than I am. You have run this thing far enough."

Metzker had a loaded whip in his hand and was about to strike Duff when the younger man landed a solid blow with his fist. It was a frontier fight, no holds barred. But soon the larger antagonist had the smaller one on the ground and was mauling him unmercifully, when the crowd pulled him off. Then everyone went to the bar. Duff called for drinks. He and Pres bumped glasses. Just when Duff thought the incident was forgotten, Metzker, without any provocation, struck him on the upper lip. Taking up a glass, he was about to hurl it at Duff when a bystander shouted: "Set that glass down. If you strike him with that glass I will kill you!"

According to Duff's story, that was the last time he saw Metzker that night. Stealing a quilt from a buggy and wrapping it around himself, Metzker sought a place to sleep. But before calling it a night, he appears to have had another brawl, this time with a bystander named James H. Norris. The next morning Metzker was observed walking up to the bar with the stolen quilt around him. His right eye was swollen shut. He bathed it with a glass of whisky, drank another glass, mounted his horse, and rode away. Duff never saw Metzker again.

On September 1, two days after quitting the campgrounds, Metzker died at the house of Ed Ormie, three miles away. A post-mortem revealed two wounds in the head of the deceased. One on the back was alleged to have resulted from a blow by Norris, who was charged with wielding a piece of wagon harness called a neck yoke. The wound over

the right eye that Duff himself had noticed the morning
after the row was attributed to a blow by Armstrong with
a slung shot. Since either blow was deemed sufficient to
have caused death, Armstrong and Norris were promptly
arrested and charged with murder in the first degree.

Murder requires malice aforethought, an anticipated design to commit the felony. Had Duff been permitted to take
the stand and tell his own story, he could have made out a
case of justifiable homicide or, at worst, manslaughter. But
in those days Illinois criminal procedure followed the English common law, which barred defendants from testifying
in their own behalf. Unfortunately for Duff, as his attorney
was soon to discover, the accounts of the incident from the
mouths of other witnesses varied in significant details from
his own story.

At the October term of the Mason County circuit court,
held at Havana, Norris and Armstrong were jointly indicted
for murder and held without bail. Norris's record was by
no means clean. Some time before, he had killed a man
named Thornbury, but managed to clear himself on a plea
of self-defense. Naturally, local feeling ran high against
him, and the ugly tide swept over Duff as well. Fearing a
lynching party, the authorities hustled the pair from the
insecure Mason County jail and lodged them across the
Illinois River in the Fulton County jail at Lewiston.

"All the bad luck in the world seemed to come to me
now," Duff later commented, for on the very day that the
indictment was handed down his father died. On his death-
bed Jack, who had wrestled with Abe Lincoln years before
in front of Offutt's store, admonished his wife: "Hannah,
sell everything to clear Duff."

Realizing that Norris's bad record would count heavily
with a jury, Armstrong's friends shrewdly advised him to
stand trial separately and in a court less dominated by
local tension. On the 5th of November, he signed an affidavit for a change of venue, alleging that he could "not receive a fair and impartial trial in this court on account of

the inhabitants of said Mason County being prejudiced against him." The affidavit had been prepared for him by William Walker, a young, inexperienced, and unlettered attorney who was at that time handling the defense of both prisoners. The court granted his plea, and his case was transferred to the Cass County seat of Beardstown. The providential nature of the move soon was revealed when, on November 7, a Mason County jury found Norris guilty of manslaughter and the court sentenced him to serve eight years in the state penitentiary.

For the first time Lincoln now stepped into the Armstrong case. At the November term of the Cass circuit court, he happened to be in Beardstown assisting the district's leading lawyer, J. Henry Shaw, in defending a divorce action against Jonathan Gill. Shaw and Lincoln were beaten; the divorce was granted, and the custody of the child given to the mother, but the matter of alimony went over to the May term of court. With some of his sporadic secretiveness, Lincoln kept his own counsel about Armstrong. Shaw, who was later to be associated with the prosecution of Duff, was amazed when, on November 19, Lincoln moved that Duff be admitted to bail, arguing "hotly" for the motion. Judge James Harriott denied the motion, and Duff remained in jail for almost six months more.

When, on the evening of May 6, 1858, Lincoln arrived at Beardstown again, he momentarily set aside issues of large moment to make his appearance in the alimony action and to defend Armstrong. In fact, the early days of May of that year were among the busiest of his whole career. He had already announced his candidacy for the United States Senate, within a month he was to sound an ominous warning to the Republican convention at Springfield that "a house divided against itself cannot stand," and in his spare moments he was giving a good deal of thought to preparing for his midsummer debates with Stephen A. Douglas, from which he was to emerge with national stature.

The morning of Friday, May 7, came in warm and sultry.

When the doors opened, crowds stormed into the little brick courthouse, still standing in Beardstown. With aisles packed, doorways jammed, and spectators dangling their legs from every windowsill, the temperature kept rising, until by midday the courtroom resembled an oven. Judge Harriott, who had deemed it to be in the public interest to keep Duff locked up, presided. The state's attorney, Hugh Fullerton, conducted the prosecution. He was reinforced by J. Henry Shaw, serving as special counsel employed by the Metzker family to make doubly sure that justice would take its course. Shaw and Lincoln had only just made an appearance on the same side in the alimony matter, but the latter continued strangely closemouthed about his connection with the Armstrong case. The first intimation Shaw had that Lincoln would defend Armstrong was when the Springfield attorney took his place across the counsel table.

Fully realizing that even a bad case might be retrieved if entrusted to a sympathetic jury, Lincoln and Walker, who was also retained by the Armstrongs, showed unusual care in the selection of jurors from among the talesmen in homespun and brogans. Soon the regular panel was exhausted by challenge, with but four jurors obtained, and a second venire of fifty was summoned. Lincoln shrewdly gambled that a jury of young men would be more sympathetic to a defendant tried for the consequences of a brawl than one displaying advanced arteriosclerotic symptoms. One by one the superannuated were challenged by the defense. As Milton Logan, the foreman of the jury later reminisced: "I was then in my twenty-eighth year and was the oldest member of the jury. Ben Ayr, who had but a month before reached his majority, was the youngest. As I remember, I do not believe the average age of the jury was over twenty-three years."

Walker had furnished his senior counsel with his notes on the evidence in the Norris trial, and as a result Lincoln was well prepared for the case the prosecution would build. But that case was indeed formidable. A procession of a

dozen witnesses, two of them reluctant, took the stand to
hammer home the accusation that Armstrong had hit Metzker over the right eye with a slung shot. Some had jour-
neyed as far as a hundred and sixty miles to appear in court.
The defense just could not allow their stories on the direct
to stand uncontested.

Most of the cross-examination was entrusted to Walker.
According to Abram Bergen, a spectator located not more
than four feet from the counsel table, Lincoln sat motion-
less during most of the state's testimony and stared at the
wall. Only in a few cases did he personally cross-examine.
But even in these, where he felt that the witness was telling
the truth as he saw it, he refrained from browbeating tactics.
His attitude was folksy. He was among friends. This is how
Lincoln handled one such witness, a lad named William
Killian.

"Where do you reside?"

"Clary's Grove."

"Are you the son of Jim Killian, and your mother's
maiden name was Sparks?"

"Yes, sir, you are right," the witness answered.

"Well," said Lincoln somewhat aside, "if you take after
your father, you are a bright boy, and I knew your mother
well."

That was all. No attempt to confuse, humiliate, or impugn the credibility of the son of old acquaintances.

Despite this surface informality, Lincoln's cross-examination was never casual, but was based on painstaking preparation and a mastery of the strength and weakness of his
adversary's case. "I am never easy now when I am handling
a case," he once confessed, "until I have bounded it north,
bounded it south, bounded it east, and bounded it west." In
addition to being prepared for the evidence and arguments
on both sides, Lincoln was a stickler for real proof—proof
beyond the probability of doubt. Years earlier, when poring
over lawbooks, he was struck by the failure of the texts to
make clear the meaning of "demonstrate." "I worked until

I could give any proposition of the six books of Euclid at sight," he later remarked. "I then found out what 'demonstrate' meant." In the Armstrong trial he bided his time, but when the crucial witness for the state appeared, Lincoln would furnish a demonstration of the verification of evidence which has become a legend of the American bar.

The state's star witness was a Petersburg housepainter named Charles Allen. It was his testimony at the Norris trial that had scored most heavily with the jury which had brought in a verdict of guilty. Lincoln could not afford to let him score again. While Allen had shown no reluctance to testify against Norris (in fact, he seemed eager to do so), he tried hard to avoid involvement in the Armstrong case. He ignored a summons to appear for the state and seems to have been staying at a tavern in Virginia, Illinois, some dozen miles away, apparently with the connivance of the Armstrong boys. Since the failure of the state's star witness to appear would have meant a continuance of the case and further time in jail for Duff, Lincoln thought it better that he take the stand. Nevertheless, it was necessary to issue an attachment for contempt against him, and for John Huston, deputy to Sheriff James A. Dick, to arrest him and bring him to court in time for the trial. That Allen was obviously not anxious to help out the state must be borne in mind when his conduct on cross-examination is reviewed.

Fullerton, on the direct, brought out that Allen had clearly seen Duff strike Metzker with a slung shot. If uncontested, this testimony would have sealed the verdict against the prisoner. Lincoln took over the cross-examination himself. No stenographic record of the *Q.* and *A.* was made by circuit courts in those days, nor is any local newspaper account extant, but from a variety of spectators, including Foreman Logan, it is possible to reconstruct the exchange between Allen and Lincoln with every likelihood of authenticity.

LINCOLN: Did you see Armstrong strike Metzker?

ALLEN: Yes.

LINCOLN: About how far were you from where the affair took place?

ALLEN: About forty feet. I was standing on a knoll looking down at them.

LINCOLN: Was it a light night?

ALLEN: Yes, it was.

LINCOLN: Was there any moon that night?

ALLEN: Yes, there was a full moon, and it was shining almost as bright as day.

LINCOLN: About how high was the moon?

ALLEN: About where the sun would be at ten o'clock in the day.

LINCOLN: Are you certain there was a moon that night?

ALLEN: Yes, sir. I am certain.

LINCOLN: You are sure you are not mistaken about the moon shining as brightly as you represent?

ALLEN: No, sir. I am not mistaken.

LINCOLN: And you are sure it was a full moon.

ALLEN: Yes, positive.

LINCOLN: Did you see Armstrong strike Metzker by the light of the moon and did you see Metzker fall?

ALLEN: I did.

LINCOLN: What did Armstrong strike him with?

ALLEN: With a slung shot.

LINCOLN: Where did he strike Metzker?

ALLEN: On the side of the head.

LINCOLN: Will you show the jury just how the blow was struck?

Allen rose and went through the motion of striking an overhand blow, "just as he saw me do by the light of the full moon," Duff later recalled. Lincoln had him repeat the performance.

LINCOLN: About what time did you say this happened?

ALLEN: About eleven o'clock at night.

• • •

Two significant issues of fact had been raised in this exchange. Allen had asserted that Armstrong had attacked Metzker with a slung shot and that it was light enough to see the blow clearly at a distance of forty feet. At the appropriate time Lincoln would tear into both these assertions.

Now it was the turn of the defense to present its case. Eight of Lincoln's witnesses testified that Duff had done nothing more than defend himself with his fists against a foe who towered over him by a head. Each one categorically denied that he had seen the slung shot used to attack Metzker. One witness for the defense might easily have got out of hand. That was Will Watkins, a young Petersburg farmer and the reputed owner of the slung shot. A short time after the trial, one of the jurors named Brady was on a cattle-buying trip in Watkins's neighborhood and swapped stories about the case with him. Watkins told him that, before the trial, Lincoln had asked him to come to Springfield. In an office interview he questioned him about the slung shot, seeking to learn how it happened to be lost and then located near the very spot where Metzker was killed. Watkins replied that, before going to sleep that night under his wagon, he had laid the slung shot on the coupling pole of the vehicle. The next morning, completely forgetting about the precarious spot on which the weapon was perched, he drove away, and the slung shot had evidently dropped to the ground. So far, so good. But Watkins went on to intimate that he knew too much to make a good defense witness. When he started to talk freely, Lincoln, like a good attorney who did not wish to hear anything that might affect his objective handling of the defense, stopped him abruptly.

"All I want to know is this," Lincoln asked. *"Did you make that slung shot, and did Duff Armstrong ever have it in his possession?"*

Although Watkins was reassuring on both scores, he went on to warn Lincoln: *"On cross-examination they may make me tell things I do not want to tell."*

Lincoln kept this warning in mind. On the direct Watkins

swore that the slung shot in evidence was his and not Duff's. His detailed description of how he made it carried conviction. He had filled an eggshell with lead, poured molten zinc on it, covered up the unfused mass with a piece of calfskin sewn with a squirrel-skin string, and fastened the slung shot to his wrist with the skin of a groundhog.

"Was it continuously in your possession on the night of the fight?" Lincoln asked.

"Yes," Watkins replied.

"Then how did it happen to be found on the campgrounds that night?"

This question gave Watkins an opportunity to tell the jury the story he had previously told Lincoln, of placing the slung shot on the coupling pole, and its accidental dropping to the ground.

So scrupulously had Lincoln narrowed his questions to the ownership of the slung shot and the explanation of its discovery that the prosecution, failing to perceive the witness's tension on the stand, never realized that Watkins actually was an eyewitness to the brawl. Had he been pressed very hard on cross-examination he would have been forced to admit that he saw Duff strike Metzker over the eye, *not* with the slung shot, *but with an old-fashioned wagon hammer!* Lincoln's superior preparation and the prosecution's insufficient alertness lost the state a major scoring opportunity.

Lincoln's skillful handling of the medical testimony served as a booster shot for the defense. Dr. B. F. Stevenson, the prosecution witness, had ignored two summonses and was finally taken up on the same warrant issued for the arrest of Allen. When he took the stand, it was quite obvious that he did so reluctantly. The testimony of this prominent New Salem citizen, later to found the Grand Army of the Republic, was refuted by one of Lincoln's own witnesses, Dr. Charles E. Parker. Using a skull to make his points, he demonstrated to the jury how the fracture over the right eye might well have been caused either by a fall suffered by the deceased or by the blow on the back of the head attributed to Norris. Now, several defense witnesses had sworn that Metzker, either thoroughly inebriated or badly stunned, had great difficulty keeping upright in the saddle on his way home and actually fell from his horse a couple of times. Dr. Parker's testimony gave significance to these falls and served to confirm Lincoln's own hypothetical reconstruction of the circumstances of the fatality. According to Lincoln and Parker, either Metzker himself was accountable for his own death or a man already convicted of the crime. This all-too-pat solution could do no one any harm, least of all Armstrong. Judge Harriott later maintained that it was Parker's testimony that weighed most heavily for the defense rather than the more dramatic refutation of the star witness yet to come.

When the defense rested, Fullerton and Shaw still felt that they had proved the state's case overwhelmingly. But, knowing Lincoln's effectiveness in addressing juries, the prosecution might well have been on guard. Lincoln would have thoroughly agreed with a more recent master of trial practice, Emory R. Buckner, who has pointed out that "the most important arrow in the quiver of a trial lawyer is the last one, the summation." One clipped but eloquent memorandum for a summing-up to a jury indicates how seriously Lincoln took his jury speeches. In that case a widow of a Revolutionary soldier had had her pension halved by a rapacious agent. Himself a veteran of a frontier episode magnified as the Black Hawk War, Lincoln could be counted on to leave no stone unturned for veterans and their widows. His notes ran as follows:

No contract. Not professional services. Unreasonable charge. Money retained by defendant—not given by plaintiff. Revolutionary War. Describe Valley Forge privations. Ice. Soldiers' bleeding feet. Plaintiff's husband. Soldier leaving home for army. SKIN DEFENDANT. Close.

Herndon attests that Lincoln made the most of the soldier's bleeding lower extremities and the snows of Valley Forge, and that the defendant was skinned to the entire satisfaction of the jury. But Lincoln in his jury speeches eschewed showy oratory. He had nothing but contempt for flowery windbags. "He must ape Demosthenes even if the subject is only pip," was one of his barbed comments about a fellow attorney.

Walker, Lincoln's junior associate, led off the summation for the defense. When he finished, Lincoln rose. The courtroom was sweltering. Lincoln, who was wearing a rumpled old linen suit, soon removed his coat. As he came to grips with the case, he threw off his vest. Then he unfastened his collar, often stopping to wipe the sweat off his face with a red silk handkerchief. As usual, a single gallus did duty for both during most of the forensic effort, as the other suspender, of knitted wool, soon slipped off his shoulder. Like many giants, Lincoln's voice was high-pitched and thin, but with remarkable carrying power. When he began his speech to the jury, his voice sounded shrill and piping, but the tones became fuller as he warmed up and gained momentum.

Lincoln struck a sentimental note at the start. He stressed his own ties to the Armstrongs, how kind they had been to him. "Abe did his best talking," Duff later recounted, "when he told the jury what true friends my father and mother had been to him in the early days, when he was a poor young man at New Salem. He told how he used to go out to Jack Armstrong's and stay for days; how kind my mother was to him, and how, many a time, he had rocked me to sleep in the old cradle. He said he was not there pleading for me because he was paid for it" (an obvious dig at Shaw, who was paid a fee by the Metzkers to assist in the prosecution); "but he was there to help a good woman who had helped him when he needed help."

Having established a sympathetic rapport between the jurors, the prisoner's family, and himself, Lincoln abruptly tore into the prosecution's case. Speaking slowly and carefully, he reviewed the whole testimony, item by item, and picked it to pieces. He laid stress on the nature of the wound, which generally gives a clue to the weapon used. The fracture over the eye, he argued, was a consequence of the blow on the back of the head by the neck yoke. Reviewing Dr. Parker's testimony, Lincoln eliminated the slung shot as the weapon that accounted for Metzker's death.

But the climax of his summation was reached when he came to the state's star witness, Allen. It has been the fashion of romanticists to tell how Lincoln floored the housepainter by introducing the almanac in evidence while Allen was still on the stand and by demanding that the witness read the appropriate entry for the night of August 29. But the reminiscences of spectators, jurors, and the prisoner himself discredit this legend. Lincoln shrewdly held his surprise blow almost for the last.

On the morning of the trial, Lincoln sent Duff's cousin, Jake Jones, to a drugstore to procure an almanac. Jake brought back a *Jayne's Almanac.* In introducing the evidence for the defense, Lincoln had remarked to Judge Harriott that he assumed that the court would take judicial notice of the almanac, but in order that there might be no question on that point he offered it as part of the evidence for the defense. Then, at a recess of the court, he took the blue book out of his capacious hat and handed it to Sheriff Dick, with the request that it be turned back to him when called for. When Lincoln reached the point in his summation where he was dissecting Allen's testimony, he asked for the almanac.

"Now I will show you," Lincoln asserted, "that this man Allen's testimony is a pack of lies; that he never saw Armstrong strike Metzker with a slung shot; that he did not witness this fight by the light of the full moon, for the moon was not in the heaven that night." He then opened the almanac to the date of the fatality and proceeded to read the entry. According to the almanac, the moon was within an hour of setting and not high up in the sky at the time of the alleged murder, and instead of being full, as Allen had asserted, it had barely passed the first quarter. A roar of laughter swept the courtroom. Seldom has a state's witness been discredited as completely and suddenly as was Allen. Lincoln passed the almanac to the judge and the prosecuting attorneys and then handed it to the jury for their inspection. Lincoln then pointed out that, since Allen could not be trusted in so crucial a matter as the position of the moon, his whole testimony must be received with caution.

The only objection was raised by Fullerton, who said: "Mr. Lincoln, you are mistaken. The moon was just coming up instead of going down at that time."

Lincoln retorted: "It serves my purpose just as well, just coming up, or just going down, as you admit it was not over- head as Mr. Allen swore it was."

The state's attorneys then sent out for another almanac, which was procured from the office of the probate judge in the same building. The entry for the date in question sub- stantially agreed with Jayne's. And that was the last time the state referred to the Almanac. No further objection was raised to its authenticity, and in their closing to the jury neither attorney for the prosecution mentioned the embar- rassing matter. The silence of the prosecution has much significance because of the canard that circulated during the Lincoln-Douglas debates, only a few months after the trial, and cropped up again during the Presidential campaign of 1860, that the almanac Lincoln used was for the year *pre- vious* to the date of the murder. The story appears to have been invented by a pettifogging local attorney named Car- ter, and to have been reiterated by Shaw, Lincoln's adver- sary in the Armstrong case, who nevertheless insisted that "Mr. Lincoln was entirely innocent of any deception in the matter." Sheriff Dick, at the instigation of the Democrats, compounded the confusion with an affidavit that he did not notice the year covered by the almanac. Carter was mo- tivated by pure spite. According to Bergen, he had only one case for jury trial at that term, and Lincoln "for a five-

dollar fee had run Carter's worthless, litigatious client out
of court on a motion for security for costs." Carter was in
a mood to be easily satisfied that Lincoln was capable of
any chicanery.

Like many other legends, this piece of fiction had hoary
roots. Back in 1786 an attorney for a highwayman in
County Mayo, Ireland, produced a copy of *Ryder's Almanac* to prove that on the occasion of a robbery the moon
had not risen until three o'clock in the morning, long after
the crime alleged to have been committed. After acquittal
it was discovered that the attorney had submitted a doctored edition. The trick bcame a part of Anglo-American
legal folklore and was appropriately attached to the most
celebrated almanac case in American history when in point
of fact nothing of the kind occurred. The malicious twist
made the story more palatable to Lincoln's enemies.

Apart from the unlikelihood that Lincoln would resort to
so cheap and risky a trick of deception (and a review of
Lincoln's legal career will show that he was incapable of
altering evidence), it seems incredible that the fifteen persons who examined the almanac at the trial would not have
noticed the substitution. "It was one for the year in which
the murder was committed," Milton Logan, the foreman
of the jury later insisted, and "there was no trick about it";
and another juror, John T. Brady, was equally positive
about its authenticity. While a *Jayne's Almanac* for that
year and area has never been located since, astronomical
computations reveal that the moon set in Cass County, Illinois, that Saturday night at five minutes after midnight—
in other words, that the astronomical data in the almanac
Lincoln offered as a defense exhibit closely conformed to the
actual fact.

But granted that Allen was lying and that the moon was
in reality close to setting, one question must still be met.
Could he have had sufficient light to see what he declared
he saw *without* illumination from the moon? Duff Armstrong himself answered this question many years later.

"The truth is," Duff admitted, "there was no moon that night. If there was, it was hidden by the clouds. *But it was light enough for everybody to see the fight. The fight took place in one of the bars, and each bar had two or three candles on it.*" In other words, the phase of the moon was nothing more than a decoy, and the prosecution was too inept to recognize it for what it was.

The shrewd interrogation about the moon and the palpably false answers suggest a relationship between defense counsel and the state's star witness quite different from tradition. No question about the moon had been asked Allen at the previous trial. An inspection of any standard almanac would have readily revealed the moon's position. Hence, the witness's behavior on cross-examination hardly seems rational unless he was answering questions that had been planted. To Allen the revelations from the almanac could not have been nearly so stunning a surprise as they must have been to the prosecution staff.

Despite the effective disposal of the state's chief witness, there was one peril ahead: the ticklish job of analyzing the testimony of the jittery owner of the slung shot, Will Watkins. Lincoln carefully reviewed Watkins's identification of the slung shot as his own and not Duff's. Taking out his knife, he cut open the slung shot to show that it was made just as Watkins had stated, that the two different metals had failed to fuse. Then he passed the weapon around for the jury to examine. After the trial was over, Lincoln handed the slung shot to Shaw, with an enigmatic observation: "Here, Henry, I'll give you this to remember me by."

Having demolished the state's case with sledgehammer blows, Lincoln returned to the cabin on the hill. He took the jury to the bedside of Jack Armstrong, whose death had been aggravated by news of his son's arrest. Lincoln asked the jury to cast their eyes on Jack's widow in mourning weeds, now sobbing quite openly. His fiery mood behind him, Lincoln was now tender and pathetic. "The last fifteen minutes of his speech," Walker told Herndon, "were as eloquent as I ever heard, and such the power and earnestness with which he spoke that jury and all sat as if entranced and, when he was through, found relief in a gush of tears. I have never seen such mastery exhibited over the feelings and emotions of men as on that occasion." "He carried us with him as if by storm," Logan, the jury foreman, recalled. Even the counsel for the prosecution was moved. "There were tears in Mr. Lincoln's eyes while he spoke. But they were genuine. It was the most touching scene I ever witnessed," observed Shaw. According to his opponent on that occasion, it was the jury speech, not the cross-examination of Allen or the use of the almanac, that carried the day. "I have said it a hundred times that it was Lincoln's *speech* that saved that criminal from the gallows," Shaw always insisted.

"I hope this man will be a free man before sundown." With these words Lincoln returned to his chair.

Even the state's attorneys were subdued, and the closing by the prosecution was a perfunctory effort incapable of puncturing the mood that Lincoln had spun. While the state was summing up, Lincoln sat at the defense table preparing instructions to the jury. These, along with instructions submitted by the prosecution, were included in the judge's charge. The gist of them was that if the jury had any reasonable doubts whether Metzker came to his death by the blow on the eye or the blow on the back of the head, they were to find the defendant not guilty unless they believed from the evidence that he had acted in concert with Norris.

As the jury filed out of the courtroom, Lincoln reached over and put his arm about Hannah's shoulders. She was still distraught. "Hannah, your son will be cleared before sundown," he said *sotto voce*, but not without being overheard by at least one of the jurors as he was leaving the box. Hannah went over to Thompson's hostelry and waited. The first ballot stood three for acquittal and nine for conviction. Foreman Logan and two others stood out against the rest.

While the battle in the jury room continued, judge and attorneys went over to the tavern for supper. Duff, who stayed in the courtroom with his brother Jim and the sheriff, tells the rest of the story:

> As soon as the judge and the lawyers got back from supper the jury was brought in. They had to pass me, and I eyed them closely for some hopeful sign. One of them looked at me and winked. Then I knew it was right, and when the foreman handed up the verdict of "not guilty" I was the happiest man in the world, I reckon.

While Judge Harriott felt that the medical testimony was most conclusive, the jury, according to Logan, was swayed by the general "force of Mr. Lincoln's argument" as well as by "the falsity of the testimony of Allen."

Lincoln had a messenger run over to Thompson's to tell Hannah the good news. Her own story is moving. "I went up to the courthouse," she later recalled. "The jury shook hands with me, so did the court, so did Lincoln. We were all affected and tears streamed down Lincoln's face. He then remarked to me: 'Hannah, what did I tell you? I pray to God that William may be a good boy hereafter, that this lesson may prove in the end a good lesson to him and to all.'"

Hannah expressed her gratitude and asked Lincoln what he would charge her, reminding him that she was poor. "Why, Hannah," Lincoln said tolerantly, "I shan't charge you a cent—never. Anything I can do for you I will do for you willingly and freely, without charge."

The Armstrong case is as interesting for what it suggests about Lincoln's own attitude toward his client as for what it reveals about Lincoln as a jury lawyer. Duff's attorney had been far from guileless in his handling of the witnesses. From his private examination of Watkins he must have had grave misgivings about the innocence of his client. His dragging in the irrelevant but dramatic detail of the moon's phase and its position was a daring gamble. He

took a chance that the somnolent prosecution would fail
to perceive its irrelevancy, and he won. Probably, if pressed,
Lincoln would have replied very much in the vein of that
other great jury lawyer, Jeremiah Mason of New England,
the mentor of Daniel Webster. Years after he had defended
a Methodist minister, the Reverend Ephraim K. Avery, for
the murder of Sarah Maria Cornell in Tiverton, Rhode
Island, someone had the temerity to ask Mason if he believed Avery innocent. His reply was in the best traditions
of the legal profession: "Why, do you know, I never thought
about it that way, at all."

VIII

The Fate of the Flagrant Adulterer

Dan Sickles flaunts the unwritten law

No greater commentary on the revolution in moral standards over the past century can perhaps be found than in
the different ways in which society treated Dan Sickles on
the eve of the Civil War and Dr. Robert C. Rutledge Jr.,
in the years following the Second World War. The latter
did exactly what Sickles had done and on the identical
provocation. Finding that his wife had been unfaithful to
him, he stalked her seducer to a Cedar Rapids hotel room,
and, according to the prosecution, deliberately stabbed him
to death. Convicted of second-degree murder in 1949 in one
of Iowa's most sensational trials, he was sentenced to seventy years in prison. Despairing when the Iowa Supreme
Court upheld the conviction, the twenty-nine-year-old up-
holder of the sanctity of the marriage bed attached a rubber
hose to the exhaust pipe of his tightly closed car, got inside,
started the motor, and secured his release from punishment
in a way not anticipated by the law.

Rutledge was convicted, Sickles freed. A moral climate
in Dan Sickles's day very different from our own largely
explains the opposing verdicts. The Sickles case is a notorious example of the propensity of juries to establish new
law by judging the law as well as the fact in defiance of
explicit instructions from the bench. When that happens in
a criminal case and the accused is acquitted, the court is
powerless to do anything about it. It has been demonstrated
that procedural safeguards do not invariably assure the
acquittal of an innocent man. Conversely, a clear violation
of the law may go unpunished if the jury approves the conduct of the accused. When the jury takes the latter course,
its conduct is not necessarily without pattern or purpose. As

Learned Hand has pointed out, the finality of the jury's verdict "introduces a slack into the enforcement of law, tempering its rigor by the mollifying influence of current ethical
conventions."

The Sickles case might have passed for another run-of-
the-mill triangle slaying, just another sordid shooting by
a husband of his faithless wife's seducer. But the chief
actors in the tragedy happened to be celebrities in their own
right. If that were not enough to galvanize public attention,
the episode was given an unusually macabre twist when it
turned out that the bullet-riddled torso was that of the
district attorney for the city of Washington. To a generation not easily shocked by defaulting mayors or bribe-
fattened legislators the fate of a flagrant adulterer who also
doubled as the chief law-enforcement officer of his community dramatized the clay-like underpinnings of Olympian
figures. Accordingly, when the deceased's successor in office
moved that the court adjourn in honor of his memory, the
press was mordant in its criticism.

Everybody in Washington save Dan Sickles seemed to
know that his wife, Teresa, and Philip Barton Key, son of
Francis Scott Key, the author of *The Star-Spangled Banner*,
were having an affair. Preoccupied with his political career
in Congress, Sickles, who represented New York and was
looked upon as a white-haired boy in Democratic party
circles, ignored the danger signals posted all around him.
Despite previous warnings, it took an anonymous letter to
shake him out of his complacency. One evening after a
dinner party at the Sickleses' mansion, built a generation before by Commodore Stockton, the butler brought Dan Sickles a letter. Absent-mindedly he thrust it into his pocket
and went off with his guests to a ball at Willard's Hotel.
It was not until his return home well after midnight that,
in emptying his pockets, he came across it again. What
Sickles read was written in an obviously disguised hand and
seemed intentionally unpolished:

Washington, February 24th, 1859.

Hon. Daniel Sickles

Dear Sir:

With deep regret I enclose to your address the few lines, but an indispensable duty compels me so to do, seeing that you are greatly imposed upon.

There is a fellow, I may say, for he is not a gentleman, by any means, by the name of Phillip Barton Key and I believe the district attorney who rents a house of a negro man by the name of Jno. A. Gray situated on 15th Street between K and L Streets for no other purpose than to meet your wife, Mrs. Sickles. He hangs a string out of the window as a signal to her that he is in and leaves the door unfastened and she walks in and sir I do assure you *he has as much use of your wife as you have.*

With these few hints I leave the rest for you to imagine.

Most Resply,

Your friend,

R. P. G.

Who Sickles's informant was has never been determined. The handwriting, which bears certain disguised feminine characteristics, may well have been that of a castoff rival of Teresa for Key's affections, or a suitor led on by that coquette up to a point where he was crazed with jealousy, or one of those poison-pen wielders who get a virtuous satisfaction out of spoiling other people's fun. But those who knew the impetuous Sickles intimately would be sure to prefer an anonymous letter to a direct vis-à-vis approach. Gossip about the pair went back at least a year. At that time a young clerk in the Department of the Interior whose infatuation for Teresa went unrequited happened to encounter her and the debonair district attorney when they made what seemed like an unconventional call at a tavern

outside of Washington in the course of one of their riding
jaunts. Key's rival did quite a bit of talking until Sickles
called him on the carpet and dared him to prove his insinuations. The thoroughly scared lad backtracked completely.
At that time Key glibly assured Sickles that his interest in
Teresa was purely platonic and, considering the disparity
in age, one might even say paternal. Outwardly, at least,
Sickles appeared completely satisfied.

Why so sophisticated a man of the world as Dan Sickles
should have permitted his young, dazzling, and passionate
wife to be constantly squired by the handsomest wolf in
Washington now seems incomprehensible. But Dan had
been similarly generous when, a few years before, he had
permitted Teresa to act as an official hostess for an elderly
bachelor, Ambassador James Buchanan, whose First Secretary he was. Sickles's casual attitude started tongues wagging throughout London. The petite, exquisitely formed
Latin beauty would have been a *femme fatale* in any society. Sickles had wooed and won this daughter of the
maestro of an Italian opera company at the home of the
fabulous Da Pontes in New York. Charming, exotic, child-
like, and self-willed, five years married but still only
twenty-two, Teresa could not be expected to find marriage
a completely absorbing occupation once the grand passion
that had drawn the couple together had chilled and her
husband's political career proved an ever growing competitor for his attentions. On any stage Teresa would have
insisted on the spotlight. Mated to an ambitious extrovert,
she should never have been taken for granted.

Probably no one was more surprised than Key himself
when he found that he was trapped by his passions. The
Capitol's Casanova, known as a lavish spender, was equally
fond of horses and women. He held so secure a social position that he could dare to attend a formal party in riding-
togs, whip under arm. Hitherto this devil-may-care wid-
ower, father of four children, had conducted his amours
with some degree of conventional circumspection; but only

shortly before the tragedy he had boasted to an intimate
that he was all for "French intrigue and romance, with a
good spice of danger in it." When Key abruptly forsook the
company of Washington belles and attached himself so con-
spicuously to the young wife of a bosom friend, Washington
dowagers began to cackle. But the district attorney and his
inamorata heedlessly wove a web of intrigue about themselves. Love had made them, as Iago would have put it.

> as prime as goats, as hot as monkeys,
> As salt as wolves in pride, and fools as gross
> As ignorance made drunk.

That Dan Sickles was able to sleep after receiving the
incriminating note was belied by his haggard and distraught
appearance the next morning. En route to the Capitol he
stopped off at a telegraph office and wired his friend Manny
Hart, Collector of the Port of New York: "PLEASE COME AT
ONCE. I NEED YOU." Hart, not realizing the extreme urgency,
replied that he could not get away for a few days. Sickles
then confided in George B. Wooldridge, clerk of the House,
who proceeded to verify the fact that Key and Mrs. Sickles
had been seen entering the house on Fifteenth Street on
the previous Wednesday afternoon. Sickles confronted a
now thoroughly frightened Teresa and forced her to write a
confession. Unhinged by the revelations, Sickles broke down
and sobbed the night through. The next morning he sent for
Wooldridge and another friend, the Tammany politician
Samuel F. Butterworth. "I am a dishonored and ruined man
and cannot look you in the face," Sickles repeated over and
over again.

Key had engaged a room at the Cosmos Club, across the
park from the Stockton mansion. There, with the aid of an
opera glass, he could make out a signal from the Sickles
residence. Perplexed by Teresa's failure to communicate
with him for several days and sensing that something was
tragically wrong, he dashed out of the club and twice passed
in front of the Sickles residence raising and lowering his
handkerchief three times. This was a prearranged signal be-

tween the lovers. Butterworth, the principal witness of the fatal incident, who left town to avoid prosecution as an accessory and failed to make an appearance at the trial, reported the events from this moment:

Mr. Sickles came into the library and said that he had "seen the scoundrel making signals"; and he added, "My God! this is horrible!" I said, "Mr. Sickles, you must be calm, and look this matter squarely in the face. If there be a possibility of keeping the *certain knowledge* of this crime from the public you must do nothing to destroy that possibility. You may be mistaken in your belief that it is known to the whole city."

He instantly replied, "No, no, my friend, I am not. It is already the town talk!" I then said, *"If that be so, there is but one course left for you, as a man of honor— you need no advice!"*

After a few moments' silence Mr. Sickles said that he was "satisfied that Mr. Key had been in the habit of making his signals from a window of the Clubhouse opposite; and what surprised him very much was that his wife strenuously denied this, though freely confessing her guilt." He then walked into the hall, and said to me, "Come, go over with me to Stewart's room in the Clubhouse, and he may be able to inform me whether Key has a room there, and for what purpose he uses it." I assented, and walked out into the street, supposing that Mr. Sickles was following me. I left the house for this sole purpose.

When I left Mr. Sickles in the hall I am satisfied he had no weapons on his person. He was without his overcoat. He said nothing to me about weapons, or the probability of encountering Mr. Key. I walked slowly down the Avenue on the side south to the corner, and as I was crossing the street I saw Mr. Key advance a few steps toward me. He saluted me, saying, "Good

morning, Mr. Butterworth. What a fine day we have!"
I responded and said, "Have you come from the Club?"
He said, "I have." I asked, "Is Mr. Stewart in his
room?" He answered "Yes, and he is quite unwell." I
then said, "I am going to see him. Good morning," and
turned to leave him. As I did so I saw Mr. Sickles, for
the first time after leaving his house, coming rapidly
down 16th Street, on the side next the square, and then
near the corner. I had walked about thirty feet on my
way to the Club when I heard Mr. Sickles exclaim, in
a loud voice, *"Key, you scoundrel, you have dishonored
my house—you must die!"*

I turned immediately, and saw Mr. Key thrust his
hand in his vest or side coatpocket, take a step in the
direction of Mr. Sickles, and, simultaneously, I heard
the discharge of a pistol. Mr. Key then rapidly advanced on Mr. Sickles, seized him with his left hand by
the collar of the coat, and seemed to make an effort to
strike with something in his right hand, which I then
supposed to be a weapon. Mr. Sickles backed into the
middle of the street, when he succeeded in extricating
himself from Mr. Key's grasp, drew a pistol from his
overcoat pocket, presented it at Mr. Key, who retreated
backward up 16th Street toward the Club, and threw
something at Mr. Sickles. Mr. Sickles followed, and
when within ten feet, fired. I saw Mr. Key was
wounded. He staggered toward the sidewalk, saying,
"Don't shoot me!"

He leaned for a moment against a tree when Mr.
Sickles advanced upon him, exploded a cap, and fired a
third time. As Mr. Key was falling Mr. Sickles frequently exclaimed:

"YOU VILLAIN, YOU HAVE DISHONORED MY HOUSE, AND
YOU MUST DIE!"

He uttered these words again while standing over Mr.
Key with his revolver in his hand. I took no part in the
contest.

Ironically, the "something" that Key hurled in desperation at Sickles was the opera glass employed in his intrigue.

Butterworth's denial that he had participated in the shooting was literally true. As the staff artist for *Leslie's* depicted the grim incident, Sickles's friend, who had done a perfect job of needling the distraught husband, leaned comfortably against a picket fence while Sickles proceeded to finish off Key. Sickles fired first with a Colt. When that failed to go off a second time, he used a derringer at close range. Then, with deliberation, he set the cap on the Colt again and aimed once more at Key's stomach. After the third shot a member of the club rushed over and grabbed Sickles by the arm. Key was carried to the clubhouse, where he soon expired.

The violent outburst served to restore Sickles's poise. He calmly strode over to the home of Attorney General Black and gave himself up. After a coroner's jury concluded that "the deceased met death from the effect of pistol shots fired by the Hon. Daniel E. Sickles," he was committed to jail. Refusing bail, Sickles shrewdly figured that his incarceration would win him public sympathy. Perhaps he had not reckoned on the foulness of an unventilated, fetid District of Columbia jail. After battling with bedbugs for four nights, he was moved into the warden's cleaner quarters. In this privileged location the prisoner planned his defense and held court, seeing Cabinet members, intimate friends, his wife's grief-stricken parents, and his little daughter. Even President Buchanan sent Sickles a comforting note, though he abstained from visiting the jail. In a mood of compassion Dan agreed to return to his wife the wedding ring that in his anger he had pulled off her finger and broken.

Sickles's ordeal was given conspicuous coverage by the press. Editorials and letters revealed the country to be sharply divided on Dan's culpability. Many felt that the world was well rid of Key. Others, as for instance the *Washington Star*, questioned whether Sickles had the right to protect his "marital honor" by taking the life of an unarmed man. Unless his conduct as a husband had been scrupulously correct, that paper argued, with a scarcely veiled insinuation about the prisoner's own extramarital sex life, "he could scarcely plead the justification of wounded honor." So the debate waxed furiously while the nation awaited the trial in the Criminal Court of the District of Columbia.

As trial time drew near, rumors circulated that Key's friends would rebut the plea of justification by introducing evidence to the effect that "there were certain physical reasons to make any recent criminal intercourse on the part of the deceased impossible." According to report, witnesses were being rounded up in both New York and Washington to testify to Sickles's hardly impeccable private life. The deed, the celebrities, the circumstances, and the scandal all pointed to a memorable trial, and the public was not to be disappointed. *Harper's Weekly* saluted the opening of the trial as "a valuable precedent for our courts," and remarked that "it is being closely watched by the whole people—especially by that part of them who are not in the habit of restraining their passions within limits of law and morality."

When, on Monday morning, April 4, 1859, Dan Sickles stood trial for the murder of Philip Barton Key, police battled with a mob of sensation-seekers who sought admittance in the dingy, cramped, fetid courtroom of the Washington City Hall. Upon Key's successor, the square-set, athletic Robert Ould, as United States District Attorney, was thrust the thankless burden of the prosecution. Humorless, solid rather than brilliant, Ould was impaled on the horns of a dilemma. To be defeated would reflect on his competence as a prosecutor. To be overzealous would make him *persona non grata* with top Democrats from the President down and antagonize a large segment of the public who already regarded Sickles as a martyr. The deceased's relatives had provided Ould with an associate counsel, the wiry and restless James M. Carlisle, whose mordant thrusts were to prick the defense time and again in the course of the trial.

For his defense Sickles selected a lavish battery of top legal counsel. Heading his staff was James T. Brady, the extremely personable New York jury lawyer, celebrated for his clever handling of witnesses, himself a bachelor, but a stout defender of women's rights. Suave and courteous in manner, Brady was the direct antithesis of Edward M. Stanton, who was associated with him in Sickles's defense. Already renowned as one of the nation's outstanding constitutional lawyers, Stanton went at a point hammer and tongs, and though the bane of court stenographers because of his rapid-fire delivery, he had the knack of injecting some of his own abundant vigor into the weakest cause. His victories in court were a tribute to his acute analytical powers and his extraordinary pre-trial preparation. Thickset, medium in height, with black curly hair crowning a massive head, and a luxuriant crop of whiskers concealing jaw and chin, Stanton could transfix a witness with so fierce a look that he earned the sobriquet of "black terrier." The third big gun in Sickles's arsenal was an experienced New York criminal lawyer named John Graham, like Brady a bachelor. Graham's impassioned manner and facile eloquence, spiced with apt Biblical quotations, were calculated to mesmerize the most obdurate jury.

It took three days to agree on a jury. Although oddly enough a relative of Barton Key had served on the grand jury that returned the indictment, the prosecution had enormous difficulty in securing an objective panel. Some seventy-two out of the seventy-five interrogated on the first day expressed sympathy for Dan Sickles. That was a straw in the wind. Only one let fall an expression of animus toward the prisoner, a big, elderly man, with English whiskers and a Dutch phlegm, who remarked that, in his opinion, "he who does a wilful murder ought to suffer for it." The fact that two hundred talesmen were excused for bias in favor of the prisoner underscored District Attorney Ould's difficulties. Dan Sickles's peers were solid, undistinguished men—several grocers, two farmers, a couple of merchants, a gents'-

furnishings specialist, a tinner, a shoemaker, a coachmaker, and a cabinetmaker. How would each in turn have behaved had he come home and found his best friend in bed with his wife? For the three weary weeks of the trial Dan Sickles sat in the prisoner's dock, which looked like a cattle crate, and anxiously scanned the faces of the jurors to detect their reactions to the testimony as it was unfolded.

From the opening gun it was clear that the government would seek to cut the ground from under the anticipated defense pleas of insanity and justification. Ould's attack was brief but savage. Pointing out that the accused chose the Sabbath to perpetrate this "deed of blood," he compared the "unarmed and defenseless victim" with the accused.

The prisoner at the bar had come to that carnival of blood fully prepared. He was a walking magazine. He was not only fully provided in the number of his firearms, but had also taken care to supply himself with their different varieties, each one of which, doubtless possessed its peculiar excellence for the murderous work. To a nice and close calculator the contingency of an anticipated collision might call into requisition both derringer and revolver. If before the time of meeting any such idea had passed through the mind of the prisoner at the bar, as would seem to be indicated not only from the number and variety of his firearms, but from the temporary armory with which he was provided, to wit, a convenient overcoat on an inconveniently warm day, it would seem that he did not reason carelessly. Against this moving battery which could place itself in any position like a piece of flying artillery on a field of battle, the deceased interposed nothing, and had nothing to interpose save the physical strength which, when governed by presence of mind, ever was but feeble at best; a poor and feeble opera glass, which, even when thrown with well directed aim, was comparatively harmless; and last of all, the piteous exclamations which, however they might have moved other men, in this case, let me state, fell upon ears of stone.

The evidence in this case, gentlemen of the jury, will show to you from the first act in this tragedy down to its full fruition, through each and every successive scene of horror—not only that the deceased was un-armed, but that the prisoner at the bar knew such was the fact; that he must have known it when the first shot was fired at the corner; that he must surely have known it when, subsequently, the exclamations of the de-ceased were ringing in the air; and that, if possible, more certainly still he must have known it when he stood bravely over his victim, revolver in hand, seeking to scatter the brains of one who had already been mor-tally wounded in three vital parts, and whose eyes were being covered with the film of death. I say not this, gentlemen of the jury, for the purpose of inflaming your minds against the prisoner at the bar, but as an illustra-tion of the common law, that homicide with a deadly weapon, perpetrated by a party who has all the advan-tage on his side, and under circumstances indicating cruelty and vindictiveness, is murder, *no matter what may be the antecedent provocations in the case.*

The strategy of the prosecution was to concentrate its fire on the deed itself, to stress the deliberate nature of the killing, and to avoid at all costs any allusion to Sickles's provocation. Oulds called to the stand a procession of eye-witnesses of the shooting, including the famous inventor of the reaper, Cyrus H. McCormick, who happened to see the affray from a window of his residence opposite. Another was James H. Reed, a wood and coal dealer, who testified that after the first shot Key took cover behind a tree, only to be fired at a second time when he imprudently exposed himself. "After the second shot he exclaimed he was shot, and re-treated to the pavement. Key's back was towards the man who fired when he retreated." Then, when Key slumped to the ground, Sickles shot him a third time while he was lying on the pavement, despite Key's cry: "Don't shoot." Edward Delafield, Jr., stated that the first shot did not seem to take effect, for Key ran toward a tree screaming: "Don't shoot, don't shoot me, don't murder me!" According to this witness, Sickles's second shot was fired while Key was down on the pavement. "Sickles put the pistol to his breast and fired. Sickles cocked the pistol and put it near the head of Key and pulled the trigger. The cap missed." Thomas G. Martin, a Treasury clerk, heard Sickles shout: "He has violated my bed." With minor variations the same scene was depicted by Eugene Pendleton. Then the state wound up its case by introducing, over the objections of the defense, the derringer, Colt, and ball which had so abruptly ended Key's amatory adventures.

So far only fragments; but pieced together, they made a composite picture of cold-blooded murder. The prosecution had refrained from calling Samuel F. Butterworth, realizing perfectly well that he would prove a hostile witness. The defense accordingly moved to compel the district attorney to put him on the stand. Sickles's staff argued that Butterworth had testified before the coroner's inquest. But Ould avoided an obvious trap. He refused, acutely aware that the law does not permit a party offering a witness in proof of his cause to impeach his reputation for truth or to impugn his credibility. But his explanation served to invest his refusal with an aura of mystery. "I do so for reasons which I shall keep locked within my own breast, but which, I have no doubt, are well known to counsel for defense." After all, many people insisted, Butterworth was the principal witness to the shooting. Why should he not be called to tell his story? It seemed as though the prosecution was actually suppressing evidence that might clear the accused, but the fact was that Butterworth had discreetly fled from the District of Columbia.

Graham's opening, a grandiose effort that few criminal

lawyers of the present generation could match, gained quick
recognition as a forensic classic. He also chose to stress the
desecration of the Sabbath. But the man who profaned that
day, he contended, was not the injured husband, but "a confirmed, habitual adulterer." "We find him," he told the jury,
"besieging with most evil intentions that castle where, for
their security and repose, the law had placed the wife and
child of his neighbor." The events that transpired were
somewhat oversimplified in the interest of the accused. "The
injured husband and father rushes upon" the adulterer "in
the moment of his guilt, and under the influence of frenzy
executes upon him a judgment which was as just as it was
summary."

Graham quickly placed his case on the grounds of higher
law. Does this act render "its author amenable to the laws
of the land?" he asked the jury. "You are here to fix the
price of the marriage bed," he told them. "You are here to
say in what estimation that sacred couch is held by an
honest and an intelligent American jury." It was a trite but
emotionally effective touch when the eloquent Graham, ever
pat with a quotation, drew the obvious parallel between
Othello and Sickles:

> *But alas! to make me*
> *A fixed figure for the time of scorn*
> *To point his slow, unmoving finger at,*
> *Oh! Oh!*

With biting irony the defense counsel tore into the prosecution's picture of "the prisoner coming to his carnival of
blood," of his being "a walking magazine," of his "adding
mutilation to murder," of his "standing bravely over his
victim." Denying that the defendant had acted with malice,
Graham asked rhetorically:

> Do you mean to tell me that the ordinary symptoms
> of a wicked, depraved, malignant spirit attend the act
> of the husband who slays the man who has polluted his
> wife? What distinction, then, do you draw between the

case of a man who slays in order to commit a crime, and that of the man who slays in order to prevent the commission of a crime? Unless, gentlemen of the jury, you are prepared to find that the act of the husband who vindicates his marriage bed, by slaying the man who dares to defile it, is symptomatic of a "wicked, depraved and malignant spirit," there would seem to be an end of the case, upon this branch of it.

What Sickles did was abundantly justified by Scriptural law, Graham argued. His quotations ranged from Genesis through the New Testament. " 'And they shall be one flesh' says the Book of Genesis, and Matthew quoted Jesus as stating: 'What God hath joined together let no man put asunder.' " Biblical law not only regarded the marriage bed as sacred but punished adultery by death. The fact that adultery was not punished as severely under the civil law did not mean, Graham contended, that "the adulterer shall go unpunished. No. *It throws you upon the law of your heart.* There is the repertory of your instincts. Go by them, and you reflect the will of Heaven, and when you execute them, you execute its judgment." Perhaps never before had the case for the "unwritten law" been pleaded so adroitly.

With considerable ingenuity Graham now found support in the Bible to bolster up the most vulnerable spot in the defense's case—Dan Sickles had not killed Key immediately upon receiving confirmation of the latter's treachery, but waited for several days. Graham defended the time gap by reminding the jurors of the vengeance inflicted by Absalom upon the traducer of his sister. "You will perceive, gentlemen of the jury," he informed them, "that this killing took place *two years* after the offense which provoked it was committed, and the punishment which was inflicted for the killing was that 'the king kissed Absalom'!" But how immediate must the slaying be after discovery of the wrong? Graham resolved that crucial issue in this fashion:

Our proposition is this, that to catch the adulterer
in the fact means to catch him *so near* the fact as to
leave no doubt as to his guilt. If you caught the adulterer turning out of the bed in which your wife was, the
coition would not then be taking place, but would you
not then be pardoned for killing him? If you caught him
coming out of a room where she was, in such a state as
to indicate what he had been doing, would you not then
be pardoned if you killed him? You would have the
same right as if you caught them in actual coition. The
question is, not as to how you catch them, but are the
parties guilty, and are you satisfied and convinced of
their guilt? Whether the fact actually takes place before the eyes of the husband, if he becomes satisfied of
it by irrefragable proof, is perfectly immaterial.

Finally, Graham insisted that the provocation so unbalanced the prisoner's mind as to exonerate him from all the
legal consequences of his acts. This was the second string
to the defense's bow—emotional insanity. Homicide, counsel
told the jury, when committed in a transport of rage, is not
a crime "when the provocation is sufficient to justify the
mental condition." Graham's masterly résumé of the facts
in the case was shrewdly calculated to put the jury in a receptive mood for considering the monstrous provocation:

It is important for you, gentlemen of the jury, to
know some of the facts of which he was aware at the
time of his collision with the deceased. He knew when
he met Mr. Key on the afternoon in question that he
was about his house for the purpose of making an assignation with his wife. He knew that he had hired a
house but a few blocks from his mansion, where he met
his wife. He knew that he had the aid of a park, and a
club house, and an opera glass, which enabled him to
see whether or not it was safe for him to approach his
habitation. This thing was well considered by Key!
He hired the house in a part of the city from which he

thought no witnesses could come against him; in a part of the city populated chiefly by blacks, where, from his legal knowledge, he knew that facts seen by them were not seen at all. All the weapons which, as an adulterer, he required, he had about him on the afternoon of this fatal occurrence. He wanted no derringers to accomplish this end. And although there is no proof before you to show that he was not armed at that time, the evidence to be adduced on the part of the defense will be that he was a man who was in the habit of carrying arms. He was provided, no doubt, with all that was necessary to protect his life. At all events, he was furnished with all the means serviceable to him in the pursuit of his adulterous intentions—his white handkerchief, the signal of assignation—the adulterer's flag—and the other appliances of an adulterer's trade.

Mr. Sickles knew that Key was in the habit of carrying his opera glass. He knew that he was in the habit of availing himself of the club house and park, and that he had been frequently seen about there for the purpose of making an assignation with his wife. He had no knowledge that he was coming there that afternoon, and he saw him without any forewarning whatever. But he knew what the purpose was that brought him there. What, then, must have been the condition of his mind? Mr. Sickles did not invite him to that vicinity. The meeting was the result of accident, and when his eyes rested upon the destroyer of his happiness, he associated him at once with the facts he knew, and went forward in the transport of his rage to the consummation of the deadly scene. I state these facts that you may be able to appreciate the point I am discussing.

Is it possible that, under these circumstances, Mr. Sickles could have acted in cold blood? Was it possible for him to know what he did of the relations of Mr. Key and his wife, and yet look upon him, even though he saw him accidentally, and preserve his equanimity?

If Mr. Sickles was excited, was it an instance of passion unduly excited? If he was in a state of white heat, was that too great a state of passion for a man to be in who saw before him the hardened, the unrelenting seducer of his wife? Mr. Key did not yield to temptation in an erring moment. It was not while any sudden fit was on him, he deflowered the wife of his friend! It was a deliberate and systematic crime from beginning to end.

Graham's opening had now consumed the better part of three days. So unsparingly had he given of himself that he was fast approaching total exhaustion. But he mustered every ounce of reserve strength for a stinging attack on the character of the dead district attorney, a man "selected to conserve the cause of public morality and public decency." "It was his business," Graham charged, "to see that your houses were protected against seducers and adulterers, and every other species of criminals." Yet, robing himself in the "garb of hypocrisy," he had the effrontery to come into this very court and to hunt down "with almost unparalleled success the very worms that crawl upon the face of the earth, while full-grown men in crime, such as he himself was, were permitted to stalk about this community, not only unpunished but not even admonished or reproved."

Such was the character of the adulterer. But who was the woman with whom he committed the adultery, Graham now asked. "Young enough to have been his daughter . . . susceptible to the attentions of men" . . . not fully impressed with the gravity of the marriage vow. Upholding a feudal conception of matrimony that must have seemed less out of date in the age of Buchanan and Victoria than later in the era of the emancipated woman, Graham pointed out that Mrs. Sickles "did not comprehend fully the meaning of the terms by which *she had surrendered herself, body and soul, to the ownership and control of her husband.*"

Reviewing the curious relationship between Sickles and

Key, Graham maintained that on the Congressman's part it was a "sincere friendship," on the district attorney's a "professed or avowed friendship." One can bear the wrong of a stranger with patience, defense counsel declared, but the double-dealing of a friend becomes "intolerable." Having undermined the moral fabric of that friend's behavior, Graham prepared his audience for a scathing denunciation of his conduct:

Why was Mr. Key constantly in the vicinity of Mr. Sickles' house? We will show you that he lived in another part of your city, a very considerable distance from it. Yet he was in the habit of riding by it on horseback at all hours, and of showing himself off in every way he could to the greatest advantage. In his intercourse with Mrs. Sickles, too, he resorted to and practiced all the blandishments, which adulterers study and cultivate, to reach the target they have set before them. How did he make his assignations? If he encountered her in the President's mansion, he made them there. If in the mansion of some Senator, he made them there. He tainted with his vile appointments, the atmosphere which your wives and daughters—the virtuous females of this district—were obliged to breathe. The very air about was laden with them. He followed his object wherever she went. She could hardly get more than a hundred feet from her house before he was unexpectedly by her side. If she walked, he was on foot. If she was riding in a carriage, it was stopped, and he got in, and rode with her for two or three hours; and the directions to the driver were, that it must be driven through the back streets. He became a subject of kitchen comment. He was called by the servants "Disgrace." That was the name bestowed upon him by the kitchen department of Mr. Sickles's house. The District Attorney of the County of Washington had become a by-word and a reproach in the kitchen of one of the houses in the district; and as often as he entered the house, or was seen approaching it, the remark was made, *"Here comes Disgrace."* Even the servants in the house felt the pressure of his infamous attentions to the defendant's wife.

Calling the roll of cases where juries had refused to convict on the ground that the homicide had been incited by exceptional provocation, Graham laid most stress on the Singleton Mercer case. In that trial in 1843 a New Jersey jury had acquitted the prisoner, charged with killing the man who had raped his sister. Closer to home, however, was the Jarboe case, prosecuted in the very same Washington Criminal Court some years before by none other than the late Philip Barton Key. In that case a brother had avenged the seduction of his sister. Judge Crawford, now presiding over the Sickles trial, had then ruled that the prisoner's mental state at the time of the homicide was a question for the jury. It took the Jarboe jury just fifteen minutes to acquit the enraged brother, but obviously Key learned nothing from this inglorious defeat.

So far Graham had talked about honor, but perhaps this jury of tradesmen and men of middling property wondered why Sickles was not content to have sued Key for damages and thus written off the whole ugly episode. In his closing remarks Graham thought it expedient to dispose of this alternative:

> Gentlemen of the Jury, shall the abominable doctrine go forth from this Court that pecuniary compensation is the only mode of stanching the bleeding wounds of a husband? What is the effect of that doctrine? It tells every man that if he will pay the price which a jury may set upon his seduction or his adultery, he can enter any house he pleases and rifle it of its purest contents. Is that to be the doctrine of your District? Are we to have a mere list of rates, or a mere tariff of charges? Is the lower house of infamy to fix one, and the higher house of infamy to fix another? Shall an American jury

say to the seducer or adulterer what he shall pay for
his crimes? The very moment you act upon that principle you tell every libertine he may enter any house
in your District, if he is only ready to foot the bill
which shall be presented by an American jury, and
stand clear of all human or divine accountability.
In God's name repudiate that principle from your verdict.

The defense now called its witnesses to establish the emotional instability of the prisoner at the time the homicide
was committed. Of these, by far the most impressive was
the prominent Democratic politician and bosom friend of
Sickles, Robert J. Walker, former Senator from Mississippi
and one-time Secretary of the Treasury. Visiting Sickles on
the day of the tragedy, Walker reported that the Congressman became "convulsed" and "threw himself on the sofa,
covering his face with his hands." He then broke into "an
agony of unnatural and unearthly sounds, the most remarkable I ever heard—something like a scream, interrupted by
violent sobbing. His condition appeared to me frightful;
appalling me so much that I thought if it lasted much
longer he must become insane. He was indulging in exclamations about dishonor having been brought on his house,
his wife, and child. He seemed particularly to dwell on the
disgrace brought upon his child." Walker accompanied
Sickles from his residence to jail. On cross-examination by
Carlisle, the former head of the Treasury Department, described Sickles's condition as "an agony of despair, the most
terrible thing I ever saw in my life," adding this damaging
blow to the government's cause: "I feared if it continued he
would become permanently insane. His screams were of the
most frightful character. They were unearthly and appalling."

Walker's testimony caused Sickles to break down. He
sobbed like a child. Stanton asked that the cross-examination be temporarily halted until the prisoner could pull him-

self together. Manny Hart and Isaac Bell propelled Sickles from the courtroom, and Sickles's infectious grief communicated itself to his father, who followed the group, weeping. Hardly an eye in the courtroom was dry.

The defense was now preparing the stage props for the most dramatic moment in the trial. Teresa's chambermaid, Bridget Duffy, recounted on the direct that, returning to the house late Saturday afternoon, Sickles refused to eat, but went directly to his room. Soon she heard loud talking in Mrs. Sickles's bedroom and then, at Sickles's request, signed a paper, which was also attested by Octavia Ridgeley, Teresa's companion. Teresa did not go to bed, but dropped, exhausted, to the floor, where she spent the night. Having laid a proper foundation for the document, Brady then announced abruptly: "This paper we propose to read in evidence. It is Mrs. Sickles's statement to her husband, and is as follows":

I have been in a house in Fifteenth street with Mr. Key. How many times I don't know. I believe the house belongs to a colored man. The house is unoccupied. Commenced going there the latter part of January. Have been in alone with Mr. Key. Usually stayed an hour or more. There was a bed in the second story. I did what is usual for a wicked woman to do. The intimacy commenced this winter, when I came from New York, in that house—an intimacy of an improper kind. Have met a dozen times or more, at different hours of the day. On Monday of this week, and Wednesday also. Would arrange meetings when we met in the street and at parties. Never would speak to him when Mr. Sickles was at home, because I knew he did not like me to speak to him; did not see Mr. Key for some days after I got here. He then told me he had hired the house as a place where he and I could meet. I agreed to it. Had nothing to eat or drink there. The room is warmed by a wood fire. Mr. Key generally goes first. Have walked there together say four times—I do not think more; was there on Wednesday last, between two and three. I went there alone. Laura was at Mrs. Hoover's. Mr. Key took and left her there at my request. From there I went to Fifteenth street to met Mr. Key; from there to the milk woman's. Immediately after Mr. Key left Laura at Mrs. Hoover's. I met him in Fifteenth street. Went in by the back gate. Went in the same bedroom, and there an improper interview was had. I undressed myself. Mr. Key undressed also. This occurred on Wednesday, 23d of February, 1859.

Mr. Key has kissed me in this house a number of times. I do not deny that we have had a connection in this house last spring, a year ago, in the parlor on the sofa. Mr. Sickles was sometimes out of town, and sometimes in the Capitol. I think the intimacy commenced in April or May, 1858. I did not think it safe to meet him in this house, because there are servants who might suspect something. As a general thing, have worn a black and white woolen plaid dress, and beaver hat trimmed with black velvet. Have worn a black silk dress there also, also a plaid silk dress, black velvet coat trimmed with lace, and black velvet shawl trimmed with fringe. On Wednesday I either had on my brown dress or black and white woolen dress, beaver hat and velvet shawl. I arranged with Mr. Key to go in the back way, after leaving Laura at Mrs. Hoover's. He met me at Mr. Douglas'. The arrangement to go in the back way was either made in the street or at Mr. Douglas', as we would be less likely to be seen. The house is in Fifteenth street between K and L streets, on the left hand side of the way; arranged the interview for Wednesday in the street, I think, on Monday. I went in the front door, it was open, occupied the same room, undressed myself, and he also; went to bed together. Mr. Key has ridden in Mr. Sickles' carriage, and has called at his house without Mr. Sickles' knowledge and after my being told not to invite him to do so, and against Mr. Sickles's repeated request.

                                    Teresa Bagioli.

This is a true statement, written by myself, without any inducement held out by Mr. Sickles of forgiveness or reward, and without any menace from him. This I have written with my bedroom door open, and my maid and child in adjoining room, at half past eight o'clock in the evening. Miss Ridgeley is in the house, within call.

                                    Teresa Bagioli.

Lafayette Square, Washington, D. C., Feb. 26, 1859.

Mr. and Mrs. Pendleton dined here two weeks ago last Thursday, with a large party. Mr. Key was also here, her brother, and at my suggestion he was invited, because he lived in the same house, and also because he had invited Mr. Sickles to dine with him, and Mr. Sickles wished to invite all those from whom he had received invitations; and Mr. Sickles said "do as you choose."

                                    Teresa Bagioli.

Written and signed in presence of O. M. Ridgeley and Bridget Duffy, February 26, 1859.

Immediately District Attorney Ould was on his feet with violent and profuse objections. The document was hearsay, a communication between husband and wife, parties excluded by law from being witnesses for or against each other. It was not essential to prove the prisoner's insanity. Brady and his associates retorted fiercely; they .argued that the confession was essential to show the cause of the frenzy that the previous witness had described. In refutation Carlisle hit below the belt. There is a certain type of man, he insinuated, "safe, quite safe from insanity, from such a blow as that—the confirmed adulterer, the open shameless profligate—the man nurtured in brothels, the man breathing all his life the atmosphere of adultery and seduction; if there be such a man, he is certainly safe from the visitation of insanity because his familiar plaything has turned and wounded him. . . . Now," he contended, "to offer evidence of the fact of the adultery with the prisoner's wife as the ground to impute to him insanity, necessarily opens inquiry of the sort I have indicated."

Judge Crawford put a momentary halt to the threats and wrangling by excluding the confession on the strange ground that it would have an injurious effect on the relations of husband and wife. Just how the relations of this particular husband and wife could have been more seriously injured he failed to make clear, nor how it would be humanly possible for a jury to ignore such a sensational morsel despite the strictest injunctions. In fact, the long-awaited confession was the big story of the trial. The first page of the April 23 issue of *Harper's Weekly* was devoted exclusively to a facsimile of Mrs. Sickles's statement. So far as the public was concerned, the document cut the ground from under the prosecution, but its distribution to the news services by the defense did irreparable damage to the reputation of Teresa Sickles and served as a reminder that the age of chivalry was dead.

How to circumvent this technical curb and get the story of Teresa's adulterous behavior before the jury was now the main task of the defense. Their key witness was Sickles's friend and confidant George B. Wooldridge, who described on the stand the behavior of the prisoner on the day of the shooting. As Key passed the house waving his handkerchief and looking up toward Mrs. Sickles's windows, Dan burst into the library shouting: "That villain has just passed my house!"

"When you saw him at the Capitol on Saturday did he make any communication to you at that time?" Brady demanded.

Ould objected, and there ensued another interminable debate. Stanton called on the court to heed "the ordinary feelings of humanity" and to admit this evidence by a third

party when the communication between husband and wife
had already been excluded: "This evidence should not be
excluded in order that vengeance might obtain the blood
of this prisoner who was so fiercely hunted." Ould jumped
to his feet, his face livid. He would let his argument and
conduct in the case stand before the court and the world "in
contrast with the disreputable rant which this counsel had
exhibited," he shouted, and, continuing in satiric vein, he
attacked the defense lawyers for their conduct in the trial,
for calling murder "gentleness" and malice "good feeling."
Stanton, quick to resent the imputation, retorted that the
law enunciated by the prosecutor was "not adopted to our
state or society." Under such a law those who were "malig-
nantly" seeking his client's blood would "lead him to the
gallows." *I cannot reply to the counsel's remarks. I defy
them! I scorn them! I don't fear them!*" Stanton's bold tack
had created a sensation in the courtroom. Carlisle now intervened in Ould's behalf, but his stinging sarcasm was
hardly calculated to ease frayed nerves. The long-suffering
judge finally interposed: "Really, gentlemen, this thing
must be interrupted." Again the court hit the defense a body
blow by ruling that the communication of Wooldridge to the
prisoner could not go to the jury to show the prisoner's insanity. With difficulty Stanton curbed his temper. "Your
Honor will recollect," he reminded him testily, "that we are
trying to get in evidence to save the prisoner's life!"

Stymied twice in an effort to bring before the jury the
sordid story of Key's adultery, the defense now called to the
stand a string of witnesses to tell what went on in the house
on Fifteenth Street. But the one who might have been most
informative, John A. Gray, who had rented the house to
Key, was not permitted to testify on the ground that he was
a Negro. Crawford's third adverse ruling infuriated Stanton. "The prosecution, in their thirst for blood," he shouted,
"have not only forgotten the institution of slavery, but
modern society and law as well." Carlisle, quick to capitalize on the fact that there were slaveholders on the jury,

assailed Stanton for his "anti-slavery speech." But again Stanton proved that he was not easily intimidated. "The doctrines which I have maintained here today in defense of homes and families," he declared, "will be the proudest record I can leave to my children."

Hampered by a series of partisan rulings from the bench, the defense still managed to get a good deal of the Fifteenth Street story into the record. Realizing the drift of the evidence, Carlisle remarked that the witnesses "were sliding along in the direction of giving evidence of adultery." The defense had a perfect right to prove the adultery, Brady rejoined, in order to show that "in point of law and in reason the deceased was killed in the act." It was one thing to seek to prove the insanity of Sickles; that was proper, Carlisle conceded. But it was another matter to delve into the alleged cause of the insanity. To do so would be to introduce evidence of adultery by the back door.

Over the week-end the court took the issue under advisement. Then came the first technical break for the defense. On Monday, April 18, Judge Crawford ruled that the evidence the defense sought to include was admissible on the ground that Sickles at the time of the shooting had exclaimed that Key had dishonored his bed. Graham's clever use of the Jarboe case now bore dividends, for Crawford held that his admission of evidence of the seduction in that earlier case was a precedent to justify his present ruling. Accordingly, the court then permitted the anonymous letter to Sickles to be introduced in evidence. When Wooldridge was recalled to the stand, he was allowed to tell his story of his inquiries into the occupancy of the house on Fifteenth Street. Sickles's confidant emerged from a rough cross-examination comparatively unscathed.

Now the backstairs gossipers had their fling. Coachman John Thompson stated with evident relish that Key came to the Sickles house practically every night when Dan was in New York, staying as late as one o'clock in the morning. Teresa and her caller would lock the study, and, from noises

that were heard through the locked door, it was apparent
that suspicious use was being made of the sofa. "I knew they
wasn't at no good work," was the classic understatement of
the trial. Nancy Brown testified that she saw Key go into
the Fifteenth Street place on the fatal Wednesday. Some
time later Teresa was observed going in the back way. A
white string hung from the upstairs shutters and fluttered
in the breeze—Key's indiscreet signal, which notified the
whole neighborhood. As other testimony disclosed, Teresa,
on observing the signal, would dart between the Negro huts
like a frightened rabbit, skurry up the blind alley, and
sneak into the trysting-place by a back gate. Sometimes
she was in morning dress, sometimes in a conspicuous dis-
guise, with her face enveloped in a closed hood.

With the close of the defense's case, the district attorney
stated that, in consequence of the admission of evidence
proving the adultery, the prosecution would now withdraw
its objection to admitting the confession. This offer was
declined by his adversaries. "The case of the accused is
closed," Brady reminded Ould. "The prosecution must
therefore pursue such course on their part as they may deem
advisable."

Now both sides proposed instructions that they requested
the court to give the jury. The prosecution insisted that the
killing amounted to murder even in the face of Key's adulterous relations with Sickles's wife unless it could be proved
that the defendant was in fact insane at the time of the commission of the act. The defense, on the other hand, requested
the court to leave the determination of whether the act was
murder or justifiable homicide to the jury. If it was found
that Sickles killed Key while the latter "was in criminal
intercourse with the wife of the former," the defense contended, "the prisoner could not be convicted of *either* murder
or manslaughter." Not only that, but if, from the evidence,
the jury believed that Sickles's mind was impaired at the
time of the act, he was not guilty of *any offense whatsoever*.

After Carlisle proceeded to contest each of the defense

propositions, Stanton then took over the task of refuting the prosecution. Judged by present-day standards, his forensic effort was a typical overblown piece of Victorian rhetoric, an ingenious thesaurus of aphorisms on the sanctity of the family. But its immediate impact on jury and spectators alike was devastating. Realizing that common-law precedents were cold comfort to the defense, Stanton dismissed them as originating in the age of the Stuarts. That was an era of vice and profligacy. This, he implied, was an era of virtue. With considerable ingenuity Stanton likened the protection of a wife's honor to the defense of one's property. The wife is the property of the husband, Stanton argued, and the husband has as much right to kill her seducer as he would to shoot a burglar who breaks into his house. If this obsolete concept of the relations of husband and wife appeared anachronistic to his associate, James T. Brady, staunch defender of female emancipation, the latter kept a discreet silence. Warming up to his subject, Stanton hurled Jovian thunderbolts at the jury. There is a higher law, the law of God, which commands "that no man shall look on woman to lust after her." Developing this theme, he asserted:

> The penalty for disobedience to that injunction did not originate in human statutes; it was written in the heart of man in the Garden of Eden, where the first family was planted, and where the woman was made bone of man's bone, flesh of man's flesh. No wife yields herself to the adulterer's embrace till he has weaned her love from her husband; she revolts from her obedience, and serves the husband no longer. When her body has once surrendered to the adulterer, she longs for the death of her husband, whose life is often sacrificed by the cup of the poisoner or the dagger or pistol of the assassin.

Despite the polygamous practices of the Mormons of his day, it appeared inconceivable to Stanton that a person

might find monogamy just plain monotonous or that some
women might require a good deal more sexual activity than
others.

Coming to grips with a crucial issue, Stanton ingeniously
argued that Sickles had really killed Key *in flagrante
delicto*. The act of adultery, he contended, was not "limited to the fleeting moment of sexual contact," but includes
"every proximate act in furtherance of, and as a means to,
the consummation of the wife's pollution." The adulterer
lying in wait around the husband's house was as much taken
in the act, he insisted, as the luckless fellow interrupted in
bed with another man's wife. Key's action in taking Teresa
to the "guilty den" on Fifteenth Street "in order there to
enjoy her" surpassed "all that has ever been written of
cold, villainous, remorseless lust." Nor could the wife's consent be invoked to shield the adulterer, since she was incapable by law of "consenting to any infraction of her husband's marital rights."

Stanton's inspired eloquence created a sensation in the
courtroom, and the court was unable to suppress the spontaneous outburst of prolonged applause that greeted the
conclusion of his remarks. Stanton had declaimed in the
manner of a stern Old Testament prophet. The district attorney rested his case on the charitable New Testament dis-
pensation. If Christ could forgive the adulteress, why could
we not forgive the adulterer, he asked the jury. After all,
he curtly added, a woman's chastity lies in her own keeping.

> The very moment you invoke the law of force for the
> protection of female honor, that moment you sacrifice
> female honor. If it must be protected by the sword, the
> knife, and the pistol, it stands unworthy of protection.
> Unless it be that God-ennobling nobility in and of it-
> self, and unless it exists of itself and for itself, it is un-
> worthy to be cherished or known.

The judge's instructions, pedantically enunciated, provided small comfort for the defense. Crawford pointed out

that the intervening of even as little as a day between the knowledge of the adultery and the act served to make the homicide deliberate and, therefore, murder. In this instruction he followed a celebrated opinion of Chief Justice Ruffin of North Carolina. According to that jurist, where a husband heard of the adultery of his wife, no matter how well authenticated the information might be, and killed either the wife or her paramour, he did so *"not upon present provocation, but for a past wrong."* The effect of the adultery, according to Ruffin, would at most reduce the grade of killing from murder to manslaughter. Despite the attitude of the man in the street or in the jury box, Ruffin's views have been restated time and time again by the appellate courts of this country. As regards the defense of temporary insanity, Crawford properly placed the burden of proof on the defense.

Despite these rulings solidly resting upon precedent, the defense was not noticeably downcast. It had staked all on the willingness of the jury to prefer the unwritten law to the law as the judge had expounded it, and its confidence in Sickles's acquittal was widely shared outside the courtroom. The battle of the defense had been unremitting, whereas Ould's lack of vigor was unfavorably noticed. The defense had made a point of loudly arguing issues of inadmissible evidence in such a way as to place before the jury many facts that counsel knew the court would never let them hear as testimony. The district attorney, on the other hand, had pursued a more scrupulous course. When he had discussed certain debatable evidence that he proposed to present by way of rebuttal, he had done so out of the hearing of the jurors. In a rough-and-tumble brawl the defense had proved more battle-hardened.

Veterans at the bar were astounded when, on the twentieth and last day of the trial, defense counsel proposed that the case be submitted to the jury without further discussion. A weary, battered D.A. concurred. That so important a criminal case, involving path-breaking issues of

law, should go to the jury without a summing up would
seem a hazardous proceeding. Brady and Stanton gambled.
The jury was now in their pockets. Why antagonize them
with summations rehashing ground thoroughly familiar to
everyone in the courtroom? Minutes passed. When the jury
failed to come back at once with a verdict of acquittal, there
was some shaking of heads about the defense's course. The
first ballot showed seven for acquittal, two against, three
on the fence. The foreman, a Know-Nothing partisan, naturally antipathetic to Tammany, the party of New Hibernia,
needed a lot of persuasion to be won over. Finally the division narrowed down to a single holdout. This was an elderly
gentleman who, unswayed by arguments and imprecations,
suddenly left the heated group, knelt in a corner in prayer,
and returned shortly to make the verdict unanimous. In all,
the jury was out a bare seventy minutes, and when the foreman answered "Not Guilty" to the query of the clerk, tu-
multuous cheers drowned out the pounding of the judicial
gavel. Stanton had the last word: "I now move that Mr.
Sickles be discharged from custody." The court so ordered.

Macaulay's description of the way London greeted the
acquittal of the bishops under James, in a far nobler cause,
seems to match the behavior of Washingtonians that spring
afternoon of 1859. Only the paroxysms of bobbysoxers paying tribute to a popular crooner seem comparable in our
own age. Like David before the ark, folks literally danced
in the streets, according to an A.P. reporter's account. When
Sickles left the courtroom, a frenzied crowd tried to take
the horses from the carriage and draw him through the
streets themselves, but the police intervened. Stanton,
Brady, and Graham were publicly serenaded for their val-
iant efforts.

Elsewhere the acquittal was received with mixed emotions. The press of his own city felt that Sickles should retire from Congress or at least withdraw from the public gaze
for a comfortably long period. Many people were shocked at
the cold-blooded manner in which Key was killed, and

equally stunned by Sickles's readiness to heap disgrace on an undefended Teresa to save his own neck. By forcing his wife to sign the confession, a virtual death warrant so far as her future domestic happiness was concerned, Sickles had revealed a brutal streak. Slowly realization dawned that the dishonor Sickles so glibly talked about was the wound to his self-esteem that the scandal had inflicted. Many people felt that an overwhelming egotism rather than an over-powering love had prompted Sickles to dispose of his rival.

As for Teresa, "lift her up tenderly in your thoughts, all gentle souls," one newspaperman pleaded. Even Dan felt that he had been too harsh on the girl. To everyone's utter astonishment, but to his own credit, he took her out of her parents' home, her temporary refuge, and set her up once again as mistress of his household. Typical of Sickles's warm, impulsive nature, the reconciliation served as a re-buke to the scandalmongers. "I am not aware of any statute or code of morals which makes it infamous to forgive a woman," he asserted stoutly. Although attacked by some diehards, Sickles received a batch of letters felicitating him on his "noble act." "I feel the whole is softened and wrong greatly mitigated by this deed of forgiveness," wrote Stephen Gooding in July of '59. But another, less charitable correspondent reminded Sickles that had he been possessed by that spirit of forgiveness "a few months earlier in your career, the *dead* might also have been forgiven and you have been saved a heavy sorrow." But intimate fellowship between the couple was never restored. Sleepless, disconsolate, broken in health, Teresa gradually failed, and she died some eight years after the trial, still a young woman. As for Sickles, he demonstrated that extraordinary resiliency which stamped his entire career.

Harper's Ferry and Fort Sumter soon buried the Key affair in yesterday's news. Sickles found the war a release from his private misfortunes. After distinguishing himself by his brilliant conduct at Gettysburg, where he left a leg on the field of battle, Sickles served as a special envoy to

Latin America for Lincoln, acted as military governor of
the Carolinas under Johnson and, finally, under Grant, became American Minister in turbulent Spain. There, to the
delight of gossips, he continued his erotic adventures, like a
latter-day Aaron Burr, this time with no less a personage
than that Spanish siren the ex-queen Isabella. Soon dubbed
"Le Roi Américain de l'Espagne," Sickles arranged a
mariage de convenance with a lady of the Spanish court in
order that he might carry on his affair with his sex-ridden
royal paramour with less obvious surveillance. That second
marriage proved even less stable than the first. And so this
avenger of flagrant adultery spent his declining years. Part
hero, part fraud, the man who established the "unwritten
law" in the United States was a dismal failure as a husband.

IX

The Treason Trial of John Brown
minor prophet or major lunatic?

Had John Brown been tried according to the rules of criminal procedure and due process as they are understood today, he might never have been invested with the mantle of martyrdom. In the first place, his case would in all probability never have gone to trial. In the light of the background of insanity in Brown's family, the court in most states would today assign an alienist to investigate the accused's mental condition. The question of sanity would be resolved before the trial proceeded. If the judge, in his discretion, allowed the jury to get the case before taking this step, he could still consider such evidence before sentencing. If even then he declined to take insanity into consideration, the governor could be expected to conduct a hearing on this point to stay execution.

But on still other grounds John Brown's trial was flagrantly unfair. The right of the accused to a reasonable time to prepare for trial was shockingly violated. Brown was forced to stand trial the very same day he was indicted. Scrupulous though the court was to provide the accused with competent trial counsel, it erroneously denied him the right to engage lawyers of his own choice. When, finally, his own counsel took over, they were given no time to familiarize themselves with the case against their client.

To this catalogue of judicial errors must be added a last one: John Brown was tried and sentenced for a crime of which he could not conceivably have been guilty. How the accused could have committed treason against Virginia when he was neither a citizen nor a resident of that state and owed it no allegiance was never clarified by the law-enforcement authorities. Objectivity and reason gave way to

hysteria and vigilantism. This was no time for technicalities. It was enough that John Brown be convicted of a crime
carrying the capital penalty and that the sentence of the
court be carried out with expedition.

To understand how a fanatic like John Brown was able
to precipitate a series of crises that culminated in his fantastic trial for treason in 1859, one has to retrace the course
of a whole generation in American life—at least as far back
as 1831. In that year occurred two momentous events in the
history of the slavery controversy. On January 1 there appeared the first issue of the *Liberator*, the formal launching
of William Lloyd Garrison's violent attack on Southern
slaveholding. In midsummer came the first serious Negro
insurrection since the American Revolution, the ferocious
attack on the whites of Southampton County, Virginia, led
by a superstitious Negro preacher named Nat Turner and
some seventy followers. A savage manhunt resulted in the
massacre of many Negroes and in Turner himself being
tracked down, tried, found guilty, and executed.

The appearance of a determined and even rabid aboli-
tionism in the North was matched by the blooming of a
widespread psychosis in the slave states on the score of
potential Negro uprisings. This hysteria indubitably contributed to defeating by the narrowest of margins the pro-
posals of the advocates of slave emancipation in the Virginia General Assembly during the winter of 1831–2. These
historic debates marked a turning-point. Henceforth the
Southern states, instead of preparing the ground for the
ultimate liberation of the Negro, adopted a series of repressive measures designed to tighten slave discipline and discourage the numerical expansion of free men of color.

Out of the continuous and expanding efforts of Northern
abolitionists to induce slaves to flee from bondage arose
some of the most dramatic trials in American history. The
Federal fugitive-slave law, on the books since 1793, was
countermanded in the Northern states by various personal-
liberty laws. In 1842 the Supreme Court, while sustaining

the right of a slaveowner to recover his runaway slaves despite the conflict between state statutes and Federal law, held that it was the prerogative of the Federal government to carry out the law. The Fugitive Slave Act of 1850, which was part of the Compromise of that year, was savagely manhandled by Theodore Parker and John Greenleaf Whittier. Seward's assertion that there was a "higher law" above the Constitution was now taken up by Wendell Phillips, with the result that Federal marshals were openly resisted in the Northern states when they attempted to return runaway slaves to their Southern owners. In 1851 a score of free Negroes broke into the Boston courthouse and whisked away a captured runaway named Shadrach. A few months later Boston was again thrown into a frenzy of excitement when a Negro named Sims was taken into custody as a fugitive of a Georgia planter. City Marshal Tukey, to whom the anonymous notes in the Webster trial had been addressed, had the courthouse barricaded with iron chains, and a huge police force guarded every foot of approach to the building to prevent a rescue. "The Courthouse is in fetters!" cried the abolitionists, "bound to the Georgia cotton presses!" Despite inflammatory meetings, as combustible as any assemblage since the days of Sam Adams, Chief Justice Shaw refused to be intimidated by pressure tactics. Although he regarded slavery as a moral wrong, he nevertheless upheld the Fugitive Slave Act.

Again three years later the fever chart mounted when Phillips and Parker induced a mob armed with clubs and axes to break into the jail and rescue an escaped slave named Burns. The mob was driven off by pistol-shot, and when Burns was conveyed to a cutter for return to his master, church bells tolled and homes were draped in black. Indictments for riot brought against Phillips and Parker were quashed on technical grounds. The tragic predicament of arrested fugitive slaves was dramatically highlighted in 1856 when an escaped Negress named Margaret Garner killed her three-year-old daughter and severely wounded two of her other children rather than allow them to be taken back across the Ohio to Kentucky. Finally, in 1857, in the most catastrophic legal decision in the annals of the Supreme Court, that tribunal, by a divided opinion in the Dred Scott case, denied to a Negro the right to plead in the Federal courts as a citizen and went so far as to declare, quite gratuitously it seemed to many, that the old Missouri Compromise on the slavery issue was unconstitutional. Only the states, so the majority held, could prohibit slavery within their boundaries.

While the issue of slavery was being fought out in the courthouses of the land, the halls of Congress resounded with fierce debates on the sectional conflict. In the same year as the Burns case Stephen A. Douglas greatly exacerbated the tension between the sections by securing the passage of the mischievous Kansas-Nebraska Act, which left the question of slavery to the decision of the people of the states when admitted. Although there was no sound economic reason why slavery should have taken hold in Kansas, and, contrariwise, that "peculiar institution" seems to have already reached its natural geographic limits, both pro- and anti-slavery forces soon engaged in an undeclared civil war to organize the territory in accordance with their respective convictions.

Here it is that John Brown first appears as an apostle of direct action and "higher law." A failure as a businessman and a farmer, he had migrated from Connecticut to Ohio and then settled near Osawatomie at the outbreak of the Kansas troubles. In 1856 he led four of his sons and three others on a private military expedition known as the Pottawattomie Massacre. First a Tennessee poor white named Doyle and two of his sons were shot and hacked down with swords. Then Brown's men dragged a proslavery politician named Wilkinson out of bed and cut his throat, and they terminated the bloody night's work by seizing Dutch Bill Sherman, cutting off his head, cracking open his skull, and dumping him in the creek.

An immense egoist, eager to command, emotionally unstable, yet sustained by strong moral convictions, Brown now assumed the role of a minor prophet. He naïvely explained the shocking assassinations with the observation that the victims had "each one committed murder *in his heart* and according to Scripture they were guilty of murder and I felt justified in having them killed." God, he maintained, had used him as an instrument "to kill men; and if I live, I think he will use me as an instrument to kill a good many more." With a price on his head, Brown left Kansas, only to return two years later with the alias of Shubel Morgan and involve himself in the extremely risky operations of the underground railway to Canada. Unfortunately, one of Brown's associates felt it necessary to murder a slave-owner in the course of liberating a runaway slave.

The ability of John Brown to win friends for his conspiratorial plans is a tribute not alone to his powerful personality but also to the gradual discrediting of the older ideas of nonresistance to force still clung to by William Lloyd Garrison. A more militant group of abolitionists were now in the saddle, ready for the conclusive encounter. Equally ready were the Southern irreconcilables, who were proceeding to supplant the more conciliatory statesmen in their region. Those who promoted Brown's operations included such responsible persons as Theodore Parker, Boston's Unitarian leader and antislavery firebrand, who was conveniently absent abroad at the time of the raid, Gerrit Smith, the New York philanthropist, Thomas Wentworth Higginson, long identified with the cause of the Negro, Dr. Samuel Gridley Howe, the humanitarian and educator, Franklin B. Sanborn, a social reformer, and George Luther Stearns, a public-spirited Boston merchant. To Gerrit Smith and other backers Brown unfolded his plan for a military campaign "in slave territory east of the Alleghenies." He then read them a constitution he had drawn up in the Rochester home of Frederick Douglass, the ex-slave and militant Negro leader, who at the very last disavowed the proposed attack on the Federal government and warned Brown that "he was going into a perfect steel-trap, and that once in he would never get out alive." Brown's constitution, ratified at a meeting of a handful of white and Negro followers at Chatham in Canada, denounced slavery as violative of the Declaration of Independence and singled out the Dred Scott decision for special attack. Curiously reflecting the dangerously militaristic outlook of this latter-day Cromwell, it provided that no peace treaty could be ratified save by the president of his new government, the vice-president, a majority of Congress, the Supreme Court, *and* the general officers of his army. "A piece of insanity," von Holst characterized this document, but, visionary though it seems today, it was shrewdly calculated to furnish a moral justification for Brown's treasonable purposes.

When it appeared that Brown could not be dissuaded from his military coup, his prominent supporters began to be uneasy. "Our dear old friend has made up his mind to this course, and cannot be turned from it," explained Gerrit Smith. "We must support him. *I see no other way.*" Brown tossed aside practical objections to his chimerical military plans with the Scriptural text: "If God be for us, who can be against us?"

After much talk—too much, in fact—much correspondence, and the procurement of arms, the commander-in-chief of the "Provisional Army" (eighteen men in all) struck his great blow for the liberation of the slaves on Sunday, October 16, 1859. The scene was Harper's Ferry; the immediate objective, the Federal arsenal. Crossing the Potomac, Brown seized control of the bridge, cut the telegraph wires, and overpowered the few civilian guards at the arsenal. Had he stripped the arsenal of arms needed for his full-dress insurrection and then fled to the hills, he might have been able to carry on a guerrilla campaign for some time. Instead he committed a series of fatal and inexplicable blunders. Not only did he linger on with his pathetically small force, but he divided his few men by sending a raiding party beyond

Bolivar Heights to seize Colonel Lewis W. Washington, great-grandnephew of the first President. Then, wasting precious time on silly symbolism, he forced the captive to turn over to him the sword that Frederick the Great had given the general. After stopping the 1.24 a.m. train east-bound for Baltimore and killing a free Negro in the process, Brown's men unaccountably let the train proceed east. As a result, the Federal and state governments received news of the coup and could take prompt military measures. Mean-time a local physician named John D. Starry, the Paul Revere of Harper's Ferry, put spurs to his horse and roused the citizens of Charleston, eight miles away. Several com-panies of militia were called out, and they proceeded to cut Brown's line of communication back to Maryland and to bottle up his forces in the fire-engine room within the ar-mory, where prominent townsmen were held as hostages.

President Buchanan, now thoroughly aroused, ordered Colonel Robert E. Lee to the scene with a detachment of marines. Lee tried to smash down the engine-house door with sledgehammers, and, when the door failed to yield, called on the insurgents to give up. Brown refused. Lee then ordered his men to batter down the door with a heavy lad-der. When they broke through, the survivors within fired and one marine was mortally wounded.

The scene confronting the attackers was pitiful. Ten of Brown's followers lay dead or dying, including one of his own sons. "If you must die, die like a man," Brown had told him. Despite this tragic denouement, Brown was amazingly composed. Another badly wounded son lay beside him. He used one hand to feel the lad's pulse, the other to hold his rifle. As Lieutenant Green rushed in, Colonel Washington pointed Brown out to him, saying: "This is Osawatomie." Green lunged at Brown with his light sword and then show-ered blows upon his head. The bayonet quickly ended the resistance of the rest. Both Brown and his principal lieu-tenant, the handsome Aaron Dwight Stevens, adventurous ex-soldier whose sentence of death for mutiny had been commuted by President Pierce, were painfully wounded. Brown's hair was matted and tangled, his face, hands, and clothes smeared with blood. With four balls in his body, two of them in the head and neck, Stevens's condition was critical.

Brown and Stevens were removed to the armory office. Lying on "miserable shakedowns," covered with some old bedding, the captives were there examined on the afternoon of October 19 by a group of prominent citizens, including Colonel Lee, Jeb Stuart, to go down in history as America's greatest cavalryman, Governor Henry A. Wise and Senator J. M. Mason, both of Virginia, Congressman Vallandigham of Ohio, Colonel Washington, Andrew Hunter, the state's special prosecutor, and Charles James Faulkner, temporarily serving by court order as Brown's attorney. The first four were destined to play important roles in the Confederacy, and Vallandigham was to become a leader of the Northern fifth column. Despite wounds and captivity Brown cleverly fenced with his interrogators, who sought futilely to get the insurrectionary to name his backers.

MASON: Can you tell us who furnished money for your expedition?

BROWN: I furnished most of it myself. I cannot implicate others. It is by my own folly that I have been taken.

MASON: If you would tell us who sent you here—who provided the means—that would be information of some value.

BROWN: I will answer freely and faithfully about what concerns myself—I will answer anything I can with honor, but not about others.

VALLANDIGHAM: Mr. Brown, who sent you here?

BROWN: No man sent me here. It was my own prompting and that of my Maker, or that of the devil whichever you please to ascribe it to. I acknowledge no master in human form.

VALLANDIGHAM: Did you get up the expedition yourself?

BROWN: I did.

MASON: What was your object in coming?

BROWN: We came to free the slaves, and only that.

MASON: How do you justify your acts?

BROWN: I think, my friend, you are guilty of a great wrong against God and humanity—I say it without wishing to be offensive—and it would be perfectly right for anyone to interfere with you so far as to free those you wilfully and wickedly hold in bondage. I do not say this insultingly. I think I did right and that others will do right who interfere with you at any time and all times. I hold that the golden rule, "Do unto others as you would have that others should do unto you," applies to all who would help others to gain their liberty.

VALLANDIGHAM: Have you had any correspondence with parties at the North on the subject of this movement?

BROWN: I have had correspondence.

A BYSTANDER: Do you consider this a religious movement?

BROWN: It is, in my opinion, the greatest service a man can render to God.

BYSTANDER: Do you consider yourself an instrument in the hands of Providence?

BROWN: I do.

His interrogators then informed Brown of a published letter by Gerrit Smith criticizing moral suasion and advocating an insurrection in the South as the only effective way of achieving Negro emancipation. When asked what he thought of Smith's views, he replied: "I agree with Mr. Smith that moral suasion is hopeless. I don't think the people of the slave states will ever consider the subject of slavery in its true light till some other argument is resorted to than moral suasion." Then he went on to warn the slavocracy: "I wish to say, furthermore, that you had better—all you people at the South—prepare yourselves for a settlement of that question that must come up for settlement sooner than you are prepared for it." When a bystander characterized Brown's immediate purposes as "fanatical," he retorted: "And I think you are fanatical. 'Whom the gods would destroy they first make mad,' and you are mad."

Inept as a military adventurer, Brown now used the armory and later the courthouse as a forum for his political views. From the moment of his capture until his execution he showed courage and dignity, impressing all who had contact with him with his strong moral fervor. "They are themselves mistaken who take him to be a madman," remarked Governor Wise after this interrogation. "He is a fanatic, vain and garrulous, but firm, truthful, and intelligent." The Old Dominion's Governor later spoke of Brown at this time as "a broken-winged hawk lying upon his back, with fearless eye, and talons set for further fight if need be."

The prisoners were promptly transferred by train to Charlestown in the joint charge of the sheriff of Jefferson County and the United States marshal of the Western District of Virginia. No one was sure whether the Federal government or the state would initiate the prosecution, though there was no question but that Brown, in seizing a Federal arsenal and proclaiming a new constitution, had committed treason against the United States. At the same time his forces had carried out murder within the state of Virginia. With his eye on the main political chance, Governor Wise decided that to turn the prisoners over to the United States would appear to be an abdication of the state's right to act in the case. Furthermore, a Federal prosecution would most certainly postpone the moment when Brown and his cohorts would pay the penalty for their wild deeds. The spirit of lynch law had taken a vise-like grip on the area. If the Governor did not act fast, vigilantes would act for him. To the authorities it seemed imperative to move just as rapidly as the law would permit.

Fortuitously, from the Governor's point of view, the law and the court calendar combined to offer the prosecution an opportunity for a quick trial. The Virginia Code provided that a prisoner indicted for felony was to be arraigned and tried at the same term "unless good cause be shown for a continuance." It so happened that the grand jury was then in session, and that Judge Richard Parker, of Winchester, had just begun the semiannual term of the circuit court. Thus, in ordering John Brown to stand trial in the state courts one week after his capture, the Governor made due obeisance both to sectional feeling that this wrong should be speedily avenged and to considerations of state prestige, so precious in ante-bellum days.

While many Northerners thoroughly disapproved of Brown's desperate course and hoped that he would suffer the fullest penalty of the law, there was a fairly universal feeling in that part of the nation that the prisoner was being railroaded to trial with an indecent haste that violated the spirit if not the letter of the Anglo-American tradition of due process in criminal cases. But in dealing with Brown, Virginians exhibited none of that lethargy which Yankees attributed to those residing below Mason and Dixon's line. In fact, it is doubtful if any American state trial since the War for Independence has ever moved with such celerity.

On October 25, just one week after Lee's capture of the armory, Brown was brought before the magistrate's court in Charlestown for a preliminary examination. Although Charles B. Harding, county attorney, was technically in charge of the prosecution, the authorities had little confidence in this inflated windbag. A physical wreck, Harding could not be counted on to stay sober at the right time. "If you shut your eyes and listened for the first few minutes you would think Patrick Henry had returned to earth," was the way one of his associates described a typical Harding speech. "After that he dwindled away into ineptitudes." Needing a man with an inflexible determination to match his own, Wise virtually supplanted Harding by appointing as special prosecutor an able local lawyer named Andrew Hunter. Every inch a Southern statesman in bearing, Hunter believed in observing what he called "the judicial decen-

cies," but in "double quick time." "There must be no delay
in trying Brown and Stevens," he insisted. "As to the latter," he warned Wise, "*he will probably die of his wounds if
we don't hang him promptly.*"

Haste marked every step in the preliminary proceedings.
Had it not been for Brown's courage and his flair for dramatics, the hearing before the magistrates would have been
a routine affair as planned. When the court inquired if
Brown had counsel, the prisoner rose with an obvious effort
and replied:

Virginians, I did not ask for any quarter at the time
I was taken. I did not ask to have my life spared. The
Governor of the State of Virginia tendered me his assurance that I should have a fair trial; but, *under no
circumstances whatever will I be able to have a fair
trial.* If you seek my blood, you can have it at any moment, without this mockery of a trial. I have had no
counsel; I have not been able to advise with any one.
I know nothing about the feelings of my fellow prisoners, and am utterly unable to attend in any way to
my own defense. My memory don't serve me. My
health is insufficient, although improving. There are
mitigating circumstances that I would urge in our favor, if a fair trial is to be allowed us. But if we are to
be forced with a mere form—a trial for execution—
you might spare yourselves that trouble. I am ready for
my fate. I do not ask a trial. I beg for no mockery of a
trial, no insult—nothing but that which conscience
gives, or cowardice, would drive you to practice. I ask
again to be excused from the mockery of a trial. I do
not even know what the special design of this examination is. I do not know what is to be the benefit of it to
the Commonwealth. I have now little further to ask,
other than that I may not be foolishly insulted only as
cowardly barbarians insult those who fall into their
power.

Had the magistrates' ears been more perceptively at-
tuned, they might have heard William Kidd, but one of a
long line of victims of political trials, making the same argument in almost the same language. But the time was hardly
propitious for historical parallels. The magistrates simply
would not brook any delay, and ordered the prisoners sent
on to the circuit court of the county for trial.

Congressman Charles J. Faulkner and Lawson Botts were
assigned to defend the prisoners. In view of Brown's feeling
that the court's action was not bona fide, but a "mockery,"
Faulkner withdrew from the case after the preliminary examination. Botts, a grandson of the Benjamin Botts who
was counsel for Aaron Burr in the Richmond treason trial
over half a century earlier, was an able trial lawyer, who
later gave his life to the Confederate cause on the battle-
field. When the prosecutor asked Brown whether he would
accept the counsel assigned by the court, he replied:

> I wish to say that I have sent for counsel. I did apply,
> through the advice of some persons here, to some per-
> sons whose names I do not now recollect, to act as coun-
> sel for me, and I have sent for other counsel, who have
> had no possible opportunity to see me. I wish for coun-
> sel if I am to have a trial; but if I am to have nothing
> but the mockery of a trial, as I have said, I do not care
> anything about counsel. It is unnecessary to trouble
> any gentleman with that duty.

"You are to have a fair trial," Harding assured him. At
long last each of the prisoners agreed to the court's assignment.

When at two o'clock that same afternoon the circuit court
opened with Judge Parker on the bench, the tranquillity of
the mellowed county seat of Charlestown was rudely punctured. Outside the courthouse the scene was reminiscent of
the Anthony Burns trial in Boston, except that in this case
the mob would have liked nothing better than to lynch the
prisoner rather than liberate him. Cannon were trained on

this red brick Georgian structure, later to be damaged by shellfire during the Civil War. A detachment of militia guarded all approaches to the building. Sixty-three years later the scene was virtually duplicated when three persons were tried in that very same courthouse on treason charges as an aftermath of the miners' armed march in Logan County and their entrenchment on a mountain ridge, withstanding successive attacks during a four-day battle with armed deputies. On that latter occasion one of the convicted defendants received ten years' imprisonment.

When a threatening mob is outside a courthouse, nobody inside the building is likely to ignore it, least of all the judge. Judge Parker had good reason to believe that unless there was a prompt trial Brown and the remnants of his captive army would be torn from the minions of the law and summarily dispatched. The court, therefore, wasted no time, but proceeded at once to charge the grand jury. The bill of indictment that was promptly brought in contained three counts: (1) for "traitorously" making rebellion and levying war against Virginia; (2) for conspiring to start a slave insurrection; and (3) for the murder of four whites and one Negro. All were capital offenses. The Governor and the prosecution easily satisfied themselves that Brown was a traitor despite the fact that the accused was neither a citizen nor a resident of that state. But when, in April 1861, Wise conspired to capture the identical arsenal at Harper's Ferry and by this act of treason against the Federal government forced the hand of the Virginia legislature to pass the Ordinance of Secession, it is doubtful whether he put himself in the same category as John Brown. It was Brown's militancy, not his fate, that inspired him. "Take a lesson from John Brown," Wise then insisted.

Brown and his chief lieutenant were arraigned together. Both were in bad physical shape. Breathing with great difficulty, Stevens had to be carried into court on a mattress. In the jailer's opinion Brown was malingering, but nevertheless

it was necessary to bring him into court on a cot. Since
Faulkner had withdrawn from the case, the court now appointed Thomas C. Green, mayor of Charlestown and later
to distinguish himself on the state bench, to share the defense burden with Botts. Before being formally arraigned,
Brown addressed the court:

> I do not intend to detain the Court, but barely wish
> to say, as I have been promised a fair trial, that I am
> not now in circumstances that enable me to attend a
> trial, owing to the state of my health. I have a severe
> wound in the back, or rather in one kidney, which en-
> feebles me very much. But I am doing well, and I only
> ask for a very short delay of my trial, and I think I
> may get able to listen to it; and I merely ask this, that,
> as the saying is, "The devil may have his dues," no
> more. I wish to say, further, that my hearing is im-
> paired, and rendered indistinct, in consequence of
> wounds about my head. I cannot hear distinctly at all;
> I could not hear what the Court has said this morning.
> I would be glad to hear what it said on my trial, and
> am now doing better than I could expect to under the
> circumstances. A very short delay would be all I would
> ask. I do not presume to ask more than a very short de-
> lay, so that I may in some degree recover, and be able
> at least to listen to my trial, and hear what questions
> are asked of the citizens, and what their answers are.
> If that could be allowed me, I should be very much
> obliged.

Under normal circumstances such a request for a continuance is automatically granted. But there was nothing normal about this trial. Parker required little prompting on the
part of Hunter to rule that Brown's plea must wait until
the arraignment. The reading of the verbose indictment took
all of twenty minutes, during which period both Brown and
Stevens were compelled to stand, the latter having to be

held up by two bailiffs. Each of the prisoners pleaded not guilty and expressed a desire to be tried separately. The prosecutor then informed the court that the state elected to try Brown first.

Botts now repeated Brown's request for a delay of two or three days. Hunter insisted that, in view of the atmosphere of the countryside, any delay was dangerous, and that, furthermore, Brown was physically capable of standing trial. To remove all doubts about the actual condition of the prisoner, he asked the court that the accused be examined by the jailer and a physician. The court then called on Dr. Mason, the physician who attended Brown, to testify regarding his condition. The doctor expressed the opinion that Brown's wounds were not such as to affect his mind or recollection. Then one of the jail guards attested to Brown's customary garrulousness. This was sufficient for the court. The motion for a continuance was denied.

The selection of a jury was the next order of business. All those who were present at Harper's Ferry during the insurrection and witnessed the prisoner commit the acts for which he was about to be tried were, naturally, excluded. When the court and counsel had agreed on twenty-four veniremen as competent jurors, the prisoner's counsel were permitted to challenge eight peremptorily. Finally, out of the sixteen remaining, twelve were drawn by ballot. All this had been accomplished before the afternoon was over. Probably no jury in an American state trial has ever been impaneled so rapidly.

The state was now ready to proceed with its case. A night's rest appeared to have refreshed Brown who came into the court the next morning walking unassisted. But he did not maintain this upright position for long. Almost immediately he stretched himself out on his cot, at full length, within the bar. Now came a crucial defense move that caught both prisoner and prosecution by surprise. Lawson Botts proceeded to read a telegram he had received only that morning:

Akron, Ohio, Thursday, Oct. 26, 1859

To C. J. Faulkner and Lawson Botts:

John Brown, leader of the insurrection at Harper's Ferry, and several of his family have resided in this county many years. Insanity is hereditary in that family. His mother's sister died with it, and a daughter of that sister has been two years in a lunatic asylum. A son and daughter of his mother's brother have also been confined in the lunatic asylum, and another son of that brother is now insane and under close restraint. These facts can be conclusively proven by witnesses residing here, who will doubtless attend the trial if desired.

A. H. Lewis

Botts then explained that when he had read the telegram to Brown in jail the prisoner denied that there ever had been insanity in his father's family, though he admitted that there had been repeated instances on his mother's side. His first wife had also shown symptoms, which were evident as well in his first and second sons by that wife. How about Brown himself? One of his intimates, W. S. C. Otis, forwarded an affidavit, later used in an effort to secure a reprieve, in which he asserted:

I have known John Brown for fifteen years and never saw any business transaction conducted by him which indicated a sane mind—except while engaged in Summit County in growing sheep and wool. After opening a house in Springfield, Mass., and engaging in that business, he became involved in transactions and difficulties which indicated conclusively that *whenever under great mental excitement he was clearly insane.*

Brown disdained the plea of insanity. Raising himself on his cot, he declared:

I will add, if the court will allow me, that I look upon it as a miserable artifice and pretext of those who ought to take a different course in regard to me, if they took

any at all, and I view it with contempt more than
otherwise. As I remarked to Mr. Green, insane persons,
so far as my experience goes, have but little ability to
judge their own sanity; and, if I am insane, of course,
I should think I know more than all the rest of the
world. But I do not think so. I am perfectly unconscious
of insanity, and I reject, so far as I am capable, any
attempt to interfere in my behalf on that score.

Once more Botts pleaded for delay, this time on the
ground that a telegram had been received the previous day
informing Brown that counsel from Cleveland was leaving
that night. Brown's Virginia attorney argued that the prisoner could have a fairer trial if the defense were conducted
by counsel of his own choosing than if he were defended by
counsel assigned by the court. Hunter rejoined sharply that
he was getting a fair trial, according to the laws of Virginia.
Seconding the special prosecutor, Harding addressed himself to the question of the prisoner's physical condition,
called the court's attention to the fact that Brown had the
previous afternoon pretended that he was unable to walk
and yet had walked back to jail at the close of the session
without apparent difficulty. Botts had raised two fundamental issues which should not have been casually dismissed: the prisoner's sanity and his right to his own choice
of counsel. But Parker was too impatient to get on with the
trial to do other than sustain the prosecution. No one was
surprised when he ordered that the jury be sworn and the
trial proceed.

Opening for the state, Harding asserted that the prisoner's
whole object was "to rob Virginia's citizens of their slaves
and carry them off by violence." But he was gratified to
be able to point out that these acts had been committed
"against the wills of the slaves, all of them having escaped,
and rushed back to their masters at the first opportunity."
Considering the character of Botts's local clientele, it took
a good deal of courage for him to retort that "it was due to

the prisoner to state that he believed himself to be actuated by the highest and noblest feelings that ever coursed through a human breast, and that his instructions were to destroy neither property nor life." Hunter then informed the jury that the state treason law under which Brown was indicted was much broader than that of the Federal government and that the guilt of the prisoner would be proved "in the clearest manner" by some dozen witnesses "unless limited by lack of time." Asking for a consideration of the case "with fairness and impartiality, and without fear, favor or affection," he demanded that the prisoner be meted out the penalty "which law denounces, which reason denounces, which our safety requires, and which the laws of God and men approve."

The state then put its witnesses on the stand to tell the facts of the raid, the killing of the victims, and the purposes of the insurrection. Most effective of the state's witnesses was Colonel Lewis Washington, who on direct examination related a stirring tale of the attack:

Between one and two o'clock Sunday night, while in my bed at my house, five or six miles from Harper's Ferry, I was awakened by hearing my name called in the hall. I supposed it was some friends arrived who, being acquainted with the house, had come in through the kitchen without making any noise. I got up and opened the door into the hall, and before me stood six men, three armed with Sharp's rifles, leveled and cocked. I recognized Cook, Coppoc, and another white man whom I afterward recognized as Kagi. There were also two Negro prisoners. The fourth, Stevens, was in command, with a revolver in his right hand, and in his left a lighted flambeau, made of pine whittlings. As I opened the door, one of the men said, "Is your name Washington?" Said I, "That is my name." Perhaps Cook, who was of the crowd identified me, as he told me afterward he was taken there for that purpose.

I was then told I was a prisoner, and one of them said, "Don't be frightened." I replied, "Do you see anything that looks like fright about me?" "No," he said, "I only want to say that if you surrender and come with us freely you are safe."

I was struck with the number of men sent against me and asked what need there was of so many as there was no danger of an unarmed man in his nightshirt resisting an armed force. I was told to put on my clothes, and complied. "Perhaps," said I, "while I am dressing, you will be so good as to tell me what all this means?" I inquired what the weather was outside, and one of them advised me to put on an overcoat as it was rather chilly. Another said they wanted my arms, and I opened the gun closet for them to help themselves. They then explained their mission, which they represented to be purely philanthropic, to wit: the emancipation of all the slaves in the country.

After I was dressed Stevens said to me, "Have you got any money?" I replied, "I wish I had a great deal." "Be careful, sir," said he. I told him if I had money I knew how to take care of it, and he could not get it. Said he, "Have you a watch?" My reply was, "I have, but you cannot have it. You have set yourselves up as great moralists and liberators of slaves; now it appears that you are robbers as well." "Be careful, sir," said he again.

I told them I was dressed and ready to go. They bade me wait a short time and my carriage would be at the door. They had ordered my carriage for me, and pried open the stable door to get it out. They had harnessed the horses on the wrong side of each other, and I tried to induce them to correct the mistake, which they did after driving a short distance, but being harnessed wrong and rather spirited animals, they would not work well.

Colonel Washington suspected that his captors were robbers, and was surprised when they took him directly to the armory. There Brown invited him in to a comfortable fire. He indicated that later on he would formally propose that each of the captives there assembled should ransom his freedom by sending "a stout Negro man" in his place. Washington was determined not to agree to such an arrangement, but the ransom proposal never took concrete form. Breakfast for the entire company of forty-five—Brown's insurgents and the prisoners—was ordered at the Wager House, but neither Washington nor Brown himself ate anything. "All of us, I think," the witness declared, "were afraid that the employees had poisoned the food." Colonel Washington had asked Stevens as a personal favor to return to him the old sword presented by Frederick the Great to George Washington, which had been taken from his house along with other arms. "In the present improved state of arms," Washington pointed out, this was merely a museum piece. Stevens promised to see to it, and when his prisoner reached the armory he found the sword in John Brown's hands. "I will take especial care of it and I shall endeavor to return it to you after you are released," Brown told him. All day Monday Brown carried the sword, but when the marines attacked he laid it on a fire engine, where Washington retrieved it after the rescue.

Upon the announcement of the arrival of the militia, Brown came into the room and picked out ten of us, whom he supposed to be the most prominent men. He told us we might be assured of good treatment, because in case he got the worst of it in the fight, the possession of us would be of service in procuring good terms; we could exercise great influence with our fellow citizens; and as for me, he knew if I was out I should do my duty, and, in my position as aide to the Governor, I should be a most dangerous foe. Then we were taken

into the engine house and closely confined. Two of our
number went backward and forward repeatedly to con-
fer with citizens during the negotiations, and finally
remained out altogether, leaving the eight who were inside when the building was assaulted and captured by
the marines. During Monday various terms of capitulation were proposed and refused and at night we requested our friends to cease firing during the night, as,
if the place should be stormed in the dark, friends and
foes would have to share alike. In the morning Capt.
Sinn, of Frederick, announced the arrival of the United
States marines. During the night he had brought in Dr.
Taylor, of Frederick, to look at the wounds of old
Brown's son. The surgeon looked at the man and promised to attend him again in the morning if practicable,
but about the time he was expected hostilities commenced.

Colonel Lee, who commanded the United States
forces, sent up Lieutenant Stuart to announce to Brown
that the only terms he would offer for surrender were,
that he and his men should be taken to a place of safety
and kept unmolested until the will of the President could
be ascertained. Brown's reply was to the effect that he
could expect no leniency, and he would sell his life as
dearly as possible. A few minutes later the place was
assaulted and taken. In justice to Brown, I will say that
he advised the prisoners to keep well under shelter during the firing, and at no time did he threaten to massacre us or place us in front in case of assault. It was
evident he did not expect the attack so soon. There was
no cry of surrender by his party, except from one young
man, and then Brown said, "Only one surrenders."
This fellow, after he saw the marines, said he would
prefer to take his chance of a trial at Washington. He
had taken his position and fired one or two shots when
he cried, "Surrender." There were four of Brown's party
able to fight when the marines attacked, besides a

Negro, making five in all. This Negro was very bold at
first but when the assault was made, he took off his ac-
coutrements, and tried to mingle with the prisoners, and
pass himself off as one of them. I handed him over to
the marines at once, saying he was a prisoner at all
events.

Cross-examined on whether the marines fired after they
broke into the engine-house, Washington replied that he
could not tell, owing to the noise and confusion. He did
admit, however, that Brown's conduct was "not rude or in-
sulting to us," and that he had heard Old Osawatomie direct
his party not to fire on any unarmed man.

The trial now took a weird turning. On the morning of
the third day Botts informed the court of the arrival of
George M. Hoyt, of Boston, who had come to assist counsel
for the prisoner. But twenty-one years of age and looking
no more than nineteen, the callow Bostonian at once
aroused the suspicions of the prosecution. "A beardless boy
came in last night as Brown's counsel," Hunter wrote Wise.
"I think he is a spy." But the acute intuition of the special
prosecutor, unsupported at the time by documentary proof,
was not sufficient to bar Hoyt from attending the trial and
making contact with the prisoner. Hoyt had been retained
by John W. Le Barnes, of Boston, ostensibly to serve as
Brown's counsel but really to send back information on the
military situation in Charlestown, the number and distribution of the troops, and the approaches to the jail. He had
walked right into a bear trap. How intelligent men of the
world like Thomas Wentworth Higginson, Frank B. Sanborn, and Le Barnes could have hatched so harebrained a
scheme as to stage a jail break in the most heavily guarded
town in all America surpasses understanding. When Hoyt
revealed the rescue plot to Brown, the prisoner, intent on
martyrdom, said he would have no part in it. Higginson even
sent Brown's wife to see him in an effort to induce him to consent to the plan; but Brown telegraphed that she was not to

come, and she never got farther than Baltimore. Frustrated
in this direction, the Boston firebrands concocted a scheme
to kidnap Governor Wise and hold him as a hostage for
Brown's safety. Even on the eve of the execution rescue
plans were still stirring. One of the most significant of the
extant letters to John Brown was a short note, dated Boston,
November 1, 1859, on the eve of Brown's sentencing, which
reads:

> My brave but unfortunate friend,
> Protract to the utmost your trial. Your delivery is at
> hand.
>
> W. L. G.

Obviously, the chagrin of Brown's friends at the tragic termination of the putsch had emotionally unhinged them.

Only once during the course of the trial did John Brown
cry out. That was when Henry Hunter, son of the special
prosecutor, testified. The elder Hunter fought aggressively
to keep out of the trial evidence showing that his own son
and George W. Chambers had shot down William Thompson, a Brownite, on the Harper's Ferry bridge *after* he had
been taken prisoner. Unless it could be shown that Brown
had knowledge of the shooting, he contended, such evidence
was not admissible. But in one of the very few rulings favorable to the defense, Judge Parker admitted the testimony.
Despite the acute embarrassment of the prosecutor sworn
to enforce the law, his son told a forthright tale:

> After Mr. Beckham, who was my grand uncle, was
> shot, I was much exasperated, and started with Mr.
> Chambers to the room where the man Thompson was
> confined with the purpose of shooting him. We found
> several persons in the room, and had levelled our guns
> at him, when Mrs. Foulke's sister threw herself before
> him and begged us to leave him to the laws. We then
> caught hold of him and dragged him out by the throat,

he saying: "Though you may take my life, eighty million will rise up to avenge me, and carry out my purpose of giving liberty to the slaves." We carried him to
the bridge, and two of us, levelling our guns in this
moment of wild exasperation, fired, and before he fell,
a dozen or more balls were buried in him. We then
threw his body over the trestlework and returned to
the bridge to bring out the prisoner, Stevens, and serve
him in the same way. We found him suffering from his
wounds, and probably dying. We concluded to spare
him, and start after the others, and shoot all we could
find. I had just seen my beloved uncle and best friend
I ever had shot down by those villainous Abolitionists,
and felt justified in shooting any that I could find. *I felt
it my duty, and I have no regrets.*

This defiant, blood-curdling admission was too much for
Brown's fast-ebbing patience. Rising from his mattress, he
got up on his feet and addressed the court:

May it please the Court: I discover that, notwithstanding all the assurances I have received of a fair
trial, *nothing like a fair trial is to be given me,* as it
would seem. I gave the names as soon as I could get
them of the persons I wished to have called as witnesses, and was assured that they would be subpœnaed.
I wrote down a memorandum to that effect, saying
where those parties were; but it appears that they
have not been subpœnaed as far as I can learn; and now
I ask if I am to have anything at all deserving the name
and shadow of a fair trial, that this proceeding be de-
ferred until tomorrow morning; for I have no counsel,
as I before stated, in whom I feel that I can rely, but I
am in hopes counsel may arrive who will attend to seeing that I get the witnesses who are necessary for my
defense. I am myself unable to attend to it. I have
given all the attention I possibly could to it, but am
unable to see or know about them, and can't even find

out their names; and I have nobody to do any errand,
and I have not a dime. I had two hundred and fifty or
sixty dollars in gold and silver taken from my pocket,
and now I have no possible means of getting anybody
to go my errands for me, and I have not had all the
witnesses subpœnaed. They are not within reach, and
are not here. I ask at least until tomorrow morning to
have something done, if anything is designed; if not, I
am ready for anything that may come up.

Despite the consternation that Brown's unwarranted re-
pudiation of his own counsel caused in the courtroom, he
calmly proceeded to lay himself down again. Drawing his
blanket over himself, he closed his eyes as though in peaceful slumber. The star had spoken his lines. Why bother
about the rest of the play? But Brown's disavowal put
Hoyt, that jittery neophyte, completely lacking in trial experience, in an unenviable, not to say unanticipated role, at
least momentarily. Upon his slim shoulders rested the sole
responsibility for the life of the accused. Even a more mature
advocate might have been overwhelmed by the equivocal
honor. Now each of Brown's attorneys in rapid succession
addressed the court:

HOYT: May it please the Court; I would add my voice
to the appeal of Mr. Brown, although I have had no consultation with him, that the further hearing of the case may
be postponed until morning. I would state the reason of this
request. It was that I was informed, and had reason to believe, that Judge Tilden of Ohio was on his way to Charlestown, and would undoubtedly arrive at Harper's Ferry at
7 o'clock tonight. I have taken measures to insure that
gentleman's arrival in this place tonight, if he reaches the
Ferry. For myself, I have come from Boston, travelling
night and day, to volunteer my services in defense of Brown.
I could not undertake the responsibility of his defense as
I am now situated. The gentlemen who have defended
Brown acted in an honorable and dignified manner in all

respects, so far as I know, but I cannot assume the responsibility of defending him myself for many reasons. First it would be ridiculous in me to do it, because I have not read the indictment through—have not, except so far as I have listened to the case and heard counsel this morning, got any idea of the line the defense proposed, and have no knowledge of the criminal code of Virginia, and no time to read it. I had no time to examine the questions arising in this defense, some of which are of considerable importance, especially that relative to the jurisdiction over the Armory grounds. For all these reasons, I ask the continuation of the case till tomorrow morning.

BOTTS: In justice to myself I must state that, on being first assigned as counsel to Mr. Brown, I conferred with him, and at his instance took down a list of the witnesses he desired subpœnaed in his behalf. Though it was late at night, I called up the sheriff and informed him that I wished subpœnas to be issued early in the morning. This was done, and there are here Messrs. Phelps, Williams, and Cross, and they have been examined.

GREEN: Mr. Botts and myself will now withdraw from the case, as we can no longer act in behalf of the prisoner, he having declared here that he has no confidence in the counsel who have been assigned him. Feeling confident that I have done my whole duty, so far as I have been able, after this statement of his, I should feel myself an intruder upon this case were I to act for him from this time forward. I had not a disposition to undertake the defense, but accepted the duty imposed on me, and I do not think, under these circumstances, when I feel compelled to withdraw from the case, that the Court could insist that I should remain in such an unwelcome position.

When Judge Parker now declared that "the idea of waiting for counsel to study our code through could not be admitted," Botts felt impelled to take a strong stand, but one that did him credit:

I have endeavored to do my duty in this matter, but I cannot see how, consistently with my own feelings, I can remain any longer in this case when the accused whom I have been laboring to defend declares in open court that he has no confidence in his counsel. I make this suggestion, that as I now retire from this case, the more especially since there is now here a gentleman from Boston who has come on to volunteer his services for the prisoner, that the Court allow him this night for preparation. My notes, my office, and my services are at his command. I will sit up with him all night to put him in possession of the law and facts in relation to this case. I cannot do more; in the meantime, the sheriff can be directed to have the other witnesses here tomorrow.

The court, at last recognizing the iron determination of Brown's counsel, declared that it could not compel Botts and Green to remain on the case. A postponement until the following morning was magnanimously granted. Except for the brief delay, Brown gained nothing by his tactics save to ensure his martyrdom. The next day Samuel Chilton, an experienced Fauquier County criminal pleader, and Hiram Griswold, of Cleveland, recently a state senator, were introduced to the court as new counsel for the prisoner. Parker graciously granted them a few minutes to interview their client, but denied them a short delay of even a few hours to read the indictment and the record of the preliminary examination. "The trial must go on," the court ordered quite arbitrarily. Since Brown had been forced to accept counsel not of his own choosing and then, when his own lawyers did enter the case, they were not given sufficient time to prepare the defense, it could have been properly argued that at no stage of the trial was the accused represented by counsel *except nominally*. Today, following the rule in the Scottsboro case, the Supreme Court would be bound to reverse Brown's conviction. But when the prisoner went to trial there was no

Fourteenth Amendment on the books to restrain violations of due process by state courts.

In the afternoon session Chilton sought to compel the prosecution to elect one count in the indictment and abandon the others, but the court ruled that, as the trial had begun under the indictment, it must continue to a conclusion, when, Judge Parker conceded, the defense might move to arrest the judgment. The court's ruling stands as good law at the present day.

Despite the lack of preparation by Brown's new counsel and the complete exhaustion of young Hoyt, who protested that he had had an average of no more than two hours' sleep over the past five days, the court seemed under some fixation to wind up the case. All the evidence was in, Parker insisted; let them get on with the trial. Accordingly each side prepared to sum up. Harding began for the state. Reviewing the testimony, he stamped as absurd the prisoner's contention that he should have been treated according to the rules of honorable warfare. Denouncing Brown as the commander of a band of murderers and thieves, the state's attorney declared that the prisoner had forfeited all rights to protection of any kind whatsoever.

But the summations were not destined to proceed without interruption. What Brown's counsel had not been able to secure by their forensic efforts the prisoner himself again obtained by craft. Feigning illness, which the court physician would not authenticate, he once more had to be carried into court on a cot. Although Brown's behavior seemed transparent, Parker felt it the better part of discretion to grant a postponement over the week-end. Having won this little victory, Brown got off the cot and walked back to jail. Under different circumstances behavior such as Brown's would have made the accused liable to punishment for flagrant contempt of court. But this was a capital case. When a man faces virtually certain death, a prison term for contempt holds no terrors for him. It might even be welcomed as actually delaying the day of his execution. Such a result would have been diametrically opposed to what his enemies devoutly desired.

Griswold led off on Monday morning with the summation for the defense. Punching at the glaring weakness in the indictment, he contended that Brown could not be guilty of treason against Virginia unless he were a citizen of that state. "We maintain," he argued, "that this prisoner was not bound by any allegiance to this state and could not, therefore, be guilty of rebellion against it." Griswold went on to belittle the character of Brown's accomplishments and to deny that the accused could have constituted any real danger to the state of Virginia.

It is not true that there is any danger from the popular feeling. It is not true that there is danger to the State, either from within or without. Think of it, gentlemen, calmly and dispassionately. Here stands a man of whom you know something. He is a man of indomitable will, of sleepless energy of purpose, possessed of a spirit of perseverance that turns back from no difficulty, and endowed with a constitution that will endure and overcome everything. He, with all these qualities fitting him for such an enterprise, was engaged for months and months prosecuting it, and how did he succeed? Despite all his efforts, despite those energies of mind and body which he threw into the work, and that unbending will of his which never faltered nor slept, he was able throughout the length and breadth of the United States to gather round his standard some twenty-one men, both black and white. Can it be supposed, gentlemen, for a moment, that there is fear to be apprehended from such a man, who, in the zenith of his power, when he had a name in history, and when something might be hoped for the cause in which he was engaged, could only, throughout the whole country, raise twenty-one men?

Is it to be supposed for a moment, I ask, now, when
he is struck down to the earth, his few followers scat-
tered or destroyed—now, when the fact is known that
the South is alarmed and armed in every direction
ready to repel any enterprise of this kind, that anything is to be feared? No, gentlemen, there is not the
remotest danger of your ever again witnessing in your
State anything akin to that which lately occurred. I do
not know whether it is necessary for me to make these
remarks. I know it is the duty of the jury to be blind
to everything that bears not upon the case. Justice is
represented as blind, seeing nothing, but dealing only
with the facts which relate to the case. I believe you
will take this case and deal with it fairly, and dispose
of it under the ruling of the court.

Any notion that this local jury could consider the facts of
the case "calmly and dispassionately" was swiftly disabused when Andrew Hunter in his summation proceeded to
whiplash the prisoner. "He wanted the citizens of Virginia
calmly to fold their arms and let him usurp the government,
manumit our slaves, confiscate the property of slaveholders,
and without drawing a trigger or shedding blood, permit
him to take possession of the Commonwealth and make it
another Haiti." Brown knew what he was doing and was
ready to abide by the consequences. "That proves malice,"
Hunter contended. "We therefore ask his conviction to vindicate the majesty of the law." Dealing inferentially with
Griswold's allusion to "Justice," the special prosecutor
placed "Justice" in the "center upon which the Deity sits."
"There is another column which represents mercy," but lest
the jury get any foolish notions, he quickly added: "You
have nothing to do with that. It stands firmly on the column
of justice. Administer it according to your law—acquit the
prisoner if you can—but if justice requires you by your
verdict to take his life, stand by that column uprightly, but

strongly, and let retributive justice, if he is guilty, send him before that Maker who will settle the question forever and ever."

The state had spoken. It took the jury nearly three quarters of an hour to return with a verdict of guilty. When the foreman answered the clerk's query, Brown sat up on his cot, then turned to adjust his pallet, and composedly stretched himself upon it. But he remained silent. At long last the martyrdom had come that he had so eagerly craved. Chilton's motion in arrest of judgment was argued on November 1, and on the following day was overruled. The most memorable moment of the trial was now at hand. The clerk asked John Brown whether he had anything to say why sentence should not be pronounced upon him. Always a supreme moment for professional agitators, the prisoner was certain to exploit it to the fullest. In a perfectly calm voice and with a self-possession that was remarkable under the circumstances, Brown delivered this extemporaneous utterance:

I have, may it please the Court, a few words to say.

In the first place, I deny everything but what I have all along admitted, of a design on my part to free slaves. I intended certainly to have made a clean thing of that matter, as I did last winter when I went into Missouri, and there took slaves without the snapping of a gun on either side, moving them through the country, and finally leaving them in Canada. I designed to have done the same thing again on a larger scale. That was all I intended to do. I never did intend murder or treason, or the destruction of property, or to excite or incite the slaves to rebellion, or to make insurrection. I have another objection, and that is that it is unjust that I should suffer such a penalty. Had I interfered in the manner, which I admit, and which I admit has been fairly proved—for I admire the truthfulness and candor of the greater portion of the witnesses who have testified in this case—had I so interfered in behalf of any of the rich, the powerful, the intelligent, the so-called great, or in behalf of any of their friends, either father, mother, brother, sister, wife, or children, or any of that class and, suffered and sacrificed what I have in this interference, it would have been all right, and every man in this court would have deemed it an act worthy of reward rather than punishment. This Court acknowledges, too, as I suppose, the validity of the law of God. I see a book kissed, which I suppose to be the Bible, or at least the New Testament, which teaches me that all things whatsoever I would that men should do to me, I should do even so to them. It teaches me further to remember them that are in bonds, as bound with them. I endeavored to act up to that instruction. I say I am yet too young to understand that God is any respecter of persons. I believe that to have interfered as I have done in behalf of His despised poor, is no wrong, but right. Now, if it is deemed necessary that I should forfeit my life for the furtherance of the ends of justice, and mingle my blood further with the blood of my children and with the blood of millions in this slave country whose rights are disregarded by wicked, cruel, and unjust enactments, I say let it be done.

Let me say one word further. I feel entirely satisfied with the treatment I have received on my trial. Considering all the circumstances, it has been more generous than I expected. But I feel no consciousness of guilt. I have stated from the first what was my intention, and what was not. I never had any design against the liberty of any person, nor any disposition to commit treason or excite slaves to rebel or make any general insurrection. I never encouraged any man to do so, but always discouraged any idea of that kind. Let me say also in regard to the statements made by some of those who were connected with me, I fear it has been stated by some of them that I have induced them to join me;

but the contrary is true. I do not say this to injure them, but as regretting their weakness. Not one but joined of his own accord, and the greater part at their own expense. A number of them I never saw, and never had a word of conversation with till the day they came to me, and that was for the purpose I have stated. Now, I am done.

Brown was then sentenced by the Court to be hanged in public on the 2nd of December. Subsequently, the Court of Appeals refused to grant his counsel a writ of error, and Brown's fate rested in Governor Wise's hands. The Governor received the customary batch of crank letters, which, of course, he ignored. He did feel impelled, however to reply to an appeal for clemency addressed to him by New York's pro-Southern mayor, Fernando Wood, a leading Northern Democrat who was soon to try to take New York City out of the Union. Wise did not mince words. Denouncing the view that the state "had better spare a murderer, a robber, a traitor, because public sentiment elsewhere will glorify an insurrectionist with martyrdom," he retorted that since such views were so widely held, "it is time to do execution upon *him and all like him.* And I therefore say to you firmly that I have precisely nerve enough to let him be executed. He shall be executed as the law sentences him, and his body shall be delivered over to surgeons and await the resurrection without a grave in our soil."

But had Wise been sincere in demonstrating the measure of his intestinal fortitude, he would have ordered a stay of execution until the question of Brown's sanity had been properly determined. Such an act would have required the kind of courage to which ambitious politicians have a natural aversion. Since Wise's day Virginia has made amends for his unpardonable oversight. While a majority of the states of the Union execute a person charged with a crime only if he is capable of knowing that he was doing wrong, in the Old Dominion, even when the accused does know that the act is wrong, he still is excused if he is incapable of controlling the impulse to commit it. Assuming its application at a time of political hysteria, so liberal an interpretation of insanity as the present Virginia rule would save a person like John Brown from being executed regardless of how shocking his offense.

During his last days on earth Brown received numerous messages of sympathy and encouragement, but one stinging epistle must have recalled to him a bloody night on the Pottawattomie.

Chattanooga, Tennessee, Nov. 20th, 1859.

John Brown,

Sir:

Altho' vengeance is not mine, I confess that I do feel gratified to hear that you were stopped in your fiendish career at Harper's Ferry, with the loss of your two sons, you can now appreciate my distress in Kansas, when you then and there entered my house at midnight and arrested my husband and two boys, and took them out of the yard and in cold blood shot them dead in my hearing. You cant say you done it to free slaves. We had none and never expected to own one, but has only made me a poor disconsolate widow with helpless children, while I feel for your folly I do hope and trust that you will meet your just reward. O how it pained my heart to hear the dying groans of my Husband and children. If this scrawl gives you any consolation you are welcome to it.

MAHALA DOYLE

N.B. My son John Doyle whose life I beged of you is now grown up and is very desirous to be at Charlestown on the day of your execution, would certainly be there if his means would permit it that he might adjust the rope around your neck if Gov. Wise would permit it.

M. DOYLE

On the day of the execution the condemned man was taken to the cells of his five confederates. Four of them who had been steadfast received his benediction. But to John E. Cook, who had given damaging testimony, Brown said: "You have made false statements that I sent you to Harper's Ferry." As he left his cell for the last time, he handed a prophetic final message to one of the attendants, which read: "I, John Brown, am now quite *certain* that the crimes of this *guilty land* will never be purged *away* but with blood. I had *as I now think* vainly flattered myself that without *very much* bloodshed it might be done."

Turning to the sheriff, he told him he was ready. After his arms were pinioned he proceeded to the door calm and even cheerful, wearing a black slouch hat and the same clothes he had worn during the trial. Outside the jail six companies of infantry and one of horse were deployed. Virginia was taking no chances on a last-minute rescue operation. An open wagon with a pine box awaited the prisoner. Brown climbed up on the wagon and sat down on his own coffin. On reaching the scene of execution the prisoner got out of the wagon and with a firm step ascended the scaffold, which sat on a low rounded knoll. "This is a beautiful country," Brown remarked. "I never had the pleasure of seeing it before." No longer the malingerer, he was supremely courageous at the last. Behind the gibbet stood "Stonewall" Jackson commanding a howitzer unit. More obscurely, in a Richmond company, stood the sinister figure of John Wilkes Booth, shouldering a rifle. A hatchet blow severed the rope that held the trapdoor on which Brown stood. "So perish all such enemies of Virginia!" Colonel Preston solemnly declared. "All such enemies of the Union! All such foes of the human race!"

And thus ended the earthly career of John Brown. But finis had not been written to his story. "John Brown still lives," the *Springfield Republican* commented on the day after the execution. To Emerson and countless others in the North, John Brown had "made the gallows glorious like the

cross." Henry Wadsworth Longfellow, under date of December 2, recorded in his diary: *"They are sowing the wind
to reap the whirlwind, which will come soon."* Lincoln was
more dispassionate when he soundly observed that Brown's
beliefs on the "wrong" of slavery "cannot excuse violence,
bloodshed, and treason. It could avail him nothing that he
might think himself right."

But in that gathering storm Lincoln's objectivity could
not stem the fury of sectional hates. Testifying to a trans-
figuration without parallel in American history, men in blue
were soon to march, muskets to their shoulders, tramping
to the refrain of "John Brown's body lies a-mouldering in
the grave." Significantly, before many months had passed,
a version of the same refrain bespoke a new vindictiveness
and determination: "We'll hang Jeff Davis to a sour apple
tree."

"Bury the South together with this man," a later minstrel
sang in memory of the furious force that was John Brown.

X

Ordeal by Jury

the trial of the Chicago anarcho-communists

Just who hurled the bomb into Chicago's old Haymarket Square on the night of May 4, 1886 remains a mystery to this very day—perhaps one of the best-kept secrets in the annals of extremist labor groups. Neither the police investigation, nor the trial evidence, nor the appeal record, nor the commutation hearings ever conclusively identified the unbalanced fanatic who stood in a noisome alley and let loose a charge of dynamite that was to change the entire direction of the American labor movement.

But this is not a detective story. It is the story of a trial, a criminal trial with political overtones, a trial conducted in an atmosphere of hysteria over the public safety. It was that kind of trial where the jurors had their minds made up before they heard any of the testimony, where the prosecutor's prejudicial and inflammatory tactics served as a smoke screen to conceal his bad logic, and where the judge's every ruling betrayed his flagrant partisanship. Instead of affixing individual culpability for the crime, the verdict expressed society's condemnation of an entire group for a program of ideas and action deemed inimical to the general welfare.

Despite the shock of the Haymarket massacre the community had not been unprepared. Chicago's laboring population, living in squalor, exploited by low wages and long hours, were sullen and discontented. Swept along on the national tide of the eight-hour movement, packing-house workers, machinists, printers, and drygoods clerks were all prepared to strike if this demand, among others, was not met. By May 1 these strike threats had attained a screaming crescendo. Meantime a little group of extremists, bap-

tized in the European revolutionary movement, were seeking to exploit labor's anxieties for their own spurious ends.
Hypersensitive to social injustice, these revolutionaries had
long since moved beyond Marxian socialism and embraced
the gospel of Bakunin—anarchism. "Tremble, oppressors
of the world!" the anarcho-communists proclaimed when
that pugnacious social revolutionary Johann Most set foot
on American soil in 1882. Though few listened, least of all
native labor uninfected by European notions of caste and
privilege, the agitators in some centers like Chicago kept
the pot simmering with appeals to violence and class hate.
The *Alarm*, organ of the anarchists, published incredible
items like these:

> Dynamite! Of all the good stuff, this is the stuff.
> Stuff several pounds of this sublime stuff into an inch
> pipe, plug up both ends, insert a cap with a fuse at-
> tached, place this in the immediate neighborhood of a
> lot of rich loafers who live by the sweat of other peo-
> ple's brows, and light the fuse. A most cheerful and
> gratifying result will follow. . . .

> All governments are domineering powers, and any
> domineering power is a natural enemy to all mankind,
> and ought to be treated as such. *Assassination will re-
> move the evil from the face of the earth.*

To the anarchists the eight-hour issue was merely a means
to an end. By attaching themselves to the movement like a
fungus growth on a healthy plant they were actually discrediting legitimate trade-unionism.

May 1 saw a gigantic labor parade, its ranks swollen by
the huge outpouring of workers on strike for ten hours' pay
for eight hours' work. The next day, Sunday, was suitably
quiet, but on Monday violence broke out on Black Road
near the McCormick plant, when strikers attacked scabs.
The police then joined in with club and revolver. One striker
was killed and several wounded. The Black Road riot was
grist for the mill of the adherents of violence, of men like

August Spies, who had not only witnessed the McCormick affray but personally harangued the strikers. Spicing his news story with that combination of melodrama and hyperbole so characteristic of news coverage in the *Arbeiter-Zeitung,* Spies produced an inflammatory product:

REVENGE! WORKINGMEN! TO ARMS!

Your masters sent out their bloodhounds—the police—they killed six of your brothers at McCormick's this afternoon. . . .

To capitalize on police brutality at Black Road a mass meeting was called for the very next evening, May 4, to be held in the Old Haymarket, now at the intersection of Desplaines and Randolph Streets in Chicago's Loop district, a sordid "Skid Row," lined with flophouses, pawnshops, and missions. Handbills announcing the meeting read: "WORKINGMEN ARM YOURSELVES AND APPEAR IN FULL FORCE!" But despite these histrionics the turnout was disappointingly small.

The agitators who addressed the Haymarket crowd were well known in Pinkerton circles. Spies and Albert R. Parsons boasted long records as revolutionary publicists and organizers. Only three days earlier the *Chicago Mail,* in a vitriolic editorial, warned its readers against the unholy pair. "They haven't got one honest aim nor one honorable end in view." With remarkable prescience that paper continued: "MARK THEM FOR TODAY. KEEP THEM IN VIEW. HOLD THEM PERSONALLY RESPONSIBLE FOR ANY TROUBLE THAT OCCURS. MAKE AN EXAMPLE OF THEM IF TROUBLE DOES OCCUR."

In opening the meeting shortly after eight thirty, Spies launched at once, in German, into a savage denunciation of McCormick as "responsible for the murder of our brothers." "Hang him!" cried some of the more responsive in the audience. Around nine o'clock Parsons took up where Spies left off. "It behooves you," he shouted, "as you love your wife and children, if you don't want to see them perish with hunger, killed or cut down like dogs in the street, Americans, in the interest of your liberty and your independence, to arm, to arm yourselves." In turn Parsons was followed by Samuel Fielden, a veteran of direct action, who now faced a formidable competitor in the drizzle that forced about three fourths of the twelve hundred spectators to leave for shelter. "You have been robbed, and you will be starved into a worse condition," the slightly dampened speaker insisted.

It was now twenty minutes past ten. Fielden was warming up for his peroration when suddenly a police cordon of a hundred and eighty men, led by Inspector Bonfield and Captain Ward, advanced upon the square. To Ward's demand that the meeting disperse, Fielden retorted: "We are peaceable." Nevertheless, he, Spies, and others began to descend from the wagon that had served them as a speaker's platform.

Suddenly a dynamite bomb hurtled through the air, exploding among the front rank of police. Panic swept the crowd. Re-forming their ranks, the enraged agents of law and order now fired into the mass of spectators, who fled for their lives. Policeman Degan had been killed almost instantly, six other officers later died of injuries, and seventy were wounded. In addition, at least one spectator was fatally shot and perhaps as many as sixty injured.

"Hang them first and try them afterwards," was the reaction of the average Chicagoan to the suspected anarchists. Responsible labor leaders, from Terence Powderly down, denounced the bomb-throwing. Inflamed patrioteers asked for stricter immigration laws, coupled with a more active deportation policy. Assisted by Pinkerton agents, the police quickly rounded up all the well-known anarchists, including the Haymarket speakers, Spies and Fielden. But no trace could be found of that inflammatory spellbinder Parsons. Significantly, none of those arrested was charged with throwing the bomb. But the tactics of the prosecution were not long concealed. On the day after the tragedy a coroner's jury found "that Mathias J. Degan had come to his death from a bomb thrown by a person or persons unknown, but *acting in conspiracy* with August Spies, Albert Parsons, Samuel J. Fielden, and others unknown." Following this pattern, the grand jury charged some ten individuals with being accessories before the fact to the murder of Patrolman Degan and with a general conspiracy to murder. These ten were August Spies, Michael Schwab, Samuel Fielden, Adolph Fischer, George Engel, Louis Lingg, Albert R. Parsons, Rudolph Schnaubelt, William Seliger, and Oscar Neebe. Still others were indicted for conspiracy and riot.

Left-wing circles managed to persuade two youthful attorneys, Sigismund Zeisler and Moses Salomon, to defend the anarchists. The pair made up in courage what they lacked in trial experience. No lawyer of standing would touch the case until, finally, William Perkins Black, a liberal-minded corporation attorney, and William A. Foster, a competent trial lawyer imported from Iowa, agreed to join the defense forces. The state's case was prosecuted by Julius S. Grinnell, state's attorney, who leaned heavily on his two young assistants, Francis W. Walker and Edmund Furthman, as well as on George C. Ingham, specially retained to help in this case. The prosecution team worked around the clock to have their case ready for trial date.

June 19, some six weeks after the fatal bomb-throwing, marked the opening of the trial in the Cook County Criminal Court. Presiding was Judge Joseph Easton Gary, whose reputation for competence, solidly grounded on some twenty-three years' service on that bench, was matched by his fame as a martinet. If any judge in the Chicago area could have assured the defendants a fair trial, this quondam carpenter seemed the least objectionable. But even Gary could not escape the climate of opinion that blanketed the Windy City much as the stench of the stockyards permeated to its remotest alleys when the prairie wind was right.

Closely guarded, the prisoners sat to the left of their counselors' table. Spies, with waxed mustache, had about him a Prussian military air. Schwab and Fielden, with their ascetic faces and deceptively mild demeanors, might have been taken for a pair of underpaid German schoolteachers. Fischer, Engel, and Neebe were nondescript weaklings in appearance. Only the wild-eyed Lingg suggested the criminal type in the Lombrosian sense.

To conservatives it did not seem surprising that there was not a native American in the lot, for Albert R. Parsons had taken flight at the time of the bomb-throwing and a systematic manhunt had still failed to locate him. The fact that the Alabaman agitator's ancestors had come over in that very crowded second voyage of the *Mayflower,* that he had turned scalawag to his political advantage in Texas during Reconstruction, and then, upon moving to Chicago, had drifted into left-wing labor circles, served to make him the special focus of public hate. One might expect anything from foreigners. From an American, hardly bomb-throwing!

Scarcely had the preliminary examination of talesmen begun when William P. Black entered the courtroom with a companion at his elbow. The prosecutor leaped to his feet.

"I see Albert R. Parsons, indicted for murder, in this court, and demand his instant arrest!" he shouted.

Black's plans for a dramatic delivery of the defendant into the custody of the court were now rudely punctured, and he retorted sharply: "This man is in my charge and such a demand is not only theatrical clap-trap, but an insult to me!"

Parsons was too much the extrovert to miss a performance in which he could enjoy top billing. At the same time, in fairness to him, he appears to have been moved by a sense of loyalty to share the lot of his associates picked up in the police dragnet which he had evaded. In giving himself up, Parsons had signed his own death warrant. Had he waited until the jury had been impaneled, he would have been

given a separate trial. This would have meant a delay until
the clamor had at least partly subsided—a priceless advantage.

"I present myself for trial with my comrades, Your
Honor."

"You will take a seat with the prisoners, Mr. Parsons,"
Judge Gary directed, alone in the courtroom in concealing
his astonishment.

Like other political trials before and since, the Haymarket case was really over, technically, before it had begun. The examination of jurors started on June 19 and
lasted until the 16th of July. In the course of that circus
marathon 981 talesmen were interrogated. Each of the eight
prisoners was entitled to twenty peremptory challenges
(disqualifying a juror without assigning cause), in all, 160,
which were used up long before the end of the questioning.
The state, entitled to an equal number, challenged only
fifty-two talesmen peremptorily. Grinnell was obviously
much less dissatisfied with the panel than the defense, and
with good reason. The fact that the court found it necessary
to excuse 757 prospective jurors upon challenge for cause,
chiefly by the defense, speaks eloquently of the state of
public prejudice. So desperate was the situation that Judge
Gary deemed it expedient to exercise considerable latitude
in qualifying jurors who had formed opinions.

Now, in a case as shocking and as widely publicized as
the Haymarket affair only a knave or a fool could have
failed to form an opinion on the responsibility of the prisoners for the crime, but Judge Gary's obvious pressure to
get twelve men into the jury box and to move the case into
gear was a major ground for appeal and for the widespread
dissatisfaction that soon arose over the course and conduct
of the trial. More than any other trial issue, Gary's rulings
on qualifying jurors served to invest the defendants with the
spurious cloak of martyrdom. To the defendants' advocates
Judge Gary resembled Procrustes, the ancient Greek robber

at Eleusis who had an iron bedstead on which he placed
his victims. If the body of the unfortunate was too short for
the bed, he stretched its limbs until they just fitted. If it
was too long, he lopped off a portion. In the same way, it
seemed to the friends of the Chicago anarchists, the most
transparent rules of law were put on a Procrustean bed in
the Haymarket case and tortured until they fitted the facts.

Judge Gary's behavior in court was as objectionable to
friends of the defendants as his rulings. "He seemed to treat
the affair as a Roman holiday," one eyewitness later reminisced. Sitting on the bench alongside the jurist were usually
several lady friends, with whom he chatted, and when this
did not provide him with sufficient distraction, he would
work out puzzles. Alert to overrule every motion of the defense, he seemed otherwise quite casual for one on whom
rested the responsibility for assuring a fair trial to the eight
prisoners before him on capital charges.

Take the examination of James H. Walker. Walker admitted that he had formed an opinion on the question of
the guilt or innocence of the defendants, that he still entertained that opinion and had expressed it to others. Asked
whether this opinion would influence his verdict, he replied: "Well, I am willing to admit that *my opinion would
handicap my judgment, possibly.*"

Q.: Now, considering all prejudice and all opinions that
you now have, is there anything which, if the testimony
were equally balanced, would require you to decide one way
or the other in accordance with your opinion or your prejudice?

A.: If the testimony was equally balanced, I should
hold my present opinion, sir.

Q.: Assuming that your present opinion is that you believe the defendants guilty—or some of them—now suppose,
if the testimony were equally balanced, your present opinion would warrant you in convicting them, you believe,
assuming your present opinion is that they are guilty?

A.: I presume it would.

Q.: Well, you *believe* it would—that is your present belief, is it?

After Walker was challenged for cause by the defense, the court then took a hand in the interrogation:

JUDGE GARY: Mr. Walker, I suppose you know that the law is that no man is to be convicted of any crime unless the evidence upon his trial, unless that evidence proves that he is guilty beyond a reasonable doubt?

WALKER: Yes, sir.

GARY: Now, this confusion about opinions and verdicts I want to clear up if I can. I suppose that you know that no man is to be tried upon prior impression or prior opinion of the jurors that are called into the case.

WALKER: Yes, sir.

GARY: But only upon the evidence. That you are familiar with, of course. Now, do you believe that you can fairly and impartially render a verdict without any regard to rumor and what you may have in your mind in the way of suspicion and impression, etc., but do you *believe* that you can fairly and impartially render a verdict in accordance with the law and evidence in the case?

WALKER: I shall try to do it, sir.

GARY (interrupting): But do you *believe* that you can sit here and fairly and impartially make up your mind from the evidence whether that evidence proves that they are guilty beyond a reasonable doubt or not?

WALKER: I think I could, but *I should feel that I was a little handicapped in my judgment,* sir.

GARY: Well, *that is a sufficient qualification for a juror in the case. Of course, the more a man feels that he is handicapped, the more he will be guarded against it.*

Immediately defense counsel was on his feet making exception to the remark of the court made in the presence

of a large number of talesmen awaiting examination.
The court overruled the challenge for cause, to which
the defendants' attorneys objected. Gary had left the
defense no alternative but to challenge Walker peremptorily.

After the defense had challenged Leonard Gould for cause
when that excessively conscientious talesmen admitted that
he was in doubt whether he could render "an absolutely impartial verdict," the court interposed:

GARY: Make up your mind as to whether you believe
you can fairly and impartially render a verdict in accordance with the law and the evidence. Most men in business
possibly have not gone through metaphysical investigations
of this sort, so as to be prepared to answer offhand without
some reflection?

GOULD: Judge, I don't believe I can answer the question.

GARY: Can't you answer whether you believe you
know?

GOULD: I should try. If I had to do it I should do the
best I could.

The court attempted vainly three or four more times to
get a categorical reply, then, before giving up, Gary made
one more stab:

GARY: Have you a belief one way or another whether
you can or cannot?

GOULD: If I were to sit on the case I should get just as
near to it as possible, but when it comes to laying aside all
bias and all prejudice, and making it up in that way, it is a
pretty fine point to them.

GARY: Not whether you are going to do it, but what
you do believe you can—that is the only thing. You are not
required to state what is going to happen next week, or the
week after, but what do you believe about yourself, whether
you can or cannot?

GOULD: I am just about where I was when I started.

GARY: This question, naked and simple of itself, is, do you believe that you can fairly and impartially render a verdict in the case with the law and the evidence?

GOULD: *I believe I could.*

As with Walker, the court, having worn down the talesman's intellectual resistance, then overruled the challenge for cause; whereupon the defense was forced to use up another precious peremptory challenge.

If there was any objective visitor in the courtroom, the judge must have seemed to be engaging in a transparent bit of coaching. Similar rulings were made by the court when a talesman stated that he now believed the newspaper accounts and rumors, on which he formed and expressed his opinion, or that "some of them are guilty," or that it would take "pretty good evidence" or "a large preponderance of evidence" to change his present opinion. In fact, Gary seemed ready and anxious to qualify jurors who indicated quite frankly, as did Rush Harrison, that unless "strong evidence of their innocence" was introduced, they would vote for conviction.

Handicapped by such rulings, the defense picked the best jury obtainable under the circumstances, probably as impartial a group of rather youngish white-collar workers and businessmen as could have been assembled in the entire area. But that these twelve entered the case with a prejudice against anarchists in general and had already prejudged the specific issues should be abundantly clear from a review of the examination of the twelfth juror, Harry T. Sandford, a twenty-seven-year-old railroad clerk. On questioning by Black, Sandford admitted that he had formed an opinion as to the guilt or innocence of the defendants, but maintained that he could nonetheless fairly and impartially listen to the testimony. He also confessed to a "decided" prejudice against Communists and anarchists, but insisted that despite such opinions he could render a fair and impartial verdict. Then the state's attorney took up the interrogation:

GRINNELL: Have you ever said to anyone whether or not you believed the statements of fact in the newspapers to be true?

SANDFORD: I have never expressed it exactly in that way, but still I have no reason to think they were false.

GRINNELL: Well, the question is not what your opinion of that was.

SANDFORD: Well, I don't recall whether I have or not.

GRINNELL: So far as you know, then, you never have?

SANDFORD: No, sir.

GRINNELL: Do you believe that, if taken as a juror, you can try this case fairly and impartially and render a verdict upon the law and the evidence?

SANDFORD: Yes.

GARY: The juror is qualified in my opinion.

BLACK: We challenge the juror for cause and except to your Honor's ruling.

To many laymen Judge Gary seemed to have stretched the pertinent provision of the Illinois Revised Statutes barring disqualifications of a juror to the very limit of its distention. The state law provided that where the juror had formed an opinion but stated upon oath "that he believes he can fairly and impartially render a verdict therein in accordance with the law and the evidence, and the court shall be satisfied of the truth of such a statement," he had not disqualified himself. Judge Gary was an easily satisfied man, but the Supreme Court in affirming the conviction maintained that the kind of opinions held by Juror Sandford were not the "strong and deep impressions" that Chief Justice Marshall described in the Burr trial. Technically, the defendants were on trial for murder. Any prejudice against radicals, regardless of how deep-seated, did not, in the judgment of the appellate court, render a juror incapable of trying the murder issue fairly and impartially.

But any idea that the defendants' ideologies could be kept separate from their actions was swiftly dispelled by State's Attorney Grinnell's opening for the prosecution:

> Gentlemen: For the first time in the history of our country are people on trial for their lives for endeavoring to make Anarchy the rule, and in that attempt for ruthlessly and awfully destroying life. I hope that while the youngest of us lives this in memory will be the last and only time in our country when such a trial shall take place. It will or will not take place as this case is determined.
>
> In the light of the 4th of May we now know that the preachings of Anarchy, the suggestions of these defendants hourly and daily for years, have been sapping our institutions, and that where they have cried "murder," "bloodshed," "Anarchy," and "dynamite," they have meant what they said, and proposed to do what they threatened.

These wild-eyed anarchists, these advocates of solution by dynamite, were "the biggest cowards that I have ever seen in the course of my life," Grinnell charged. "Like cowards contemplating crime," they sought to establish an alibi for the 4th of May. But before dealing with the events of that evening, Grinnell went back to the Black Road episode. He accused Spies of acting "unmanly," of provoking a mob to "rush on McCormick's." These were not the tactics advocated by legitimate trade-union leaders. They wanted eight hours, "but Spies is not anxious for eight hours," Grinnell charged. "We will prove that in this case." The prosecutor pressed home the attack. Referring to Spies's participation in the Black Road episode, Grinnell charged:

> If the laboring men—if the bosses and employers in the city of Chicago on the 1st day of May had universally acceded to the eight-hour project, Spies was a dead duck; they would have had no further use for him,

and he didn't want it. Therefore he went down there
and exasperated the people, and he made a speech. The
police didn't come on the ground until after McCormick's was attacked, and until after stones and bombs
were used, or pistols and lead against McCormick's factory. What does Spies do, this redoubtable knight? He
runs away and gets home just as soon as he can.

Turning to the immediate background of the Haymarket
incident, the state's attorney characterized the "Revenge"
circular that Spies then wrote in its German original as constituting "not only treason and Anarchy but a bid to bloodshed and a bid to war." The inflammatory handbill was followed up by the appearance in the *Arbeiter-Zeitung* of the
code letter "Y," which to the conspirators meant: "Come
Monday night." In this way the anarchists got in contact
with their special armed cell. Meeting on Monday evening
in a dingy basement beneath a saloon, Fischer, Lingg, Engel,
and other conspirators agreed on the word *"Ruhe"* as a code
for "war." That word, Grinnell charged, actually did appear
in the *Arbeiter-Zeitung* on Tuesday morning, "and in a
double lead, with an emphasis under it, before it, and behind
it." Lingg, the bomb-maker, then agreed to manufacture the
bombs. Engel was the brains behind the master plan.

Now, gentlemen, just look at this plan, and this is the
plan that Engel told them should be performed. They
were to get these bombs; certain of them were to be at
the Haymarket Square, where this meeting was; and in
this meeting, mind you, in this conspiracy meeting the
program was that there should be at least twenty-five
thousand laboring men present; that they would not
hold the meeting down on the square, but that they
would get up in the street, because they were out in a
great open place there, the police could come down on
them and clean them all out; but they must get back
where the alleys were, instead of holding the meeting
down here where it was advertised. You see there are

two blocks here. Instead of holding the meeting on this broad spot here [indicating on the map], they were to hold it up here; and that very thing was discussed down there that night in the conspiracy meeting, as to the feasibility of holding it here where the police could corner them. Then these individuals with the bombs were to distribute themselves in different parts of the city. They were to destroy the station houses; they were to throw bombs at every patrol wagon that they saw going toward the Haymarket Square with police officers. They expected there would be a row down there at the Haymarket Square, of course. There was going to be one bomb thrown there at least, and perhaps more, and that would call the police down; but the police must be taken care of and must not be permitted to go, and they were to be destroyed, absolutely wiped off from the earth by bombs in other parts of the city.

So much for the conspiracy. But the indictment was for murder, and the actual murderer was not named. This blatant fact was carefully skirted by the state's attorney. "It is not necessary in a case of this kind," he argued, "that the individual who commits the exact and particular offense —for instance, the man who threw the bomb—should be in court at all." He need not even be indicted. Once it was ascertained that a murder had been committed, the question for the jury to determine, Grinnell pointed out, was "not only who did it, but *who is responsible for it, who abetted it, assisted it, or encouraged it.*" Perhaps none of these men personally threw the bomb, Grinnell generously conceded, but it would be proved that "each and all abetted, encouraged and advised the throwing of it, and therefore are as guilty as the individual who in fact threw it. They are accessories."

Such was the state's case, but as the people's evidence was unrolled, it soon became clear that Grinnell had been over-optimistic in describing the proof in his possession. The

prosecutor was to discover that it was a lot easier to establish the existence of a widespread anarchist conspiracy on
the eve of the Haymarket tragedy than to demonstrate that
the defendants were accessories to the murder of Patrolman
Degan.

The state's chief witness to the "Monday night conspiracy" was Gottfried Waller, who escaped trial by turning
state's evidence. A savage cross-examination revealing suspiciously intimate relations between Waller and the police
in the days right after the bomb-throwing could not efface
the damning effect of the informer's testimony. As soon as
the trial was over, Waller discreetly left for Hamburg, bury-
ing his past under an assumed name.

Waller had documented the conspiracy, but failed to name
the actual bomb-thrower. The state now called to the stand
its most sensational witness, Harry L. Gilmer, who had
stopped at the Haymarket meeting about a quarter to ten
on his way home. Fortuitously, just as the police moved in,
Gilmer saw a man step down from the speaker's wagon and
join a small group standing on the south side of the alley.
This man held the bomb while Spies, in Gilmer's story under
oath, supplied the match with which the fuse was lit. Then
the man took two steps forward and tossed the bomb into
the street. Who was the bomb-thrower? Shown a photograph of Rudolph Schnaubelt, a fugitive from justice, he un-
hesitatingly identified him as the culprit. In his court testimony he described the bomb-thrower as being five feet ten
inches in height, perhaps one hundred and eighty pounds in
weight, with a light sandy beard. But according to a *Chicago Times* reporter, Gilmer had given him a significantly
different description on May 5, the very day after the
bomb-throwing, when his recollection should still have been
quite sharp. At that time he depicted him as being of medium height, with whiskers and a soft slouch hat, "but his
back was turned to me." It is also significant that in his
account to the reporter he had maintained that the man
who threw the bomb also lit the fuse. It was not too diffi-

cult to discredit Gilmer. His statement that Spies lit the bomb was never corroborated, but thirteen witnesses agreed that Spies did *not* leave the wagon until some time after the police arrived and that he did *not* enter the alley. The state's character witnesses were tepid in their support of Gilmer, but nine of his neighbors or acquaintances appearing as witnesses for the defense did not hesitate to label him a notorious liar. Nevertheless, Gilmer's testimony was corroborated in part by M. M. Thompson, who claimed that prior to the meeting he had seen Spies pass something to another man who bore a likeness to a photo of Schnaubelt. But this evidence stood in direct contradiction to other testimony for the state.

William Seliger, who turned state's evidence, then put the finger on Louis Lingg, his tenant, charging that Lingg, together with the witness and three other German comrades, had manufactured bombs in considerable quantity, and that they were placed in the passageway of a saloon, whence some ten persons had procured infernal weapons. The state now put on the stand scientific experts who testified that similar metal was used in the Haymarket bomb and in Lingg's homemade explosives that the police had succeeded in running down. A fuse and fulminating cap were also found in the pocket of Fischer's coat at the time of his arrest. This evidence served to connect Lingg with the crime even though it was definitely established that the bombmaker was nowhere near Haymarket Square the night of the tragedy.

In short, there seemed little doubt by the time the state had completed its case that the defendants had advocated resort to dynamiting and had arranged to have bombs manufactured. Theodore Fricke, business superintendent of the *Arbeiter-Zeitung*, testified that he had seen Johann Most's inflammatory pamphlet *Science of Revolutionary War* in the building of the anarchist newspaper, and was present when it was sold at anarchist picnics and at meetings at which Spies, Parsons, and Fielden were present. When de-

fense counsel Black objected to this line of inquiry, Judge
Gary replied in prejudicial vein: "If men are teaching the
public how to commit murder, it is admissible to prove it if
it can be proved by items." Predicting that such explosives
would "form a decisive element in the next epoch of the
world's history," the author of that fantastic literary effort
explicitly instructed social revolutionaries in the way to
manufacture a bomb.

To show that the anarchists had edited and distributed
literature advocating bomb-throwing was a task less than
Herculean. But, in view of the difficulty in pinning the crime
on any one of the prisoners, the specific advice of the
Arbeiter-Zeitung, under date of March 16, 1885, now took
on sinister overtones. *"Has the deed been completed,"* that
frenetic organ counseled, *"then the group of action dissolves
at once according to an understanding which must be had
beforehand, leaves the place of action, and scatters in all directions."* How perfect, if unintended, a description of what
may have happened at the old Haymarket!

With a judicious mixture of logical analysis and character
annihilation the defense set to work to dampen the flames
of prejudice that threatened to sweep all before them. "Mr.
Grinnell," Salomon asserted in opening for the prisoners,
"failed to state to you that he had a person by whom he
could prove who threw the bomb, and he never expected to
make this proof until he found that without this proof he
was unable to maintain this prosecution against these defendants; and it was as this case neared the prosecution
end of it that the State suddenly changed front and produced *a professional tramp* and *a professional liar,* as we
will show you, to prove that one of these defendants was
connected with the throwing of it. . . . We do not intend to
defend against Socialism; we do not intend to defend
against Anarchism," Salomon shrewdly concluded. "We expect to be held responsible for that only which we have
done, and to be held in the manner pointed out by law."

The defense fired its heaviest gun at the outset. Mayor

Carter E. Harrison, who was present during the first part
of the Haymarket meeting, related on direct examination
that he found the meeting lacking in inflammatory character. He testified:

I did in fact take no action at the meeting about dis-
persing it. There were occasional replies from the audience, as "Shoot him!" "Hang him!" or the like, but I
don't think from the directions in which they came,
here and there and around, that there were more than
two or three hundred actual sympathizers with the
speakers. Several times cries of "Hang him!" would
come from a boy in the outskirts, and the crowd would
laugh. I felt that the majority of the crowd were idle
spectators, and the replies nearly as much what might
be called "guying" as absolute applause. Some of the
replies were evidently bitter; they came from immediately around the stand. The audience numbered from
800 to 1,000 people. The people in attendance, so far as
I could see during the half hour before the speaking
commenced, were apparently laborers or mechanics,
and the majority of them not English-speaking people,
mostly Germans. There was no suggestion made by
either of the speakers looking toward calling for the
immediate use of force or violence towards any person that night; if there had been, I should have dis-
persed them at once. After I came back from the
station [house, where he had reported to Captain Bon-
field] Parsons was still speaking, but evidently approaching a close. It was becoming cloudy and looked
like threatening rain, and I thought the thing was about
over. There was not one-fourth of the crowd that had
been there during the evening, listening to the speakers
at that time. In the crowd I heard a great many Germans use expressions of their being dissatisfied with
bringing them there for this speaking. When I went to
the station during Parsons' speech, I stated to Captain

Bonfield that I thought the speeches were about over;
that nothing had occurred yet, or looked likely to occur,
to require interference, and that he had better issue
orders to his reserves at the other stations to go home.
Bonfield replied that he had reached the same conclusion from reports brought to him, but he thought it
would be best to retain the men in the station until the
meeting broke up, and then referred to a rumor that he
had heard that night, which he thought would make it
necessary for him to keep his men there, which I concurred in. During my attendance at the meeting I saw
no weapons at all upon any person.

As the mayor left in the middle of Parsons's talk, it was
necessary for the defense to piece together a connected account of the entire meeting from other testimony. A travel-
ing salesman named Barton Simonson told how the unfavorable weather virtually broke up the assemblage, that some
in the crowd had shouted: "Let's adjourn," to which Fielden
replied that since he was about through, there was no need
to adjourn. In other words, according to the defense story,
the meeting was about over when the police poured into
the square. Right before the bomb went off, Simonson distinctly heard words coming from the vicinity of the wagon
which sounded like "peaceable meeting." The clue to just
why the police found it necessary to break up a meeting
that was below average in inflammatory content and virtually at an end may be found in Simonson's reported conversation with Captain Bonfield at the stationhouse just before
the Haymarket speeches:

> I asked him about the trouble in the southwestern
> part of the city. He says, "The trouble there is that
> these"—whether he used the word "Socialists" or
> "strikers" I don't know—"get their women and chil-
> dren mixed up with them and around them and in front
> of them, and we can't get at them. I would like to get
> three thousand of them in a crowd without their women

and children"—and, to the best of my recollection, he added, *"and I will make short work of them."*

Cross-examination failed to shake Simonson's story or his insistence that he "did not see a single shot fired from the crowd on either side of the street." In answer to a prosecution query as to his present employment, he replied laconically: *"My firm discharged me."* Both sides rested.

The closing arguments dragged through nine oppressively stifling August days. The people's summation was begun by Assistant State's Attorney Walker, who instructed the jury that under the laws of the state of Illinois the accessory to a murder is as guilty as the principal and that the conspiracy statute was ample to hold every one of these defendants —"even if they number three thousand"—guilty of the murder of Mathias Degan. Zeisler, in closing for the prisoners, hammered away at the fact that it was "not only necessary to establish that the defendants were parties to a conspiracy, but it is also necessary to show that *somebody who was a party to that conspiracy had committed an act in pursuance of that conspiracy.* Besides that, it is essential that the State should identify the principal." If the principal could not be identified, then no one could be held as accessory. Upon this theory, argued Zeisler, "the case must stand or fall," and it was for this reason, he frankly admitted, that the defense was compelled to impeach the testimony of Harry Gilmer, whose evidence was crucial for the people's case. Ridiculing the notion that a social revolution could have been inaugurated by the homemade bombs produced by Lingg, Zeisler concluded on a note of outraged indignation. He could not bear to see the accused convicted upon testimony "like that of Harry L. Gilmer. . . . I am now exhausted. I can do no more." Nevertheless, in his closing remarks he warned the jury against Ingham's probable arguments: "Do not allow yourselves to be deceived by declamation. Analyze the facts. The prosecution want you to believe that Schnaubelt threw the bomb, and that Spies and Fischer assisted him, and that the others were in the conspiracy. Either you believe Gilmer or you must acquit the defendants. There can be no middle ground. *Unless Schnaubelt is the principal and the others are his accessories, you must acquit these men!"* Do not compromise. If need be, "sit there until doomsday."

To Ingham, summing up for the people, Zeisler's logic was about as palatable as nicotine sulphate is to an aphid. He preferred a flagrant appeal to the passions of the jury to a cold analysis of his adversary's contentions. "Have you ever read any of the writings of the Communists of France," he asked, "the men who substituted a prostitute for the image of the Virgin Mary and made the streets of Paris run with blood? These defendants have the same literary style." Leaving the bloodshed of *l'année terrible* that France would never forget, he came back to the state's case. How about Gilmer's credibility? Ingham's prejudicial argument completely evaded the real issue: was Gilmer lying?

> An attack was made upon Gilmer, and witnesses were brought to asperse his character who were busy putting up their cent per cent shanties while he was bearing his breast to the bullets of the enemies of his country under the glorious Stars and Stripes. Fielden and Parsons often said that they would like to take the black flag and march up and down the avenues of the city and strike terror to the hearts of the capitalists. Why did they choose the black flag? The flag which represents their principles is the flag of the pirate, which now and always meant, "no quarter"; a flag that means, for men, death; for childhood, mutilation; for women, rape. That was the flag under which the defendants marched. Between them and Gilmer I would not hesitate for an instant.

Ingham's rabble-rousing seemed to unbalance William Perkins Black. Speaking last for the prisoners, he imprudently chose to match passion with passion. With cutting sarcasm he pointed out that so long as the mayor was at the Haymarket meeting, Bonfield could not act, but no sooner was Harrison's back turned than the police officer showed that he could not get to the square quickly enough. Whereas Foster had been careful to repudiate the defendants' utterances and to base his plea on the lack of evidence to link them with the bomb-throwing, Black, with reckless courage but poor judgment, now uttered a declamation in defense of terrorism which seemed to be directed more to appeasing his clients than to persuading the jury. "Jesus, the great Socialist of Judea," he told the jury, "first preached the socialism taught by Spies and his other modern apostles. John Brown and his attack on Harper's Ferry may be compared to the Socialists' attack on modern evils. Gentlemen, the last words for these eight lives. They are in your hands, with no power to whom you are answerable but God and history, and I say to you in closing only the words of that Divine Socialist: 'As ye would that others should do to you, do you even so to them.' "

State's Attorney Grinnell's closing argument stands as a classic example of how to prejudice a jury by a judicious sprinkling of substantive matters not in evidence, misstatements of issues, abusiveness to the defendants, and inflammatory appeals to the passions of the jury:

GRINNELL: The proof has been submitted; everything has been done for the defense that could be done. Gentlemen, it is time in all conscience that you did have a judgment; and if you have now prejudice against the defendants under the law as the Court will give it to you, you have a right to have it. Prejudice! Men, organized assassins, can preach murder in our city for years; you deliberately under your oaths hear the proof, and then say that you have no prejudice!

BLACK: If the Court please, I desire to note an exception to what seems to me an offense against propriety in the course of this argument. In the position that he occupies I do not think it is proper that he should speak of these defendants, the men of whose guilt is the question under consideration, as he has done now, as assassins, and I desire to note an exception to the use of such a term.

THE COURT: Very well, save the point upon it.

Black's exception was thoroughly justified, as it is improper and highly prejudicial for a prosecutor to stigmatize the defendant.

GRINNELL: Before I proceed further in the discussion of this case I wish to suggest to you something that may be in some measure personal to the prosecution, not in the way of apology. We stand here, gentlemen, as I told you yesterday, already with the verdict in our favor. I mean in favor of the prosecution as to the conduct of this case, but if it had not been for the testimony of Gilmer what would the defense have done in this case?

BLACK: If the court please, I desire to note an exception to that statement by the State's Attorney—the statement that there has been given a verdict already in favor of the prosecution.

THE COURT: Save the point upon it.

BLACK: It is an outrageous statement.

Ridiculing Black's portrait of the prisoners as humanitarians, Grinnell attacked furiously. "Don't try, gentlemen," he warned, "to shirk the issue. Law is on trial. Anarchy is on trial. The defendants are on trial for treason and murder."

BLACK: The indictment does not charge treason; does it, Mr. Grinnell?

GRINNELL: No, sir. I will make a suggestion to you, gentlemen, upon that. Under the laws of this State, if an individual is guilty of treason his punishment is death. Punishment for the offense of treason, under the laws of this State, is death. There is no mitigation, no palliation, no chance for the jury to hedge on the offense. For that offense you cannot say that this man shall have a few years in the penitentiary, and that one a few more, and that one shall suffer the extreme penalty of death. No; it is death. But treason, gentlemen, can only be committed by a citizen. You and I can commit treason. None of these defendants except Parsons and Neebe, according to the statement of Mr. Foster, can commit treason under the laws. Why? Because they are none of them citizens.

Grinnell had covered up his prejudicial injection of an issue which was not on trial by a flagrant appeal to nativist feeling. He was now ready to conclude his summation to the jury:

> You stand between the living and the dead. You stand between law and violated law. Do your duty courageously, even if that duty is an unpleasant and a severe one. Gentlemen, I thank you most sincerely for the kind attention you have given to me these many hours.

Whatever slim chances the defendants may have had for an acquittal or at least a hung jury vanished utterly when Judge Gary instructed the jury. On all the principal points of law at issue he ruled for the people. His definition of the crime of conspiracy was so broad that even though some of the defendants were not present when the crime was committed and the actual murderer remained unidentified, they could be found guilty of murder. As one penetrating commentator on the trial has observed, the question of how an unknown person may be shown *"beyond a reasonable doubt"* to be a member of a conspiracy makes "fascinating speculation." But the court went a good deal farther and instructed the jury that if any two or more of the defendants had conspired together to excite the people to sedition, tumult, or riot, and in furtherance of such objectives any of those so conspiring had advised publicly in print or speech the commission of murder, without designating time, place, or occasion at which it should be done, or if as a result of such encouragement a murder was committed, then all such conspirators were guilty of murder.

In three hours the jury reached a unanimous decision. At ten o'clock the morning of August 20 the foreman reported the verdict:

> We the jury find the defendants, Adolph Spies, Michael Schwab, Samuel Fielden, Albert R. Parsons, Adolph Fischer, George Engel, and Louis Lingg guilty of murder in the manner and form as charged in the indictment, and fix the penalty at death. We find the defendant Oscar E. Neebe guilty of murder in the manner and form as charged in the indictment, and fix the penalty at imprisonment in the penitentiary for fifteen years.

Even the state's attorney had considered the case against Neebe extremely shaky and would have dismissed it had his staff not insisted that such an action would have an injurious effect on the case against the other prisoners. For the evidence against Oscar Neebe had merely revealed that he had a copy of the "Revenge" circular in his possession, was a member of the anarchist group, and had collected in his home some firearms and a red flag, which a search without warrant a few days after the Haymarket incident had brought to light.

Despite the fear of the police that the announcement of the verdict would set off a hostile demonstration, the Chicago anarchists seemed strangely subdued. Outside the Criminal Court building a huge crowd cheered the verdict, and their spontaneous reaction was shared by the American press. The *Chicago Tribune* commented in an optimistic vein that "the verdict of the Chicago jury will check the emigration of organized assassins in this country." "They will have all the rope they want, and more, too," was the caption under a characteristic Nast cartoon in *Harper's Weekly,* showing seven nooses dangling from a stark scaffold labeled "The Law."

Nobody was the least surprised when Judge Gary denied a motion for a new trial. Before sentencing the prisoners he asked them whether they had "reasons why sentence should not be pronounced." Standard practice in criminal trials, this invitation provided these professional fire-eaters with a forum for their philosophy. Speaking first and interminably, Spies denied categorically that he and his comrades had anything to do with the bomb-throwing. "Before this court and before the public which is supposed to be the State, I charge the State's Attorney and Bonfield with the heinous conspiracy to commit murder." For the latter he reserved his most sulphurous epithets, stigmatizing the police officer as "the man who would bring a blush of shame to the managers of the Bartholomew night," "the illustrious gentleman with a visage that would have done excellent service to Doré in portraying Dante's fiends of hell." For a brief moment, when Spies was able to transcend his personal plight, his remarks constituted a heroic defiance of the social order:

If you think that by hanging us you can stamp out the labor movement—the movement from which the downtrodden millions, the millions who toil and live in want and misery—the wage slaves—expect salvation— if this is your opinion, then hang us! Here you will tread upon a spark, but there, and there, and behind you and in front of you, and everywhere, flames will blaze up. It is a subterranean fire. You cannot put it out. The ground is on fire upon which you stand. You can't understand it. You don't believe in magical arts, as your grandfathers did, who burned witches at the stake, but you do believe in conspiracies; you believe that all these occurrences of late are the work of conspirators! You resemble the child that is looking for his picture behind the mirror. What you see and what you try to grasp is nothing but the deceptive reflex of the stings of your bad conscience. You want to "stamp out

the conspirators"—the agitators? Ah! stamp out every
factory lord who has grown wealthy upon the unpaid
labor of his employees. Stamp out every landlord who
has amassed fortunes from the rent of over-burdened
workingmen and farmers. Stamp out every machine
that is revolutionizing industry and agriculture, that
intensifies the production, ruins the producer, that
increases the national wealth, while the creator of
all these things stands amidst them, tantalized with
hunger! Stamp out the railroads, the telegraph, the telephone, steam and yourselves—for everything breathes
the revolutionary spirit. You, gentlemen, are the revo-
lutionists. You rebel against the effects of social conditions which have tossed you, by the fair hand of fortune, into a magnificent paradise. Without inquiring,
you imagine that no one else has a right in that place.
You insist that you are the chosen ones, the sole proprietors. The forces that tossed you into the paradise,
the industrial forces, are still at work. They are growing more active and intense from day to day. Their
tendency is to elevate all mankind to the same level, to
have all humanity share in the paradise you now monopolize. You, in your blindness, think you can stop the
tidal wave of civilization and human emancipation by
placing a few policemen, a few Gatling guns, and some
regiments of militia on the shore—you think you can
frighten the rising waves back into the unfathomable
depths whence they have arisen, by erecting a few
gallows in the perspective. You, who oppose the
natural course of things, you are the real revolution-
ists. You and you alone are the conspirators and de-
structionists!

"Call your hangman!" he concluded. "Truth crucified in
Socrates, in Christ, in Giordano Bruno, in Huss, in Galileo,
still lives—they and others whose number is legion have
preceded us on this path. We are ready to follow."

In its icy logic Oscar Neebe's attack seemed unanswerable:

> They found a revolver in my house, and a red flag
> there. I organized trades unions. I was for reduction of
> the hours of labor, and the education of laboring men,
> and the re-establishment of the *Arbeiter-Zeitung*—the
> workingmen's newspaper. There is no evidence to show
> that I was connected with the bomb-throwing, or that
> I was near it, or anything of that kind. So I am only
> sorry, your Honor—that is, if you can stop it or help
> it, I will ask you to do it—that is to hang me, too; for
> I think it is more honorable to die suddenly than to be
> killed by inches. I have a family and children; and if
> they know their father is dead, they will bury him.
> They can go to the grave, and kneel down by the side of
> it; but they can't go to the penitentiary and see their
> father, who was convicted for a crime that he hasn't
> had anything to do with. That is all I have got to say.
> Your honor, I am sorry I am not to be hung with the
> rest of the men.

There was something refreshing about Louis Lingg's brazen defiance:

> I tell you frankly and openly, I am for force. I have
> already told Captain Schaack, "If they use cannon
> against us, we shall use dynamite against them." I re-
> peat that I am the enemy of the "order" of today, and I
> repeat that, with all my powers so long as breath re-
> mains in me, I shall combat it. I declare again, frankly
> and openly, that I am in favor of using force. You
> laugh! Perhaps you think, "You'll throw no more
> bombs," but let me assure you that I die happy on the
> gallows, so confident am I that the hundreds and thou-
> sands to whom I have spoken will remember my words;
> and when you shall have hanged us, then, mark my

words, they will do the bomb-throwing! In this hope do
I say to you! "I despise you. I despise your order, your
laws, your force-propped authority." Hang me for it!

Speaking last and longest, Parsons launched into a savage
attack on the prejudicial atmosphere in which the case
against him was conducted, and insisted that he and the
other accused men had not received a fair trial.

You ask me why sentence of death should not be pronounced upon me, or what is tantamount to the same
thing, you ask me why you should give me a new trial
in order that I might establish my innocence and the
ends of justice be subserved. I answer you and say that
this verdict is the verdict of passion, born in passion,
nurtured in passion, and is the sum total of the organized passion of the city of Chicago. For this reason I
ask your suspension of the sentence, and a new trial.
This is one among the many reasons which I hope to
present before I conclude. Now, what is passion? Passion is the suspension of reason; in a mob upon the
streets, in the broils of the saloon, in the quarrel on the
sidewalk, where men throw aside their reason and resort to feelings of exasperation, we have passion. There
is a suspension of the elements of judgment, of calm-
ness, of discrimination requisite to arrive at the truth
and the establishment of justice. I hold that you cannot dispute the charge which I make, that this trial has
been submerged, immersed in passion from its inception
to its close, and even to this hour, standing here upon
the scaffold as I do, with the hangman awaiting me
with his halter, there are those who claim to represent
public sentiment in this city—and I now speak of the
capitalistic press, that vile and infamous organ of monopoly, of hired liars, the people's oppressor—even to
this day these papers, standing where I do, with my
seven condemned colleagues, are clamoring for our

blood in the heat ·and violence of passion. Who can deny this? Certainly not this Court. The court is fully aware of these facts.

Moving off comparatively solid ground, Parsons slipped easily into the quicksands of the philosophy of violence. It takes money to buy Winchester rifles, he argued, and workers do not have that kind of money. But the dynamite bomb costs six cents as against eighteen dollars for the Winchester rifle. That is the difference. Gunpowder, he continued in a historical résumé, came as a democratic instrument, and today it comes "as the emancipator of man from the domination and enslavement of his fellow man." Force, he argued, is the law of the universe, "and this newly discovered force makes all men equal." A later generation in the atomic age would find much the same arguments persuading a Klaus Fuchs and the Rosenbergs. "I have nothing, even now, to regret," Parsons asserted.

The last anarchist had spoken. In sentencing the prisoners Judge Gary felt it incumbent on him to expose them to a lecture on the American way of life:

> I am quite well aware that what you have said, although addressed to me, has been said to the world; yet nothing has been said which weakens the force of the proof, or the conclusions therefrom upon which the verdict is based.
>
> The people of this country love their institutions. They love their property. They will never consent that by violence and murder their institutions shall be broken down, their homes despoiled, and their property destroyed. And the people are strong enough to protect and sustain their institutions and to punish all offenders against their laws. And those who threaten danger to civil society if the law is enforced are leading to destruction whoever may attempt to execute such threats.
>
> It only remains that for the crime you have committed—and of which you have been convicted after a

trial unexampled in the patience with which an outraged people have extended you every protection and
privilege of the law which you derided and defied—the
sentence of that law be now given. In substance and
effect it is that the defendant Neebe be imprisoned in
the State Penitentiary at Joliet at hard labor for the
term of fifteen years.

And that each of the other defendants, between the
hours of ten o'clock in the forenoon and two o'clock in
the afternoon of the third day of December next, in the
manner provided by the statute of this State, be hung
by the neck until he is dead. Remove the prisoners.

Judge Gary's final words precipitated an epochal fight to
save the lives of the eight anarcho-communists. Black took
the case to the Illinois Supreme Court, where it was argued
in March 1887. His cogent reasoning suggested certain alternative hypotheses to explain the bomb-throwing:

The instructions embody the erroneous rulings which
were applied to the introduction of evidence. They permit the finding of these men guilty, when for aught that
appears in this record, your Honors upon your consciences will be compelled to say that the bomb may
have been thrown by somebody in no way connected
with these defendants, directly or indirectly. It may
have been done by an enemy of theirs. It may have
been done by some man acting upon his own mere
malice and ill-will. It was thrown outside of the purpose
of the Haymarket meeting. It was thrown in disregard
of the arrangement and understanding for that meeting.
It was thrown to the overthrow of the labor and the
effort that these men were then giving their lives to,
namely, the establishment of the eight-hour day. It
brought to an end their efforts. It disappointed their
hopes. It was not of their devising. The records show it.

The record fails to show who threw that bomb. And
the question is, whether upon the barbaric *lex talionis*

that whenever a man was slain a man of the opposing
faction must be slain, these seven men shall die, because seven policemen, whom they did not like as a
class, and who certainly did not love them, have died?
You know the barbarians never stopped to fix individual responsibility for the crime. They simply said:
"One of ours is dead, and we cannot rest until one of
theirs die for him!" It has been so here.

His argument fell on deaf ears. On September 14 the conviction was affirmed, Chief Justice Magruder delivering the
opinion of the court. The defense forces were then strengthened by the addition of John Randolph Tucker, who had
served as Attorney General of Virginia during the Confederacy and was a leading constitutional lawyer; Roger A.
Pryor, an ex-Confederate brigadier general, who was a
prominent member of the New York bar; and that consummate Yankee politician Benjamin F. Butler, who had won
the undying hatred of Southerners by his implacable administration of military affairs in the conquered city of New
Orleans. Having made suitable obeisance to North and
South, the defense felt prepared to carry the fight to the
Supreme Court, but Chief Justice Waite failed to find that
a Federal issue had been raised.

Now upon the shoulders of Governor Oglesby rested the
final decision, and during the fall of 1887 he was deluged
with petitions inspired by such public figures as William
Dean Howells and Henry Demarest Lloyd to commute the
death sentences. Even Spies, Schwab, and Fielden, chicken-
hearted in the end, addressed a statement of penitence to the
Governor, in which they declared, hypocritically, that "if,
in the excitement of propagating our views, we were led
into expressions which caused workingmen to think that
aggressive force was a proper instrument of reform, we regret it." Later, to clear his name among the comrades of any
imputation of acting the renegade, Spies asked the Governor
to take his life and let the other prisoners go. But there was

a solid core of resistance to mitigating the punishment. "It was to the common interest of all Americans that the Chicago dynamiters be hung," Theodore Roosevelt shouted from out west, and tycoons like Marshall Field made no bones about their opposition to clemency. To add to the travails of the prisoners, four tiny dynamite bombs were found in Lingg's cell on November 6. Parsons screamed: "It is a mare's nest, a canard, a put-up job to create a sensation and manufacture public prejudice! The story is too thin! It won't wash!" But Parsons talked just once too often, for three days later Lingg blew off the lower half of his face with a small bomb, apparently smuggled to him at the last moment. He died six hours later.

Oglesby's announcement was anticlimactic. He commuted to life imprisonment the sentences of Fielden and Schwab, but refused to intervene for the four remaining prisoners. At eleven thirty on the morning of November 11, 1887 the trap was sprung. Spies's last words were meant to be prophetic: "There will come a time when our silence will be more powerful than the voices you strangle today!"

In 1892 a political overturn in Illinois placed a Democrat in the gubernatorial chair. John Peter Altgeld, a courageous reformer, was far more receptive to petitions for pardon than his predecessor, Governor Fifer. "If I decide they were innocent I will pardon them, by God, no matter what happens to my career!" Altgeld declared. His pardon message, eighteen thousand words in length, in which he freed Fielden, Neebe, and Schwab, proved dynamite, in its content as explosive as the bomb hurled six years earlier in Haymarket Square. Altgeld charged that all eight had been railroaded, that the jury had been packed, and the judge's instructions improper. Referring to the accusations that "the judge conducted the trial with malicious ferocity" and that "such ferocity of subserviency is without parallel in all history," Altgeld found them sustained by the trial record and other documents submitted to him. In short, concluded the Governor, *the trial was not fair.*"

Seldom has any political figure in American history been subjected to the storm of abuse that now buffeted Altgeld. In an apostrophe "To Anarchy," the New York *Sun* closed on this hysterical note:

> *O wild Chicago, when the time*
> *Is ripe for ruin's deeds,*
> *When constitutions, courts, and laws*
> *Go down midst crashing creeds,*
> *Lift up your weak and guilty hands*
> *From out of the wreck of States,*
> *And as the crumbling towers fall down*
> *Write* ALTGELD *on your gates!*

Defeated when he ran for re-election, Altgeld, the honest liberal, was the most tragic victim of the Haymarket bomb-throwing, while the miserable wretches who were the beneficiaries of his amnesty went into well-deserved obscurity.

If you happen to be in Union Park at the north end of "Labor Row" in Chicago, you may want to visit the monument by Johannes Gelert commemorating the policemen who lost their lives in the Haymarket Riot. But out in the suburbs, in Forest Park, that community of the quick and the dead, another bronze monument, about the same size and equally expensive, stands in Waldheim Cemetery. The sculptor, Albert Weiner, cast a bronze figure of Justice crowning a dying worker with a laurel wreath, and inscribed to the men hanged for the Haymarket Riot. Here memorial services for Engel, Fischer, Parsons, and Spies are observed every year.

And that is all that is left of the Haymarket affair. Even the old site has disappeared. But every so often some old-time radical politician after a few beers at a Montparnasse café gets confidential and asserts that he knew for a fact that Schnaubelt, the permanent fugitive from American justice, or perhaps some other psychotic firebrand, really threw the bomb. But of proof there is none. Sixty-six years is a long time, and nobody really cares any more.

Morally, the Haymarket prisoners did not come into

court with clean hands. They may not have perpetrated the crime for which they were convicted, but the probabilities are very strong that the bomb was thrown by a member of their anarcho-communist group. In fact, unless their whole previous careers amounted to a living lie, the prisoners should have exulted in the deed. That was not enough to convict them, however; regardless of how foul a prisoner's political or moral creed may be, he still is entitled in an American court to a fair and impartial trial.

And this the eight Chicago anarchists most certainly did not receive.

XI

The Case of the Morphine Murder

*wherein a glass-eyed corpse confounds the
Philadelphia expert*

Invariably when a person is convicted of a capital crime on
circumstantial evidence alone, a substantial segment of the
public can be counted on to cry out: "Unfair!" Since juries
reflect such emotional attitudes, they are likely to prove
obstinate and unreasonable in the face of damning evidence
and to give the accused the benefit of every doubt, no matter how slim. An outstanding example is close to home.
Consider the case of Benjamin Feldman, the Brooklyn druggist, acquitted in 1949 in his third trial for fatally poisoning
his wife by strychnine. On their deathbeds both his wife
and his mother-in-law, who had predeceased her, frantically pleaded: "Don't touch my feet!" The characteristics
of strychnine poisoning were clearly indicated in each case.
But the jury was not convinced beyond a reasonable doubt
that the prescription the druggist had handed to a nurse to
administer to his wife contained the fatal dose of strychnine.
The cold fact is that one who premeditates murder is hardly
likely to make advance arrangements for witnesses to be
present at the moment of the crime.

In the days before scientific methods were applied to
crime detection such reluctance to condemn on circumstantial evidence had a considerable measure of justification.
But there is far less justification for it at the present time.
In the century between the anatomical reconstruction of
Dr. Parkman's skeleton and the positive identification of
the wood in the ladder used in kidnapping the Lindbergh
baby impressive strides have been taken in scientific crimi-
nology.

Of all categories of murderers, the principal beneficiaries

of the notorious reluctance of jurors to convict on circumstantial evidence have been poisoners. In earlier times, when post-mortem examination of corpses was forbidden, poisoners plied their craft with little fear of detection. The introduction of the practice of performing autopsies where deaths occurred under suspicious circumstances merely challenged the ingenuity of latter-day Borgias. Arsenic, white, soluble, and virtually tasteless, was the readiest poison at hand, as it was easily procured for the ostensible purpose of killing rats. Even after the discovery in 1836 of the Marsh test for its detection, arsenic still headed the list of preferred poisons, though it was being constantly pressed by such rivals as aconitine, belladonna, chloroform, strychnine, morphine, and the cyanides. Poisoners continued to calculate their chances of escaping detection, and found them good. They counted on the fact that, despite advances in chemistry and forensic medicine, the crime of poisoning still remains difficult to prove. It is a rare occasion when scientific evidence can conclusively establish whether or not a lethal dose was self-administered. Furthermore, on casual diagnosis the symptoms induced by most poisons can easily be mistaken for other diseases. No one knows this better than a pharmacist, a physician—or a medical student.

The poisoner of Helen Potts Harris gambled that both or either of these difficulties would be sufficient to save him from the chair. And had it not been for a devastating piece of cross-examination which the prosecution's extraordinary grasp of medical information made possible, he would have gone free. Numerous poisoning trials in American criminal history preceded the Carlyle Harris case, and still more were to follow. Back in 1832 Lucretia Chapman, enamored of a visiting Spaniard, went on trial for feeding her husband arsenic in his gruel. Elaborate testimony was then admitted by the court revealing contemporary techniques for detecting that particular poison. Modern methods for analyzing strychnine were demonstrated in the trial of George C. Hersey at Dedham in 1867 for the murder of his fiancée. In fact, when the Harris case broke, the American public had scarcely recovered from the sensational trial in Boston of Sarah Jane Robinson, a systematic poisoner, who murdered for insurance. But no previous murder case had involved such complicated toxicological evidence, and few cases showed more thorough mastery by both sides of medical and scientific data. In his long experience in criminal cases Judge Smyth, who presided over this trial, observed that he had never seen better preparation. In fact, the Carlyle Harris case was par excellence a trial by experts.

Now, if there is any one type of witness of which jurors are normally suspicious it is the expert. Persons in that category have come to be regarded as either masters of equivocation, skilled in using obscure and misleading phrases, or downright perjurers who will take either side for a fee and the attendant publicity. To laymen one of the most baffling phases of expert testimony is the fact that so often experts squarely contradict one another on simple matters of fact falling directly within their field of experience. Medical testimony offers innumerable examples where experts have slugged it out in the courtroom. In fact, some authorities in forensic medicine insist that the expert should not sit on the fence, that he should take a categorical position. Such counsel not only is unrealistic, but, if literally followed, is likely to impale the expert on the horns of an ethical dilemma. The medical facts are not infrequently highly complex, and inferences are expected to be drawn from isolated cases. In poisoning, it is one matter to isolate and identify the poison employed; it is quite another to state categorically that the particular poison may or may not have caused death. An honest expert may prefer one theory but recognize that another may be equally feasible. The incompetent or conscienceless "expert" is often the one who is most glib and dogmatic. Unfortunately, the fact that the experts are chosen by the parties, makes them assume the role of advocates, and the result is confusion compounded. For instance, a few years after the Harris case the most eminent authorities in England on the subject of poisons took the stand in the trial of a former medical man named Palmer, accused of murdering his friend by strychnine. These experts then proceeded to disagree completely on whether or not strychnine leaves traces in the body. While such disagreements have served to bring expert testimony into disrepute, they are life-sustaining to the accused, the case against whom must be proved beyond a reasonable doubt.

To understand why Carlyle Harris became one of the most notorious poisoners of his generation it is necessary to move back in time to a winter's night in the year 1889. Three thousand people had braved the icy blasts to jam the Metropolitan Opera House in New York City to capacity. The attraction: a well-known temperance lecturer who wrote under the name of Hope Ledyard. Her subject was "How to Bring Up Children." In an appropriate introduction the presiding officer pointed out that no one was better qualified than the lecturer of the evening to talk on the subject, in view of the "lovely family" she herself had raised. One of the members of that adorable family who was in the audience that evening was the speaker's son, Carlyle W. Harris, who, in scarcely three years, was to be electrocuted for having committed one of the foulest murders in the annals of the state. The fate of Hope Ledyard's son served to confirm the public's suspicion that child-guidance experts were immensely competent in the rearing of all children except their own.

Hope and her son spent the summer of '89 at Ocean Grove, a New Jersey seaside resort. At the Coleman House Ball, the big event of the summer, held at near-by Asbury Park, they met pretty Helen Potts and her family. Helen, a sweet, eighteen-year-old, fell in love at first sight. Carlyle Harris was a handsome lad, three years her senior, who had just finished his first year at the College of Physicians and Surgeons in New York after trying his hand at bookselling and at acting with a professional troupe. To an artless girl like Helen, Carlyle had glamour and sophistication. Unfortunately for her life expectancy, the object of her love did not share his mother's strong moral views. A late Victorian, he was in fact a throwback to the Restoration era. Brought up in the home of a teetotaler, he had not the slightest aversion to alcoholic beverages. During one summer at Asbury Park he had spent a night in the lockup for running a blind pig, disguised as the Neptune Club. For his type each generation has its own characterization—a Don Juan, a sheik, a wolf. All would aptly fit this *jeune homme fatal*. Puzzled though we remain about his motivations at times, we are certain about one thing: toward females Carlyle Harris's intentions were strictly dishonorable.

Once when a Scranton friend had plied him with sufficient liquor, Harris explained his technique. He never had any difficulty in persuading a girl to go to bed with him, he boasted. His almost infallible formula was a bottle of ginger ale heavily loaded with whisky. But he admitted that this did not prove effective on two occasions.

"What did you do in those two cases?" his friend asked.

"On those two occasions I married the girl, but married her under assumed names."

The latter course seemed the only alternative open to Carlyle Harris in his heady courtship of Helen Potts. Reared in a strict moral atmosphere, daughter of a middle-class family that had never even visited a theater, Helen was determined to get her man but to keep her virtue. Whether or not Helen's mother, who engaged a flat in New York that fall, suspected Harris's real intentions is not clear, but she soon found it necessary to caution him against too frequent visits at her home, and then, some months later, in January 1890, to tell him point-blank: "You cannot be engaged to my daughter. She is fond of you, but you are as yet only a medical student, and in your second year at college. Both families could not but be averse to any engagement under such circumstances."

Harris moved fast. On February 8 he persuaded Mrs.

Potts to allow him to take Helen down to the Stock Exchange, where his brother, McCready, was employed. But McCready never met the couple that day, for the nearest they got to Broad and Wall Streets was the City Hall, where Alderman Rinckhoff married them under false names. Carlyle used the name of Charles. Helen was married under the name of Helen Neilson, her middle name. They returned home with a graphic account of a mildly bearish setback on the Exchange that day, which they probably learned from newspaper accounts. But of the marriage not a word was said to Mrs. Potts.

Having accomplished his objective, Harris's ardor soon waned. His calls on the Pottses' household were now irregular and widely spaced. As Harris's passion cooled, Helen wilted rapidly. Feeling that a change of scene might perk her daughter up, Mrs. Potts took Helen back to Ocean Grove. But there was one obstacle to continued secrecy of the marriage relationship, a secrecy deemed so vital by Carlyle Harris. Helen was pregnant. One night Harris bungled an attempt to perform an abortion. Disturbed by her daughter's ailing health, Mrs. Potts sent the girl off to her uncle, a physician in Scranton named Dr. Treverton, who quickly diagnosed the cause of her nausea and listlessness. When Helen confided in him, he summoned Harris, but that scoundrel denied the legality of their marriage and declared that he was in fact secretly married to someone else. The name of this other woman never was revealed. Dr. Treverton then decided that there was no alternative but to perform an abortion, which he did with the assistance of another local physician.

The scene now shifts from Scranton, Pennsylvania, to Canandaigua, New York, where a stunning-looking young woman of easy virtue was having an assignation with Harris while she was stopping as a guest at the home of some respectable friends, a Mr. and Mrs. Latham. Their suspicions finally aroused, the Lathams entered her bedroom one evening without knocking and at an embarrassing moment. But before interrupting the couple and sending Harris packing, they had overheard a conversation with sinister overtones. The man who had once boasted that he never "got in any scrape" he could not get himself out of was overheard telling his paramour that he didn't have a nickel and that the best thing for her to do would be to marry some rich old man. She was quoted later as having asked: "How will that help if I get married?"

Harris's reply: "Oh, that will be all right. I can easily fix that. I'll mix him a pill and get him out of the way at short notice."

The casualness of this observation doubtless weighed heavily in the balance against Harris in the minds of twelve jurors whom he had never anticipated meeting under such fateful circumstances.

Back in New York City, Harris was obsessed with the need for keeping his marriage to Helen Potts a secret. Helen's mother, once she was informed of the true relationship between the couple, was equally determined to make the wedding legal. In the presence of his attorney she demanded that he produce the wedding certificate. Harris admitted that he had burned it, but his lawyer agreed to send over to the Health Department for a copy. When it was produced, it was found to have been issued under false names. "I thought that we might get tired of one another," Harris explained to his mother-in-law, "and if we were married under false names we could some day drop the whole matter and nobody would be the wiser."

Mrs. Potts was properly indignant. "With my daughter! You were going to drop the whole matter, and nobody would be the wiser!"

Finally, under pressure from his own lawyer, Harris signed an affidavit affirming his marriage, which was given to Mrs. Potts along with a copy of the marriage certificate. Then Harris escorted his mother-in-law to the ferry and exacted a promise from her that she would send Helen to the fashionable Comstock School for Young Ladies, then

situated opposite the reservoir on the present site of the
Public Library on Fifth Avenue. Harris was now under
some strange compulsion to have Helen return to the city,
where she could be under his surveillance. In one letter he
wrote to her: "For God's sake, do as I say in this matter,
and go to that school." But when Helen complied, Carlyle
showed her that his affections had completely cooled. In
desperation, her mother wrote to him on January 15, 1891,
urging that on the *8th of February*, the anniversary of the
secret marriage, the couple be married "in a Christian way."
On January 20, Harris replied: "All your wishes shall be
complied with *provided no other way can be found of satisfying your scruples.*"

For Harris little time remained. It so happened that during
that same month he was attending Dr. George L. Pea-
body's lectures at the medical school, and that, coincidentally, the eminent pathologist was holding forth on the toxi-
cology and pharmacology of morphine. Accordingly, when,
on January 20, Harris walked into Ewen McIntyre's drugstore and handed the clerk a prescription that he took from
his pocket, he was well posted on morphine dosages and the
physiological effects of that drug. His prescription provided
for twenty-seven grains of quinine and one grain of morphine and was to be made into six capsules, one sixth of a
grain of morphine and four and a half grains of quinine in
each capsule. Two days later he gave these capsules to
Helen when she complained of a headache. He instructed
her to take one each night. The very next day he took a
steamer for Old Point Comfort.

Obedient and trusting, Helen did exactly what her medi-
cal-student spouse had told her. But the effects were dis-
turbing. She wrote to him at Old Point Comfort: "I have
taken one of your pills. They do not help me. Your remedy
is worse than the disease." He replied: *"Try another."* She
took a second and a third and then stopped. On Carlyle's
return from Virginia on January 31, he persuaded her to
take the fourth and last capsule in the box. Helen retired

at about ten o'clock that night. At ten thirty she was
awakened by her three roommates, who had just come in.
She is reported to have exclaimed: "Girls, I have had such
a beautiful dream. I could dream on forever. I have been
dreaming of Carl." But before the girls had turned in for
the night, she remarked: "I feel numb all over. I feel so
queer, girls, I wish you would come and see what is the
matter with me." Within an hour Helen was in a profound
coma, from which she could not be aroused. Around midnight Dr. Fowler was called in. By that time he observed
that she had lost complete control of her muscles and was
not only totally unconscious but completely comatose, and
the pupils of her eyes were *symmetrically* contracted. Her
face was blue, her body bathed in a cold sweat. Calling in
a Dr. Bauer, Dr. Fowler tried everything—digitalis, atro-
pine, strong black coffee, and, as her breathing almost
ceased, artificial respiration.

For five hours the two physicians worked over this unconscious girl. A search of her room quickly revealed the
pill box carrying a label with the initials "C. W. H., student—one before retiring." "Send for this man," Fowler requested; "there is some terrible mistake here." Harris arrived at six and explained that each capsule contained a
sixth of a grain of morphine and four and a half grains of
quinine. "One sixth of a grain of morphine never caused the
condition there is here. There is some terrible mistake,"
Fowler insisted, and demanded that Harris go back to the
druggist to check the prescription.

But here is where the murderer made his first fatal slip.
An innocent man would have frantically asked the druggist:
"What have you put in those pills? The lady I gave them
to is dying." Instead, Harris, calm and completely self-
possessed, merely asked the clerk to read him the prescription from his record book. Harris wrote it down in his own
notebook, commented: "Ever so much obliged," and left.
That was all! When he was told by the physicians that his
wife was dying of morphine poisoning, his only reaction was

to ask whether he personally would be liable. When informed that she had died, he exclaimed: "Great God, what will become of me?"

Then the murderer made his second mistake. That afternoon, when interrogated by the coroner, he produced one of the capsules that he had prescribed for her, commenting: "There were six of them. I kept two out. Here is one of them, and here is the box they were in. You can take that one. You will find it right."

This action served as the main link in the chain of circumstantial evidence soon to be forged against Carlyle Harris. It was to be the contention of the prosecution that he had taken out two of the capsules in order to protect himself if any suspicion attached to him afterward. Then he unloaded one of the remaining four capsules and substituted three grains of morphine for the quinine in it. When Carlyle kept persuading Helen to take more capsules, he could not have known which of the four contained the lethal dose, as quinine and morphine in capsule form resemble each other very closely. But once she had taken three, it became a certainty. Harris's filling out the prescription was no casual act. The day after Helen's death he remarked to a classmate at the medical school: "How fortunate it was that I signed myself 'student' at the end of it!" When he was asked to explain himself, he added that if he had signed himself "M.D.," which he was not, he might have got "into trouble." Now he was in the clear.

Harris prudently absented himself from the funeral of Helen Potts, who was buried in New Jersey. Had not the suspicions of the New York *World* been aroused by the peculiar circumstances of her death and its reportorial bloodhounds been unleashed to track down clues, this might have been the perfect murder that Harris had planned it to be. But it did not take the *World* long to unearth evidence of the secret City Hall marriage. In fact, so thorough was the *World's* detective work that the district attorney's preliminary tasks were comparatively simple. An autopsy, fifty-six days after Helen's death, disclosed in the stomach the presence of morphine but *not* of quinine, supporting the state's theory that morphine had been substituted for the contents of the quinine capsule.

Carlyle Harris's trial, held in the old Court of General Sessions in January 1892, had to compete in public favor with Adelina Patti, who was then giving sensational performances at the Metropolitan, and Mme Modjeska, who was playing to packed houses in *Countess Roudine* at the Union Square Theater. But thousands fought with police to get into the courtroom every day of the three-week period the trial consumed. Many brought along their lunches in order not to have to yield their places during the noon recess.

Presiding over the trial was Recorder Frederick Smyth, dreaded by underworld habitués for his severe sentences. As one Irish wit at the New York bar put it, "There's Smyth—he is a good judge, a foine judge, but he thinks ivery man ought to go to prison at least wance." The trial rapidly developed into a personal duel between Francis L. Wellman, then a talented assistant district attorney, short and stout, affecting the fashionable Kaiser Wilhelm mustache, and tall, tense, bespectacled William Travers Jerome, still a fledgling at the bar, but headed for a career as one of the city's most brilliant prosecutors. The wearisome labor of picking a jury consumed three days. Significantly, only two bachelors were chosen. The trial bristled with exceptions and wrangling, and the judge's patience was at the breaking-point on many occasions. Once when Jerome accused Wellman of advising a state's witness who was an embalmer to "work the testimony about the embalming fluid for all it's worth," Wellman shouted: "That's a God damned lie!" Recorder Smyth chose that moment to leave the room rather than permit the dignity of the bench to become further ruffled. Betting was even, a *Herald* reporter stated, that there was going to be a fight.

From Wellman's opening to the jury it was clear that the

state would rest its case on circumstantial evidence. Before
the jurors' eyes, strands of suspicious circumstance were
woven into a rope that gradually tightened around the prisoner's neck. With hand lifted and index finger pointed ac-
cusingly at the prisoner, Wellman hammered home each
damning fact:

In closing this case it will be for you and me, gentlemen, to clear the atmosphere and to try, through the
doubts raised by the defense, to get at the real truth of
the matter and mete out justice to this defendant.

The questions you must bear in mind are these: Did
Helen Potts commit suicide? Why, she was happy. She
was in love with this prisoner. She was well. Her mother
will tell you that she was very happy that day, and had
been all along. Her roommates will tell you she was
both happy and contented. Miss Day, who spent the
last evening with her, will tell you that she was well,
happy, in a peaceful frame of mind and contented.
Had she any cause to commit suicide? Had she the
means of committing suicide? Was there any drug
found in her bedroom but this one box marked
"C. W. H."?

Was it the "druggist's awful mistake"? The analysis
of the remaining capsule, the care with which it was
compounded, and its having been checked by a second
clerk when the morphine was first weighed out—all
will bear you evidence that it was not the druggist's
mistake.

What did Helen die of? Natural causes or disease?
The autopsy shows a perfectly healthy body. All the
doctors agree morphine caused the death, and that three
grains had been taken.

The last and important question is, Who administered the poison? I ask you, who had a motive to do it?
Who said he "would kill her before the marriage should
be made public"? Was the marriage about to be con-

summated by a Church marriage? Was Harris tired of
his secret wife? Had he neglected her? Was he faithful
to her, or did he want to get rid of her? Did he, as he
said to Miss Schofield, "wish she were dead," and he
"were well out of it," or, as he wrote to Mrs. Potts, had
he "found some other means of satisfying her scruples"?

Those, gentlemen, are the questions that you are to
keep constantly before you in this case. If, in the end,
nothing succeeds in convincing you of this man's guilt,
in God's name let not the innocent suffer. But if, on the
other hand, all the facts and all the circumstances satisfy your minds of his guilt, then the best interests of
society *demand* his conviction.

From the beginning to the end of the trial, the morphine
capsules kept on bobbing up. Jerome went to Ewen Mc-
Intyre's drugstore and ordered some capsules like those
which Harris had procured. Coming up to the judge's railing, the defense attorney then apologized for "invading the
sacred precincts." He had with him an old-fashioned druggist's scale with horn cups suspended from a crossbeam by
cords. Driving a nail into the railing at the corner, he hung
the scales on it. During this piece of carpentry some good-
natured badinage was exchanged by counsel:

WELLMAN: What have you there? Howe's scales?

JEROME: No, druggist's scales. Don't you know the
difference?

WELLMAN: Are you going to weigh yourself?

JEROME: Well, I'm not going to weigh you. You're too
big for Howe scales.

WELLMAN: Why don't you get a pair of hay scales?

The scales finally arranged, Jerome asked a pharmacist
witness to fill the cup nearest him with five grains of quinine. Wellman kept up a cross-fire of objections during
this operation. Then Jerome had the witness remove the

weight and place morphine in the other cup until it bal-
.anced the quinine. Objection was made to the use of morphine crystals, but finally the weighing was accomplished.
Jerome had succeeded in demonstrating that the crystal-
lized morphine was half the bulk of the quinine. Then he
carried his scales over to his table and dropped them with
an air of triumph.

"Thus far I am more than satisfied," Carlyle Harris told
a *World* reporter that afternoon.

But the major engagement of the experts had barely begun. For several days all eyes in the courtroom had been
riveted on a short, rotund, bald-pated gentleman, with
thick pince-nez and whiskers arranged after the manner of
the Poughkeepsie Smith brothers. This was Professor Rudolph A. Witthaus, of the New York University medical
staff, who was known to be the star expert for the prosecution. Quietly, without warning, and in the most unconcerned
manner, Wellman said simply: "Now, Professor Witthaus."
A buzz ran from one end of the courtroom to the other as
Wellman's major witness took the stand. The professor followed up a lengthy explanation of laboratory procedures
with these answers:

Q.: Now, then, as a result of your analysis, did the
stomach, contents and membrane contain morphine?

A.: They did.

Q.: Did the intestines contain morphine?

A.: They did.

Q.: Did the stomach and the membrane contain quinine?

A.: No, they did not.

Q.: Did the intestines contain quinine?

A.: They did not.

Q.: Is quinine as stable as morphine?

A.: It is.

Q.: If quinine had been taken in the same quantity as
the morphine, would you expect to find it?

A.: I would.

Q.: If twenty-five to thirty times as much quinine had been taken as of morphine, what would you expect to find?

A.: Certainly I would expect to find the quinine certainly as readily, or more readily, than I did the morphine.

This was the climactic point toward which Wellman had been skillfully maneuvering the state's circumstantial case, and William Travers Jerome cross-examined the professor relentlessly for eight hours without eliciting any more than a repetition of his statements on the direct examination. Even if his tenacity proved futile, Jerome in this exchange with the expert had demonstrated an amazing capacity for digesting and mastering scientific data far outside the field of the law.

The defense rested entirely on the testimony of medical experts who sought to cast doubt on the prosecution's theory that morphine was the cause of death. After eliminating such natural causes as heart disease, brain tumor, apoplexy, and epilepsy, the defense narrowed the causes of death down to two—morphine poisoning and uremic poisoning. If we assume, the defense argued, that the deceased had a latent kidney disease, would it not be likely that such a condition would have been aggravated by small doses of morphine? Would not such a dosage as the sixth of a grain admittedly contained in Harris's capsules have induced uremic coma and ultimately caused the death of Helen Potts? Was not there as much likelihood that hers was the coma of kidney disease as of morphine poisoning? All that the defense needed to do was establish that *one or the other* diagnosis might have been *equally correct* in order to raise a reasonable doubt in the minds of the jury. Carlyle Harris might then have walked out of the courtroom a free man. Because of this conflict of the experts over a crucial issue, "nine out of ten think the jury will disagree," a *World* reporter commented at this stage of the trial.

To scuttle the hypothesis that morphine poisoning was the only possible cause of Helen's death, the defense brought from Philadelphia Dr. Horatio C. Wood, a nationally known expert on the subject of uremic poisoning. Of all the authorities quoted by the defense, Dr. Wood had been the only one whose eminence was recognized by experts for both sides. Each expert had agreed that there was no abler diagnostician than Dr. Wood. When the physician took the stand, the spectators saw a stocky, stoutish man, with iron-gray beard and thick iron-gray hair that stood out from his head as if in indignant protest against comb and brush. He proceeded to speak in a hesitant manner—the kind of witness who calculates the effect his answer will have on the case and weighs his reply accordingly. His answer to Jerome's climactic question closed the direct examination:

Q.: Now, doctor, I want to put to you a hypothetical question, put by the District Attorney to some gentlemen who were called, some scientific men who were called here to testify as to their opinion, excluding from the question by Mr. Wellman results said to have been obtained from such autopsy and examination as I have described. Doctor, in your opinion as a scientific man, assuming those facts in the hypothetical case to be true, as stated in that question, can you state, or can medical science state, from what the girl died?

A.: I should be unable to state, sir. My own belief is that in the present state of medical science no accurate opinion could be passed upon [the cause of her death]. The symptoms are compatible with various conditions other than that of morphine poisoning.

This was the turning-point of the trial. Dr. Wood had made a profound impression on judge and jury alike. A flush of color stole into Harris's white face, and his mother beamed upon the jurors. Wellman, commenting later on his own handling of the cross-examination of this crucial witness, stated that he "sparred for an opening with the determination to strike quickly and to sit down if he got in

one telling blow." How well he succeeded is borne out by the
stenographic report of the testimony at this point:

Q.: You live in Philadelphia?

A.: Yes, sir. I always have except when I was in the
army.

Q.: Are we to understand you as swearing that Miss
Helen Potts did not die of morphine poisoning?

A.: I don't know, sir, what you understand. I don't
swear to that.

Q.: Do you swear what she died of?

A.: I don't swear what she died of.

Q.: I understood you to say that it was your opinion
that the symptoms of morphine poisoning could not be
sworn to with positiveness. Is that correct?

A.: I said nothing of the sort, sir. I don't think it can
be done with positiveness.

Q.: Have you never diagnosed a case of morphine poisoning except where you have had an autopsy?

A.: I have. I have always had a history.

Q.: Do you wish to go out to the world as saying you
have never diagnosed a case of morphine poisoning excepting where you have had an autopsy?

A.: I do not. I have not said so.

Q.: Then you have diagnosed a case on the symptoms?
Answer yes or no. I want a categorical answer: Have you
diagnosed a case of morphine poisoning on the symptoms
alone?

A.: I would say that that question could not be answered categorically, because the word "diagnosed" is used
with two different meanings. When a doctor is called to a
case he has to make what is known as a working diagnosis;
but that diagnosis is never—I wouldn't say never—but
often not a positive diagnosis. It is really a suspicion, or
may be a suspicion upon which he acts. I can't remember at
present having ever made such a diagnosis as this without
a history, because I don't remember a case of morphine poi-

soning in which no history was given, and as in the case
which I narrated a while ago, when the diagnosis was made
as it proved to be, on a false history, I made a false working
diagnosis, which was corrected by the post-mortem.

Q.: When was your last case of opium poisoning—just
the name of it?

A.: The name of the person?

Q.: Well, you can state the fact if you don't want to
give the name. I don't mean to ask any improper questions,
you understand.

A.: I can't remember which was the last. I think the
last was a case some years ago. I have had no recent case of
severe opium poisoning.

Q.: How many years ago?

A.: (hesitating) It may be eight or ten years ago.

Q.: Was it a case of opium poisoning?

A.: Morphine poisoning.

Q.: Was there an autopsy?

A.: No, sir.

Q.: How did you know it was a death from morphine
poisoning if, as you said before, such symptoms cannot be
distinguished?

A.: I found out from the apothecary that the woman
had taken seven grains of morphine.

Q.: And before you knew she had taken morphine you
didn't know what was the trouble?

A.: I simply didn't know when I first commenced. It
was a case where I simply knew what was to be done. I
didn't stop to make a diagnosis.

Q.: You made no diagnosis at all?

A.: I made what I call a working diagnosis.

Q.: What did you do?

A.: I put the woman down and commenced artificial
respiration.

Q.: Well, you would do that with morphine poisoning,
wouldn't you?

A.: I certainly should.

Q.: That was about eight years ago. Do you remember the case you had before that?

A.: I remember another case.

Q.: When was that?

A.: That was a still longer time. I guess probably twenty years ago.

Q.: And that was the next case before this?

A.: No, I don't say that.

Q.: Well, give me the next case before this one. You had a case eight years ago. Now when was the next one? One case twenty years ago?

A.: I remember another case probably between those. I don't know the date.

Q.: About how many years ago?

A.: Fifteen probably.

Q.: Did you know then what the person had taken?

A.: Yes, I knew what the person had taken, to the best of my memory.

Q.: You had a case twenty years ago and you knew what was taken then?

A.: Yes.

Q.: So that within twenty years you can remember three cases you have had of morphine poisoning, can you?

A.: Opium poisoning. Yes, sir.

Q.: Was there more than one of those three cases that was morphine poisoning?

A.: No, sir. One was with Dover's powder.

Q.: Then you have had one case of morphine poisoning in the last twenty years?

A.: (very subdued and obviously uncomfortable) One case that I distinctly remember. Yes, sir.

Q.: And are you willing to come here from Philadelphia and state that the New York doctors who have gone on the stand for the People and who attended this patient, and who said that they had attended *seventy-five* similar cases, and were constantly having them—and who testified as a

XI *The Case of the Morphine Murder* 351

matter of fact that this was a case of morphine poisoning—
that they had seen the patient and had treated her—will
you say with one experience in twenty years, come here and
say that you don't believe that they can tell what they saw
or what she died of?

A.: Yes, sir. Only I deny part of the statement.

Q.: Now, you state, do you not, that the symptoms of
morphine poisoning could not be told with positiveness?

A.: Yes, sir.

Q.: That that was your best opinion, based upon your
reading and upon your own experience, your own experience in twenty years being confined to one case. Is your
reading confined to your own book?

A.: No, sir. I say no.

Q.: But I suppose you embodied in your own book the
results of your reading, didn't you?

A.: I tried to, sir.

Q.: Allow me to read to you from page 166: (reading)
"I have thought that inequality of the pupils"—that is
where they are not symmetrically contracted—"I have
thought that inequality of the pupils is proof that a case is
not one of narcotism; but Professor Taylor has recorded a
case of opium poisoning in which it occurred." *So that until
you heard of the case that Professor Taylor had reported in
which inequality of the pupils occurred, your opinion up to
that time was that it [asymmetrical contraction of the pu-
pils] never had occurred?*

A.: (extremely agitated) Yes, sir.

Q.: (very loudly) Well, sir, did you investigate that
case far enough to discover that Professor Taylor's patient
had *one glass eye?*

A.: I have no memory of it.

Q.: Well that has been proven here to be the case. You
would better go back to Philadelphia, sir."

The witness, in the words of one newspaperman, "hurried
away from the witness stand with that pained expression

sometimes visible in the face of a picnicker who has sat on
an anthill." He looked almost as small, according to another observer, "as one of the brain hemorrhages which he
had testified had caused death." Perhaps the best comment
on his performance was made by the Philadelphia expert
himself when he later remarked that he had "gone to New
York only to make a fool of myself and return home again."

To catch the witness in this fateful slip the prosecution
had examined the reports of six thousand cases of morphine
poisoning, including the case of the glass-eyed patient reported by Professor Taylor. As the attending physicians
had stated that the pupils of the eyes of Helen Potts were
contracted to a pin-point and *symmetrically* so—an invariable symptom in coma from morphine poisoning and distinguished from coma of kidney disease, where the pupils
would be *asymmetrical* (one dilated, the other contracted)
—the defense never recovered from the body blow dealt its
chief expert. Only a few moments after this debacle, Jerome,
whose nerves were not equal to the strain, broke down in
the midst of cross-examining an expert for the state, shouting: "I can't go on with the case. I—my mind—I won't go
on!" The recorder adjourned the trial until the following
Monday, when Jerome's associate, John A. Taylor, who was
more at home at a literary tea than in a sordid criminal
trial, advanced some highly ingenious but implausible arguments to take the minds of the jurors off the dramatic
events of the previous session.

Francis Wellman's closing address bolted the death-cell
doors behind the defendant. He reminded the jury of Victor
Hugo's account of the octopus, that eight-armed cepha-
lopod, described as having the "aspect of scurvy and gangrene." To protect itself this "devil fish" shoots out onto
the surface of the water a dark fluid from its "ink bag" and
then seeks escape in the darkness. That is exactly what the
defense had been doing, Wellman contended. But the prosecution, through a proper combination of common sense,
sound reasoning, and true evidence, was seeking to clear

these blackened waters and bring the retreating octopus
back for punishment. Actually, this huge mass of testimony,
he then told the jury, can be reduced to two main questions:
"Did Helen Potts, into whose death we are inquiring, die
from natural causes, or was she taken off by the foul means
of poison, and, if the latter proposition be sanctified by the
evidence, then comes the important question: Was the prisoner at the bar the author of her death?" Wellman proceeded to confine his arguments to these two lines of inquiry:

It is alleged by the prosecution that Helen Potts died
by morphine poison. Does the defense deny it? Who has
gone on the witness stand and said that she did not die
of morphine poison? Indeed, reference was even made
here by the counsel for the defense to the fact that the
Coroner's jury, made up of distinguished physicians,
after hearing evidence in this case, had decided that
Helen Potts did die of morphine poisoning, and of
nothing else; and at this trial they have brought no
one here to deny this assertion of the People. They have
simply tried to befog the minds of the jury; they have
tried to raise a "reasonable doubt." They have tried to
use their "ink bag" by bringing doctors here who
should state that it was not "certain," that it was not
"absolutely sure" (that is the form in which they put
their questions to the physicians), that she died of
morphine poisoning. What else could she die of? Gentlemen, do you remember the first day or two of this
trial, when Dr. Fowler was on the stand and was being
cross-examined? At that time Helen Potts apparently
had all the diseases known to medicine. It was epilepsy,
it was most likely heart disease, it was a brain tumor,
it was apoplexy, it was kidney disease. Finally, they
concluded to drop one after the other of these diseases,
until now it is no longer an "idiosyncrasy for morphine," it is no longer the possible fatal effects of a

small dose of morphine, but it is either a minute, infinitesimal hemorrhage of the pons,[1] so small that the naked eye could not discover it at the autopsy, or else it is a latent disease of the kidneys, so latent that the naked eye could not observe it after death. And they ask you on these mere suppositions and without any proof to set this man free!

Recognizing the irrational character of Harris's motivation—to preserve the secrecy of his marriage—Wellman shrewdly pointed out that what would be a motive to such "a blatant libertine" might "well be no motive, thank God, to you or me." Reporters at the trial were profoundly impressed by Wellman's peroration, which had been suggested by that shady shyster William F. Howe, who, in a purely disinterested spirit, had a habit of counseling his friends in the district attorney's office about ways of convicting other lawyers' clients. Howe advised Wellman to take the jury on a rhetorical tour to the grave "of this poor poisoned girl," that he then turn to Harris and shout: "You dare not go to that spot. You put her there, she whom you swore to love, cherish, and protect, and you would hear through the sod which covers her remains the cry of 'MURDERER! MURDERER!'" Wellman followed Howe's broad outline, adding some embellishments of his own. It was pure corn, but effective.

I well remember once seeing an old engraving, an English picture, which represented the first trial by jury. The twelve men were assembled in the open field, no house inclosed them. It was a murder trial, but it was far different from this murder trial, for here we have the accused and his family and friends sitting about him and appealing to you for your sympathy. There the jury were collected on the commission of the crime, and at their very feet lay the body of the dead.

[1] Nerve fibers of the brain at the anterior end of the medulla oblongata.

One relative of the deceased was bending over the lifeless form, her locks falling upon his face as her tears fell in her agony of grief. A male relative stood over the prostrate form pointing with one hand to the accused and with the other to the gaping wound through which the life tide had gone. That was an ancient trial by jury, and here, in closing this trial, I ask you to remember the dead. I ask you to go with me to that lonely churchyard, and stand for a moment with me by the grave of this unfortunate girl. Let us there with bared heads, say a few words in praise of her innocent young life—she who had a right to live for years in this garden of God's beauty, suddenly taken off and hurled into eternity. Let us write an epitaph on her tomb. *"Murdered innocence."*

Would to God, gentlemen, we could call her back. Would to God we could bring her back to life once more and could put her loving hand in his, and send them out into the bright world *forgiven,* wiser and better for this sad experience, to live their lives together as man and wife, according to God's holy ordinance. But it is too late. She has gone. Her lovely spirit has left the earth. The die is cast. A terrible doom has settled over this defendant. And we can now only listen to the command of the great Jehovah, *"Whosoever sheddeth man's blood by man shall his blood be shed!"*

Judge Smyth quite correctly charged the jury that circumstantial evidence is legal evidence. If all the circumstances point toward guilt, the judge instructed, the jury would be bound to regard such evidence, circumstantial though it be, in the same way they would consider direct or positive evidence. But if the facts were susceptible to two opposing interpretations, then in criminal cases the accused is entitled to receive the benefit of the more favorable construction. The record of the trial concludes:

THE COURT: Now, gentlemen, you may render any one

of these verdicts. Guilty of murder in the first degree, guilty
of murder in the second degree, guilty of manslaughter in
the first degree, guilty of manslaughter in the second degree,
or not guilty; any one of these verdicts which you believe
the evidence warrants.

The jury retired at 9.28 p.m.

At 10.48 p.m. the jury returned to court and stated that
they had found the defendant *guilty of murder in the first
degree*.

Harris, who never took the stand, accepted the verdict
with the same icy aplomb he had exhibited throughout the
trial. His mother fainted and had to be carried out, but the
son was imperturbable. "Got a match?" he asked, and
lighted another cigar. When he was arraigned at the bar
for sentencing, he listened politely to a savage castigation
of his moral character by the Recorder. In reviewing the
facts of the case, Smyth made some slight error in a date.

"Pardon me, your Honor," Harris interrupted, "it was the
eighteenth and not the nineteenth."

"That is a matter of slight importance!" the judge
brusquely replied.

"I beg your Honor's pardon," Harris retorted, "you see, I
have never been sentenced to death before, and am not as
familiar with the procedure as might be."

Despite the heroic labors of Jerome and Taylor on his
behalf, Harris was dissatisfied with his trial counsel and in
desperation turned to the notorious firm of Howe & Hummel
to handle his appeal. But the change of counsel brought no
change in his fortunes. The Court of Appeals unanimously
sustained the verdict. Judge John C. Gray, in an opinion
for the court, maintained that there was not a single fact in
the record "to help out the presumption of the defendant's
innocence." As they stood at the bar to hear the decision
of New York's highest court, Howe, who had become extremely fond of Harris, handed him a flask of whisky.

Harris in turn theatrically handed Howe an envelope containing a pair of diamond cuff-links, Helen's last present to him. "I am sure she would want you to have them," he said with pious hypocrisy. Howe could always be counted on to squeeze the last tear out of his auditors even if he had to carry half an onion inside a pocket handkerchief.

Howe and Hummel responded in characteristic fashion to aid that "noble and persecuted youth." From their own casting agency, aptly termed "a veritable cesspool of perjury," they came up with several persons who made perjured affidavits to the effect that Helen had been addicted to the use of morphine. But Recorder Smyth refused to reopen the case. Enough misguided sentiment had by now been whipped up in Harris's behalf to cause Governor Flower to appoint ex-Senator George Raines to take testimony to determine whether there was any reason for the exercise of executive clemency. But even more convincing testimony of Harris's guilt (including Helen's last statement to her friends) was admitted than at the original trial, and Flower very properly refused to intervene.

We should like to think that, lying in the death cell awaiting the Governor's decision, Harris, like Richard III, was haunted by his victim's ghost. But on the part of this inordinately egotistical exhibitionist there was never the slightest trace of remorse. On May 8, 1893 he walked calmly into the execution chamber, fixed his steel-blue eyes on the electric chair, and declared:

"I have no further motive for concealment, and I desire to state that I am absolutely innocent of the crime for which I am to be executed."

Then he was strapped into the chair, and the current was turned on.

XII

The Triangle Fire Case

triumph for perjury

A just verdict is one founded on the truth. When the facts at issue are either withheld or distorted, a fair trial cannot be had. The overzealous prosecutor who feeds a witness pat stories or improperly coaches him may, perhaps unwittingly, contribute to a miscarriage of justice. A more sinister obstruction to fair trial procedure is the not uncommon practice of bribing or threatening witnesses. The witness who unexpectedly proves uncooperative, refuses to repeat on the stand his pre-trial statements, or goes so far as to give the lie to his earlier accounts can unfairly trap the side that called him. The most flagrant recent example to come to mind is the case of Harry Gross, the Brooklyn bookmaker. Brazenly defying Judge Samuel Leibowitz, he refused to tell in court what he had told the grand jury about his illegal pay-offs to high police officials. The judicial threat that the balky witness would "rot in jail" for his criminal contempt failed to make him talk, and the state's case collapsed dramatically. Perhaps no trial better illustrates the way in which a combination of overcoached, if honest, witnesses and downright perjurers served to defeat the ends of justice than the Triangle fire case.

The story of the trial takes us back to the year 1911. It was the last Saturday in March. The time was a quarter to five. In the Triangle Waist Company, which occupied the three top floors of the Asch Building, a ten-story loft at Washington Place and Greene Street in lower Manhattan, the bell had just rung for "power off." Most of the girls working in this rush season had left the tables for the washrooms. Suddenly a fire was discovered in a rag bin between two cutting-tables on the Greene Street side, probably from a match or a lighted cigarette dropped by a cutter in some old waste. Some of the men tried to extinguish it with fire-pails, but the fire soon kindled the "stretches" of lawn laid out on the cutting-tables for Sunday work. Someone tried to use the stand-pipe hose in the hall, but the valve wheel would not turn. It was rusted, and the hose, wherever it was folded, was rotten.

On the street, a hundred feet below, a passer-by heard a sound "like a big puff," accompanied by smoke and flame and the crash of glass falling from the eighth-floor windows that had blown out. Almost immediately a sheet of flame poured out of the windows, and, as a fire-fighter described it, "veiled into the windows of the ninth and tenth floors as if drawn by a magnet."

For the six hundred Triangle employees it was now a question of getting out alive. A dozen workers on the eighth floor took to the fire escape, which ended five feet from the ground in a closed court, soon engulfed in flames. Unable to descend to the ground, they broke into windows on the sixth floor, where they were found later, bleeding and hysterical. Had all the employees tried to escape this way, it would have taken them three hours to make the descent, and most certainly the frail trellises would have collapsed under the weight.

On the Washington Place side the girls on the eighth floor rushed to the stairway exit door, only to find it locked. They screamed and beat on it with their fists, but they could not open it. Another door gave way, and more than two hundred panic-stricken girls threw themselves down the unlighted winding stairs. One of the girls fainted at the seventh floor, and a milling mass soon piled up on her. On the ninth floor the girls rushed madly for the elevators. One of the elevator men fled from his post in panic, but a passer-by ran the elevator for trip after trip, packing in twenty-five to thirty girls each time, until those above who could not wait any longer flung themselves down the shafts. Above one elevator on the Greene Street side nineteen bodies were

found. On the Washington Place side the elevator finally
gave way from the weight of screaming girls who hurled
themselves down on top of it. Others then slid down the
ropes. Many bodies were tightly wedged between the car
and the shaft. Fortunately, nearly all the workers on the
tenth floor escaped by using the Greene Street stairway to
the roof.

When the fire-trucks raised their extension ladders, they
found that they reached only to the sixth story. Then a
new fourteen-foot rope net was stretched. Three girls
jumped together from the ninth floor, and the firemen were
jerked headlong in upon their mangled bodies as the nets
broke under the impact, equal to sixteen tons. "Nobody
could hold a life net when those girls from the ninth floor
came down," Battalion Chief Worth later testified, adding:
"there were so many bodies hitting the ground that it was
impossible to see them. You did not see them. You heard
the impact of the bodies hitting the ground." Last to jump
were a man and a girl, both afire. Kissing each other ar-
dently, they entwined their arms about one another and
dropped deliberately off the ledge. At least fifty women and
girls died in such falls. Broken bodies littered the streets
and prevented fire-fighting apparatus from being maneu-
vered into position.

The tragedy consumed a mere ten minutes, but when the
total fatalities were finally compiled, they had reached the
appalling number of 146. Under a leaden sky, between pave-
ments lined with miles of open umbrellas like mourning
bands, fifty thousand persons marched in a five-hour-long
funeral procession in tribute to the victims. Bearing a banner with the legend: "We Mourn Our Loss," inscribed below a triangle, these workers and many who stood in tribute
along the line of march willingly gave up a day's pay to
honor the dead, who were buried in a common grave in the
cemetery of the Workmen's Circle.

The do-nothing Department of Buildings was at last
prodded into action. Two days after the fire that bureau

posted a notice on the door of the Asch Building declaring it unsafe. Singled out as violations of the law were the fire escapes, now warped and twisted iron, the doors of the elevator shafts, burned and charred wood, and the vault lights on Washington Place, shattered by the impact of falling bodies. It was another case of locking the door after the stable had burned down.

There had been warnings from responsible persons that such a disaster could be expected. For about a decade the sweatshop garment-manufacturers had been migrating from the East Side tenements to more respectable locations in the new skyscrapers that were then dotting the Manhattan landscape. Once the Department of Buildings had given its approval to these loft buildings, with their steel frames and masonry construction, originally designed as warehouses, it made no follow-up to check on the contents of the buildings and the uses to which they were put. Although the Fire Department had demonstrated that fire-fighters could not throw streams of water with any penetrating power above the seventh floor, and that extension ladders did not reach above that height, the Building Department allowed manufacturing to be carried on above that level. Many loft buildings, like the Asch, had no sprinkler systems. Their owners were willing to gamble. A typical floor in a garment-trade loft was littered with pasteboard boxes and rag bins. Shelves were stacked high with rolls of inflammable lawn, lace, muslin, and tissue paper. Bunches of paper patterns hung at the windows. Smoking was notorious among the cutters, but was winked at by the bosses for reasons of morale. Girls were seated at machines, back to back, packed on the floor.

Only a month before the fire, a Joint Board of Sanitary Control, representing the manufacturers, the unions, and the public, and including such representative citizens as William Jay Schieffelin, Henry Moskowitz, and Lillian Wald, had warned of fire hazards in an industry notorious for its unsanitary conditions, its overcrowding, its pollution of the air by the use of coal and gas irons, and its bad lighting. For a long time Fire Chief Croker had assumed a Cassandra-like role. But the manufacturers continued to get sizable fire insurance. It was not necessary for the policy-holders to commit deliberate arson, for these factories were like the "coffin" ships of an earlier day in England. The owner of the rotten hulk actually did nothing to sink her, but, as one old coast guardsman put it, "her'll go down, time enough, wi' the weight of her insurance, an' the things they ha' left undone."

The Triangle disaster was a shock to the city and the nation. At a huge protest meeting held at the Metropolitan Opera House the following week, a fiery redhead, Rose Schneiderman, an organizer for the shirtwaist workers, who, years later, was to help fashion Franklin D. Roosevelt's views on the trade-union movement, whipped the audience to fever pitch. Someone cried out from the gallery: "Why can't workingmen have their own legislators?" From the other side of the house came the cry: "Down with the capitalistic legislature!"

As is customary in all disasters, the public demanded a scapegoat, and Max Blanck and Isaac Harris, the factory-owners, exemplifying in themselves the popular conception of the sweatshop boss, seemed perfectly fitted for the role. In that city of almost five million souls it would have been hard indeed to have come up with a more dissembling pair of pious hypocrites. The Triangle factory had been notorious for its labor grievances. In the past, girls had been charged by the firm for needles, power, and supplies at a sizable profit to their employers and were even taxed for their chairs and for a locker in which to put away their hats. Fines imposed for goods spoiled were frequently treble the value of the actual damage. As early as 1908, Harris and Blanck had pioneered in setting up a company union known as the Triangle Employees Benevolent Association, but differences of opinion soon broke out between the members and the bosses. In the fall of 1909, Triangle employees met with officers of the shirtwaist-makers Local 25 of the International Ladies Garment Workers Union and the United Hebrew Trades in a room on Clinton Street, with shades drawn and doors bolted. The Triangle espionage demonstrated its efficacy by the dismissal a few days later of some union sympathizers on the pretext of lack of work. Since Triangle simultaneously advertised for other workers, Local 25 had no alternative but to call a strike on the ground that the firm had locked out its employees.

Within a few weeks the fighting spirit of the strikers was at the breaking-point. "Gorillas" had been hired to beat up the men pickets, and prostitutes had been stationed by the firm in front of the factory to waylay the women. Then Harris and Blanck proposed an employers' protective association to fight the union. Up to this point the strike had attracted little public sympathy, but when the president of the New York Women's Trade Union League was arrested for picketing the factory, the metropolitan press began to feature the strike. At a mass meeting in Cooper Union in November, the crowd of shirtwaist workers were stampeded into voting a general strike by the eloquence of Clara Lemlich, a young girl still in her teens. Two thousand hands were raised in prayer: "If I turn traitor to the cause I now pledge may this hand wither from the arm I now raise." But the police and the courts seemed in league with the strike-breakers. In sentencing one picket Magistrate Olmstead shouted: "You are on strike against God!" George Bernard Shaw cabled a characteristic retort: "DELIGHTFUL. MEDIEVAL AMERICA ALWAYS IN THE INTIMATE PERSONAL CONFIDENCE OF THE ALMIGHTY." At this point prominent women of affairs rushed in to the support of the striking girls, with a Hippodrome mass meeting in December sponsored by Mrs. O. H. P. Belmont, the banker's wife, Anne Morgan, J. P.'s sister, Elizabeth Marbury, and the Reverend John Howard Melish, rector of Holy Trinity Church in Brooklyn and more recently associated with less popular causes. As a result of this unexpectedly strong public support most manufacturers found it expedient to make a compromise settlement with the union, which amounted to a substantial victory for labor. But within the Triangle factory much bitterness survived. After the fire ugly rumors were afloat in the trade that the bosses had kept the doors locked not so much for fear of the girls' taking the firm's property with them on the way *out* as to keep labor agitators from getting *in*. This was never proved.

District Attorney Charles S. Whitman, who within a year was prodded into action by a *World* reporter, Herbert Bayard Swope, to break the vise of the underworld on the police system, was now goaded by an aroused citizenry to secure indictments against Blanck and Harris for the death of one of the shirtwaist workers, Margaret Schwartz. The charge was manslaughter in the first and second degrees. Up to this point Harris and Blanck had been extremely maladroit in their public relations, but they now revealed some of that innate shrewdness which had made them leading manufactures in their field. For counsel they turned to Max D. Steuer, shining light of the East Side bar, who accepted what seemed to everyone a thankless assignment.

Despite the lapse of nine months between the tragic fire and the start of the trial, public excitement had by no means abated. The scene of the trial was the old Criminal Courts Building known as the Tombs, a brownstone monstrosity in bastard Egyptian style, massive, dark and gloomy, with an air of grim portentousness suitable to the sordid business with which it was concerned. "Abandon hope, all ye who enter here," might well have been carved on its extravagantly thick walls, or, at least, "Be Sure to Get a Clever Lawyer." That latter injunction the defendants had scrupulously followed. When Harris and Blanck were brought to the building on the first day of the trial a hysterical mob waylaid them, holding up photos of deceased relatives and shouting: "Murderers! We want justice!" The trial in the Court of General Sessions was presided over by Justice Thomas T. C. Crain, a Tammany wheel horse; and the active conduct of the prosecution was entrusted by Whitman to Assistant District Attorneys Bostwick and Rubin.

From the state's opening it was evident that it intended to prove that the ninth-floor exit door on the Washington Place side was locked at the time of the fire and that this violation had been the direct cause of the death of one of the 146 victims, Margaret Schwartz. This was the nub of its case. A cavalcade of witnesses who took the stand for the state testified that they had never seen the door opened and were positive that nobody had ever been seen to pass through it. The most sensational witness on the first day of the trial was a seventeen-year-old-girl waist worker, Katie Weiner, who was dressed in deep mourning, with a big picture hat made out of black velvet adorned with small flowers. She said she was cutting lace on the ninth floor when the fire started.

"When was the first time you heard that there was a fire?" asked Bostwick.

"I heard some one cry 'Fire!' and it seemed a long way off," she began. "In less time than I can tell it all became confusion about the ninth floor. Girls ran about shouting and fighting to get out. Some crowded about the elevators, and others about the Greene Street stairway. I rushed to the table where my sister worked and she wasn't there. Then I began to cry, but something told me that would do no good, and then I saw my sister near the window. I started to run toward her, but the smoke was so dense that it choked me, and I could not reach her. I shouted to her but she didn't hear me, and that was the last I saw of her then. I was at a loss to know what to do for a time, but I saw many girls about the Washington Place door, and ran there. Just as soon as I started to the Washington Place door, some one said: 'Girls, it's no use. The door is locked and we can't get out!' "

"Suppose we allow this girl to illustrate just how she tried to pull that door," Mr. Rubin proposed.

Katie walked over to the door nearest the judge's bench and pulled and twisted with all her might. The jurors rose in their seats to get a better view.

"It seemed as though I had been standing at that door for three minutes," she continued. "Again I saw the Washington Street elevator come up. Once more I was pushed back by the crowd. All around me I saw flames spreading. The car was crowded and was on its way downstairs again. I don't remember just how it all happened, but as the car passed the floor the door was left open and I got hold of the cable and swung myself toward the car. I think I landed on top of the car. My feet were up in the air and my head downward. My ankles were hurt. I must have landed on top of a lot of girls. In that way I made my escape and finally reached the street."

"Did you see your sister?" asked Bostwick.

"Yes—I—saw her, but she was dead."

"What was your sister's name?" asked Steuer, taking up the cross-examination.

"Her name was Rosie, and she was only eighteen years old."

"Don't you know that your mother has sued Harris and Blanck for a very large sum of money?" asked Steuer, getting in a characteristic light jab, which at that point did little damage.

"My mother never spoke about that to me," replied the witness.

Score round one for Bostwick and Rubin.

The next day the prosecution continued to hammer away at the locked door. Its purpose, the state sought to show, was to compel the girls to leave nightly by way of the Greene Street door, where a watchman was stationed. This was standard practice in the garment trades. Every night the watchman would search the bags and pocketbooks carried by the girls in order to make sure that they took nothing of value belonging to Messrs. Harris and Blanck. This evidence supported the public findings of a joint committee from the Cloakmakers' Union and the Cloak Manufacturers' Association that in twenty-two shops the doors leading to hall and stairway were habitually closed during the day.

On cross-examination Steuer held up a good-sized ladies' handbag. The witness conceded that some of the girls carried bags something like it.

"Just open it and see for yourself how big it is," said Steuer, tossing the bag over to Assistant District Attorney Rubin. Unsuspecting, he opened the bag and drew out four thin silk waists.

"Oh," said Bostwick, "we will concede that the bags carried by the girls were big enough at times to hold waists such as are shown here to the jury."

Steuer handed the waists back to Mr. Blanck, who carefully folded them and put them in a bundle. If he could not controvert evidence of rigid inspection, he could at least plant in the jury's mind some understanding of its expediency.

On the third day of the trial the defense scored heavily. On direct examination the state's witness, a Negress named Christina Lang, was placed on the stand to give testimony along the lines of a preliminary statement she had made to Assistant District Attorney Koenig.

"Did you ever know there was a door at the Washington Place side of the ninth floor?" asked Bostwick.

"No," replied the witness.

"Miss Lang," demanded Steuer, "did you see people coming in and out of that door, during the eight weeks you worked there?"

"Yes, sometimes only. I seen them go in and out of that door sometimes," the witness answered, to the consternation of the prosecution. Bostwick and Rubin were on their feet instantly.

"Didn't you say on April 28 in the District Attorney's office, 'I never knew there was a door there'?" shouted Bostwick.

"I don't remember," was the answer.

Steuer objected, but was overruled. "From the day of that fire until this moment," he asked, "did you get a letter from Harris and Blanck or see Harris and Blanck or see any one from a lawyer's office?"

"No."

"For whom are you working now?" asked Judge Crain.

The witness said she was unemployed.

At this point Assistant District Attorney Koenig entered the room and took a seat close to the witness stand.

"Don't you remember stating to Mr. Koenig that you never knew there was a door at the Washington Place side?" Bostwick asked for the second time.

"Yes," replied the witness.

"And when you made that statement was it true?"

"Yes."

During this exchange Steuer objected vehemently, insisting that the state could not be permitted to impeach its own witness. But Crain allowed this line of question to be continued.

"Didn't you refuse to attend this trial and say so to a subpœna server?" thundered Bostwick.

"I was sick at the time," replied the woman.

"Now you pay attention to me," interposed Judge Crain, who had been scrutinizing the witness carefully. "Did you ever see that door at the Washington Place side on the ninth floor?"

"I had seen that door," replied the Negress. "Yes, I had seen it opened and seen girls pass through that door during the day."

"And a little while ago you said you had never seen that door," snapped Bostwick in disgust.

In permitting the state to impeach its own witness, the court had exercised sound judgment. To the general rule that forbids one side from impugning the credibility of witnesses it calls to the stand, the weight of authority makes a significant exception. Where the evidence takes the party by surprise and is contrary to the examination of the witness preparatory to the trial, such questioning is permitted. Only by disclosing flat contradictions in the witness's stories can a party be protected against an artful and unscrupulous person. At Bostwick's request Crain instructed the witness not to leave the courthouse and warned her not to talk to any person about the case. The reluctance of this witness to appear at the trial should have been sufficient warning to the state against using her. Calling her to the stand constituted merely one of a series of blunders that Steuer was to capitalize heavily.

In his cross-examination Steuer sought to portray Harris and Blanck as humanitarians concerned about the welfare of their workers. "Don't you know," he asked Josie Nicolosi, a pretty, dark-eyed teen-ager, "that Mr. Harris and Mr. Blanck even had a phonograph playing for you during luncheon hours so you girls might enjoy yourselves and dance?"

"Yes, I remember that," she replied, neatly coupling her categorical answer with a statement damaging to the other side. "But that phonograph only played while there was a strike in the shop. They wanted to treat us very nicely."

Steuer should have seen the red light and stopped there, but he plunged ahead: "And Mr. Blanck even gave prizes for dancing?"

"He did, but the moment the strike was over that stopped, too."

Hoist by his own petard, he had failed to recognize in this young girl a witness with an unerring instinct for a trap. It was a variation of the classic exchange: "Do you know the defendant? Yes—to my cost!" Even the most experienced lawyers are time and again caught off balance by the hostile woman witness alive to the dramatic possibilities of the situation. Perhaps Steuer had momentarily forgotten Rufus Choate's humorous instruction to a young attorney: "Let me give you my dying advice—never cross-examine a woman! It is of no use. They cannot disintegrate the story they have once told, they cannot eliminate the part that is

for you from that which is against you. They can neither
combine, nor shade, nor qualify. They go for the whole
thing; and the moment you begin to cross-examine one of
them, instead of being bitten by a single rattlesnake, you
are bitten by a whole barrel full. I never, except in a case
absolutely desperate, dare to cross-examine a woman." But
Steuer was willing to gamble once again, and on that last
occasion his intuition was to pay off.

For five whole days Steuer fought desperately to keep from
the jury the lock with the shot bolt which was found on the
ninth floor of the Asch Building. Although Bostwick had
called witness after witness to prove the finding of the lock
near the burned door, Judge Crain sustained Steuer's objections to its admissibility until a more solid foundation
could be laid. Finally Bostwick succeeded in tracing the
lock from the manufacturer to the locksmith who installed
it. Thereupon Judge Crain admitted it in evidence.

Despite a few setbacks, the state had scored heavily in
the first week of the trial, but the climactic moments were
reserved for the resumption on the following Monday, when
the state sought to prove that Margaret Schwartz had been
at the locked door and was overpowered by the flames in a
futile effort to open it. To back up this charge, the state
called its star witness, Kate Alterman, who was working on
the ninth floor at the time of the fire. In answer to Bostwick's questioning she declared:

"When the alarm was raised I was in the dressing room
with Miss Schwartz. We ran out together and saw a great
crowd near the door on the Washington Place side. I saw
Mr. Bernstein, a brother of the superintendent, trying to
open that door, but he couldn't budge it. I ran over to the
windows, but there was nothing but flames around them.

"I saw Margaret once more—trying to open the door I
had just turned away from. I pushed her aside and tried the
door myself, but I could not open it. It was locked. Margaret was kneeling at the door when I noticed her again, a
moment later. Her hair was loose and the hem of her dress

was on fire. She was using all her strength to turn the knob.
She was tearing at it. Then she screamed: 'The door is
locked! I am lost! Open the door! Open it! Open it!'"

There was absolute silence in the courtroom as Miss
Alterman reached the climax. Bostwick's voice fell almost
to a whisper as he put the next question: "And then—what
became of Margaret?"

"That was the last I saw of her," was the low reply.

Miss Alterman turned then to an account of her own escape from the factory.

"I ran to the sink," she said, "and wet my hair. I saw
Mr. Bernstein flying around like a wildcat, putting his head
out of the windows and pulling it back again. Then I took
my fur coat, turned it inside out and put it on that way. I
picked up some unfinished dresses from a table that had
not yet caught fire, wet them and wrapped them about my
head.

"Purple flames were following me along the floor. My
pocketbook, which I had in my hand, caught fire, and I
pressed it to my breast to put out the flames. I ran then for
the door on the Greene Street side of the building. Smoke
and flames were all around me, and finally my dress began
to burn.

"A girl caught me around the waist as I ran. I begged her
to let me go, but she wouldn't. I knew I couldn't save myself if I had to drag her along with me. I struck her, I hit
her, I kicked her away from me. I don't know what became
of her, but I reached the stairs and I was safe."

Steuer could not let Katie's dramatic and damaging story
go unchallenged. It seemed a little too pat. On cross-examination he got her to admit that she had come from her home
in Philadelphia two weeks before and that, though she had
been ready at any time, she had been held as the very last
of the state's witnesses. Having duly impressed the jury
with the fact that she was the state's most important witness, he then proceeded step by step to discredit her testimony.

Q.: Before you came down here this last time, to come down every day for two weeks, when did you see anybody from the District Attorney's office before that?

A.: Saturday.

Q.: You were down here Saturday, too, were you?

A.: Yes, sir.

Q.: And did you go anywhere with Mr. Rubin and Mr. Bostwick?

A.: Yes, sir.

Q.: They took you up to the building, did they?

A.: Yes, sir.

Q.: And they went along?

A.: Yes, sir.

Q.: And they pointed out to you where the Washington Place door is?

A.: (indignantly) I had to point it out to them.

Q.: You were taken right over to the Washington Place door, weren't you?

A.: I took *them* to the Washington Place door.

Q.: They didn't know where it was?

A.: I don't know whether they knew or not, but they asked me to show it to them.

Q.: Well, they took you all around the floor, didn't they?

A.: I took *them* all around the floor, I.

Q.: *You* took Mr. Bostwick and Mr. Rubin all around the floor?

A.: Yes, sir.

Q.: You had never gone there before in all the two weeks you were in New York, had you?

A.: No, sir.

Q.: And how was the appointment made for Saturday?

A.: Mr. Rubin told me to come, he wants to see me. He showed me the plan and asked me to show on the plan where I saw Margaret last; I couldn't show him very well on the plan for I picked it in my mind the place as it was before the fire, and he couldn't make out very well with me there, and he took me to the place and told me to show him exactly the place.

Q.: All that you have told us about that, was that she was right up against the door, isn't that so?

A.: She was right near the door.

Q.: Well, now, that was right alongside of the Washington Place door?

A.: She was right near the door with her hands at the knob.

Q.: With her hands at the knob?

A.: At the knob.

Q.: But you couldn't tell him that before you went up to the loft?

A.: Well, I don't believe I told him—I think I told him, I am not sure, though, for when I gave my statement first I was sick that time.

Q.: And so you did not make it the same way as you are making it now?

A.: *I made it the same way, just the same way.*

Q.: Did you tell then that she was with her hand on the knob?

A.: I don't remember exactly whether I told the knob, or not, for it was nine months ago.

Q.: Now, I want you to tell me your story over again just as you told it before?

A.: What kind of a story do you mean?

Q.: You told us before that you had gone to the dressing room, do you remember that?

A.: Yes, sir, before I heard the cry of fire.

Q.: And then it was in the dressing room that you heard the cry of fire?

A.: Yes, sir.

Q.: Now tell us what you did then when you heard the cry of fire?

A.: I went out from the dressing room, went to the Waverly side windows for fire escapes. I didn't find any. Margaret Schwartz was with me; afterwards she disappeared. I turned away to get to the Greene Street side, but she disappeared, she disappeared from me. I went into the toilet rooms, I went out from the toilet rooms, bent my face over the sink, and then I went to the Washington side to the elevators, but there was a big crowd, and I saw a crowd around the door, trying to open the door; there I saw Bernstein, the manager's brother, trying to open the door but he couldn't; he left; and Margaret was there, too, and she tried to open the door and she could not. I pushed her aside. I tried to open the door, and I could not, and then she pushed me aside, and she said, "I will open the door," and she tried to open the door, and then the big smoke came and Margaret Schwartz I saw bending down on her knees, her hair was loose and her dress was on the floor a little far from her, and then she screamed at the top of her voice, "Open the door! Fire! I am lost! My God, I am lost, there is fire!" And I went away from Margaret. I left, stood in the middle of the room. That is, I went in the dressing room, first, there was a big crowd, I went out of the dressing room, went in the middle of the room between the machines and examining tables, and then I went in; I saw Bernstein, the manager's brother, throwing around the windows, putting his head from the window—he wanted to jump, I suppose, but he was afraid—he drawed himself back, and then I saw the flames cover him, and some other man on Greene Street, the flames covered him, too, and then I turned my coat on the wrong side and put it on my head with the fur to my face, the lining on the outside, and I got hold of a bunch of dresses and covered up the top of my head. I just got ready to go and somebody came and began to chase me back, pulled my dress back, and I kicked her with the foot and she disappeared. I tried to make my escape. I had a pocket-book with me, and that pocketbook began to burn, I pressed it to my heart to extinguish the fire, and I made my escape right through the flames—the whole door was a flame, right to the roof.

    Q.: It looked like a wall of flame?

A.: Like a curtain of fire.

Q.: *Now, there was something in that that you left out,*
I think, Miss Alterman. When Bernstein was jumping
around, do you remember what that was like? Like a wildcat, wasn't it?

A.: Like a wildcat.

Q.: You left that out the second time. You did leave
that out, didn't you, just now, when you told us about Bernstein, that he jumped around like a wildcat?

A.: Well, I didn't imagine whether a wildcat or a wild
dog; I just speak to imagine just exactly.

In disclosing the literal parallelism between her first and
second accounts, Steuer hammered home to the jury the lack
of spontaneity in her answers. Once Katie got into the swing
of her story, she stuck pretty close to lines obviously memo-
rized. Again he took her over the same ground on the burning ninth floor. Again she gave the same story—Bernstein
"jumped like a wildcat on the walls," somebody pulled her
dress, and she kicked with her foot, she pressed her purse to
her heart when it started to burn, and as she ran through the
fire she saw "the whole door was a flame, it was a red curtain
of fire, and I went right on to the roof."

Q.: You never spoke to anybody about what you were
going to tell us when you came here, did you?

A.: No, sir.

Katie denied that she had talked with her family or anyone
else about it.

Q.: *You didn't study the words in which you would
tell it?*

A.: *No, sir.*

For a third time Steuer led the girl through her ordeal.
Once more she told of Bernstein's "throwing around like a
wildcat," of the woman who began pulling her dress and
whom she had to kick with her foot to free herself, and of

running through the Greene Street door, which was in flames. "It was a red curtain of fire on that door, to the roof."

Q.: *You never studied those words, did you?*

A.: *No, sir.*

Bostwick could not allow Steuer's insinuations to remain unchallenged. On redirect examination he asked the witness: "Now, Miss Alterman, each time that you have answered Mr. Steuer's question you have tried to repeat it in the same language that you first told it here in Court, have you not?" "Yes, sir," she replied. "And you remember every detail of that story as well today as if it happened yesterday?" "Yes, sir." "And it is all true." "All true, yes, sir."

But Steuer was not satisfied by these answers. *"Can you tell that story in any other words than those you have told it in?"* he asked on re-cross-examination. *"In any other words?"* queried the witness pathetically. *"I remember it this way, just exactly how it was done."*

When Bostwick asked Miss Alterman to tell the jury why she tried to repeat her story the last time in the very same language she had previously used to Mr. Steuer, she answered with pathetic logic: "Because he asked me the very same story over and over, and I tried to tell him the very same thing, because he asked me the very same thing over and over."

When Katie Alterman stepped down from the stand she had not been contradicted at a single point, but Steuer's ruthless cross-examination left an impression that the state's star witness had been over-coached. This tendency of witnesses on the stand to repeat pat versions of some occurrence is well illustrated by a reminiscence of Justice McGoldrick, who tells of a truck-driver who repeated on the stand an account of an accident in identical language. "How long did it take you to memorize how this accident happened?" he was asked on cross-examination. "Four years," he blurted out; then looking quizzically at his questioner, he added: "It's four years since the accident happened, isn't it?"

Steuer was always to insist that his handling of Katie Alterman stood out as one of his most effective pieces of cross-examination in a career studded with forensic triumphs. Underneath his patient and even gentle manner he had demonstrated that instinct for the jugular vein which was to keep him in the first rank of notable trial lawyers. At the Triangle fire trial he did not rant. He did not pound the rail of the jury box. When he spoke to the jurors he often pitched his voice so low that judge and prosecution attorneys had to ask him to speak up in order to find out just what was going on. But behind his simple, direct manner was a carefully calculated technique for impressing jurors. In defending Harris and Blanck he sat at the counsel table alone, as was to be his invariable custom. Across from him a battery of state's attorneys were crowded around the other table. He let them play Goliath; he would be David. These and other little stage tricks, like never carrying a briefcase in order not to give the jury the wrong impression, almost unfailingly paid dividends. While Steuer could make adult dissemblers tremble, his talents were never better mobilized than when he had to handle inexperienced, half-educated teen-agers. His mordant prodding was illustrated at a later day in the savage cross-examination of Sarah Schoenfeld, a grade-7B schoolgirl, who was a key witness in the morals case brought against Tex Rickard. Sarah's story may have been true in general outline, but Steuer was able to trip her up on small details and to tarnish the impression she had first made on the stand of being an innocent and artless adolescent.

In resting its case, the state had shown that employees believed that the Washington Place door was not to be used by them, but that they were required to pass a watchman at the Greene Street door; that the Washington Place door was locked at the time of the fire, that no fire drills were ever held in the Triangle factory, and that inflammable refuse frequently accumulated on the floor.

Then Steuer paraded a group of witnesses—employees, salesmen, and customers—who testified that there was always a key in the door in question, attached to it with a piece of string, that the door opened without any difficulty—in fact, was always kept open—and that Mr. Blanck himself personally tried every door every day. To clear the defendants of any criminal negligence, Steuer sought to show that they were unaware of fire violations in their plant. To this end he brought down from Albany Commissioner John Williams of the Department of Labor. Williams put in evidence report blanks of his subordinates which revealed that the last factory-inspection report made prior to the fire had been satisfactory. For a moment the production of the cards in evidence appeared to be a risky move on Steuer's part as they showed that the inspectors had recommended certain desirable changes; but Steuer was quick to bring out that they had given this advice *not* to Harris and Blanck but to Edna Barry, the telephone operator. Why they failed to inform the employers personally, the commissioner was unable to explain, and he seemed not at all unhappy to quit the witness stand.

The state now introduced rebuttal evidence to stress the perjured nature of much of the testimony. It was disclosed that a number of witnesses who now repudiated the preliminary statements they had made to the district attorney were given raises in pay. District Attorney Whitman charged that the superintendent of the factory was in the lobby at the grand-jury hearing, seeking to intimidate girl witnesses. Whitman had rushed from the grand-jury room shouting: "I'll punch your face in," and ordered him out of the building. The most damning testimony to be offered by any of these rebuttal witnesses came from Robert Wolfson, formerly a head cutter with Harris and Blanck. Before he quit the firm, a few days after the fire, Harris remarked to him, according to his testimony: "The dead are dead and must be buried, but the living must keep on living. Of course the door was locked. Why should I let them rob me of my fortune?" Steuer immediately sized up Wolfson as a dangerous witness, and his testimony went virtually unchallenged.

Before the case went to the jury, it was apparent that in a contest between "inspired" recollection testimony for the state, on the one hand, and obviously perjured testimony for the defense, on the other, the jury might very well give the accused the benefit of the doubt. Even allowing for the terror and panic of the scene and for the notorious inability of witnesses to the same event to agree on exactly what happened, there was no question but that wholesale portions of the testimony were perjured. Mrs. O. P. H. Belmont, who in the recent past had followed labor troubles in the Triangle factory very closely and was a spectator at the trial, was forthright in her comments. "The trial is a travesty of justice," one reporter quoted her as saying. "All these witnesses should be sworn on a Jewish Bible, and then we might get different testimony. To swear a Jewish person on a Christian Bible is of no more use than if you swore them on a cuspidor."

The enormity of the disaster and the impossibility of fixing responsibility accentuated the public's shock at the degree to which perjury was so obviously committed. But competent authorities maintain today that anywhere from twenty-five to seventy-five per cent of the testimony offered by witnesses for the defense on the direct point at issue in the ordinary run of criminal trials is perjured, and in divorce cases as much as ninety per cent. "Show me an eyewitness and I will show you a liar," is an aphorism that trial experience underscores. In the face of such scandalous practices the general public remains astonishingly cynical and complacent. Unfortunately for justice, in the Triangle fire case there was no Brougham to rip and tear the defense witnesses, no man on the prosecution staff of the caliber of that eminent British barrister who almost a century earlier excoriated the paid witnesses—imported character assassins, he called them—after they had testified to the improper behavior of Queen Caroline. For some inexplicable reason Messrs. Bostwick and Rubin muffed an easy play, and with it the ballgame.

As though the contradictory testimony did not present sufficient difficulties for the prosecution, the requirements of the New York penal law, as interpreted by Judge Crain, added an insuperable obstacle. The accused were on trial for manslaughter in either the first or the second degree. This meant that it was necessary, under the code, to show that the homicide had resulted from a misdemeanor or an attempt to commit one, or that Margaret Schwartz's death was the direct consequence of the culpable negligence of the accused. Judge Crain's charge virtually constituted a directed verdict of acquittal. Manslaughter was a felony, he pointed out, and unless it could be shown that the accused were *aware* of the violations, they could not be found guilty. It must be shown *"beyond a reasonable doubt,"* Crain charged, that the door was locked *with the knowledge of the defendants,* and that the locking of the door caused the death of Margaret Schwartz.

It took the jury only one hour and forty minutes to bring in the expected verdict of not guilty. But even the jurors' consciences were troubled by the result. One of them, Victor Steinman, told a reporter of the *Evening Mail:*

> I believed that the Washington Place door, on which the district attorney said the whole case hinged, was locked at the time of the fire. But I could not make myself feel certain that Harris and Blanck knew that it was locked. And so, because the judge had charged us that we could not find them guilty unless we believed that they *knew* the door was locked then, I did not know what to do.

When asked just why he could not feel beyond a reasonable doubt that the owners knew the door was locked, Steinman presented this logical reconstruction of the events during the panic:

> Because the evidence was so conflicting and because so many of the witnesses on each side were lying. They told their stories like parrots, and I could not believe them. All I felt sure of was that the door had been locked. I believed that piece of charred wood and the lock with the shot bolt that the State put in evidence. But then I believed also the testimony that the key was usually in the door and that it was tied to it with a piece of string.
>
> So there was the thought in my mind that during the first rush for that door some panic-stricken girl might have turned the key in an effort to open it. And if that was so, then Harris and Blanck could not have known of it, as the judge demanded they should, to be convicted.

While the case against Harris and Blanck was wrecked by the technicalities of the criminal law, there is no question that Steinman and other jurors would have known their duty had the factory inspectors been on trial instead of the employers.

For Harris and Blanck their ordeal was not quite at an end. Fearful of a crowd of several hundred relatives of the victims of the fire who had gathered outside the criminal courthouse after the verdict, the two employers managed their exit from the building as unobtrusively as possible. They left the courtroom through the judge's chambers, then passed through a pen reserved for detained prisoners, and, accompanied by five uniformed policemen, quit the building by the Leonard Street exit.

Suddenly someone in the crowd spotted them. Then David Weiner, whose seventeen-year-old sister Rosa was killed in the fire, thrust himself up to her former employers, shook his fist at them, and cried shrilly: "Not guilty? Not guilty? It was murder! Murder!" The Italians among the crowd began to sneer: "Not guilty? This, America—fine country for justice!" Harris and Blanck and their friends scampered down Lafayette Street to the nearest subway entrance. David Weiner kept shouting: "Not guilty? Murder!" until he collapsed and had to be taken to a hospital.

Since the evidence against Harris and Blanck for the death of Margaret Schwartz was considered the strongest of that in all the cases against them, the district attorney's office never brought to trial the other manslaughter indictments. They could have been made to stand trial 145 times more without violating the constitutional prohibition against double jeopardy. But there were still heavy damage suits pending. Three years after the fire it was reported that the families of twenty-three girl victims agreed to accept seventy-five dollars apiece in full settlement of their claims against the liability company that covered the factory. "It seems little enough," commented the *Evening Post*, "but, to be sure, they could console themselves with the thought that it was nearly four times as much as the twenty dollar fine which Chief Justice Russel of the Court of General Sessions imposed upon Max Blanck," one of the Triangle partners, "two and a half years after the fire, for keeping the door of another factory locked." Max Blanck was what educators today would call a slow learner.

Had Steuer lost his case, it is doubtful whether the social consequences of the Triangle fire would have been as far-reaching. Responsible public opinion was outraged by the verdict. Morally if not legally the defendants were considered blameworthy for a fire which resulted from that greed and indifference they shared in common with hundreds of other factory-owners. The *Tribune* forthrightly attacked the verdict as "revolting to the moral sense of the community," but the Socialist *Call* was too pessimistic when it predicted that "the authorities will forget the case as speedily as possible."

While the prosecuting arm of the law quickly lost interest, responsible state officials, the public, and labor did not forget. A terrific impetus was given to the organization of labor in the needle trades. From the tragedy really dates the rise of the I.L.G.W.U. as a great force in city and nation. Governor Dix moved swiftly. A state factory-investigation commission, with Frances Perkins as its first executive officer, supported enthusiastically by two political fledglings, Robert F. Wagner and Alfred E. Smith, made radical recommendations, which the legislature enacted. A drastically revised and stringent building code was adopted and the labor laws of the state were completely refashioned, with new curbs on the hours of the labor of women. But one imperious young state senator seemed quite untouched by these humanitarian impulses. As Franklin Delano Roosevelt later commented to Frances Perkins, "You know, I was an awfully mean cuss when I first went into politics."

XIII

The Clergyman, The Choir Singer, and the Pigwoman

Jersey justice in the Hall-Mills case

Shot through from beginning to end with incompetent bungling and climaxed by palpable melodramatics, the state's handling of the Hall-Mills murder mystery defies comparison for its ineptitude. The case revealed how far out of line prosecutors may go when they yield to newspaper pressure or are stirred by political ambitions. It proved how ugly rumor and malicious gossip are often impossible to convert into authenticated testimony that will stand up in court. It gave one jury an opportunity to rise above the class animosities that had placed in jeopardy the lives of the affluent and socially prominent defendants. Its ugly wounds still unhealed, the Hall-Mills case stands as the most fascinating unsolved murder mystery of our era.

Other murders have remained unexplained, but seldom apart from detective fiction has a crime produced so many different suspects each possessed with a strong motive for the killings as in the Hall-Mills tragedy. In fact, not since Lizzie Borden was acquitted back in 1893 of the ax murder of her parents has a crime furnished so many clues that led down so many blind alleys. But while the Borden killings seem senseless, the double slaying of the rector and his paramour appears well motivated. The murder of Joseph B. Elwell is another opaque mystery, but there was no established motive for the killing of the bridge expert. So, too, with the butchery of Cleveland's torso murderer who worked out on Jackass Hill; this diabolically clever fiend, like Jack the Ripper, ran amuck but managed to outwit the law. The criminal files are jammed with unsolved murders, but the

Hall-Mills case remains unique. And the trial was on a par
with the crime.

This cause célèbre dates from the morning of September
16, 1922, when the bodies of the Reverend Edward Wheeler
Hall, the forty-one-year-old rector of fashionable St. John's
Church, New Brunswick, and Mrs. Eleanor Mills, a choir
singer in that same church, were discovered under a crab
apple tree on the old Phillips farm off De Russey's Lane, a
little over a mile from their respective homes—a setting as
appropriate and improbable as any in the annals of crime.
A .32 caliber bullet had entered the top of the minister's
head and passed out through the lower part of his skull.
Three bullets had plowed into Mrs. Mills's skull, one passing through, two remaining embedded in the brain tissues.
The choir singer's throat had been cut by two slashes of a
knife, and her head was nearly severed. Even a casual examination indicated that the bodies had been arranged by
someone with either a macabre brand of humor or an over-
developed sense of the proprieties. The rector and the choir
singer lay side by side under the tree, his arm under her
head, their faces covered by a Panama hat and a scarf
respectively. Mrs. Mills's skirt was properly smoothed down,
but the rector's gold watch was missing as well as a wallet
supposed to have contained about fifty dollars.

Two clues were found at the scene of the murder, stage
props arranged by the murderer or by some subsequent
visitor to the scene either to defy or to mislead police investigators. Incriminating letters from Mrs. Mills to the
rector were strewn over the dead bodies, and the Reverend
Mr. Hall's calling-card was propped against his shoe as
though to ensure adequate identification. The ghoulish
scene was a perfect candidate for Mme Tussaud's chamber
of waxwork horrors.

Her letters sizzled. "Sweetheart, my true heart," Eleanor
Mills confessed, "I could crush you—oh, I am so happy tonight! So happy I could dance wildly." She felt impelled to

provide documentation. "I'm not pretty. I know there are girls with more shapely bodies, but I'm not caring what they have. I have the greatest part of all blessings, a noble man's deep, true, eternal love, and my heart is his, my life is his; poor as my body is, scrawny as my skin may be; but I am his forever. How impatient I am and will be! I want to look up into your dear face for hours as you touch my body close." Then a more sober note: "What a muddle we are in! But I will be content. I WILL." But married to a dull, unimaginative, thoroughly unromantic church sexton, Mrs. Mills was in fact anything but content.

The rector's own love letters, a smoking cache later released by an attorney for Eleanor Mills's daughter, disclosed that her passion was not unrequited. "Darling wonder heart," the man of the cloth wrote his inamorata, "I just want to crush you for two hours. I want to see you Friday night *alone by our road*, where we can let out, unrestrained, that universe of joy and happiness that will be ours." Revolting against the conventional morality of his church and the frigid stuffiness of his marital life, he tossed discretion to the winds and confessed to his "gypsy": "I just want to hold you; there is a peace then that nothing else brings." Without appreciating his role in the history of the drama, the Reverend Mr. Hall had given the hinterland a sort of preview of the passion-consumed missionary in *Rain*, soon to begin an extraordinary run on Broadway. Both clerics had discovered sex and could not escape its clutches.

The chronology of the fatal 14th of September must be scrutinized for further clues to the crime. Some time after five o'clock that afternoon Mrs. Mills tried to reach the rector by telephone. Mrs. Hall answered, and informed her he was not at home. When Hall arrived around dinnertime, he appears to have called Mrs. Mills back. Miss Opie, Mrs. Mills's neighbor, who took messages for the choir singer, was positive that she called across to the Millses' house and got no answer. About 7.30 she told Mrs. Mills about the call. Mrs. Mills dressed, went to a near-by store, and telephoned the Hall residence. The rector answered on the upstairs extension. From the gist of his rather cryptic remarks over-heard by Louise Geist, a maid in the Hall household, he appears to have made a date for 8.15. Then, remarking to Louise: "Isn't this a lovely evening?" he went out the front door and was never seen alive again. When Mrs. Mills was about to leave, her husband called out: "Where are you going?" Her taunting answer was more meaningful than she intended: "Follow me and you'll find out!"

Mrs. Mills's husband and the rector's wife and in-laws appear to have covered considerable territory that night. Mills went out around eleven o'clock, dropped in at the church, and then went back to bed. Mrs. Hall retired about 11; her brother Willie, before 9.30. Henry, another brother, asserted he had been at Lavalette on a fishing trip, and was not seen in the vicinity until the following morning at 7.30 a.m., and then by a person whose testimony was never cor-roborated. Mrs. Hall spent a restless night. Around 2.30 she rose, noted that her husband had not returned, and wakened Willie. The pair dressed and walked to St. John's Church, little more than two blocks away. The church was dark and locked. Then they walked past the Mills residence, but, seeing no lights, went back home. Mills also appeared equally edgy. Before 2 a.m. he got up, dressed, and went to the church to see if he could find his wife. He later insisted that he was back at 2.30, and, if his story is true, he must have missed Mrs. Hall and Willie by at most a few minutes. For the rest of the night Mrs. Hall went sleepless. At 6 a.m. she called the police, guardedly asking whether any "casual-ties" had been reported. It was not until evening that she notified the police that her husband was missing.

At the outset the authorities had to determine how the killings had taken place and who possessed a motive for the crime. They had to consider the possibility, regardless of how tenuous, that this was a murder and suicide—the rector slaying in desperation and then ending his own life. But this explanation was quickly dismissed. The condition of the corpses raised a strong presumption of a double murder. Bobbing up intermittently throughout the long investigation was the hypothesis that the fatalities were the result of robbery. Supporting this theory was the fact that the rector's money and watch were missing. But watch and wallet may well have been pilfered by someone who stumbled across the bodies. This was murder—murder prompted by hate, jealousy, or lust, universal impulses to felonious action. Now, both Mrs. Hall and Mr. Mills had solid motives, but the subsequent actions of the widow and members of her family provoked far more gossip than did the behavior of the sexton.

When a murder has occurred, even the most matter-of-fact routine takes on an incriminating coloration and the most commonplace actions are closely screened for evidence of consciousness of guilt. People raised their eyebrows when they heard that Mrs. Hall had asked the police about "casualties." When she sent her brown coat off to be dyed, presumably for the period of mourning, and chose a Philadelphia firm instead of a local establishment, her action seemed highly suspicious, particularly since she did not use the mails or an ordinary common carrier but entrusted the coat to a relative, who sent it by express from her own house.

The mutilation of Mrs. Mills's body pointed to a person who was either unbalanced or fired by venom, if not both. What better suspect than Mrs. Hall's eccentric brother Willie, who seemed to fit the role like a glove? Willie was definitely different. He spent his time haunting the local firehouse and riding about town on fire-trucks and laundry wagons. Everyone in town seemed to know that Willie was regarded by the family as incapable of handling his own financial affairs. In addition, Willie just happened to own a .32-caliber revolver, which he used to brandish before the housemaids. When the police located it, they found that the firing pin had been filed down so that it would not shoot. Mrs. Hall's explanation was that her husband had done

this two years previously for safety's sake. Then why keep
the revolver at all, gossips asked. Again, a seemingly routine
action on Willie's part took on a sinister meaning. On the
Saturday after the crime was committed, he ordered a
brand-new suit and sent two badly spotted old ones to the
dry-cleaners.

From the moment the crime was discovered, the detection of the perpetrators was beset with one difficulty after
another. The orchard where the two bodies were found was
close to the Raritan River just over the boundary of Somerset County, whereas both the slain clergyman and the choir
singer had been residents of Middlesex. Hence both county
prosecutors felt it incumbent on themselves to set in motion
the creaking wheels of the law. Middlesex moved on the
theory that the murder did not actually take place where
the bodies were found but that the corpses had been transported by the murderer over the county line and then laid
side by side under the crab-apple tree. Detectives soon
accepted the theory that the couple were murdered at a
site reported to have been owned by the Carpenders,
wealthy relatives of the Halls, more than five miles from
the Phillips farm. This theory rested on the uncovering of
a bloodstained handkerchief and a woman's sidecomb. But,
even granting this unproved assumption, as long as there
was a possibility that the victims were carried over the
line before they died, Somerset was bound to take action.
Between the two counties over fifty thousand dollars were
spent on the original investigation without even settling
the locus of the crime, let alone determining the guilty
party.

All clues seemed to point in one direction, but the authorities with strange perversity moved in a directly opposite
course. The public was astounded when on October 9 a
nineteen-year-old lad named Clifford Hayes was arrested
for the murders. Hayes's connection with the crime rested
on the slenderest foundation. On the night of the rector's
last tryst Pearl Bahmer, a fifteen-year-old factory girl,

made a date with a sordid character by the name of Raymond Schneider. Schneider took Pearl to a movie and then walked her home. There her father, Nick, a Hungarian saloonkeeper, proposed that she take a stroll with him as he needed to shake off the effect of some of his own potations. Schneider seems to have had reason to be jealous of Pearl's companion, who later was jailed for incest. He proceeded to follow the pair with his friend Clifford Hayes. Traversing Easton Avenue, he came to De Russey's Lane, where he saw a man and a woman he thought were Pearl and her escort. Then Schneider lost sight of them, but kept beating the brush until the early hours of the morning. On Saturday morning Pearl again dated Schneider. For some unexplained reason he headed her straight for De Russey's Lane, though Pearl testified: "I was never in this lane with him before." They soon stumbled upon a couple lying in the grass, completely immobile. Schneider kept on walking in a hurry. Pearl shouted: "Come here, Ray, just a minute, the people ain't breathing!" On the girl's insistence, the couple went to a near-by house and had the police notified.

Schneider, who had acted jittery from the moment of the discovery of the bodies, cracked under pressure and accused Hayes of having killed the couple in the mistaken belief they were Pearl and her father. "So it was all a mistake, was it? My God—what a mistake!" was the comment of the choir singer's husband on the news of Hayes's arrest. Pinning the crime on Hayes seemed to fit too patly the theory clung to by Mrs. Hall and her family that the killings were the result of mistaken identity. But no motive for Hayes's alleged actions ever could be established. Schneider's own story fell apart at the seams, and the accuser was himself prosecuted and convicted of perjury. When the state at long last settled on more probable suspects and brought them to trial, it was careful not to put either Pearl or her former boy friend on the stand.

This false lead had a discouraging effect on the bumbling investigation. It faltered, flagged, and finally slumbered. In

the course of time Prosecutor Beekman of Somerset died
and Prosecutor Stricker of Middlesex resigned. Key witnesses were permitted to leave the jurisdiction. One of the
maids in the Hall household went back to Scotland. The
mechanic who filed down the firing pin of Willie Stevens's
gun vanished. The whereabouts of the state trooper who
was reputed to know more about the case than anybody
else were unknown. The evidence gathered at the scene of
the crime was fouled up. Dr. Hall's cuff links, shirt, collar,
and calling-card were lost track of, and Willie's revolver
was returned to the Hall household. Most amazing of all,
some of the most crucial records in the case, including the
minutes of the grand jury and affidavits of witnesses, mys-
teriously disappeared.

But two incidents, perhaps not unrelated, brought the
case back into the headlines some four years later. In the
summer of 1926 Arthur S. Riehl, of Roselle Park, New
Jersey, filed a petition for the annulment of his marriage
to Louise Geist, maid in the Hall household at the time of
the murders. Riehl charged that "before the marriage the
respondent carefully and deliberately withheld from your
petitioner the fact that she had knowledge of the doings of
certain of the principals in the well known Hall-Mills
case." Later, Riehl went on, his wife told him that the
rector was an "old buddy" of hers, and that she herself had
visited the Phillips farm with Mrs. Hall's husband. According to Riehl's account, Mrs. Hall, believing that the rector
and Mrs. Mills planned to elope on the night of September
14, had Willie and Louise drive with her to the Phillips
farm around ten p.m. Riehl alleged that his wife was paid
five thousand dollars to keep her mouth shut, and that the
chauffeur, Peter Tumulty, paid for his home "out of this
matter."

If the divorce suit revived the smoldering rumors, a
circulation-happy newspaper editor tore the case wide open.
Philip Payne, managing editor of the New York *Mirror*,
seized on the Hall-Mills case to boom the sales of his own

paper and to outdistance the *News,* a rival tabloid from which he had been fired because of his preoccupation with a much married glamour girl of the twenties named Peggy Hopkins Joyce. Had Payne's reportorial feat taken place twenty-five years earlier, every journalist in the country would have thrown his hat in the air. But by the Harding-Coolidge era of miscalled normalcy the established newspapers, seemingly secure in their substantial circulations and enjoying the patronage of conservative advertisers, had become sedate, even stuffy, and readily accepted hand-outs from lawyers and press agents.

The coming of the tabloids marked a revival of the old techniques of yellow journalism aided and abetted by photography. Payne and men of his stamp were neither flabby nor complaisant and were not troubled by the scruples of a more ethical breed of journalists. All during the spring of 1926 the *Mirror's* news hounds were on the scent. Somehow they got hold of the secret minutes of the grand jury and proceeded to recheck the testimony of many of the witnesses before that body. Riehl's affidavit was inspired by the *Mirror* and held in abeyance until the time was right. But, far more sensational, Payne dug up the old calling-card, which experts now declared held Willie Stevens's fingerprint.

Payne scheduled the story to break on July 1 to counteract the usual summer circulation slump, but a New York subway strike held up the revelations until July 17. On that day the first page of the Hearst tabloid, the *Mirror,* was taken up with a wash drawing of the murder scene. Above it, type an inch and a quarter high screamed: "HALL-MILLS MURDER MYSTERY BARED."

Now the press was in full cry, and the hounds of the law swooped down on their prey. Although there was not the slightest evidence that Mrs. Hall planned to run away, she was routed out of her New Brunswick residence in the middle of the night and taken to the Somerville jail. Willie and Henry were also arrested, along with Henry de la Bruyere

Carpender, Mrs. Hall's cousin and a member of the New York Stock Exchange, who was held for separate trial.

Not since 1907, when Harry K. Thaw was put on trial for murdering Stanford White for the premarital seduction of his wife, the artist's model Evelyn Nesbit, had the press been so worked up about a trial as in the Hall-Mills case. Three hundred reporters descended on Somerville's handsome white-marble courthouse and battled for the sixty-seven seats assigned the working press. Sixty leased wires installed in the basement ticked off five million words of copy in the first eleven days of the trial. While the *Times*, with its penchant for accurate reporting, engaged four stenographers to present the testimony verbatim, the Hearst press imported a flock of by-line writers like Mary Roberts Rinehart, the novelist, the Reverend Billy Sunday, the evangelist, and Police Commissioner Enright of New York. Even James Mills appeared in court in the role of a reporter, and his daughter, Charlotte, a typical flapper of that day, signed her name to a ten-thousand-word story.

The trial was presided over by the elderly Justice Charles W. Parker of the New Jersey Supreme Court, with Judge Frank L. Cleary of the Somerset court, a much younger man, sitting. Back in 1922 the prosecution had exhibited indubitable symptoms of senescence, but there had been considerable face-lifting since that time. The special prosecutor for this trial was State Senator Alexander Simpson, who combined enormous dynamism with a flair for the dramatic and even the melodramatic. With his small stature, jigging movements, and fancy collars, he might have doubled in vaudeville. Reputed to have eyes upon the Democratic nomination for governor, Simpson stood to score handsomely by convicting the fashionable Stevens brood, particularly since such a victory would have been achieved over the so-called million-dollar defense staff that opposed him. Chief of that staff was the acknowledged dean of the New Jersey bar, Robert H. McCarter, a former Attorney General of the state, whose placid face scarcely prepared spectators for his not infrequent outbursts of temper. McCarter had not specialized in criminal matters, but he was ably assisted by an experienced trial counsel, Senator Clarence E. Case, Republican leader in the New Jersey upper house. Case was also reputed to have designs on the governorship, but under the standard of the elephant, not the donkey. Even before it started, the trial seemed to be rapidly shaping into a political contest.

In entrusting the prosecution to Simpson, the state had put the people's case in the hands of a man who made up in bravado what he lacked in subtlety. In his opening he plunged headlong into the murky waters of motivation. He depicted Eleanor Mills as a woman who cared for the finer things, for books and music, tied to a dull, if not stupid, clod. Hall's was the story of the handsome man married to a woman seven to ten years older than himself. "When he married her," Simpson asserted, "he got position, wealth, and refinement, but he got what men usually do get who contract such a marriage, because he found he was in a chill, cold household."

Turning his heaviest artillery on the rector's wife, he pictured her, in the conventional manner of prosecutors, as combining some of the worst traits of Messalina and Lucrezia Borgia. Mrs. Hall got possession of the love letters, Simpson argued. Then, listening in on the downstairs extension the day of the murder, she overheard a telephone conversation between Mrs. Mills and her husband. This was an appointment to meet at De Russey's Lane. "Where are you going?" she asked the rector as he was leaving the house that night. " 'I am going out.' That is all he said." Some time during the night a man placed Hall's card at the feet of the corpse to make sure that the body would not be taken to potter's field and buried unknown. "And that card was marked on the back with the left index finger of Willie Stevens." He wound up his opening by stressing Mrs. Hall's incriminating remark to the police about any "casualties" and painted the coat-dyeing episode in sinister colors.

No one could ever accuse Simpson of lack of industry. Although the case was four years old, some two hundred witnesses were rounded up, the majority by the state. Simpson started out with a slashing attack on the alibis of Mrs. Hall's brothers. John S. Dickman, of North Plainfield, and his wife, Charlotte, tapped Willie as the man who had stumbled to their door at a quarter to nine, shortly before the time the murder was believed to have occurred. Described as "excited and sick looking," Willie, according to their testimony, had told them that his sister had set him down from her car and he was lost. Then Mrs. Marie Demarest, of Piscataway, sailed into Henry's alibi by asserting that she had seen him in New Brunswick at seven thirty the morning after the murder, at a time when he had insisted he was at Lavalette, sixty miles away. But she went farther. She charged that Mrs. Hall had procured the services of Ralph L. Gorsline, a vestryman of Dr. Hall's church, and Mrs. Minna Clark, a former member of the choir, to spy on the movements of her husband and Mrs. Mills. This was a damaging blow to Mrs. Hall's steadfast protestations that she was ignorant of her husband's infidelity—protestations that never carried real conviction. To make the story more lurid, it now appeared that Gorsline, emulating the lustful behavior of his church leader, was in the murder lane with a girl from the church choir the very night of the crime. The picture of the shad-faced vestryman, who, allegedly, saw nothing incongruous about snooping on his own rector while he was indulging in some amorous activities of his own, is perhaps as ridiculous as any painted by the gossipy witnesses at this trial. Apparently De Russey's Lane must have been as crowded on the night of September 14 as a drive-in movie featuring Lana Turner.

But Simpson was not through with Gorsline. If his next witness, William Garvin, was telling the truth, Gorsline's long silence had sinister implications. According to that private detective, two weeks after the murder Gorsline came

to him to unburden his conscience. He related how that
night in the lane Henry Stevens had fired twice at his feet,
crying out: "This is none of your affair. Get the hell out of
here!" Garvin was at that time manager of the Burns Detective Agency of New York. But like so many of the fantastic stories related on the stand, Garvin's was badly
dented when his boss, William J. Burns, appeared as a
defense witness. Burns stated flatly that there was no record
of the case in the files of his concern. Finally Gorsline took
the stand. Shamefacedly he was forced to name the choir
singer he was out with the night of the murders. He admitted hearing shots and screams, but insisted that he recognized nobody. Again somebody was obviously lying.

Simpson rebounded quickly. He now put on the stand a
blushing swain named Robert Erling, who falteringly admitted that he, too, was in De Russey's Lane the night in
question and that he not only saw Mrs. Jane Gibson, the
state's star witness, riding on her jenny mule, but was
passed by two automobiles.

Now for the first time in the long tangled history of the
case the state brought so-called criminological science into
play. Several exponents of the Bertillon system were called
to the stand. The first of these, Edward H. Schwartz, the
Newark Police Department's fingerprint expert, identified
the print on the calling-card as that of Willie Stevens's left
index finger. Schwartz's testimony was crucial, and the
defense was determined to chop him down to size. Cross-
examination by McCarter brought out that the fingerprint
had not been developed at the time of the discovery of the
calling-card. For some unexplained reason it was kept in
Schwartz's safe. Then in the early summer of 1926 it was
turned over to the *Daily Mirror*. McCarter put it to him
bluntly:

"Were you not paid $10,000 for that card?"

"Oh, my God, no, no, sir! No!"

"Weren't you promised $10,000 for the card?"

"No."

After Joseph A. Faurot, a well-known New York fingerprint expert, corroborated Schwartz's identification on the
direct, McCarter held up a copy of the issue of the *Daily
Mirror* containing a photo of Willie's fingerprint. Then he
brought out in cross-examination that Faurot had gone to
the *Mirror* office on August 19 to inspect the calling-card
after a photographer from that paper and a Jersey police
official had visited him and shown him the card. How law-
enforcement officials could have allowed a piece of official
evidence to get into the hands of newspaper reporters is
hard to explain on any grounds that would not impeach the
integrity of the officials involved.

Four years of innuendo had broadcast the impression that
the case was riddled with bribery. At long last the charges
were ventilated. Other scenes in the trial may have been
more macabre and incredible. This was the ugliest. The
prosecution had finally located the missing former state
trooper, Henry L. Dickman. Where did they uncover this
paragon of law and order? In the brig on Governor's Island,
where he was serving a sentence for deserting the army
during a lost week-end that had stretched out to forty-one
days before the civilian arm of the law caught up with him.
A hard-jawed, shifty-eyed witness, Dickman, who had
originally been assigned to the Hall-Mills case, flatly stated
that he quit the case for a bribe of $2,500. That sum, he
charged, was paid him by the prosecutor of Somerset
County, Azariah Beekman. "Clear out of the case and stay
out," Beekman was alleged to have told him. Since Beekman
had been dead over a year at the time of the trial, Dickman's charges could not be controverted. "I find these
people that are making up these stories always choose dead
men," McCarter later observed. But Dickman's brazen
allegations touched off some pathetic courtroom scenes.
Old-timers, friends and neighbors of Beekman, wept openly.
On the bench Judge Cleary, Beekman's lifetime friend and
law partner, was observed to bow his head and cover his
face with both hands. In a few minutes and with a few

sentences Dickman had made himself the most detested man in Somerville. And the behavior of this cringing figure under cross-examination hardly heightened his popularity. His replies were disingenuous and lacked conviction. Money may very well have been spread around by somebody with a stake in having the investigation dropped, but Dickman's miserable reputation and his shifty conduct on the stand made it hard to believe that he, like so many other witnesses in this weird case, was not lying in his teeth. Simpson's penchant for stringing along with dubious witnesses was again demonstrated when he put on the stand a private detective named Frank Caprio, who swore that a razor Simpson sought to place in evidence had been identified by Judge Beekman as the weapon used to cut Mrs. Mills's throat. A brutal bit of cross-examining by McCarter revealed that Caprio had been convicted of obtaining money under false pretenses. "I won't offer this razor," Simpson backtracked. "I am not satisfied with the statements of this witness."

Lacking strong witnesses, the state tried to buttress its circumstantial case by pounding away at the ugly theme of bribery. Simpson was quite happy about Mrs. Mary Demarest. She swore on the stand that Felix De Martini, a private detective whom Mrs. Hall had engaged and the state had been unable to locate, had offered her $2,500 to shut her mouth against Henry Stevens's alibi. "I said, 'If I wanted to clear the mortgage off on this house, I would rather go to work in a factory in preference to taking Dr. Hall's blood money to keep my mouth shut.'" But her story did not gain in credibility when she admitted under cross-examination that, though her husband and son were upstairs at the time of De Martini's alleged visit, she never bothered to call them.

Mills's appearance on the stand was an occasion for much head-shaking. "They can't get nothing on me," he had boasted before trial. Except to describe his own ambulations on the night of the murder, his testimony on the direct was not illuminating; but the cross-examination started tongues wagging again. McCarter made Mills disclose that, in addition to being a sexton, he was also a shoemaker by trade and possessed a shoe-cutter's knife. His line of questioning was calculated to support the inference that as a sexton Mills, with free access to the rector's papers, had discovered his wife's love letters, and that when at home in his wife's absence he had located some of the rector's. As a matter of fact, he did admit finding some love letters from the rector in his wife's coat or scarf the evening before the crime, but insisted that his wife's facile explanation satisfied him. When Mills stepped down from the stand, he had shown himself to be either a first-class moron or one who played fast and loose with the truth.

Since it was Louise Geist's husband who broke the case wide open with his action for divorce, the ex-maid in the Hall household appeared to relish the opportunity of making out her disaffected spouse to be a liar. She swore on the stand that she saw Mrs. Hall put the receiver back on the hook *before* the rector began his conversation on the upstairs extension. She asserted that her mistress was at home playing solitaire at the very time the state had charged her with being at the Phillips farm. Her testimony gave just one crumb to the state. She related that on the morning after the tragedy Willie told her: "Something terrible has happened that I can't tell you about."

Louise's admission prompted Simpson to play the spotlight on Willie. He called to the stand the tailor's delivery boy, William Greelis, who swore that on the Saturday after the murder Willie gave him a suit to be "cleaned and scoured." The vest and trousers bore dark stains. How did Willie act when he handed over the clothing? He appeared nervous. He would not permit Greelis to enter or leave the house by the front door, though under normal circumstances there would seem nothing suspicious about insisting that he use the service entrance. On cross-examination Case tried to show that Simpson's attempt to read something sinister into the witness's reference to the dark spots was ludicrous. Over the protests of Simpson, he forced Greelis to admit that Willie was known to spill food on his clothes and that he had taken other stained suits of Willie's to the cleaners. Before Case finished with the witness he put to him a few deftly phrased questions:

Q.: Describe as minutely as you can how this suit of clothes was wrapped up.

A.: Well, it was folded up and just tied with a rope.

Q.: No paper around it?

A.: No paper.

Q.: Not concealed at all?

A.: No, sir.

Now back to Mrs. Hall. When Charles Stillwell took the stand, Simpson had him relate how he drove the hearse that carried Hall's body to Brooklyn for burial. He swore that on the ferryboat crossing the North River he observed Mrs. Hall lift her veil, revealing a scratch on her cheek "about an inch and a half long." This observation supported the state's theory of a scuffle under the crab-apple tree, but other attendants at the funeral, defense witnesses, were just as certain that Mrs. Hall's face was devoid of any such temporary disfigurement. Typical of the "eyewitnesses" who failed to survive rigid cross-examination was Elisha K. Sopher, who testified on the direct that, in driving home that fatal night from a meeting of the Eastern Star, he saw a car standing at De Russey's Lane. Two men and a lady were seated in the car. The lady was wearing a light coat. When the defense counsel pressed him, he admitted he could not identify any of the three.

All that the state had accomplished in ten days of testimony was to ventilate smoldering rumors and suspicions, little more. The state had still not produced an eyewitness to the murder. That was the ace up Prosecutor Simpson's sleeve. He had held in reserve his brightest spotlight for Mrs. Jane Gibson, a former circus rider turned pig-farmer, whose performance never has been topped in trial annals. Testifying at the preliminary hearing and before the grand jury, the "Pigwoman," as everybody called her, had placed Mrs. Hall, Willie Stevens, and Henry Carpender at or near the scene of the crime at the time of the murder. But her veracity was seriously impugned by Mrs. Nellie Lo Russell, a Negress, who had sworn that Mrs. Gibson was at her shack at the very time she said she was in De Russey's Lane. Senator Simpson looked into Mrs. Russell's record and discovered that she had been convicted of larceny in Philadelphia in 1921 and put on probation for a year. The state, then, was sanguine that its star witness could not be impugned.

But putting the pigwoman on the stand involved unexpected complications. On the very first day of the trial Mrs. Gibson had collapsed in the corridor of the courthouse on being confronted with her elderly mother, Mrs. Salome Cerrenner, and doubtless for good reasons. Relations between the pair seem to have been exceedingly strained, and the old lady was known to entertain entirely different views about her daughter's capacity for veracious recollection from those of Senator Simpson. Taken directly from the court to the Jersey City hospital, Mrs. Gibson, who was believed to be suffering from cancer and threatened with pneumonia, suffered a serious relapse the night before she was called to testify. She had to be given a blood transfusion.

The date, Thursday, November 19, deserves a place in the annals of the American drama, for no more theatrical scene was ever staged in an American courtroom than was put on by the little impresario at Somerville. Five hundred spectators crammed the poky courtroom built for hardly half that number, and enormous crowds battled with scores of state troopers and deputy sheriffs to force their way inside the edifice. When Mrs. Gibson's ambulance arrived, the bailiffs ordered that the aisles be cleared. The jury chairs were piled to one side to admit the stretcher, which was borne down to the prosecution table. Swathed in sheets and blankets, the patient was carefully lifted onto an iron hospital bed at the pit before the judge's bench. The bed faced the jury, but was in full view of the chairs of the defendants.

High above the bench a half circle of lights beat down full on the motionless figure. As the jury filed in, Mrs. Gibson lay with eyes closed. The hospital physician, Dr. Snyder, stethoscope peeking out of his pocket, took the patient's pulse and shoved a thermometer under her tongue. If anything else were needed to turn the courtroom into the amphitheater of a medical school, it was the pungent smells of iodoform and formaldehyde which now smothered all other odors in the room.

"Silence!" the bailiff boomed. Justice Parker and Judge Cleary now entered with a solemnity appropriate to a more dignified occasion. Then Senator Simpson stepped up to the bench. "If it please the court," he said, "the state produces the witness, Jane Gibson, and asks to have her sworn." But the defense now made its countermove. It managed to maneuver Mrs. Gibson's wrinkled mother to a position down front, where she could keep her eyes on the witness when she testified. Dressed in sober black, with red-rimmed eyes blinking uncertainly and gnarled hands folded on her lap, she kept muttering: "She's a liar—a liar, a liar, that's what she is! Ugh!"

Flanked by a white-clad nurse on one side and the physician on the other, the pigwoman, her face as white as the coverlet, proceeded from a propped-up position in bed to tell her story on direct examination.

SENATOR SIMPSON: On the night of the 15th of September, 1922, what was your occupation?

MRS. GIBSON: Farming.

Q.: Where was your farm?

A.: Hamilton Road, New Brunswick.

Q.: On that night where were you between the hours of 8 and 9?

A.: Between 8 and 9 I was sitting outside listening. I had been robbed on Sunday, or I discovered it on Monday, and I tied the dog out to a tree between the road and the house, and I listened there. I listened every night.

Q.: On Thursday night were you listening?

A.: Yes, sir, I was listening then.

Q.: What had you been robbed of on Sunday?

A.: Corn, two rows, they took all the ears off.

Q.: How many acres of corn did you have?

A.: I had twenty-three acres.

Q.: How many acres of farmland did you have?

A.: Sixty-one acres.

Q.: How many have you now?

A.: Well, not quite twenty.

Q.: When you heard the dog bark on Thursday night what did you do?

A.: I went outside and walked down where the dog was and listened, and when the dog stopped barking I walked back, and I sat on the swing and listened.

Q.: Did you hear anything?

A.: Well, then the bus passed coming from Millstone to New Brunswick.

Q.: What time did the bus pass there?

A.: A quarter to 9.

Q.: After the bus passed what did you do?

A.: Then a wagon came, a rickety old wagon that rattled and rattled and rattled.

Q.: Where did it go?

A.: It went down the road right in the middle of my cornfield.

Q.: Is that the same cornfield that had been robbed?

A.: Yes, sir.

Q.: What did you do then when you heard the wagon stop in the middle of the cornfield that they had stolen from the Sunday night before?

A.: I went to the barn and put the saddle on Jenny and I started out on the road.

Q.: Which way did you go?

A.: Toward New Brunswick.

Q.: Did you or did you not hear the wagon ahead of you as you followed?

A.: Yes, I did. It rattled and went down De Russey's Lane.

Q.: And did you keep following it?

A.: I did. When I got down in the lane the mule brayed.

Q.: What happened to the wagon?

A.: I was afraid to go too close, so I stayed about fifty feet behind. I was afraid.

Q.: After the mule brayed what did you do?

A.: Then the man got going and going and going. He got down Easton Avenue before I did. The sound of the wagon sounded like it was going to New Brunswick.

Q.: Did you see anything up to that time?

A.: Yes.

Q.: What did you see?

A.: When the wagon got out and turned around toward New Brunswick an automobile came in the lane a little ways and I saw two people.

Q.: Who were they—a man and a woman or two men or what?

A.: No, I saw a white woman and a colored man—and she didn't have no hat on.

Q.: Did you know who she was?

A.: I see her face before but I did not know who she was.

Q.: Now have you learned who she was?

A.: Yes, Mrs. Hall.

Q.: Have you learned who the man was who was with her?

A.: Yes.

Q.: Who?

A.: Stevens.

Q.: Which Stevens?

A.: Willie Stevens.

Q.: After you saw those two get out of the automobile—

A.: They didn't get out of the automobile.

Q.: Where were they?

A.: Standing in the road.

Q.: Were you on your mule then?

A.: Yes, right across from that when I looked at them. When the car backed down I went to Easton Avenue and I turned around to try to listen to the wagon, but I could not see it. Then I came around and I saw a sedan standing on the corner.

Q.: Then what did you do?

A.: Then I came back to the lane.

Q.: What lane?

A.: De Russey's Lane. I kept going up and peeking and peeking and peeking and I thought it might be some of those Italians that live in the colony back in there. Of course they heard the braying of the mule. They knew who it was that was following them and they wanted to go away.

Q.: When you went up in De Russey's Lane for the reason that you give what, if anything, did you do with the mule?

A.: Oh, I went way far back and tied her up there.

Q.: Do you know what you tied her to?

A.: Yes, two little cedar trees, and there is a stump there, too.

Q.: As you went up this lane that you describe, did you go right in the lane itself, or parallel with it, in the field?

A.: No, I did not want to go in the lane. I wanted to go in and tie the mule way back.

Q.: Where was that, in the field?

A.: Yes, in the field.

Q.: Now, after you tied your mule to the cedar tree, did you get off the mule?

A.: Oh, yes, I had to get off to tie her.

Q.: Then after you tied her, where did you go?

A.: I walked slowly to De Russey's Lane. I was going to look for the wagon and follow him on foot.

Q.: You thought he was ahead of you?

A.: Yes. I thought if Jenny brayed back there he would not think I was close by.

Q.: As you came down the lane did you hear anything?

A.: I got to where there is a big cedar tree.

Q.: What, if anything, did you hear or see?

A.: I heard mumbling voices to the left of me.

Q.: Men's voices?

A.: Men's voices and women's voices.

Q.: What did you do then, still keep coming?

A.: I stood still. They were coming closer all the time.

Q.: The voices seemed to be coming closer?

A.: Yes. Then they went over that way and came back again.

Q.: When you say that way, do you mean away from the cedar tree or toward the cedar tree?

A.: Toward the cedar tree. They were coming from De Russey's Lane right over toward the cedar tree.

Q.: Were you able to make out any words when they got closer to you?

A.: Yes.

Q.: What words?

A.: Well, the men were talking and a woman said very quick, "Explain these letters."

Q.: And what did you hear the men say, if anything?

A.: They were saying, "God damn it," and everything else. All that kind of stuff.

Q.: Did you hear more than one man say anything?

A.: Somebody was hitting, hitting, hitting. I could hear somebody's wind going out, and somebody said, "Ugh." Then somebody said, "God damn it, let go." A man hollered—

Q.: What do you mean, a man or a woman?

A.: A man hollered.

Q.: And immediately after that what did you hear?

A.: Then somebody threw a flash toward where they were hollering.

Q.: A flashlight?

A.: Yes, and I see something glitter and I see a man, and I see another man like they were wrestling together.

A pause heightened the tension in the courtroom as the nurse interrupted the questioning at this point to apply cold cream to the dried lips of the witness while the doctor continued to count her pulse. Senator Simpson fidgeted impatiently, dropping coins from one hand to the other, until the patient was ready for a resumption of the direct examination.

Q.: Did you see any faces there?

A.: Yes, I see two faces.

Q.: Have you identified those two faces since?

A.: Yes.

Q.: Who were they?

A.: One was Henry Stevens.

Q.: You need not identify the other one. Did you see Willie Stevens there?

A.: No.

Q.: You did not see his face there?

A.: No.

Q.: After you saw Henry Stevens's face did you hear anything?

A.: Yes. The light went out and I heard a shot.

Q.: Then what did you hear?

A.: Then I heard like something fall heavy. Then I run for the mule.

Q.: Did you hear a woman say anything?

A.: Yes. There were two women.

Q.: Did you hear a woman's voice after you heard the shot?

A.: One said, "Oh, Henry," easy, very easy; and the other began to scream, scream, scream so loud, "Oh my, oh my, oh my." So terrible loud.

Q.: Did you hear anything in the way of shots after the first shot?

A.: I ran for the mule after the first shot, but that woman was screaming, screaming, trying to run away or something; screaming, screaming, screaming, and I just about got my foot in the stirrup when bang! bang! bang!— three quick shots.

Q.: Three more shots?

A.: Yes, three more shots.

Q.: Then what did you do when you got your foot in the stirrup?

A.: I stumbled over a stump and I ran home then.

Q.: When you say you ran, do you mean that you ran or that the mule ran home?

A.: The mule ran home.

Q.: When you got home, what happened?

A.: I got off the mule, and then got the mule in the stable, put the mule in the barn and I got my foot wet, that is the first I missed the moccasin.

Q.: Then where did you go?

A.: And I went in the house and I sat around awhile, and I got thinking over the corn and about other things, and about the moccasin, and I was so nervous that I started back, when I found that the moon was out.

Q.: When you got back there did you see these people still there, or were they gone?

A.: After I walked over and I tied the mule, I looked around because I was sure my moccasin was there. It was bright moonlight but I could not see it because it was close to the brush and probably in the brush.

Q.: Underbrush?

A.: Underbrush; yes, sir. So I felt around. I held the mule by the bridle, and I felt around, all around the stump, all around the place, and I heard what I thought was the screeching of an owl, and I didn't think much of it at the time, but then when I heard it again I listened.

Q.: What did you find?

A.: Well, then, when I heard that screeching, why, then I stopped and listened again, and I heard it again, and I said, "Something is the matter out here," and then I listened and then I heard the voice of a man. It seemed kind of like a woman hollered along there or some one, and then I heard the voice of a man, and the moon was shining down very bright, and so I heard it again, and I looked right at the cedar, and I crossed over the lane right at the cedar, and I seen a big white-haired woman doing something with her hand, crying, something.

Q.: Standing up?

A.: No, bending down, facing something.

Q.: Was she standing up?

A.: No, kneeling down, fixing something.

Q.: Did you see who it was?

A.: Yes, the woman I seen in the lane earlier in the evening.

Q.: The same woman you say was Mrs. Hall?

A.: Yes.

As Mrs. Gibson's voice croaked this charge, her mouth twitched and her head wagged mechanically from side to side. But the weird, white-faced patient was not through. Over the vigorous objections of defense counsel, Senator Simpson had the pigwoman relate the circumstances of a call paid on her by De Martini some time after the Hall-Mills tragedy.

Q.: What did he say to you?

A.: He said, "You had better keep your mouth shut; it will pay you better to keep out of this"; and I jumped up and I said, "Who are you?" So I took the gun and banged it on the floor.

Q.: Did he stay or go away?

A.: No, he began to move. I told him to move. I said, "Move, and move quick." I was afraid of him.

Q.: When he said, "You had better keep your mouth shut and stay out of this," did he say what he meant by "this"?

A.: The Hall case.

Q.: How long was that after you had made public what you knew?

A.: Not long.

Still to come was the dramatic moment when Senator Simpson asked Mrs. Gibson whether she recognized any of the people mentioned in her account. "That looks like the lady," she croaked, pointing a stubby finger at Mrs. Hall. How about the men, the prosecutor pressed her. It so happened that Henry and Willie, who sat on either side of the widow, wore brown ties. Since Mrs. Gibson's identification was ambiguous, Simpson felt that he had to help his witness out. "Is that the man?" the prosecutor asked, pointing to New Brunswick's number-one amateur fire-fighter. Case objected to what he considered coaching, but the prosecutor retorted: "Do you want her to get out of bed and go down and put her hand on him?" After she picked out Willie, she then identified Henry Stevens as the third of the trio she had seen in De Russey's Lane.

Seldom has a direct examination been stage-managed with so many theatrical props. Grimly determined to prove Mrs. Gibson the biggest fabricator of all the state's array of disingenuous witnesses, Senator Case, suave but insistent, proceeded step by step to take the witness and her story apart. First, he sought to get the pigwoman to admit discrepancies between the account she had told two investigators back in 1922 and her tale on direct. He pressed her to admit that she then had said that she discovered the loss of her moccasin before she reached home, and that she had told an Essex County detective that she heard the shots while she was still on her mule going up De Russey's Lane. He asked her about an alleged conversation with one George Sipple, in the course of which she had been reputed to have

offered Sipple one hundred dollars to testify that he turned
into De Russey's Lane that night and saw two men and a
woman close by, and a little farther up the lane a horse or
mule ridden by a man or woman. She denied it. The hundred dollars was the figure she had set on a pair of mules,
not a bribe to suborn a witness. Why had she been unable
to identify Mrs. Hall, Willie, and Henry when confronted
with them in the prosecutor's office on October 17, 1922?
The witness hedged. Case pressed her about a reputed conversation with John Fitzgerald, a reporter for the *Camden
Daily Courier*, in the course of which she admitted not being able to identify anybody. "I told him I had nothing to
say," she replied sullenly.

But Case continued to press on relentlessly. He now confronted the witness with her testimony in the preliminary
hearing in August 1926, just three months before the trial.
On that occasion she had picked Henry Carpender's as a
face she had seen on the fatal night. She now admitted
having done so. Did she mention having seen any other
man? "No, nobody asked me that," she fenced. Case reminded her that at the August hearing she stated that she
could not make out anybody else. "I could not see; it was
dark," was her surprising admission.

The serious discrepancies in the pigwoman's accounts
over a period of four years pointed to only two possible conclusions: either her memory was faulty or she was a downright liar. But the way in which Senator Case administered
the *coup de grâce* bears comparison with the best trial work
of Lord Coleridge or Sir Edward Carson.

SENATOR CASE: You were sworn here today, I think, as
Jane Easton?

MRS. GIBSON: Both Easton and Gibson.

Q.: Which is your name?

A.: Both.

Q.: Your name is Jane Easton and it is also Jane Gibson?

A.: I acquired the name from having a farm. They always got Gibson's farm products; people got calling me Mrs. Gibson and I never said nothing.

Q.: You took title to your farm under the name of Jane Gibson, did you not?

A.: I sure did.

Q.: Therefore, if you took title to the farm as Jane Gibson, how do you explain what you have already said?

On objection from the prosecution, the question was overruled when the defense failed to explain in what way it was material. Case tried another tack.

Q.: How do you get the names Easton and Gibson?

A.: My marriage name.

Q.: And by your marriage name you mean that you were married to a man named Easton?

A.: I was.

Q.: When and where were you married to him?

A.: 1919.

Q.: Where?

A.: Somewhere in a church—the Little Church Around the Corner.

Q.: Will you tell us where you were married?

A.: I don't remember that.

Q.: Do you remember the name of the city or town in which you were married?

A.: No, I do not remember.

Q.: Do you remember the name of the State where you were married?

A.: Jersey.

Case sought in vain to get the witness to tell him the name she gave to the person officiating at the marriage ceremony. When the court barred the question as immaterial, the defense counsel brought out the fact that Mrs. Gibson's father's name was Eisleitner, but that she called herself Mary Jane Leitner, and was known variously as Jane Easton and Mary Easton. But the latter, she insisted virtuously, was after she was married. "I had a right to my marriage name, didn't I?" she protested. How about Jessie Easton? "Well, my hubby called me that—Jessie. He liked that name." Case also tried to get the witness to admit that she also at times had gone under the names of Janet Hilton and Anna King, which she denied. At this point Simpson, who was showing the strain, interposed:

"If it pleases the Court, the witness says she said the date of her marriage was 1919; she must be mistaken, because her boy is twenty-two years old." Mrs. Gibson stood by the corrected date, but still could not recall where she was married. "I don't just remember, it is a long while ago."

SENATOR CASE: How many husbands have you had?

MRS. GIBSON: How many husbands, how many husbands have I had?

Q.: Yes.

A.: I have had one husband that I can remember.

Q.: And this is who?

A.: William H. Easton.

Q.: Do you know Mr. Kesselring?

A.: He was a married man who had a baby; I could not be his wife.

Q.: Do you remember Mr. Kesselring?

A.: I remember his name, yes.

Q.: You lived with him as his wife, did you not?

A.: No, sir, I did not. I lived in the house.

Q.: Were you not married to Frederick Kesselring in Paterson on the 13th day of August, 1890?

A.: I don't remember that. I don't remember anything about such a marriage.

Q.: You don't remember anything about such a marriage?

A.: No, sir.

Q.: Do you remember that Mr. Frederick Kesselring obtained a decree of divorce from you from the Court of Chancery in the State of New Jersey on the ground of adultery?

A.: What?

SENATOR SIMPSON: I object to it unless the time is fixed.

SENATOR CASE: I will fix the time.

Q.: Do you remember that Mr. Frederick Kesselring obtained a divorce from you from the Court of Chancery in the State of New Jersey on the ground of your adultery, obtaining the final decree, filed January 4, 1899?

A.: No. That is mixed up with somebody else. That man was a married man and had a wife and baby.

Q.: Did you not live with Frederick Kesselring as his wife from on or about the date of the marriage on August 13, 1890, until about February 16, 1892, in the City of Paterson?

A.: No.

When the court, over Senator Simpson's objections, allowed the question, Mrs. Gibson insisted: "I never lived with no such person no time."

Q.: Have you ever known a man named Harry Ray?

A.: No.

Q.: You never lived with Harry Ray?

A.: Who is he?

Q.: Well, now, I am asking you.

A.: I never lived with—how many should I have—a dozen? Such talk!

Q.: Did you ever live with a man?

A.: No, I didn't.

SENATOR SIMPSON: I object, unless he specifically frames this question. She may have lived in a house or a flat. "Did you live in open lewdness or in lewdness with such and such a man without being married to him?" I do not object to. But I do object to his saying, "Did you live?"

Then Senator Case confounded the confusion by throwing in an additional name, that of Stumpy Gillan, whom the pigwoman denied ever having known.

The pigwoman had given a clinical demonstration of obsessional neurosis, of not allowing oneself to remember what could not possibly have been forgotten. But regardless of how the analysts would interpret her answers, the state's star witness had been blown sky-high. The rest of her testimony was anticlimactic. She kept denying, denying, denying that she had made previous statements in contradiction to her testimony on direct. But Senator Case was hunting for bigger game than perjury. His questions now took a turning that insinuated the pigwoman herself had a motive for the killings. Didn't she mount the mule in pursuit of someone she believed was stealing her corn? Didn't she own a twelve-gauge-barreled shotgun? She admitted ownership, but denied having a pistol. "Why did you keep that there?" Case asked. "Because when I went out at nights I would use it to scare thieves away." That was exactly what she claimed to have been doing the night of the crime. But when the defense counsel asked her: "What sort of a firearm did you take with you?" she evaded the trap. "I did not take any with me, nothing," she muttered.

With enormous patience Case had Mrs. Gibson go over her story of her return visit to De Russey's Lane that same night, either to find the man who had stolen her corn or to recover her moccasin—she never did clear this up. She asserted that she saw a woman, whom she now recognized as Mrs. Hall, kneeling on the ground, "making a funny noise."

"Shrieking like an owl, but yet you did nothing?"

"I thought the man was a colored man and she was assaulted. I thought it was none of my business."

"Now, did you think that a white woman who had been assaulted by a colored man was beyond the scope of your help and consolation?"

Over the objection of Senator Simpson, the pigwoman replied: "I didn't want to mix up in it. What did I know? When I see a white woman with a colored man—it serves them right."

Why did she fail to report the murder promptly, Case demanded. "Nobody wants to get mixed up with anybody and accuse anybody of murder, even though they do see it," she answered, and, as a later reflection: "I thought the authorities were slick enough to find out who did do it." Mrs. Gibson's final admission may have been more significant than she intended. "I didn't think anything more about it," she stated. "I thought it might have been something else. *I have shot my gun off lots of times, and people hollered and screamed, but nobody was hurt.*"

The climax of this maddening day was still to come. Just as her mattress was lifted to a stretcher and four attendants approached to remove her to the waiting ambulance, the pigwoman turned a wild face on the three defendants, shook her right forefinger at them, and snarled vindictively: "I've told the truth, so help me God; and you know it; and you know it!" Then she fell back. Perspiration stood out all over her face. Technically these remarks did not get into the record, and the jury had already gone out when the scene occurred. After three grueling hours the pigwoman enjoyed her brief triumph and was carried out. She lived another four years.

From the start of the defense case, which opened the next day it was apparent that sensationalism would be played down. There had been too much of dramatics already. Case's opening was an intimate chat with the jury. His tone was that of injured innocence. "None of the defendants were there," he contended. "None of the defendants knew anything about it, either before or after the sad, sad tragedy; knew nothing about and had nothing to do with it." After the jury had heard their story from their own lips, Case predicted, "your conscience and your minds will be free to acquit them."

Many rash assertions had been credited to Simpson in the course of the trial, none more rash, however, than his prediction that none of the defendants ever would go into the witness box. While defendants in criminal cases may, of course, exercise their constitutional privilege, the failure of a suspect in a murder case to take the stand is almost in-

variably fatal. So the defense staff must have reasoned, for
they proceeded to make a grand slam and put all four in the
box in rapid succession.

First came Henry Stevens, who took the stand on his
fifty-seventh birthday. After he completed his direct testimony supporting his Lavalette alibi, Simpson took over.
Unable to dent the story that Henry had been bluefishing
on Barnegat Bay some fifty miles away from the scene of
the murders, the prosecutor fell back on his theatrical techniques. He confronted Stevens with a gruesome anatomical
model of Mrs. Mills's head and back. Stevens seemed unmoved. After bringing out the fact that Stevens had been a
demonstrator for a firearms firm and was an expert marksman, the prosecutor put his hand on the model's throat and
remarked: "You have described cutting bluefish to clean
them. Can you tell us what kind of cuts you make in the
throat to clean bluefish?"

Unperturbed, Stevens replied: "I could not."

"You say you could not make the wounds on this figure
on the throat?"

"A bluefish is nothing like that at all," Henry pointed out
with exemplary patience. "A bluefish is a different shape in
every way."

Thus ended Simpson's confession tableau and with it the
collapse of his hypothesis that Henry had fired the shots
that killed the couple, had then crept beneath the low-
hanging crab-apple tree and, in an excess of fury, had
slashed the throat of the Mills woman. In fact, Henry was
virtually eliminated as a suspect when his alibi story was
backed by a trio of women. Mrs. Sarah M. Wilson and her
two daughters were quite positive that Stevens was at their
home at Lavalette at almost the exact time the crime was
committed.

But if the imperturbable Henry would not crack, his less
balanced brother, Willie, might be a bird of a different
feather. It seemed like a dangerous gamble. Who could
predict just what that middle-aged eccentric would say or

do under pressure? Throughout the trial he had followed
the testimony with the intense delight of a child. "There
is an irresponsible rotundity about him which suggests that
a small boy had been blown up balloon-wise and now goes
bobbing into the breeze," one reporter commented. But regardless of how upset Willie had seemed when the news of
the crime had broken and even a few months before the
trial, when he was arrested and grilled, he now seemed to
exude confidence from every pore.

What would happen when he took the stand? Willie's conduct was the surprise of the trial. Speaking like an English
vicar, he gave an intelligent, straightforward story on the
direct examination. Under Simpson's severe quizzing he remained sweet-tempered. Despite the attempt of the prosecutor to prove that he had Negroid blood and was in fact a
mental defective, Willie seemed to bear no grudge. "I still
say you have to take your hat off to Willie. Willie's all
right," Mrs. Hall remarked in one of the few manifestations
of anything like emotion she displayed throughout the trial.

Simpson had been forced to indict Henry Carpender because the pigwoman had identified him as the man who did
the shooting. Her action must have come as a shock to the
prosecutor, who had hoped she would pin the killing on
Henry Stevens. While he went through the motions of indicting the wealthy stockbroker, he shrewdly arranged to
have him tried separately, as the case against him was the
flimsiest of all. But if Simpson thought that he could keep
Henry Carpender out of his cousin's trial, he must have been
stunned when the stockbroker was called as a defense witness. Before Simpson could get his bearings, the defense had
slipped over this question: "Were you on the night of September 14, 1922, at the Phillips farm or De Russey's
Lane?" Carpender shot out: "No, I was not."

In vain did Simpson seek to strike the answer from the
record. The defense justified the question on the ground that
the pigwoman on direct examination had accused Mrs. Hall,
Stevens, *and* Carpender, and that the question went to the

credibility of the state's witness. The court sustained the defense, which once again showed that it was not asleep in matters of courtcraft.

And now the enigmatic central figure of the tragedy took the stand. Chief target of suspicion, envy, and spite, Mrs. Hall had been portrayed in the press as a cold-blooded ogre, a stone image, concealing her guilt behind the most perfect poker face since the man in the iron mask. After this build-up her behavior must have sorely let down millions of tabloid readers, for she bore herself with dignity and breeding. Dressed in black, with a touch of white at the throat, she testified in a low and cultivated voice. Her frankness on the direct was disarming. She admitted being frantic the night of the crime and going to the church around half past two in the morning. "I did not sleep all night." McCarter did not skirt the issue.

"Now, Mrs. Hall, did you kill your husband or Mrs. Mills?"

"I did not." Mrs. Hall's voice was steady.

"Did you play any part in that dreadful tragedy?"

"I did not."

"Were you in the neighborhood of De Russey's Lane or that vicinity on the night of September 14, 1922?"

"I was not."

"Have you given this jury a straightforward, accurate statement of your movements that night?"

"Absolutely."

"Was your face scratched, Mrs. Hall?"

"It was not."

"Take the witness."

That was all. Simpson rose up like an executioner. He hammered at her story from every angle, but Mrs. Hall remained unshaken. At the end of the merciless cross-examination it was Simpson, not Mrs. Hall, who had the mien of a whipped schoolboy.

Through direct testimony or insinuations the state had sought to enmesh the defendants in a network of bribery

and subornation of witnesses. For months the state had
sought De Martini, Mrs. Hall's detective. In fact, there was
a warrant out for his arrest on extradition proceedings.
Again, before Simpson realized what was happening, De
Martini slipped inside the courtroom and was on the stand.
Now a court witness, he was momentarily beyond the reach
of the warrant of arrest. The detective swore that all the
stories told about him were false. He denied ever having
talked with Mrs. Demarest or the pigwoman. He plausibly
explained that Mrs. Hall had paid him five thousand dollars
for services covering a period of five months, from October
1922 to March 1923. He figured his own compensation at
twenty dollars a day, and twelve dollars a day for each of
three operatives he had put on the assignment. On that basis
his fee did not seem excessive. As soon as the detective
stepped down from the stand, he was promptly arrested.

At this stage of the trial, when the evidence on both sides
was all in, Simpson might properly have asked himself: at
what point did the state's case go to pieces? Under cross-
fire the miserable showing of state's witnesses of the caliber
of Dickman, the former inmate of Alcatraz, started the
debacle. Senator Case's deft demonstration of Mrs. Gibson's
incapacity for veracious reporting left the state gasping, and
Simpson's failure to break down any of the defendants and
trap them into one of those improbable confessions dear to
Hollywood removed the foundations of the case. But it remained for McCarter and Case, in their overpowering summations, to topple the house of cards into the excavation.

Even before the closing speeches Simpson knew he was
whipped soundly. After twenty-nine days of courtroom dramatics involving some five thousand pages of testimony, he
virtually threw in the towel by moving for a mistrial on
the ground that some of the jurors had expressed violent
prejudices in favor of the defendants. "They would not convict if the murder was committed before their faces," he
told the court after the jury had been excluded. "You might
just as well try the case before twelve trees—perhaps with

more satisfaction, because the trees in course of time would bud and blossom, and they never will." Without comment or even calling upon the defense to argue on the motion, Parker calmly denied it.

McCarter now rose to administer the final blow. His remarks were meant for the jurors and he gave them his undivided attention. Speaking fluently and with occasional fire, he portrayed the defendants as honest, decent, church-going folk, incapable of so base a crime. If the state needed a suspect, how about James Mills, he asked. He had a motive, too, and he also had the opportunity to find the rector's letters when his wife was away on vacation in the summer of 1922. Take Mills's remarks after Mrs. Hall informed him that her husband had not been home all night. "Neither has my wife," the sexton stated, adding: "perhaps they have eloped." Thrusting his aggressive chin right at the jury, McCarter shouted: "I think that is the most significant remark of Mills." Mrs. Hall's rejoinder to the sexton bespoke an innocence of any knowledge of her husband's affairs, he argued. "That is absurd," she snapped. "What are you talking about? Perfectly ridiculous!"

It was one thing to dispose of palpable perjurers; it was another matter to explain the seemingly incriminating actions of Mrs. Hall and Willie after the crime. McCarter knew that he could not duck the story that had caused more malicious gossip than any other incident—the coat-dyeing episode. He rose to the challenge. "Why send the coat and scarf to Philadelphia?" he asked. "Because when Mrs. Hall's mother died her daughter's things were then sent to the same firm to be dyed for mourning. Mrs. Bearman took this coat home before they were sent, and she stretched it out before she packed it in a box to be sent by express to the dyers, and Mr. Chambers was there, and Mrs. Moncure Carpender was there, and they both saw the coat, and there was absolutely nothing of blood or anything else on it."

Then, turning to Willie's dry-cleaning operations, he dryly remarked: "You are like the man that the Presbyterians speak of—you see, I am a good Presbyterian—'You are damned if you do and damned if you don't.' Willie, on the other hand, sent his articles to New Brunswick to be cleaned, and he evidently is the man who spills his food on his waistcoat. And the records of the store tell us that *two* suits—ha! ha! Did he have two suits on a hot night?—*two* suits were brought there to be cleaned and scoured, just as they had been accustomed to be time and time again. Oh, damning proof of their connection with the crime!" Had Simpson been in McCarter's shoes, he most certainly would have come up with "Out, damned spot!" But the defense wasted no time on literary allusions.

At no point in his summation was McCarter more effective than in disposing of the last and possibly most damning circumstantial link to the crime—the fingerprint on the calling-card. McCarter pointed out that the experts could not find a thumbprint. "Evidently, if their story is true, William had to take time to spit on his finger, or else have some paste near by and hold that card by attrition that way, and put it down—mind you, a right-handed man—put it down without any thumb holding it behind, against a man's shoe or against a blade of grass." Having eliminated the likelihood that this print could have been put there at the time of the crime, McCarter now attacked the document as "a hocus-pocus print fraudulently put there." He charged that Schwartz had planted the fingerprint on the card, picking a similar specimen from his office files.

Case crowded the prosecution from the start. Seizing Mrs. Hall's hand, encased in a gray silk glove, he held it before the jury and exclaimed: "Is this the hand that fired the gun that killed these two people? Is this the hand that pulled the knife that cut Mrs. Mills's throat?" Inscrutable as ever, Mrs. Hall endured the scene with a resigned and weary look. Moving to the offensive, Case assailed the tactics of the prosecution. Take the cross-examination of Henry Stevens, he said, quoting from the record: "Now, Mr. Stevens, show on this model how you cut the fish?"

"Fine stuff for a drama!" Case shouted. "Poor stuff for a trial in a court of justice. Vindictive stuff. Not worthy of the state of New Jersey."

But Case was at his best in disposing of the pigwoman. He ridiculed the motion that by the light of a flashlight, which lasted a mere second, she was able to see the struggling figures, and through two rows of shrubbery, across a lane, and some distance beyond. He reminded the jury that only a few months before, she had told a grand jury that it was Henry Carpender she saw there and that he was the only man whose face she saw that night. Now she insisted it was Henry Stevens who did the shooting. And if the state wanted a probable suspect, what better one than the pigwoman herself, Case insinuated.

Simpson had the last word. Making obeisance to the custom of forensic utterance, he quoted from Euripides, Shakespeare, Byron, and Macaulay—among the few persons who had solid alibis for the night of September 14, 1922. Then, recognizing the hopelessness of his cause, he ventured to violate a basic canon of trial tactics. Shaking his finger in the face of one of the jurors, whom he denounced by name for his bias, he dared the jury to do its worst. Dancing back and forth before the jury box with the agility of an acrobat, he piled denunciations on the unbowed heads of the defendants, save for Willie, with whom he was unexpectedly gentle. "Willie Stevens was not the man, in my opinion, who did this job," he argued. "It was a crackerjack marksman who did this job and there was a fight. But Willie is in it up to his neck." Mrs. Hall was again portrayed as a woman devoid of all emotion save jealous rage, a rage that prompted her to slash her rival's throat. "Look at her eyes if you want to know the truth about this thing!" he screamed. While the jury turned toward her, Mrs. Hall's sphinxlike features were momentarily lighted up with the barest suggestion of a Mona Lisa smile.

The verdict was a foregone conclusion. Betting was ten to one against even a disagreement. When the jury filed in at about 6.45 p.m. after being out a little over five hours, they returned a verdict of not guilty. The announcement caused a tumult in the courtroom. As the reporters left to flash the news thunderous cheers rang out from the crowds massed outside the building. Governor A. Harry Moore summed up the popular reaction of fair-minded persons when he said: "I think the state has gone far enough. It's prosecution, not persecution we want."

But even then the ghost of Hall-Mills had not been laid. Risking a reopening of the entire case, Mrs. Hall and her brothers brought a libel suit against the *Mirror* for a half million dollars. But Payne had no stomach for a further fight and ran out, leaving his attorneys to settle out of court for a reputed fifty thousand dollars. Lavalette residents gave Henry Stevens a resounding vote of confidence by re-electing him to their village council, and Riehl lost his divorce action.

But the irrepressible "witness" refused to be throttled. A year after the trial a Cuban druggist wrote to the American consul at Havana to report having overheard a conversation in which an Italian accused two Germans of committing the double murder. The Italian was said to have been employed as a chauffeur by a wealthy German woman alleged to have been in love with the rector. Save for the fact that the writer of the letter could not identify the Italian nor recall the name of the German woman, he had a whopper of a story. Again in 1929 a convict named Edwin F. Allen, serving a term for forgery in an Oklahoma jail, declared that he was the man who did the shooting, for which he was paid six thousand dollars by a Connecticut dentist claiming to be related to one of the murdered pair. Allen shared credit with two accomplices, a man and a woman. The convict's story had only one flaw: he had the names right, but the year wrong. He had put the killings in 1921 instead of 1922. "Pure bunk" was the way the police characterized a tale seemingly inspired by the convict's desire to get a free ride back east. And so it went.

And if any enterprising newspaperman feels that he may still dig up some new clues in De Russey's Lane, let him save himself a trip to the scene of the crime. That romantic byway has completely buried its lurid past in a typical boomtime face-lifting. Yielding to middle-class respectability, it has become Franklin Boulevard, the center of a real-estate development. Lost forever is the rustic setting of the night of September 14, 1922, and the gnarled crab-apple tree has long since been torn limb from limb by souvenir-hunters.

XIV

The Case of Alger Hiss

"the truth, the whole truth . . ."

Perhaps the entire truth about the Hiss case will never be uncovered. Two juries have considered the evidence, and the highest court of the land has refused to intercede in behalf of the convicted man. But the mystery that enshrouds this case has by no means been resolved. There are those who believe that neither the accused nor his accuser has told all he knows,[1] and that Hiss's reticence encourages McCarthyism and the continued sniping at the liberals within the State Department. Others contend that the prosecution was more concerned with securing a conviction than with uncovering the truth, and point to the startling attacks on the validity of the corroborative evidence which have been made since the second trial. The charge that Hiss was convicted on faked evidence will have to be met squarely by the government. Regardless of the ultimate disposition of this new charge, a more fundamental question raised by the trials transcends in significance the factual issue of the accused's guilt: *was Hiss properly convicted on the law and the evidence in the case?*

The Hiss case disclosed glaring shortcomings in our criminal procedure, which both sides did not hesitate to exploit. The prosecutor's opening and summation were replete with inflammatory and prejudicial arguments and references to damaging matter not in the record. The proper procedure for identification was ignored by the government, the prosecution's witnesses seem to have been improperly

[1] In *Witness* (New York, 1952), Whittaker Chambers insists that there is *another* witness. "At least, like Hamlet, I see a cherub, who sees one."

coached, and surprise evidence was timed so that the accused could not have had an opportunity for refutation. The right of the accused to be confronted by the witnesses against him implies a right to subject their testimony to cross-examination. But the prosecutor who calls a witness to the stand for no purpose but to ask him questions that it is known in advance he will refuse to answer on the ground of self-incrimination has in effect deprived the defendant of that right of cross-examination.

Nor was the handling of the case of the accused man above criticism. Government witnesses were insulted and the word "traitor" was bandied about as freely by one side as the other even though the trial was for perjury and not for treason. In employing psychiatric testimony to impugn a witness the defense injected into both trials a highly controversial note. Some critics have contended that the field of psychiatry has not attained sufficient scientific respectability to be employed in this fashion, that at present the diagnosis of mental disease is lacking in precision and subject to the personal equation. Others argue that the use of such testimony invades the domain traditionally reserved for the jury.

The Hiss case exposed lamentable weaknesses in our jury system. Contrary to all established rules of procedure, the jurors in the first trial assumed the role of detectives and attempted to decide whether the crucial typewritten exhibits had been typed, not on the same typewriter, but by the same person. This was an issue on which no government expert had ventured an opinion. It is well recognized that for a jury to go beyond the body of testimony presented to them and pose as experts constitutes ground for a mistrial. Why did the court permit these and other deplorable lapses in accepted trial procedure to take place?

Each step in the Hiss case raised a cloud of legal and ethical issues. It started as a trial by denunciation. The charges were first brought into the open at a Congressional hearing at which virtually none of the safeguards of due process were observed. The next step, the grand-jury testimony, was planned as a trap for the accused. Since the prosecution of Hiss for espionage was barred by the statute of limitations, the government sought to circumvent this obstruction by indicting him for perjury. He was in fact, however, obliged to meet a charge of espionage allegedly committed ten years earlier, after much evidence had vanished and memories had faded. The case against the accused rested on a single witness supported by certain documentary evidence. That lone witness, a confessed ex-spy, had himself given false testimony before the grand jury, but escaped all legal punishment. The supporting evidence was brought forth under such bizarre circumstances that it called for the most meticulous scrutiny.

Doubts of the loyalty of Alger Hiss were expressed to a responsible government official at least nine years before the full extent of his alleged double-dealing was exposed. Immediately after the conclusion of the Hitler-Stalin pact a former member of the Communist underground named Whittaker Chambers called the attention of Adolf A. Berle to the nature of Communist penetration within the government. Alger Hiss was mentioned along with his brother Donald and Nathan Witt. Berle, at that time an Assistant Secretary of State, dismissed the notion as offering no "immediate danger" to the country. Investigated under the Hatch Act in 1941, Hiss was given a clean bill of health, and he continued his rapid rise in the State Department, serving as secretary general of the San Francisco Conference of '45 and becoming Director of the Office of Special Political Affairs. On several occasions William C. Bullitt, Ambassador to France, in conversations with Stanley K. Hornbeck, Hiss's superior officer in the State Department, had referred to Hiss as a fellow traveler or a Communist. Hornbeck shrugged his shoulders and did nothing. When, in November 1945, Igor Gouzenko, a former Soviet code clerk, disclosed that five different espionage rings were operating in the United States and in Canada, the rumors

against Hiss were quickly revived. He assured the then
Secretary of State, James F. Byrnes, that they were
baseless, and appears to have satisfied the F.B.I., which investigated him at this time and again in May 1947. In December 1946 Hiss was selected for the twenty-thousand-
dollar post of president of the Carnegie Endowment for
International Peace.

But the smoldering doubts about Alger Hiss were not
readily extinguished. On August 3, 1948 Whittaker Chambers unfolded his story in the hearing-room of the House
Un-American Activities Committee. This first story was a
weird tale, and his later revisions were even more fantastic. He had joined the Communist Party as far back as
1925, he told the committee, had served in fact as editor of
the *Daily Worker,* and then had been sent to Washington
as a courier between New York and an apparatus of government employees set up in the capital. Each member of
this élite group, according to Chambers, was a cell leader.
He named names: Nathan Witt, Lee Pressman, Alger Hiss,
Donald Hiss, Victor Perlo, Charles Kramer, John Abt, and
Henry Collins, with Harold Ware as organizer.[2] Finally, in
1937 Chambers, according to his account (in mid-April
1938 by his testimony at the second trial and his published
story), decided to break with the party. "I had sound reason
for supposing that the Communists might try to kill me,"
he declared. Considering the mysterious fate of Juliet
Stuart Poyntz, who also broke with the party, and the
assassination of Leon Trotsky, Chambers's alarm may have
had some basis in fact. Under examination by Robert E.
Stripling, chief investigator for the House committee,
Chambers related how he informed Hiss of his decision

---

[2] In February 1952 Nathaniel Weyl testified before the McCarran
Committee that he had been a member of the Ware group in 1934.
He names the same group as Chambers had four years previously,
including Alger Hiss. For some obscure reason he failed to mention
this fact in his treatment of the Hiss case in *Treason* (Washington,
D.C., 1950).

and begged him to break with the party. "As a matter of
fact, he cried when we separated," Chambers declared, "but
he absolutely refused to break." "He cried?" Representative John McDowell asked. "Yes, he did," Chambers replied. *"I was very fond of Mr. Hiss."* Before leaving the
stand, Chambers corroborated testimony given by Elizabeth Bentley on the previous day which had implicated
Harry Dexter White, Assistant Secretary of the Treasury.
White had been accused of working with Nathan Gregory
Silvermaster, who, it was alleged, had photographic apparatus in his basement with which he copied government
documents for transmission to a Russian spy ring.

Unlike Perlo, Kramer, Silvermaster, Abt, Witt, and Pressman (the last-named later admitted brief membership in the
party [3]), all of whom now shielded themselves behind the
Fifth Amendment, Hiss, with righteous indignation, seized
the offensive. In a wire to the House committee, in the course
of which he requested an opportunity to be heard in his
own defense, he declared: "I do not know Mr. Chambers
and in so far as I am aware have never laid eyes on him."
Hiss was given his chance on August 5. Poised and confident, he denied any affiliation with the Communists, and
seemed evasive at only one point. "You say you have never
seen Mr. Chambers?" Hiss was asked by Robert E. Stripling, committee investigator. "The name means absolutely
nothing to me, Mr. Stripling," Hiss answered. When shown
photographs of Chambers taken during 1934 and '35 and
an A.P. photo taken only a few days before the hearing,
Hiss declared: *"I would not want to take an oath that I
have never seen that man."*

Although the committee's investigator had himself admitted that "Chambers is much heavier today than he was
at that time," many people felt that Hiss's failure to make
positive identification on that occasion and again on August
16 bespoke a suspicious evasiveness. When it is borne in

[3] He testified that during the period of his own participation in
the Ware group (1934–5) Alger Hiss was not a member of it.

mind, however, that Hiss never knew his accuser under the
name of Whittaker Chambers, and that Chambers's physical appearance had markedly changed, his cautious reply
seems more understandable. At the second trial of Alger
Hiss the facts were brought out that one witness, Joseph R.
Boucot, who had rented a summer cottage to Chambers in
1935, when he was going under the name of Breen, had
similarly failed to recognize "Breen" from the two sets of
photos when he was asked by the F.B.I. to make the identification. Despite Hiss's insistence that he would rather see
his accuser before making a more categorical identification,
the committee seemed reluctant to badger him. Even
John E. Rankin, Congress's ace hatemonger, congratulated
the witness " that he didn't refuse to answer the questions
on the ground that it might incriminate him, and he didn't
bring a lawyer here to tell him what to say."

Hiss's vindication proved short-lived. Two days later
Chambers returned to the committee room and provided a
number of circumstantial details to support his charges.
Back in 1935, Chambers stated, Hiss had turned over his
dilapidated *"black"* Ford roadster to the Communist Party
when he purchased a new Plymouth. Asked about Hiss's
hobbies, Chambers was quite specific. Both Hisses shared
the same hobby: they were bird-observers. "They used to
get up early in the morning and go to Glen Echo, out by
the canal, to observe the birds. I recall once they saw, to
their great excitement, a *prothonotary warbler.*"

To the members of the House committee it now seemed
apparent that Chambers either knew the Hisses fairly intimately or had taken the trouble, for some obscure and
devious motive, to gather certain intimate details about
their private lives. When, on August 16, Alger Hiss again
appeared in the Old House Office Building, he found the
atmosphere glacial. Again he stated that the face in the
photos was "not an unfamiliar face." Refreshing his recollection, he now told the committee that in December 1934,
or January 1935, when he was counsel to the Nye Com-

mittee, he encountered a person named *George Crosley,* a
free-lance writer doing a series of articles on the munitions
investigation. When Crosley intimated that he was hard
pressed for a place to house his family, Hiss had volunteered, according to his testimony: "You can have my
apartment." In June of '35, he went on, he subleased his
apartment at 2831 Twenty-eighth Street to Crosley for the
balance of the lease and moved to a house on P Street.
Along with the apartment, Hiss, according to his own account, threw in "an old, old Ford we had kept for sentimental reasons . . . *dark blue,*" with "a sassy little trunk
on the back." How about a bill of sale? "I think I just
turned it over to him." Questioned about his hobbies, Hiss
readily admitted to being an amateur ornithologist.

"Did you ever see a prothonotary warbler?" McDowell
asked him.

Hiss did not hesitate for a moment. "I have, right here
on the Potomac." Startling as this confirmation of Chambers's story might have seemed on its face, it in fact only
substantiated the charge that the two men knew each other,
a fact that Hiss had never denied. It was entirely irrelevant
to the more serious charge, that Hiss had been in the party.

At this point, contrary to accepted standards of criminal
procedure, the House committee seemed prepared to shift
the burden of proof upon Hiss to clear himself of the
charges. Would Hiss be willing to take a lie-detector test,
Nixon now asked. Chambers had previously agreed to do
so. Hiss declined giving a categorical answer. He quite
properly pointed out that the lie-detector is not really a
test of lying but "an emotion-recording test." Even after
Hiss was told that the test would be administered by Dr.
Leonardo Keeler, of Chicago, outstanding for his operation
of the polygraph machine, Hiss asked for time before giving
his decision. Unfavorable inferences were undoubtedly
drawn from Hiss's apparent unwillingness to take the test,
but in all fairness it must be pointed out that the "lie-
detector" lacks the infallibility of the fingerprint. Scientific

studies have found the machine in error in from fourteen
to thirty per cent of the cases examined. Furthermore, sub-
normal types and the hardened criminal seem more immune to such tests than the more sensitive amateur, as they
probably have less consciousness of guilt.

Hiss's demand for a confrontation with his accuser was
immediately met by the Committee. Both men were ordered
to appear before a subcommittee at the Hotel Commodore
in New York the following day. When, on the afternoon of
August 17, Alger Hiss entered Room 1400 of that hostelry,
he appeared in anything but a co-operative mood. Obviously annoyed at certain leaks of information which had
come out of the executive sessions of the committee, he was
additionally distressed by word of the sudden death of
Harry Dexter White. "I am not sure that I feel in the best
possible mood for testimony," he observed upon entering.
After a build-up that would have satisfied Sam Goldwyn,
the great confrontation had at least been staged.

What happened in that hotel room has been so widely
publicized that it needs little elaboration. At Hiss's request,
Chambers said a few words in a rather high-pitched voice.
Hiss asked him to open his mouth "wider," and then inquired whether his accuser had not previously spoken in a
lower key. Congressman McDowell assured him that his
voice seemed "the same now as we have heard." "I think he
is George Crosley," Hiss now asserted, but asked Chambers
to talk some more. After Chambers read an extract from
Newsweek, the chief rival of *Time*, the magazine of which
Chambers was an editor, Hiss pointed out that "the voice
sounds a little less resonant than the voice that I recall of
the man I knew as George Crosley" and "the teeth look to
me as though either they have been improved upon or that
there has been considerable dental work done since I knew
George Crosley." Questioned by Representative Nixon,
Chambers admitted that he had had substantial dental
work performed on the front of his mouth since 1934, including extractions and a plate. That information, accord-

ing to Hiss, substantiated his impression that his accuser was George Crosley. "One of my main recollections of Crosley was the poor condition of his teeth." "Do you feel that you would have to have a dentist tell you just what he did to the teeth before you could tell anything about this man?" Nixon asked, his question heavily edged with sarcasm. Apparently to those who knew Chambers under one name or another before he had improved his appearance by dental work, his extremely bad teeth were an outstanding physical characteristic. Testifying at the second trial, Malcolm Cowley, the writer, recalled that when he met Chambers in 1940, the latter was unkempt, shifty-eyed, with "a bare tooth in his face." Remarking that he had a strong feeling that his accuser was Crosley, Hiss told the committee that "he looks very different in girth and in other appearances—hair, forehead, and so on, particularly the jowls." After a further exchange Hiss now interrupted: "I am now perfectly prepared to identify this man as *George Crosley.*"

One of the most serious tactical mistakes of the Hiss defense was its failure either to produce people for the House committee who knew Chambers as Crosley or to furnish such testimony at the trials. Considering the fact that Chambers had used a wide variety of aliases during the years in dispute, Hiss's identification of his accuser as Crosley would have been more readily accepted if he could have provided some corroboration. At least one such person *claims to have known Chambers as Crosley.* He is Samuel Roth, publisher of the Seven Sirens Press of New York City, who, according to an interview reported in the New York *Sun* of August 27, 1948, knew Chambers during 1926–7 and received from him in the latter year a group of poems submitted under the name of George Crosley. The defense may have feared that the government on cross-examination would have brought out the fact that Roth had been convicted four times for distributing salacious literature, including a conviction in 1929 for selling James Joyce's

Ulysses. But the fact that the government's star witness attempted to have poetry published by a dealer in pornography would have canceled whatever advantage the prosecution might have drawn from such disclosures. Here was another instance where the defense fumbled the ball. In his own published account of the trial Chambers avoids a categorical denial that he ever went by the name of George Crosley—"a name which I may possibly have used briefly," he concedes, "but of which I have no independent recollection."

The Commodore session was nearing its close. It remained only for Chambers to affirm his own story.

McDowell: Mr. Chambers, is this the man, Alger Hiss, who was also a member of the Communist Party at whose home you stayed?

Nixon: According to your testimony.

McDowell: You make the identification positive?

Chambers: Positive identification.

Striding over to Chambers, Hiss issued a ringing challenge: *"May I say for the record at this point, that I would like to invite Mr. Whittaker Chambers to make those same statements out of the presence of this committee without their being privileged for suit for libel. I challenge you to do it, and I hope you will do it damned quickly!"*

Up to this point no corroborative evidence had been offered to controvert Hiss's account. But at a public confrontation of the accused and his accuser on August 25 the committee presented documentary evidence showing that Hiss had not bought his Plymouth until *after* he had disposed of his Ford. Now Hiss found it necessary to describe the transaction more fully. It was not a gift, but a loan, he stated, perhaps not in connection with the rent, but more likely after Chambers had moved out of his apartment. Well, Hiss was pressed, how about this bill of sale showing transfer of title to the car to the Cherner Motor Co., which in turn had turned it over to one William Rosen? Was that consistent with a loan? What the hearing record did not bring out was that transfer of title to automobiles was conducted in Washington in a more formal way than in cities like New York, where it is done through the simple endorsement of an automobile-registration stub in the possession of every car-owner. Having failed to fill out such a bill of sale at the time of the gift or loan, it was not inconsistent with Hiss's story that he could have signed the document later on to accommodate Chambers when the latter wished to dispose of the vehicle. The next day Rosen was brought before the committee, but to everyone's astonishment he refused to comment on the transfer or to answer a question about party affiliation, and rested on his constitutional privilege against self-incrimination. Rosen's silence served to invest an ordinarily innocent business transaction with an aura of suspicion or even illegality. A jail sentence later imposed on him for refusing to answer a similar question before the Federal grand jury was subsequently reversed by the United States Circuit Court of Appeals. Had Rosen talked he could not have damaged Hiss any more than by his maintaining silence. In fact, it is not inconceivable that had he been willing, he could have cleared Hiss on this particular accusation.

Again Hiss took the offensive and again he was ill-advised. He now demanded that the committee put a series of questions to Chambers, among them: "I would like him to be asked whether he has ever been treated for a mental illness." Nixon's cross-examination of Hiss revealed that the witness's insinuations rested on hearsay entirely. But Hiss asked one more loaded question, which would be recalled many weeks later. "I would like him," he further demanded, "to be asked to describe the circumstances under which he came in contact with this committee and *to make public all written memoranda which he may have handed to any representative of the committee.*" Once again he challenged Chambers "to make the statements about me with respect

to communism in public that he has made under privilege
to this committee."

Chambers did not wait long. Two days later on a "Meet
the Press" radio program he asserted: *"Alger Hiss was a
Communist and may be now."* "I don't think Hiss will go
to court," his accuser observed, and when several weeks
went by and Hiss failed to carry out his threat, the spirits of
his supporters visibly drooped. During those trying weeks
Hiss was impaled on the horns of a dilemma. Even for the
innocent a libel suit is a messy ordeal. As a student of legal
history Hiss doubtless recalled the catastrophic step that
Oscar Wilde took when he was goaded into a libel suit by
the Marquis of Queensberry. "But this can't happen to me!"
Hiss must have reasoned. Chambers's assertions of Communist affiliation were so far unsubstantiated. It was Hiss's
word against Chambers's. Ten years had elapsed. How could
Chambers prove it? Hiss gambled. One month after Chambers's radio appearance, Hiss brought suit in a Baltimore
Federal court for seventy-five thousand dollars for defamation.

The libel suit turned the Hiss affair in a more sinister
direction. Chambers had to produce proof or suffer a crushing defeat. At a pre-trial hearing on November 17 in the
office of Hiss's Baltimore attorney, William Marbury,
Chambers was asked: "Do you have any documentary
proof of your assertions?" He then dumfounded his interrogators by turning over a batch of forty-seven typed copies
of official documents and some memoranda in Hiss's handwriting. These, he claimed, had been cached for him years
ago in an unused dumbwaiter shaft in the apartment house
of his wife's nephew, Nathan Levine, of Brooklyn.[4] For an

---

[4] According to Chambers's account, the papers (along with three
cylinders of undeveloped microfilm and two strips of developed film,
together with a memo allegedly in the handwriting of Harry Dexter
White) were in the identical dust-encrusted sealed envelope that had
been used for their storage more than ten years before. Daniel P.
Norman, a testing and analysis expert, however, in a post-trial affidavit, has deposed that the papers show such different characteristics

explanation of these documents, Chambers now asserted that in 1937 he had introduced Hiss to a Russian agent named Colonel Bykov, Chambers' own superior in the Communist underground. Thereafter, according to his revised story, Hiss "began a fairly consistent flow of such material as we have before us here." The routine was for Hiss to bring the documents home, Chambers said, have Mrs. Hiss type copies, and then return the papers to the files. Where the removal of papers offered difficulties, Hiss obligingly supplied notations in his own handwriting. Judge Calvin W. Chestnut agreed with attorneys on both sides that this was now a matter in the national interest, and that the documents should go to the Department of Justice. As a result, Alexander Campbell, head of the Justice Department's Criminal Division, directed U.S. Attorney McGoey in New York to order the grand jury to reconvene early in December.

With an acutely developed sense of melodrama, Chambers had withheld some evidence from Hiss's attorneys— five rolls of microfilm. Like a character in a grade-B cloak-and-dagger television script he inserted the film in the hollowed-out base of a pumpkin in a patch on his Westminster, Maryland, farm. On December 2 he extracted these items from their hiding-place and turned them over to House committee investigators. Four days later the Justice Department showed the New York grand jury enlargements of the pumpkin microfilm.

Both trials sidestepped the obvious question: of what use could such documents have been to a foreign power, and, more particularly, to the Soviet Union? The documents (covering dates running from January 5 to April 1, 1938) ranged from relative trivia to highly confidential information. One group related to Japan. It is unlikely that the Soviet Union needed this data to learn the details of

---

of aging and discoloration "that they cannot have been stored together for ten years in a single envelope" nor kept in the envelope that Chambers recovered. Norman goes further and insists that the envelope could not possibly have held *any* of the documents.

Japanese troop movements or of the five-year economic plan for Manchukuo. But the knowledge that the French Foreign Office feared that the United States might involve both Britain and itself in a conflict with Japan, leaving France so weakened that Germany and Italy would strike at once, might have fitted into the jigsaw puzzle of the ultimate plans of the West. Another group of documents might have confirmed Russia's suspicions that the Western powers were willing to appease Germany. A dispatch revealed that the military supplies France had promised Rumania on the eve of World War II "would be delivered with an eye-dropper very little at a time in return for good behavior." On the other hand, another dispatch disclosed that the Anglo-French accord vis-à-vis the Axis spelled out rearming as fast as possible, meantime speaking "softly and amiably to Germany" while completely ignoring Mussolini. A third group of documents cast light on Hitler's war time-table. For example, by January 1938 it was known in the West that Italy would not oppose Hitler's seizure of Austria. Schuschnigg described his visit to Berchtesgaden "as the most horrible day" of his life. A dispatch from Paris, dated February 15, 1938, reported that "Hitler was most loath to use force because the generals of the Reichswehr had convinced him that the army would not be in a condition to fight a major war against France and England for approximately *another year.*" How about Russia's position? A cablegram from Ambassador William C. Bullitt in the top-secret code quoted French Foreign Minister Delbos to the effect that the Soviet Ambassador in Paris had warned *"that if France should begin negotiations with Germany the Soviet Union would come to terms with Germany at once."* The date was January 25, 1938! The Russians might well have assumed that Delbos would tell Bullitt. That knowledge may well have prompted the warning in the first place.

Could this mélange of documents have served an entirely different purpose? Could they have enabled a foreign power to crack the American codes? Sumner Welles, Under Secretary of State at the time when they were presumed to have been taken, identified some of them as being in the topsecret code ("D"). Chambers, in his published account, declares that "the Russians were able to use the Hiss documents, and possibly some others, to break State Department codes." But for a foreign power to have used these deciphered papers for such a purpose, it would have been necessary for that power to be in possession of the original code text. For this purpose cables from Paris, London, Yokohama, Shanghai, Peiping, and Tsingtao would have been valueless to the Soviet unless some agent had managed to pilfer or transcribe the original dispatches or they had gone over the airwaves and been intercepted, instead of having been transmitted by cable. Such random interceptions might have provided segments of various codes, but a far simpler and more logical procedure for that purpose would have been to procure deciphered copies of dispatches sent in code from within the Soviet Union.

The facts, however, are that only one of the State Department documents in the Hiss case originated inside Russia. That was represented in the government's exhibit by a penciled memorandum in Hiss's handwriting, called for trial purposes "Baltimore 1," which was based on a rather brief cable from the United States Chargé at Moscow, the original text of which appeared in "State 1," another exhibit.[5] "Baltimore 1" contained a notation "M 28" in Hiss's personal shorthand, signifying Moscow the 28th of the current month (January). But the case for cracking the code on the basis of this cable crumbles since "State 1" is in the non-confidential Gray code, used primarily for transmittal of the text of newspaper articles or other publicly known matter. The purpose of using the Gray code was to protect the confiden-

---

[5] "State 1" concerns the mystery known as the Robinson-Rubens case, in which the American wife of a Soviet agent sought the help of the U.S. Embassy in locating her husband. Shortly thereafter she herself was imprisoned by the Soviet government.

tial codes against being broken by comparing the code text with the publicly known text of the matter transmitted. Since in "State 1," Henderson, the United States Chargé at Moscow, was repeating in his cable a telegram sent over commercial cable (the text of which the Russians would presumably have), he naturally used the Gray code. It is also significant that Hiss's handwritten memo omitted the vital word "GRAY," which precedes and ends the message. Any spy trying to help Soviet cryptographers would not have failed to include this clue.

The four penciled memoranda bore on their face evidence of being exactly what Hiss said they were—memos jotted down by him for use in conferences with his superior, Francis B. Sayre. Testifying at the second trial, Sayre confirmed Hiss's practice of making handwritten summaries of cablegrams or other papers and providing him with oral reports on dispatches sent to his office. Each of the memos, Sayre admitted, concerned a subject in which he was definitely interested. These memos were carelessly scribbled, with overwriting and interlineations. One would assume that a secret agent would have been expected to turn in cleaner copy. Would he be likely to hand over memos in his own hand and thus indelibly identify himself as the source? The same question as to the likelihood of self-identification is raised by several of the State Department documents that bear on their face the official receiving stamp of Sayre's office, and the initials of Alger Hiss signed in pencil with the stamp, in accord with routine practice. Is it credible that a spy would give himself away so obviously?

The forty-three typewritten documents, constituting copies, excerpts, or paraphrases of State Department official papers, bear on their face some evidence that they were not typed to provide the Soviet government with the kind of secret information it especially desired. Take the cable from Bullitt dated January 5, 1938, identified in the exhibits as "State 9." The two items most significant to the Rus-

sians, the delivery by France of military supplies to Rumania with "an eye-dropper," and the accord between
France and England vis-à-vis the Axis, were omitted from
the typewritten copy. This curious but possibly significant
omission of the very information the Russians would be expected to want is also evidenced in the penciled memo ("Baltimore 2") summarizing "State 2." While that memo includes the information that China had placed in France an
order for the latest type of light bomber-pursuit plane, it
omitted the illuminating comment of the French Foreign
Office that the method used by China to finance her war
orders from Russia was "a puzzle to the French."

Opinion might differ on the use to which such papers
could be put, but there was no disputing the fact that classi-
fied government documents had got into unauthorized
hands. When this evidence was submitted to the grand jury,
it seemed certain that Whittaker Chambers himself would
be indicted. Having previously denied such espionage activity under oath, Chambers was transparently guilty of
perjury. Top Justice Department officials, however, reasoned that were the informer to be indicted, no other renegade Communist would talk. To keep the grand jury from
taking action against *Time's* senior editor, Campbell found
it expedient to make an impassioned plea to the grand jury.
For a law-enforcement officer to tell a grand jury what *not*
to do constituted an extraordinary performance, but grand
juries almost invariably rubber-stamp prosecuting attorneys, and this one proved no exception. This particular
grand jury had been conspicuous for the deliberate pace it
had pursued. For some eighteen months it had listened to
evidence against subversive groups, and yet contented itself
with indictments against merely the leaders of the Communist Party, not the underground apparatus. Now, on
December 15, 1948, the last day of its statutory life, it was
suddenly prodded into bringing an indictment for perjury
against Hiss on two counts: (1) for denying that either he
or his wife in his presence had ever transmitted secret and

confidential documents to Chambers or any other unauthorized person; and (2) for swearing falsely that he had
not seen Chambers after January 1, 1937. Hiss pleaded not
guilty to each count. Meantime Chambers had relieved the
Luce organization of embarrassment by resigning from
Time, on December 10. Hiss was given three months' leave
without pay by the Carnegie Endowment. This leave was
extended in March; and in May, at his own request, Hiss's
name was not considered for re-election.

The first trial of Alger Hiss began on May 31, 1949. Presiding was Federal Judge Samuel H. Kaufman. The government's case was entrusted to Assistant United States Attorney Thomas F. Murphy, a ponderous six-footer, with walrus
mustache and deliberate manner. Lloyd Paul Stryker served
as chief of Hiss's defense staff. Short, quick, and imperious,
he was one of the most seasoned trial lawyers in the country.
Despite the enormous publicity given the case, it took
barely two hours for both sides to agree on a jury of ten
men (minor business executives and white-collar workers)
and two women (a dressmaker and a housewife). But in this
quick combing of the panel the prosecution held an overwhelming edge over the defense. The Department of Justice has at its command a full dossier on every blue-ribbon
juror. Hence a venireman who had previously shown that
he was not "reliable" could be eliminated peremptorily by
the prosecutor without having to disclose the ground.

An inept opening immediately betrayed Murphy's inex-
perience. Although he stated that the government would
corroborate Chambers's allegations by showing that the
documents were typed on Hiss's Woodstock typewriter and
the memos were in his handwriting, he nonetheless insisted:
*"if you don't believe Mr. Chambers' story, we have no case
under the Federal perjury rule."* Stryker was delighted to
narrow the issue down to "whether or not you believe Chambers." It was Chambers's word against Hiss's. Whom should
we believe? Should we accept the word of the accused, a
clean-cut, competent career servant, who had distinguished

himself at Johns Hopkins and at Harvard Law School and
had been honored by receiving the post of secretary to
Supreme Court Justice Oliver Wendell Holmes? "I shall
call, if the case gets that far, I shall summon with all due
reverence the shade of that great member of the Supreme
Court." If Stryker could have introduced ectoplasmic testimony, no one doubted that he would not have hesitated for
a moment. Hiss was eulogized for his work in the State Department, for his activity as secretary of the Dumbarton
Oaks Conference, for his leadership of the Carnegie Endowment. Garbling the most sacred allusions without a blush,
defense counsel proclaimed: "Though I would go through
the valley of the shadow of death, I will fear no evil, because there is no blot or blemish on him."

Stryker's eulogy of Hiss was followed by an excoriation
of his accuser that rivaled William Wirt's renowned blast
against Blennerhassett. "Now who is the accuser?" Stryker
thundered. A man given to many aliases, a member of a
"filthy conspiracy . . . against the land that I love and you
love," a man who wrote a despicable play about Jesus Christ
at college and was dismissed, an author of erotic poetry, a
"moral leper."

The behavior of the accused was straightforward and
honorable, Stryker contended. He had requested a hearing,
he had brought suit for libel, he had "bent heaven and
earth" to locate the typewriter owned by the Hisses which
the F.B.I. had been unable to trace. Now, with a fine sense
of theatrical timing, Stryker announced that the defense
had actually located the typewriter and secured it "from
the then owner, a truckman who had gotten it through a
long series of colored servants that they [the Hisses] had."
The defense would "consent under such reasonable provisions as his Honor may prescribe to let these F.B.I. eyes who
couldn't find it come down and look at it all they want."
Conceived as a defense move to refute any imputation of
concealment of evidence, the production of the Woodstock

typewriter seemingly provided that very link between the
Hisses and the documentary evidence without which the
entire case against the accused would have fizzled out like
a wet firecracker.

And now the "moral leper" was to have his chance to repeat in court his previous accusations. Whittaker Chambers
on direct examination seriously modified the story he had
told the House committee. He now stressed the part Hiss
had allegedly played in transmitting confidential documents. Over a steady barrage of objections, Chambers managed to bring out the alleged facts of Hiss's delivery to him
of State Department documents and copies made in the
first three months of 1938 at the Volta Place home of the
Hisses in Washington. Acting under instructions from Bykov, according to the witness's story, Hiss had brought confidential documents home and turned them over to Chambers every week or ten days. Such deliveries began in
February 1937. The routine was for Chambers to call for the
documents in the late afternoon or early evening, have them
microfilmed, turn the microfilm over to Bykov, and return
the originals to Hiss late the same night so that he could
replace them in his office in the State Department the next
morning. As Claude B. Cross, defense counsel in the second
trial, was to bring out on cross-examination, that meant for
Chambers the carrying out of a strenuous itinerary at
frantic speed. But it was all in the day's work for a dedicated Communist. Although Chambers had decided to break
with the party late in 1937, he continued the microfilming
procedure until his actual break in mid-April 1938. For
reasons he did not make explicit, he had retained samples
of such materials, which formed the basis of the government's evidence.

Chambers now for the first time added a significant detail. He recounted that in November 1937 he had borrowed
four hundred dollars from Hiss to buy a car. Both the bank
withdrawal by Mrs. Hiss of that amount on November 19,

1937 and the cash purchase of a Ford by Mrs. Chambers four days later were confirmed by officials of the bank and the motor-car company later in the trial.

"You may examine." These words, coming at the conclusion of the lengthy direct examination, scarcely prepared the witness for the bludgeoning he was to receive at the hands of Stryker. Defense counsel pommeled the witness with a series of straight smashes, but the ex-Communist courier recoiled with each blow and left his antagonist furious.

STRYKER: Mr. Chambers, do you know what an oath is?

CHAMBERS: An oath is a declaration which a man makes when he promises to tell the truth.

STRYKER: And in our courts it is an affirmation made by a man who calls on Almighty God to witness the truth of what he says, is that right?

Chambers agreed, and Stryker got down to cases. He forced Chambers to admit that he was an active Communist in October 1937, "doing what you could to overthrow this Government by force or violence, or any other means." He wrung from him the admission that he had sworn falsely when he applied for a government position in 1937. Stryker demanded to know whether or not the witness had been dismissed from the New York Public Library for stealing books. Here Chambers demurred. The books actually belonged to the Columbia University Library, he corrected. Chambers conceded that "a question of right or wrong as we ordinary Americans would see it" did not bother him in his Communist days. Stryker forced Chambers to relive his unconventional career as a youngster in New Orleans. While he denied that he had ever lived with "One-Eyed Annie, a prostitute" in a "wretched dive" in New Orleans, he admitted that when he was seventeen years old he had taken a woman named Ida Dales into his mother's home and lived with her as his wife. "And was the reason, your mother had lost one son and did not want to lose another?" Stryker demanded. "That is correct," Chambers replied. Reviewing Chambers's fourteen years spent as a Communist Party member between 1924 and 1938, Stryker asked: "Is it not true that for those fourteen years you were a traitor to the United States and an enemy to your country?" Perfectly nonchalant, Chambers shot back: "That is right."

But Murphy could not afford to have Chambers's activities characterized as "treason." "Unless he gave aid and comfort to the enemy," Murphy quite correctly pointed out, Chambers could not be guilty of treason. "He used the word 'traitor,' and admitted being one," Stryker retorted "That's out of his own mouth." The argument had descended to the juvenile "sticks-and-stones" level without adding much light on the basic issues of fact.

Then Stryker turned to a more crucial question. He forced Chambers to admit that he had been known at various times as Charles Adams, Charles Whittaker, Arthur Dwyer, Lloyd Cantwell, and David Breen. Previously Chambers had admitted on the stand that he might have been known as "Carl" and as "Crosley," and that he had also used variations of his Christian name, such as Jay Vivian, Jay David, David, David Whittaker, and Whittaker. "So you sneaked around for fourteen years under all those false names to deceive people about your real identity. Is that a fair statement?" "I think it's a beautiful statement for your purposes," Chambers rejoined. "I would say that I used false names."

Stryker then confronted Chambers with the fact that the witness's maternal grandmother had died insane after having been committed, that his brother Dick had killed himself with illuminating gas at the age of twenty-two, that Whittaker had refused to join him in a suicide pact, and that the survivor had been "immobile" for several months after his brother's death. Stryker now put into the record evidence that while Chambers was still allegedly conspiring with Hiss, he had used his real name in the Baltimore telephone directory, on the registration of his wife's automobile, on a letter applying for a scholarship for his little girl, and on the application for his government job, where in addition he had falsely represented his education and job experience. Under questioning by Stryker, Chambers insisted that when he went to Hiss's home in December 1938 to get him to break with the party, he had feared "kidnapping or assassination." "That Alger Hiss or his wife would kidnap or assassinate you?" Stryker asked. "Alger Hiss or his comrades," the witness replied.

Stryker had shown Chambers to have been a liar in the past, but that was not the issue. The question was whether he was a liar now. Stryker's questioning betrayed a failure on his part to come to grips with the crucial issue. Confronting Chambers with his denial before the grand jury that he had any "direct knowledge" of espionage, Stryker asked the witness: "Was that answer true or false?" "That answer was false." "Then you admit that you testified falsely and committed perjury before the grand jury in this building, is that right?" "That is right." Stryker's phrasing was psychologically inept. The implication of Chambers's answer seemed obvious: he was lying *then*, but he is telling the truth *now*. Profiting by this lapse, Claude B. Cross, at the second trial, phrased the question differently: "You lied either then before the grand jury or before this jury?" he asked Chambers. "That is right," the witness was compelled to answer. Again: "And you lied then or you are lying now?" "That is right."

Had Stryker in his cross-examination of Esther Shemitz Chambers been content with bringing out discrepancies in her story he would have been well-advised. Instead, he sought not only to impeach her credibility but to have her impugn her husband's character. Referring to her having withheld from an application for a kindergarten scholarship for her daughter in 1937 the fact of her husband's connection with the Communist Party, Stryker demanded: "In other words you didn't think it was very much of a misrepresentation to represent your husband as a decent citizen—" "I resent that," Esther Chambers shouted back. "My husband is a decent citizen! And he is a great man!" He was always a decent citizen even when plotting against the United States, she contended. "I believe he is a great man to live up to his beliefs. His beliefs may change—as they did." At length Judge Kaufman halted this line of questioning on the ground that Stryker was being argumentative. But the defense counsel, by baiting the witness, had aroused the sporting instincts of spectators and jurors alike in behalf of the underdog.

Stryker's curious propensity for putting the emphasis in the wrong place contributed, at least in part, to blurring certain discrepancies in the stories of Whittaker and Esther Chambers which were brought out in the course of the trial. It is a basic rule of trial practice that a witness should be discredited, if possible, while he is on the stand, Instead, comparatively long periods of time were permitted to elapse in both trials between the testimony of the Chamberses and the refutation of certain details in their accounts. As a result, these discrepancies were never brought into sharp focus, and it is doubtful whether their significance was fully grasped by either jury.

Let us consider a few of them. From July 1936 to December 1937 the Hisses occupied a house in Washington located on Thirtieth Street. In testifying before the House committee in August 1948, Chambers stated that he was sure he had stayed in that house overnight. In his pre-trial examination in the Maryland libel action in November of that year, he stated that he might have stayed there as many as ten times, sleeping in one of three bedrooms. Then in February 1949 a meeting was arranged by the F.B.I. between Chambers and two former maids of the Hisses. Chambers concededly questioned the maids about the interior of the houses occupied by the Hisses. On learning from one of the maids that there were only two bedrooms in the Thirtieth Street house—one used by the Hisses and the other by their son—Chambers told a different story. "I have no clear recollection of spending the night there," he testified at the second trial. "I have no vague recollection either." Discrepancies in Chambers's description of that house may also be significant. On November 5, 1948, about three months before he went with the F.B.I. to see the house, Chambers described the outer walls as having been in 1936 *white* clapboard with *dark green* shutters. But at the second trial he described the outer walls as "gray" or "a yellowish" color. Under further questioning Chambers shifted back to "white," which happened to be the color they had been painted in 1942. Similarly, Mrs. Chambers testified that the Thirtieth Street house "had a white or off white color," but a neighbor swore that it was *"bright yellow"* at the time the Hisses occupied it, with *"vivid blue" shutters,* and that the house was repainted in 1948, the walls gray, the blinds "dark gray-green."

Again, serious inconsistencies are found in their recollections of the Volta Place home of the Hisses, which the couple occupied from the end of 1937 to the latter part of 1943. In her testimony at both trials Mrs. Chambers recalled that this house had a brick or stone structure with an iron railing around the top which served as a vestibule for the front door. Photographs taken in 1949 did reveal such a structure. But later in the trial a neighbor testified that no such structure existed in 1938, but that instead a tree had stood in front of the house. Then a building contractor called by the defense showed in his records that he had torn down a tree at the Volta Place house and built the masonry structure in December 1946. Such discrepancies suggested that the Chamberses' testimony was based in part, at least, on the facts as they were in 1947 and subsequent years rather than in 1937.

In the hearing before the House committee Chambers gave these answers to questions by Nixon:

NIXON: Did you ever go on a trip with them other than by automobile?

CHAMBERS: No.

NIXON: Did you stay overnight on any of these trips?
CHAMBERS: No.

But in the second trial Chambers answered that on an
alleged trip to Peterboro, New Hampshire, with the Hisses
in 1937, he had made *three* overnight stops with them. The
guest book of Bleak House, the only place identified in
Chambers's story as a place where he and the Hisses stayed
overnight, contained no supporting entry.

Some of these discrepancies can be dismissed as involving
minor, not essential, details, covering an admitted acquaint-
anceship between the Hisses and the Chamberses going back
some fifteen years. But the inconsistencies in Chambers's
account of the key figure of Bykov might well constitute
a clue to his reliability and mental condition. Bykov is central to Chambers's whole story of espionage. In his testimony at the second trial Chambers stated that he informed
Hiss that "Colonel Bykov, whom I knew under the pseu-
donym 'Peter,' " wanted Hiss to turn documents over to the
apparatus. Then in January 1937 Chambers arranged a
meeting between Bykov and Hiss, which took place in a
Brooklyn movie house. At a Chinatown restaurant, following the movie, Bykov secured Hiss's agreement to procure
documents. But in the Maryland civil action he stated that
the meeting was arranged in August or the early fall of 1937.
In the trial record is an extract from an F.B.I. report of an
interview with Chambers on June 26, 1946 in which he said
that "Peter" introduced him in a theater to a person connected with Russian intelligence whom General Walter
Krivitsky later identified to him as Boris Bykov. Bykov was
"about 5 feet 7 inches tall, red hair, slightly bald, Jewish,
very shifty appearance, who spoke very little English and
poor German, was approximately 36–37 years old in 1937."
Chambers stated that he sensed that Bykov was connected
with the OGPU, and that it was his impression that he and
other secret agents of Peter were instructed to check up on
his activities and personal life. From the F.B.I. story it

would appear that Chambers met Bykov only once and
that he was a secret agent assigned to check up on him.
In his testimony at the trials Bykov was depicted as Chambers's superior and co-worker, to whom he regularly reported. After Julian Wadleigh, a confessed spy in the State
Department, stated on the stand that Chambers introduced
the "boss in the apparatus" to him as "Sasha," Chambers
on cross-examination identified Sasha as Bykov. Wadleigh
on direct stated that the right sleeve of Sasha's coat hung
loose, that he gave him the left hand when they shook hands.
Chambers, however, under cross-examination in the second
trial, provided a physical description of Bykov which tallied
closely with what he had given the F.B.I. in 1946. "Was his
right sleeve empty?" Cross asked. "Colonel Bykov had the
use of both arms," Chambers replied. Cross pressed further.
"Did he have two arms?" "Colonel Bykov had two arms." [6]
Since Chambers had previously identified the one-armed
Sasha and the two-armed Bykov as the same person, he had
now revealed a major inconsistency in his story. Was Peter-
Bykov-Sasha a one-armed or a two-armed man? Was Bykov
an OGPU agent sent to check up on him, as he had previously told the F.B.I., or was he Chambers's superior in the
espionage service? [7] Did he himself first meet Bykov at the
theater or did he arrange to have Hiss and Bykov get together at the theater? Was the second theater story a new
version superimposed upon the first? By his failure to rec-
oncile these discrepancies Chambers weakened the credibility of the Bykov-Chambers-Hiss relationship.

The government's perjury case admittedly rested on a
single witness corroborated by certain documentary evidence. To establish the source of the exhibits the prosecu-

[6] In his published story, *Witness*, Chambers writes of Bykov:
"With one hand, he would grab my sleeve. With the other he would
point . . . ." Elsewhere in the book he refers to Wadleigh's fixed impression that Bykov had only one arm as "that singular error of recollection."

[7] "I did not know the identity of the apparatus I was working
in."—Chambers in *Witness*.

tion attempted to show not only that Chambers had been engaged in providing the Russians with copies of State Department originals but that the specific exhibits in this case did in fact originate in the State Department. To prove the first point the prosecutor called Henry Julian Wadleigh, a gaunt, taut, Oxford-trained diplomat, an extrovert with a sense of the theater to match Stryker's. Wadleigh admitted on the stand that he had supplied Chambers with confidential documents. While this served to corroborate Chambers's testimony that he had been the courier for a Washington espionage group, it also gave the defense ground for its contention that Wadleigh or some other source in the State Department had actually stolen the documents that were charged to Hiss. Chambers, in addition to Wadleigh, had another source in the Trade Agreements Division, where Wadleigh worked, and a source in the Far Eastern Division. On cross-examination Wadleigh admitted that he had often dropped in at other State Department offices on business and personal calls, but, like a prisoner who confesses to embezzlement but denies burglary, he virtuously insisted that the only material he purloined was that which came over his own desk.

Could the documents themselves provide any support for the defense's position that someone other than Hiss had stolen them? There was no question that the four memoranda summarizing State Department documents were in Alger Hiss's handwriting. Eunice A. Lincoln, a State Department private secretary back in '38, positively identified them. Nor was there any doubt that the documents had come from the State Department. On direct examination Walter H. Anderson, chief of that Department's Record Division, identified fifty-five original State Department documents constituting the prosecution exhibits. In both trials Anderson was subject to masterful cross-examination revealing exhaustive trial preparation by the defense. Both Edward C. McLean, of defense counsel in the first trial, and Claude B. Cross, in the second, succeeded in having

Anderson admit that several of the documents had never been routed to Sayre's office, in which Hiss had served. One exhibit had gone to the Far Eastern Division, where Chambers had a demonstrated source of stolen documents. One *aide-mémoire,* which reached Chambers in its *German* original, had been circulated both in German and in English. Yet the German original had not gone to Hiss's office, while the *English* translation had. McLean wrung from Anderson the admission that the cables, dispatches, and "strictly confidential" reports had in fact been distributed to some fifteen agencies within the Department, where a total of 236 employees had access to them. This was something of a record in the treatment of confidential data even for a government wedded to the quintuplicate of the merest trivia. It was crucial for the defense to show that these admissions supported a reasonable hypothesis that Chambers had procured the documents from other sources and that Wadleigh, whose total deliveries to the quondam courier seem to have come to somewhere between a thousand and twenty-five hundred documents, was a likely suspect. The defense was to argue that Wadleigh's insistence that he turned over to Chambers only what he received in connection with his own work was an attempt to minimize his moral guilt. As Charles Darlington, his superior, testified, "I think there were times Wadleigh had a well developed curiosity, I might say, in a lot of things that were going on. There were occasions when . . . I would come into my room after lunch and Mr. Wadleigh would be . . . at my desk reading one of the papers."

How easy it would have been for a spy to purloin documents from Hiss's office was brought out by Federal Judge Charles E. Wyzanski. In his testimony at the second trial he stated: "I recall having gone into his office without being intercepted by anyone, or finding anyone there, and I walked directly into his office. I am under the impression that the door was open but I am not able to swear that this was the fact. . . . I went into his office and he was not there and I waited. While I waited no secretary was there, no messenger, no one except myself. He came there after I waited for, I would say, fifteen minutes."

The defense's efforts to identify the routing of the documents was crucial, since the prosecution contended that the originals of the documents that Chambers produced were all available to Hiss at the State Department. State Department routine indicated the likelihood that "State 13," one of the documents copied in the Baltimore typed material ("Baltimore 13") was never in Sayre's office, but was in the Far Eastern Division, where Chambers admittedly had one of his sources of stolen State Department documents. "State 13," a memo, partly typed, partly handwritten, is a summary of a short dispatch from the American consul at Yokohama, dated January 18, 1938, which, as appears from stamps on its face, was received in the Department on February 7, and in the Division of Far Eastern Affairs two days later. This dispatch was admittedly circulated with another dispatch ("State 13-A"), which never was routed to Sayre's office and which lacks Sayre's office stamp. If, as the evidence tends to establish, "State 13" never went to Hiss's office, the only way he could have procured it would have been by pilfering it from some other department. But since this chit summarizes information published in Japanese newspapers, it would hardly be considered worthy of the efforts of a superspy. The significance of "State 13," however, is even deeper than appears on its surface. If even *one* document among those typed on the Woodstock machine could not have been in Hiss's possession, the suspicion might well arise that someone other than the Hisses typed *all* the material.

But while it is not beyond the bounds of possibility that some person other than the accused could have purloined these documents as well as the memos in Hiss's hand, the papers typed on the Woodstock owned by the Hisses constituted on their face far more damning corroboration. The first jury was not left in doubt as to this crucial fact.

Pointer in hand before huge blowups, Ramos C. Feehan, an F.B.I. typewriter expert, gave the jury his considered opinion (based on the identity of *ten* characters) that the majority of the documents were copies typed on the Woodstock typewriter. Comparison was made between irregularities of ten letters appearing in the purloined papers and four documents concededly typed on the Woodstock in 1937 and earlier, three by Priscilla Hiss and one by her sister. The technique that Feehan used was most persuasive, as it combined a dogmatic expert opinion with a convincing demonstration from which the jurors could form their own opinions. As the defense was unable to secure a single expert of standing who was not of Feehan's opinion, Stryker refrained from cross-examining the typewriter expert. In fact, in the second trial, counsel for the defense conceded in his opening and in summation that Feehan's opinion was valid. In the long run this admission proved fatal. One could dismiss Chambers as a perjuror and psychopath, Wadleigh as a crank, the original documents as having been purloined by someone other than Hiss, but the typed copies would not vanish under some magician's wand. Nor would the outdated Woodstock.

Whatever suspicions they may have had about the Woodstock exhibit, defense attorneys took no steps to attack its authenticity until the case was presumably closed. In a motion for a new trial made in January 1952 Chester T. Lane, of defense counsel, offered what he claimed to be newly discovered evidence that (1) a technique of forgery by typewriter exists; and (2) the typewriter put in evidence at the trial as a physical exhibit was in fact a carefully constructed substitute, fabricated for the purpose of incriminating Hiss. In support of the first proposition the defense stated that a New York typewriter engineer named Martin Tytell, working simply from the sample documents typed on the Woodstock, had made another typewriter which produced typed documents virtually identical (even under microscopic examination) with those offered in evidence at the trial. Were the defense to prove this contention, it would shatter the whole "science" of positive identification of typewritten documents. To compound the confusion still further, the defense in a post-trial affidavit asserted that the serial number of the Woodstock on exhibit did not agree with its type and showed "positive signs of having been deliberately altered," with much of its type replaced and "deliberately shaped." None of this, of course, was known to either jury.

For some reason not at all clear, the defense at the trials felt it essential to show that the Woodstock was not in the possession of the Hisses at the time the papers in evidence were typed. Since the defense was to charge that Chambers had access to various houses occupied by the Hisses, it would have been more plausible to argue that Hiss's accuser had done the typing right in the Hisses' home. But the defense insisted that the machine had been turned over to the Catlett family. Mrs. Claudie Catlett, who had done housework for the Hisses in three of their Washington homes, stated on direct examination that the Hisses had given the typewriter to her children when they moved to their Thirtieth Street residence. But on cross-examination she could not remember the precise date of the gift or even whether the machine was a standard or a portable. Raymond Sylvester Catlett, Claudie's son, displayed under Murphy's cross-examination a combination of belligerence, stubbornness, and calculated confusion that left Murphy pawing the air. When asked what typing system he used, Raymond replied: "Why, my fingers." But he, too, was unable to fix with any definiteness the date when the typewriter was received.

In the second trial Murphy ridiculed the suggestion of defense counsel that by some trick Chambers had got hold of the typewriter when in possession of the Catletts and done the typing himself. The defense was never able to prove this charge. It was able to show, however, that Chambers was acutely aware of the danger of being identified as a spy through his own typewriter. He admitted disposing of a Remington portable typewriter that he had used between 1934 and 1940. He went from his Westminster farm to New York City and left the machine on a streetcar, subway, or elevated train.

CROSS: There was not any way in the world that that typewriter could be traced to you, was there?

CHAMBERS: I presume—no, probably not.

Although the defense was unable to document the hypothesis it advanced as to how the Hisses' typewriter was used to copy government papers, it counted for vindication upon the readiness of Alger Hiss to take the stand, upon the impact on the jury of an array of character witnesses of irreproachable standing, and upon discrediting Chambers by the use of psychiatric testimony. On direct examination Hiss flatly denied Chambers's accusations. He admitted knowing "Mr. Crosley" between 1934 and 1936. "I remember him," he said at the second trial, "as a short man with very bad teeth, noticeably bad teeth, the kind of teeth that riveted your attention on them because they were so bad." He declared that Chambers's story that he feared an ambush when he paid a visit to the Hisses at the Volta Place house contained "not a word of truth in any part of it," and he further reiterated that he had never until August 1948 associated George Crosley with Whittaker Chambers. Winding up the second day of direct examination, Stryker sought to blot out completely the impression left by Chambers's accusations.

STRYKER: Mr. Hiss, you have entered your formal and solemn plea of not guilty to the charges here against you, have you not?

HISS: I have.

STRYKER: And in truth and in fact you are not guilty?

HISS: I am not guilty.

STRYKER (to Murphy): Your witness.

. . .

Murphy concentrated his fire on exposing contradictions in Hiss's testimony. "Do you recall," he asked Hiss, "whether or not you told the F.B.I." that the Woodstock typewriter "was disposed of by Mrs. Hiss after 1938 to some either secondhand or used typewriter place in Georgetown?" "I did tell the F.B.I. that," Hiss admitted. "That was my impression at the time." Under cross-examination Hiss demonstrated a lawyer's precision in the exact shading of words. Once when Hiss correctly observed: "Mr. Murphy, you are characterizing what you have just read," the prosecutor blew up and demanded that the court "instruct this *character* to refrain from making remarks to me." Stryker properly objected to the comment as "offensive and improper." "Were it not for the fact that I do not want a mistrial, I would move for it!" he declared.

Murphy concluded his cross-examination on a prejudicial note. Questioned about his attitude toward the lie-detector test when the House committee had proposed it, Hiss pointed out that he had not refused to take the test but had informed the committee in a letter that he would like to consider the matter further. He heard nothing from them after that.

Q.: Well, in any event, you did not take the test?
A.: No, they dropped it, as I say.
Q. Well, you didn't come forward and insist upon it?
A. No, I did not.

Murphy's implication that the accused, if innocent, would have insisted on it not only runs counter to the presumption of innocence which is basic in Anglo-American criminal procedure but seems especially unwarranted in view of the fact that the petitioner's doubts about the scientific validity of lie-detector tests are widely shared by the courts.

The behavior of Priscilla Hiss on the stand was considered crucial by both sides. It was the hypothesis of the prosecution that Mrs. Hiss had typed the copies which were turned over to Chambers. Even many supporters of

Hiss felt that throughout the affair he was shielding his wife. But for a person with a public career at stake to be willing to shoulder the imputation of disloyalty and espionage to protect his family would seem to be carrying chivalry to its outermost limits. On the direct examination Priscilla supported her husband's story. But Murphy's raking cross-examination obviously disconcerted her. How did she account for the withdrawal of four hundred dollars from the bank? That sum was withdrawn, she insisted, to buy furnishings for the new home on Volta Place into which the Hisses were about to move. Why didn't they use their charge accounts in department stores? Because they wished to effect economies by making purchases at second-hand-shops and antique-stores, where they would have to buy for cash, she explained. From the fact that the Hisses allowed their bank balance to run down close to zero and even had to borrow from the very same bank the sum of three hundred dollars a few weeks later it might be plausibly argued that Priscilla Hiss was giving a correct explanation. Would it have been a reasonably prudent action for the Hisses to have turned over their entire nest egg to the Chamberses? Such an action hardly seems consistent with the cautious and careful type of person that Alger Hiss seemed to be.

On direct examination Priscilla Hiss had flatly denied ever having told Esther Chambers that she had intended taking courses in nursing at the Mercy Hospital in Baltimore. Murphy now read into the record a letter she had written to the University of Maryland in May 1937, applying for enrollment in a chemistry course as a prerequisite to a hospital course in medical technology she was planning to take. This was not a nursing course, but it is doubtful whether the jurors were sufficiently alert to make such fine distinctions.

No single incident in this highly controversial first trial caused more furious debate than the appearance of Associate Justices Felix Frankfurter and Stanley Reed as character witnesses for Hiss. Obviously without thinking of the effect of his behavior on the jury, Judge Kaufman rose from the bench to shake hands with the dignitaries. Justice Frankfurter, who had known Hiss since his days on the Harvard Law School faculty, testified that Hiss's reputation for loyalty, integrity, and veracity was "excellent." Justice Reed corroborated Frankfurter's character testimony. Critics were quick to charge that the two associate justices had disqualified themselves from sitting on the case if it ever came before the Supreme Court on appeal. But that was easily answered. Owing to their intimate association with the defendant, they would most certainly have disqualified themselves in any event, and they did just that when the case later came before that tribunal. It was also argued that the prosecution was placed in the position of having to impugn their testimony and that such unseemly brushes between high justices and prosecutors would in the long run tarnish the reputation of the high court. Yet the willingness of the two justices to stand up for the character of a friend under attack was by itself praiseworthy. That this testimony had some weight with the jury seems indubitable. At least one of the four jurors who held out for Hiss's innocence admitted after the trial was over that the character testimony given by the two associate justices constituted the most powerful argument in favor of the accused. For him, that testimony tipped the scales.

Throughout the trial, Dr. Carl Binger, a psychiatrist and member of the faculty of the Cornell University Medical College, occupied a seat just behind the defense table. While Chambers was on the stand, he studied the witness with the air of a man who has found an object of professional interest. Now the defense sought to put Dr. Binger on the stand despite vehement and prolonged objections by Murphy. Stryker was allowed by the court to put to the witness a forty-five-minute hypothetical question on Chambers's mental condition, but the psychiatrist was not permitted to reply. Critics of Judge Kaufman's ruling charged that

Binger's presence at the trial and the opportunity given the
defense through the hypothetical question to broadcast to
the jury its innuendoes about Chambers's mental condition
could not have failed to have a prejudicial effect. Judge
Kaufman, recognizing that this was a novel situation in a
Federal court, felt that the accused had the right "to make
this record" but that, despite the trend of judicial decisions
permitting such testimony in the state courts, the jury was
sufficiently able to appraise the testimony of all the witnesses on the basis of its own experience. Equally controversial was Judge Kaufman's ruling barring the introduction
as a rebuttal witness of Mrs. Hede Massing, the first wife
of Gerhart Eisler, notorious Soviet agent. Chambers's assertion that Hiss had been a member of an espionage ring had
not been supported by a single witness up to this point and
rested for corroboration entirely on the documents. Hence
the exclusion of Mrs. Massing's testimony on the ground
that she was being offered in rebuttal on a collateral matter
and that her appearance might be "inflammatory and prejudicial," while technically correct, was a heavy blow to the
prosecution.

Stryker's scorching summation narrowed the trial issues
to the single question of the credibility of Chambers. He
reminded the jury now of Murphy's correct but inept phrasing of the Federal perjury rule: "If you don't believe Chambers, we have no case." Pounding the rail, Stryker thundered: "I would not believe Chambers on a stack of Bibles
if the F.B.I. stacked them as high as this building! He believes in nothing; not God, not man, not the sanctity of
marriage, or motherhood, not in himself. I can't think of
any decent thing he has not shown himself against."
Charging that "roguery, deception, and criminality have
marked [Chambers] as if with a hot iron," Stryker accused
him of having fantastic political ambitions, of seeking to
become the commissar of the Communist Party. Although
there was not an iota of evidence connecting Chambers with

the Communist Party at the time of the trial, Stryker preferred to pitch his argument on an emotional level rather
than to provide a painstaking analysis of the evidence in
the case. At the end he turned to the accused. "Alger Hiss,"
he declared, "this long nightmare is drawing to a close. Rest
well. Your case, your life, your liberty are in good hands.
Thank you, ladies and gentlemen."

If Stryker's summation was objectionable, Murphy's surpassed it in seriously prejudicial content. It is a well-estab-
lished rule of criminal procedure that it is no part of a
prosecutor's duty, nor is it his right, to stigmatize a defendant. He has the right to argue that the evidence proves the
defendant guilty as charged in the indictment, but for the
prosecutor to characterize the defendant as though he were
adjudged guilty or had pleaded guilty to the charge is a
prejudicial error. In the celebrated trial of John F. Knapp
for the murder of Captain Joseph White, Daniel Webster
provided all prosecuting attorneys with a model they
would do well to study. Nowhere in his powerful and convincing summation did Webster apply any epithets to the
defendant or express any opinion of his guilt or innocence.
At the outset he made it clear that as the commonwealth's
attorney he "would not attempt to hurry the jury against
the law or beyond the evidence." His cogent analysis of the
facts pointed to the guilt of the accused. At the close he told
the jury that toward the defendant as an individual "the
law inculcates no hostility, but toward him, if proved to
be a murderer, the oaths you have taken and public justice
demand you do your duty." Many a prosecutor at the
present day would not have hesitated to characterize the
accused as "a cold-blooded killer," counting on the spine-
lessness of the bench, but Webster kept within the legitimate
bounds of a prosecutor's argument.

If Murphy had ever studied Daniel Webster he gave not
the slightest hint of it in his prejudicial summation, which
time after time skirted the borders of mistrial:

Mr. Stryker said that he was going to call the shade of Oliver Wendell Holmes and have the ghost of that revered Justice testify on behalf of the defendant. And I said to myself, if he is going to call the shade of Justice Holmes, there are a couple of shades that I would like to call here. One man's name was Judas Iscariot and the other's Major General Benedict Arnold.

But let me dwell just a moment on reputation. I daresay that Judas Iscariot had a fairly good reputation. He was one of the Twelve. He was next to God, and we know what he did. Benedict Arnold came from a fine family. . . . He was made a major general and sold out West Point. He wasn't caught. But if he had been caught, don't you think he could have had George Washington as a reputation witness?

Significantly, in his second summation, almost a verbatim copy of the first, Murphy, out of deference to Jewish members of the second jury, omitted the reference to Judas. But in both closing arguments he deliberately inflamed the jury by accusing Hiss of being a traitor, not only ignoring the strict constitutional meaning of the word, but in open defiance of the fact that Hiss was on trial for perjury, not treason. "What is the name for a government employee who takes government papers and gives them to an espionage agent?" he asked. "Inside of that smiling face, the heart is black and cancerous. He is a *traitor*." Again: "Alger Hiss, you were the traitor. Alger Hiss, your feathers are but borrowed, and you can't change those documents."

At a number of other vital points Murphy's closing arguments in either the first or the second trial exceeded the bounds of propriety. He characterized the defendant's denials before the House committee and the grand jury as "standard CP practice," and stigmatized as the "liberal approach" Stryker's charge that the questioning by the F.B.I. of one witness was "close to oppression." "This is the open season on the F.B.I.," he shouted. "Everybody is taking potshots at them. It is the party line to do it. It is the party line." Such insinuations were calculated to damage both the accused and his attorneys. It implied, without support even in Chambers's testimony or anywhere in the record, that Hiss was *now* a Communist Party member and that his counsel in the Maryland libel suit and in the criminal trials were co-operating with him in Communist tactics. It was an attempt to convey to the jury some concealed link between the defense of this case and the defense of Judith Coplon, who had just been convicted, as well as of the eleven Communist leaders then on trial. The identical unsubstantiated argument was used by the government on appeal. A fair review of the case discloses that overzealousness clearly marked F.B.I. tactics in the handling of witnesses in the Hiss case. To meet such charges with a "party line" attack not only was disingenuous but revealed a certain callousness to ordinary civil liberties.

In both his opening and his summation Murphy referred to the grand jury in such a way as to invite the present jury to believe that the questions for their decision had already been decided against the accused. At the conclusion of his opening statement the prosecutor charged:

> But when the chips were down in December in the grand jury, when the grand jury, *a body like yourself* —twice as many—called him [Chambers] and called Mr. Hiss, first one, then the other, first one, then the other—where was the truth here? Where was the truth? Did you or didn't you?
> And they indicted Hiss.

This prejudicial line was again taken up at the close of his summation:

> Finally, *you are the second jury to hear this story.* The grand jury heard the same story. *The grand jury heard this traitor* and Mr. Chambers, and that grand jury indicted Hiss. It indicted Hiss because he lied. He

lied to them, and I submit he lied to you. The grand
jury said that he lied twice on December 15th. And as
a representative of 150,000,000 people of this country, I
ask you to concur in that charge of the grand jury. I
ask you as a representative of the United States Government to come back and put the lie in that man's face.

Indubitably the most damaging of all Murphy's contentions was his unsupported argument identifying Priscilla
Hiss as the typist of the Baltimore documents. Although he
had refrained from asking the government's typewriter expert for an opinion as to the identity of the *typist* of these
documents and though no evidence was adduced at either
trial to support the conclusion that it is scientifically possible to identify a typist by comparing typing errors with
errors in standards of comparison, Murphy in his summation in the second trial gave the jury a blanket invitation:
"When you get these documents inside, these Baltimore
documents and the standards," he told them, *"look for sim-
ilarities of mistakes,* and I call to your attention the following combinations: 'r' for 'i,' 'f' for 'g,' 'f' for 'd,' and you will
see them. You will see the same mistakes on the standards,
on the Mercy Hospital letter and on the Timmy Hobson
letter, the same characteristics as you do on the Baltimore
exhibits." Aside from challenging the validity of conclusions drawn from comparing these exhibits with merely *two*
specimens of Mrs. Hiss's typing, Murphy might just as
logically and with equal impropriety have invited the jury
to compare the typing errors in the Baltimore documents
with those made in various letters typed by Whittaker
Chambers and offered in evidence by the defense. For example, while there are two instances in the Baltimore documents where the letter "r" is typed over the letter "o" or "o"
over "r," no such error is found in Mrs. Hiss's letters, but
two are located in the letters of Chambers. Again, there are
two instances in the Baltimore documents where the letter
"q" was struck instead of the letter "w" and one where "w"

was hit instead of "q." This error did not occur in Mrs. Hiss's letters but did occur once in Chambers's correspondence. Of course, Murphy refrained from asking the jury to make this test. The fact is that most of these are common errors among typists and that *the samples are too few to draw any scientific inference as to whether Priscilla Hiss, Whittaker Chambers, or some third person did the typing.*[8]

Perhaps of greater significance, in view of Chambers's literary and editorial background, are the nine instances of proofreader's handwritten transposition marks which appear in the Baltimore documents. Some of these are distinctive (see "Baltimore 8," pages 1, 6, and 13), and seem to be identical with two used in Chambers's letters. Again, the handwritten letter "d" inserted in "Baltimore 16" is definitely not in Alger Hiss's hand, but conforms more closely to the "d" as found in a letter of Chambers dated August 1, 1938.

In summing up the facts about the bank withdrawal Murphy was not completely frank with the jurors. He reminded them:

> Do you remember how shocked Mr. Stryker was when Mr. Chambers told about the $400 loan. "That's the first time you testified to that," he said . . . and what did they do with it? They fumbled; they dropped the ball on that one. . . . Where is Chambers' testimony corroborated? In what respect do we know as rational human beings that he told the truth? In what respect do we know that Hiss lied? You determine where the lie is in this case by examining and placing side by side the testimony of the Hisses and the Chamberses.

[8] Document experts engaged by the defense have deposed in post-trial affidavits that the Baltimore documents contain at least fifty typing errors not found in Mrs. Hiss's letters, which, in turn, reveal nine errors never occurring in the Baltimore items. Their conclusion is that the Baltimore documents were not typed by one person, but by two or more, and that *none* of them was typed by Priscilla Hiss.

What Murphy did not add was that it was not beyond the
realm of possibility that Chambers had first learned of
the bank withdrawals from the F.B.I., who had subpœnaed
the records of the Hiss accounts in the Riggs bank early in
February 1949, during the period when Chambers was in
daily conference with that bureau. He was not asked
whether he had learned in any way of the four-hundred-
dollar withdrawal, but was questioned by Murphy (in the
second trial) along this line:

MURPHY: Now, have you ever *seen* Mr. or Mrs. Hiss's
bankbooks or bank accounts or bank statements?

CHAMBERS: I never have.

MURPHY: Never have?

CHAMBERS: Never.

MURPHY: In no shape or form?

CHAMBERS: In no way.

Despite the deadly seriousness of the charges and the
controversial nature of the evidence, Murphy's summation
was on the plane of cheap burlesque. His attitude toward
the jury was folksy. You and I know that the ridiculous
defense of the accused should be laughed out of court. Take
the character witnesses. "What kind of a reputation did a
good spy have? Of course it must be good. The fox barks not
when he goes to steal the lamb. But we are here on a search
for truth. We are not concerned with reputations. Poppy-
cock." Take the testimony of Judge Charles E. Wyzanski of
the Federal court. Alger Hiss's reputation for loyalty, integrity, and veracity, he testified on direct examination,
was "the equal of that of anybody I have ever known."
Murphy refrained from questioning the witness. But, he
quibbled, "he doesn't tell us who [*sic*] he knows." The fact
that Wyzanski had been law secretary to two of the most
honored jurists on the Federal bench, Judges Learned and
A. N. Hand, and had served as Solicitor of the Department
of Labor prior to going on the Federal bench was disposed
of in one wisecrack. Take John W. Davis, leader of the

American bar, who had also marked Hiss "excellent." He had testified as a character witness in the trial of Judge Martin W. Manton, a Federal judge who had been convicted "in this very court," Murphy told the jury.

Considering the emotional level on which both sides had pitched their cases and the complex and contradictory nature of the evidence, it is not surprising that the first jury disagreed, splitting eight to four for conviction. Twenty minutes after starting their deliberations the jury asked for the documents in the case and, significantly, for the old Woodstock typewriter. Looking for personal characteristics of mistyping and overtyping, eight of the jurors convinced themselves that the documents were typed by the same person. Since the second jury, shortly after retiring, requested Mrs. Hiss's letters written on the Woodstock as well as the Baltimore documents, it is very likely that they also made the same improper test. But the four jurors in the first trial who voted to acquit Hiss were even more incredible. They gave as their reason "lack of confidence in the expert testimony that copies of secret State Department papers which turned up in the possession of Chambers were typed on a machine owned by Hiss." Since this point had never been contested at any time by the defense, the jurors had demonstrated such an incapacity to analyze the evidence that one wonders why so many Americans still regard the institution of the jury as a palladium of personal liberty.

The stalemate satisfied neither side. Hiss had failed to obtain vindication; the government had failed to get to the root of past espionage activity. The public wanted the whole truth and looked to the second trial for the clarification of many doubts that had not been dissolved. The second trial began on November 17, 1949, after Hiss had failed to secure a change of venue to Rutland, Vermont, which he had sought on the ground that the volume of press and radio coverage on the first trial made it impossible to obtain an unbiased jury in the Southern District of New York. It was presided over by the elderly Henry W. Goddard, a veteran with more than twenty years of service on the Federal bench. The whole tone of the trial was different. Instead of the preponderantly masculine jury of the first trial, the second jury comprised seven housewives, one optician, and four businessmen, one retired. The government, having benefited by extra time to tie up loose ends, was confident. The defense decided to play down emotionalism and replaced Stryker by Claude B. Cross, a Boston lawyer with limited criminal experience. Genial and courteous, Cross made up in analytical powers and methodicalness what he lacked in pyrotechnics. No longer were spectators entertained by snapping objections. Both sides apparently were willing to let the other have its say *ad nauseam.*

The second perjury trial has been compared to a mystery novel read a second time. Surprise and suspense were now largely gone. Nonetheless, at several points the prosecution was able to stun the defense with unanticipated blows. Countering, the defense launched a massive attack on the personality and credibility of the government's chief witness, an attack unprecedented in the history of American criminal trials.

Three controversial moves undoubtedly strengthened Murphy's case. Against the objections of the defense, Judge Goddard allowed a witness to appear even though it was known that he had claimed the privilege against self-incrimination when questioned before a grand jury. This was the mysterious William Rosen, who, through a reassignment from the Cherner Motor Company, appeared to have received Hiss's Ford. When the question of allowing Rosen to take the stand was discussed in chambers, Murphy told Judge Goddard that he proposed to ask Rosen his address, his affiliation with the Communist Party, whether he had had anything to do with the car, and whether he had any connection at all with *Chambers, Peters,* or *Hiss.* Murphy did not keep his agreement. Rosen replied to the question regarding his present address and then declined to answer the succeeding seven questions on the ground of self-incrimination. The first related to his possible connection with the Communist Party in 1936, and the remaining six to his possible connection with the Ford. Rosen denied knowing in 1936 a man known as J. Peters. "Did you in July of 1936 know the defendant, Alger Hiss?" "No, sir, I did not." Turning to defense counsel, Murphy then said: "You may examine." Why did Murphy fail to put to Rosen the question *whether he had known Chambers in 1936*? Again, under cross-examination Rosen stated that he had never seen Hiss before October 1948 in court, that he had never spoken to him in his life or had any negotiations with him.

Although Goddard cautioned the jury "that you are to draw no inference unfavorable to this defendant because of the fact that this witness, Rosen, has claimed immunity," it seems scarcely within the bounds of credibility that a jury could fail to consider it highly suspicious that a person would refuse to answer a seemingly innocent question about the purchase of an old Ford. In his summation Murphy drew a heavy inference from Rosen's silence, in flat disregard of the court's admonition that no such inference should be drawn:

> Then Mr. Chambers said he had a Ford and that he used to use it; then he said he remembered that Mr. Hiss wanted to give it away to the Communist Party so some poor worker could use it. Well, what happened with that? . . . Mr. Hiss's assignment of title; he wrote the name in himself. Then we look at the Cherner books. "We haven't got any record of it; no records are missing; they are all in consecutive order; that is our name; that is my signature," and it ends up with Rosen.
>
> Now, does that corroborate what Mr. Chambers says? "He had a Ford; he wanted to give it to the CP; he asked me; I asked Peters; he was opposed to it; finally we said, 'All right, go ahead if you want to do it.' We don't know what happened to it."

You saw what happened to it. Corroboration: Ford, disposition of the Ford.

While Kaufman had refused to allow the testimony of Mrs. Hede Massing, Goddard permitted her to tell about an alleged conversation with Hiss at the home of Noel Field in Washington in the late summer or early fall of 1935:

> I said to Mr. Hiss, "I understand that you are trying to get Noel Field away from my organization into yours," and he said, "So you are this famous girl that is trying to get Noel Field away from me," and I said, "Yes." And he said, as far as I remember, "Well, we will see who is going to win," at which point I said, "Well, Mr. Hiss,—I did not say, 'Mr. Hiss'—Well, you realize that you are competing with a woman," at which either he or I said, the gist of the sentence was, "Whoever is going to win we are working for the same boss."
>
> Now, as I say, I don't remember whether he or whether I said that, but this sentence I remember distinctly because it was very important.

On cross-examination the credibility of this former Viennese actress was rudely shaken. She had taken a false oath to obtain her passport for trips abroad as a courier and she had no recollection of the dates of her marriage to and divorce from Communist bigwig Eisler. "I have a bad memory," she was forced to concede. She admitted planning to write a series of articles with Eugene Lyons, as ghost writer, after the trial. Her sensational appearance would be expected to enhance her box-office appeal. Grave doubt was cast on her testimony by a Lithuanian refugee named Henrikas Rabinavicius. According to what she had told him at a dinner party at the home of the Eugene Lyonses, Rabinavicius stated that Mrs. Massing, in making contact with young men in the State Department, made a point of carefully concealing from them her connection with the Communist Party or Soviet espionage. When she reached the point in her tale about the remark she allegedly made to Hiss: "I am going to take this young man away from you," she turned to Eugene Lyons, according to the witness, and asked: "Gene, what did Alger Hiss say?" Lyons retorted: "I don't know what Mr. Hiss said. I wasn't there. You ought to know yourself." Under questioning by Rabinavicius, Mrs. Massing admitted that Hiss never told her that he was a member of an apparatus working for a foreign power. Rabinavicius's account tallies with Hiss's story on direct examination. Hiss confronted Mrs. Massing in December 1948. She reminded him of the dinner party and mentioned that Noel Field "was very much interested in world socialism." She made no reference to an "apparatus" or to Communism. Nevertheless, despite the serious impeachment of her credibility, Mrs. Massing was the *only* person to come forward to corroborate Chambers's accusation that Hiss was a member of an espionage apparatus. Despite inconsistencies in her gossipy testimony and her own career of disloyalty and perjury, the witness, as the former wife of a notorious Communist agent, could not fail to have had weight with the jury.

Perhaps the greatest shock was reserved for the end. As a rebuttal witness Murphy brought to the stand Mrs. Edith Murray, who testified that she had worked as a maid for the Chamberses when the couple lived in Baltimore during the years 1934 to 1936 under the assumed name of Cantwell. At their Eutaw Place home the Chamberses "didn't have any visitors, only two visitors that I know of," the witness volunteered. She then proceeded to identify these two visitors as Alger and Priscilla Hiss, but admitted that she had seen the accused only once.

The probative value of this identification was badly jarred on cross-examination when Mrs. Murray was forced to admit that she had been brought to the courthouse by the F.B.I. on November 17, the opening day of the second trial, and, in the hall outside the courtroom, had identified Hiss and his wife, apparently as they came out of the elevator.

But before doing so she had been shown their photos and told by the F.B.I. "to see if [she] could recognize them." When first shown Priscilla Hiss's picture, her reaction had been: *"It looked like—I thought maybe it was an actress or something . . . I said to myself, maybe it was in the movies."* The dramatic impact of her appearance may have given her testimony in the jury's eyes an effect wholly disproportionate to its intrinsic probative force, for, other than the Chamberses, she was the *only* witness who testified to having seen Alger or Priscilla Hiss with either of the Chamberses on any occasion that Whittaker or Esther had asserted to have occurred and the Hisses had denied. Affidavits offered by the defense *subsequent* to the trial, to the effect that the Chamberses never had a maid at their Eutaw Place residence, came too late to discredit her testimony with the jury. The government's use of surprise witnesses on rebuttal shocked some lawyers' sense of fair play. In Great Britain the prosecutor must disclose to the accused *before trial* all the evidence he intends to offer. If the prisoner is to have a proper chance to defend himself and to discredit government evidence, the introduction of the British practice should be seriously considered in the United States.

While Judge Goddard's latitude toward the strict rules of evidence proved an advantage to the prosecution, it also enabled the defense to establish a precedent. For the first time in a Federal court psychiatric experts were allowed to testify to impeach the credibility of a witness. Dr. Carl Binger had probably been itching to answer ever since Stryker in the first trial had put to him the forty-five-minute hypothetical question and Kaufman had barred his reply. Over the bitter protests of Murphy, Judge Goddard permitted a sixty-five-minute hypothetical question to be put to the witness by Cross and then permitted the psychiatrist to testify. Assuming the facts stated in the question to be true, Binger was asked, and taking into account his observation of Chambers on the stand in June and November, "have you, as a psychiatrist, an opinion within the bounds

of reasonable certainty as to the mental condition of Whittaker Chambers?"

A.: Yes, I have.

Q.: What is your opinion, Dr. Binger, of the mental
condition of Mr. Chambers?

A.: I think Mr. Chambers is suffering from a condition
known as psychopathic personality, which is a disorder of
character, of which the outstanding features are behavior
of what we call an amoral or an asocial and delinquent
nature.

Psychopathic personality is a recognized mental disease,
Binger went on to elaborate, and it includes such symptoms
as "chronic, persistent and repetitive lying," stealing, deception and misrepresentation, "vagabondage, panhandling,
inability to form stable attachments, and a tendency to
make false accusations." "There is a peculiar kind of lying
known as pathological lying," Binger went on, "and a peculiar kind of tendency to make false accusations known
as pathological accusations, which are frequently found in
the psychopathic personality." Binger then labeled as "para-
noiac" Chambers's propensity to the making of grandiose
statements in which he confused his own importance with
the realities of the situation.

The most dramatic point in Dr. Binger's testimony was
reached when he proceeded to give an analysis of a book
called *Class Reunion*, by Franz Werfel, which Whittaker
Chambers had translated in 1929. Dr. Binger felt that the
book had "extraordinary analogies" to the Hiss case. Its
central figure is Sebastian, a magistrate, a man who says of
himself: "I would lie, I would—I have no conscience. I
would stop at nothing to gain my end." Slighted by a casual
remark by his intellectually gifted friend Adler, Sebastian
fiendishly plotted his ruin. *"A work of annihilation had begun,"* Sebastian confessed, which ended with his friend's
destruction *through the falsification of documents*, a charge
that he shifted to Adler's shoulders. The defense urged that

the Sebastian-Adler relationship may have offered a clue to the Chambers-Hiss involvement.

Under cross-examination Dr. Binger conceded that he "would feel better qualified" had he more information about the first sixteen years of Chambers's life. He insisted that what he was purporting to do was to make a diagnosis, not to prescribe a treatment. He cited army experience to show that successful diagnoses of GI's had been made despite their unwillingness to co-operate. In support of Dr. Binger's opinion the defense rolled up another big gun, a Harvard psychologist named Henry A. Murray, who proceeded to corroborate the diagnosis.

In any trial when the issue is in doubt even down to the end, the attitude of the judge may easily tip the scales. While Judge Kaufman had been sharply criticized by supporters of the prosecution's case for his manner toward the government's witnesses, Judge Goddard was guilty of a number of prejudicial lapses that materially damaged the defense's case. On two occasions he contributed to discrediting important defense witnesses by observing (to Malcolm Cowley): "You are not an advocate here," and, again (to Dr. Binger): "Doctor, you are here as a witness, not as an advocate." But the real damage was done in his loaded charge to the jury. Kaufman in the first trial had instructed the jury to consider evidence of good character and reputation along with all the other evidence in the case. Goddard remarked: "It may be that those with whom he [Hiss] had come in contact previously have been misled and that he did not reveal to them his real character or acts." This was so ineptly phrased that the jury could have regarded the observation as an endorsement of the prosecution's argument against the strong character evidence. The psychiatric testimony, Goddard stated, was "purely advisory." "It is for you to say," he charged, "how much weight, if any, you will give to the testimony of experts—and of Mr. Chambers," adding that even though the jury accepted the expert's opinion as to Chambers's mental condition, they could

still find that he "was telling the truth when he testified regarding these particular matters."

But the most prejudicial lapse occurred in the judge's
charge on corroboration. While rightly instructing the jury
that they "must believe beyond a reasonable doubt that the
corroborative testimony is inconsistent with the innocence
of the defendant," he added this confused observation:

> Now, the Government says that the affair was carried
> on with great secrecy so as to escape possible detection,
> and that no one else was present when the alleged acts
> took place. The Government, however, urges that facts
> and circumstances have been proved which, it says,
> *fully* substantiate the testimony of Mr. Chambers. *This
> is an issue to be determined by you.*

The word "fully" was emphasized in a way that could not
fail to have impressed the jurors. Finally, he warned the
jury that if they found the law had been violated as charged,
"they should not hesitate because of sympathy or for any
other reason to render a verdict of guilt, as a clear warning
to all that a crime such as charged here may not be committed with impunity. *The American public is entitled to be
assured of this.*" Certainly, Judge Goddard might have
added, but did not choose to, that the American public is
also entitled to be assured that prisoners whose guilt has
not been demonstrated beyond a reasonable doubt will not
be convicted for reasons of expediency or public policy.

The jury commenced its deliberations at ten minutes
after three the afternoon of Friday, January 20. The next
morning it requested the court for instructions on circumstantial evidence and corroboration. Goddard repeated his
summary of the government's contention that its evidence
fully substantiated the testimony of Chambers. Then,
whether by intention or oversight, he omitted from his re-
charge the crucial sentence of the original charge: *"This is
an issue to be determined by you."* Probably we shall never
know whether the jury inferred from this charge that it was

not within their province to debate the issue whether or not the circumstantial evidence corroborated the sole witness. By afternoon the twelve had agreed on a verdict of guilty.

When asked whether he had anything to say at the time of sentencing, Alger Hiss stated: "I would like to thank your Honor for the opportunity again to deny the charges that have been made against me. I want only to add that in the future the full facts of how Whittaker Chambers was able to carry out forgery by typewriter will be disclosed. Thank you, sir."

And there the matter rests.

If the verdict is correct and Alger Hiss is guilty, then his shocking disloyalty was only matched by his incredible stupidity. If he is innocent, he is the victim of the most monstrous frame-up since a French captain of artillery was sent to Devil's Island on the basis of a forged *bordereau*.

BIBLIOGRAPHICAL NOTES

I. Jezebel before the Judges

Two reports of the trial are extant. The more detailed was made by an unknown friend of Anne Hutchinson and was included among the papers of her lineal descendant Lieutenant Governor Thomas Hutchinson (*The History of the Colony and Province of Massachusetts Bay,* ed. by L. S. Mayo [Cambridge, Mass., 1936], II, 366–91). A briefer version is included in *A Short Story of the Rise, Reign and Ruine of the Antinomians . . . of New England* (London, 1644). This is believed to be John Winthrop's version, with supplementary comments by the Reverend Thomas Weld. The former has been utilized in this volume, but at a few points of commentary the *Short Story* has been drawn upon for supplementary information. Both reports have been included among the tracts edited by C. F. Adams: "Antinomianism in the Colony of Massachusetts Bay," Prince Society *Publications,* XXI (Boston, 1894). In addition, that collection includes the report of the church trial at which Anne Hutchinson was excommunicated, an account attributed to Robert Keayne, the Reverend Mr. Wilson's brother-in-law, Keayne's own account of the experience of the Massachusetts emissaries who called on Mistress Hutchinson in Rhode Island, and John Cotton's apologia: *The Way of Congregational Churches Cleared* (London, 1648). Other contemporary accounts are provided by John Winthrop in his *Journal* or *History of New England,* and by Edward Johnson in his *Wonder-Working Providence of Sion's Saviour in New England,* both available in the series *Original Narratives of Early American History.* A very brief official reference to the trial is also found in *Massachusetts Bay Colony Records,* I, 207.

Some of the best treatments of the significance of the affair have been penned by Brooks Adams: *The Emancipation of Massachusetts* (Boston, 1887) ; by Charles Francis Adams: *Three Episodes in Massachusetts History* (Boston and New York, 1896), I, 366 ff.; by Daniel Wait Howe: *The Puritan Republic* (Indianapolis, 1899) ; and by George E. Ellis: *The Puritan Age and Rule in the Colony of Massachusetts Bay, 1629–1685* (Boston and New York, 1888). The theological implications of the controversy have been considered by Perry Miller: *Orthodoxy in Massachusetts, 1630–50* (Cambridge, 1933). Among the more provocative biographical studies of the principals are lives of Anne Hutchinson by Winifred King Rugg (Boston and New York, 1930) and Helen Augur (New York, 1930) ; of Wheelwright by C. H. Bell (Boston, 1876) ; and of Sir Harry Vane by James K. Hosmer (Boston and New York, 1889). For the law relating to privileged communications of clergymen, see Wigmore on *Evidence* (3rd ed.), VIII, Sec. 2394 ff., and William George Torpey: *Judicial Doctrines of Religious Rights in America* (Chapel Hill, 1948), pp. 302–4.

II. The Politicians and the Pirate

For introductory background one can hardly better the account in the 2nd edition of Captain Charles Johnson's contemporary classic: *A General History of the Pyrates* (London, 1724). The principal documents in the Kidd case are in the Colonial Office papers in the British Public Record Office, London. A judicious selection was made by J. Franklin Jameson: *Privateering and Piracy in the Colonial Period* (New York, 1923), pp. 190–257. The trial of Kidd is available in Francis Hargrove, ed.: *State Trials* (4th ed., London, 1777), V, 289–338, and that of Somers and Orford, ibid., 341–83. More recent editions were prepared by Graham Brooks (Edinburgh, 1930), who contends that Kidd was given a fair trial, and by Don C. Seitz (New York, 1936), who regards Kidd as a scapegoat. Depositions in the Kidd case before the House of Commons are found in *Journals of the House of Commons,* XIII, and, somewhat more compactly, in Leo F. Stock, ed.: *Proceedings and Debates of the British Parliaments respecting North America,* II (Washington, D.C., 1927). Further information can be found in the published *Calendar of State Papers, America and West Indies, 1699* and *1700,* and in *Acts of the Privy Council, Colonial Series, 1680–1720* (London, 1910), pp. 347, 367, 379. The pertinent records of the Massachusetts Council are in the Massachusetts Archives, State House, Boston. The agreement between Bellomont, Livingston, and Kidd is published in *New York Colonial Documents,* IV, 762–5. A facsimile reproduction of Kidd's treasure inventory is found in Ralph D. Paine: *The Book of Buried Treasure* (London, 1911), p. 82, which also reproduces the pass of the *Quedah Merchant* (p. 104). The sentence condemning Kidd's goods as droits of the Admiralty is found in R. G. Marsden, ed.: *Documents relating to Law and Custom of the Sea* (London, 1916), II, 184–6. W. H. Bonner's *Pirate Laureate* (New Brunswick, N.J., 1947) explores Kidd in legend and literature. Mr. Stanley H. Friedelbaum of the Department of History, Brooklyn College, who is writing a biography of the Earl of Bellomont under my supervision, made a number of valuable suggestions about that politician's early career.

III. The Case of the Palatine Printer

The account of the trial was published by John Peter Zenger himself as *A Brief Narrative of the Case and Tryal of John Peter Zenger, Printer of the New York Weekly Journal* (New York, 1736), which went through numerous reissues. It is reproduced in Livington Rutherford: *John Peter Zenger, His Press, His Trial, and a Bibliography of Zenger Imprints* (New York, 1904). The case is also recorded in the Minute Book of the Supreme Court of Judicature, 1732–9, Hall of Records, New York County, and referred to in the province's Council Minutes, lib. XVII, 25, State Library, Albany. Manuscript material relating to the case will be found among the James Alexander, Horsmanden, and Jay Collections in the New York Historical Society; and Alexander's brief, now in the Rutherford Collection, has been published by Julius Goebel and T. R. Naughton: *Law Enforcement in Colonial New York* (New York, 1944). The appeal of Alexander and Smith against their disbarment, December 27, 1735, is in the State Library.

The best running account of the affair will be found in the files of the *Weekly Journal* at the New York Public Library and the New York Historical Society, and other contemporary references will be found in the Cadwallader Colden Papers, New York Historical Society *Collections,* Vols. L, LI, LXVII, LXVIII; in the *Minutes of the Common Council of the City of New York* (New York, 1905), IV, *passim;* in the *Journal of the Votes and Proceedings of the General Assembly of the Colony of New York* (New York, 1764–6), Vol. I; and in the *Journal of the Legislative Council* (Albany, 1861), Vol. I. William Smith's son comments rather objectively on the trial in his *History of the Province of New York* (New York, 1830), Vol. II. C. F. Heartman's *John Peter Zenger and His Fight for the Freedom of the American Press* (New York, 1934) reproduces some of the controversial material.

The relation of the Zenger case to the broader issue of freedom of expression is considered by me in an article in *New York History,* April 1950, and by L. R. Schuyler: *Liberty of the Press in the American Colonies before the Revolutionary War* (New York, 1905). I am indebted to Mr. Irving G. Cheslaw, of the History Department, Columbia University, for a number of valuable suggestions on the trial, and to two Columbia graduate students, Mr. Carl Fryburg and Miss Anastasia Burns, for sidelights on the respective careers of Governor Cosby and James Alexander. An inadequate biography by Burton A. Konkle (Philadelphia, 1941) deals with the career of Andrew Hamilton.

IV. The Spooner Triangle Love Slaying

Peleg W. Chandler, in including the case in *American Criminal Trials* (Boston, 1844), pp. 3–58, had access to the manuscript notes of Judge Jedediah Foster, who took full minutes of the evidence, and the papers of Levi Lincoln. The latter collection, now in the possession of the American Antiquarian Society, no longer contains data for these early years. The Massachusetts Historical Society has other Lincoln letters. Further file papers and minutes of the case are found in the Records of the Superior Court of Judicature and in the Massachusetts Archives, State House, Boston. The best newspaper account of the trial and execution will be found in the issues of Isaiah Thomas's *Worcester Spy,* a complete file of which is at the American Antiquarian Society. A distant relative of Bathsheba's, Samuel Swett Green, makes a strong plea for her insanity in American Antiquarian Society *Proceedings,* new series, V, 430–6 (1888). Other local angles are stressed by Chandler Bullock: "The Bathsheba Spooner Murder Case," Worcester Historical Society *Publications,* new series, II (September 1939), 204–21. Roger Lamb, a sergeant in the Royal Welch Fusiliers, personally witnessed the execution and recorded his impressions in *Memoir of His Own Life* (Dublin, 1811), pp. 243–5. Mr. Emanuel L. Strunin, of Columbia University, contributed pertinent suggestions on the status of loyalism in Worcester County.

V. The Trial of Aaron Burr

A two-volume report of the trials of Aaron Burr, taken down in shorthand, was published by David Robertson (Philadelphia, 1818), and a more condensed one-volume version was compiled by J. J. Coombs (Washington, D.C., 1864). The Library of Congress has a collection of papers relating to the Burr conspiracy. Copies of all known papers

to and from Jefferson relating to the Burr incident have
been assembled by Dr. Julian P. Boyd and his staff at
Princeton. Some references to Wickham's role in the trial
are found in the Wickham Papers (microfilm), Alderman
Library, University of Virginia. Evidence relating to the
conspiracy also appears in *Annals of Congress, 9 Cong., 2
Sess.,* 1008–19, in *10 Cong., 1 Sess.,* 385–778, and in *American State Papers, Misc.* (1834), I, 468–645. Printed sources
that must be used with caution include *The Private Journal
of Aaron Burr . . . in Europe,* ed. by M. L. Davis (2 vols.,
1858; ed. by W. K. Bixby, 1903) ; James Wilkinson: *Memoirs
of My Own Times* (3 vols., Philadelphia, 1816) ; Mark Van
Doren, ed.: *Correspondence of Aaron Burr and His Daughter, Theodosia* (New York, 1929) ; *The Blennerhassett Papers,* ed. by W. H. Safford (Cincinnati, 1891).

Henry Adams: *History of the United States during the
Administrations of Jefferson and Madison* (Vols. II and III,
1889–90), holds that Burr plotted disunion, whereas W. F.
McCaleb: *The Aaron Burr Conspiracy* (New York, 1903)
contends that Burr sought to build a Western empire
through annexation of Spanish territories in the Southwest
and Mexico. Most of Burr's biographers, including James
Parton (1858), S. H. Wandell and M. Minnegerode (1925),
and Nathan Schachner (1937), give their hero the benefit
of the doubt; and A. J. Beveridge's *The Life of John Marshall,* Vol. III (Boston, 1916–19), is a brilliant analysis of
the trial written with that author's customary anti-Jeffer-
sonian bias. A hostile portrait of Wilkinson's role in the
Burr conspiracy is furnished in *Tarnished Warrior,* by
Major James R. Jacobs (1938), but a more objective account is found in T. R. Hay and M. R. Werner: *The Ad-
mirable Trumpeter* (New York, 1941). Like Charlemagne
and other folk heroes, Burr looms large in post-trial
literature. See S. H. Wandell: *Aaron Burr in Literature*
(London, 1936).

VI. Grand Guignol at Harvard Medical School

Few American criminal trials have been reported contemporaneously in so wide a variety of versions as was the Webster trial. One of the most useful reports was that prepared by George Bemis, one of the counsel in the case (Boston, 1850). To satisfy the voracious appetite of the American public for horror stories, the Boston and New York papers issued pamphlet reports. Versions examined include those got out by the Boston *Daily Times* and *Daily Mail* and the New York *Daily Globe*. In addition, a so-called "phonographic report" was issued by Dr. James W. Stone, and a stenographic report, most useful for *Q.* and *A.*, was published by John A. French of Boston. The case is reported in *American State Trials*, Vol. IV (ed. by J. D. Lawson, St. Louis, 1915), and in an edition by George Dilnot (London, 1928).

The legal issues raised by the Webster case were considered contemporaneously. Oakey Hall, of the New York bar, published his analysis in 1850, along with an anonymous associate at the bar, who entitled his effort: *A Statement of Reasons Showing the Illegality of That Verdict.* The most significant analysis was made by Joel Parker: "The Law of Homicide," *North American Review*, LXXII (January 1851), 178–204; the specific issue of the presumption of malice was considered by J. Gardner White: "Samuel Sumner Wilde," *Memorial Biographies of the New England Historic Genealogical Society* (Boston, 1881), pp. 368–88. Lemuel Shaw's role in the case has been considered by his biographer, Frederic H. Chase (Boston, 1918), and Dr. Leonard W. Levy, of Columbia University, who has recently completed a new and authoritative biography of the great Chief Justice, has made a number of acute suggestions.

VII. Armstrong's Acquittal by Almanac

The reconstruction of the Armstrong case has been based on recollection testimony, chiefly gathered by Herndon and located in the Herndon-Weik Collection, Library of Congress. These include letters of Walker to Herndon of June 3, August 27, September 8 and 15, 1866, and interviews in Herndon's hand with Hannah Armstrong and Judge Harriott, both undated. The Hannah Armstrong statement, with some minor errors of transcription, appears in Emanuel Hertz: *Hidden Lincoln* (New York, 1938), pp. 369–70. The alleged letter of Lincoln to Hannah Armstrong, dated September 18, 1857, and given in Gilbert A. Tracy, ed.: *Uncollected Letters of Lincoln* (Boston and New York, 1917), p. 79, is a forgery. Lincoln's request to charge the jury, which has disappeared from the court files in very recent years and is reputed to be circulating privately, is published in Hertz: *Abraham Lincoln: A New Portrait* (New York, 1931), II, 716. Post-trial correspondence with Hannah Armstrong concerning her property and her son Duff's service in the Union army will be found in the Robert Todd Lincoln Collection, Library of Congress.

Although the trial took place in Beardstown, the records of the case are now in the courthouse at Virginia, Illinois, the present county seat of Cass County. Included among these are the summonses to witnesses, receipts for witness fees, the order for change of venue, and the attachment for contempt issued against Charles Allen and Dr. B. F. Stevenson. The clerk of court in Havana, county seat of Mason County, has the affidavit for the change of venue filed by Duff Armstrong, as well as other papers in the Norris trial, including the true bill against Norris and Armstrong, the minutes in the Norris trial, and the motions of Norris's attorneys. The Norris pardon papers are in the custody of the State Archivist, Springfield.

No newspaper report of the case has survived. Beardstown's Democratic paper, the *Central Illinoisan,* is not extant for the period in question. A brief reference to the trial is found in the *Illinois State Journal,* May 26, 1858, referring to the Menard *Index* (Petersburg), no longer extant.

In gathering material for the Armstrong trial a number of Lincoln scholars were most generous with help and suggestions. Among them must be mentioned my friend and colleague Dr. Reinhard Luthin, of Columbia University; Dr. Harry E. Pratt, of Muskegon, Mich.; Mr. J. Monaghan, State Historian, and Miss Margaret A. Flint, Reference Librarian, Illinois State Historical Library; Miss Marion D. Bonzi, the Abraham Lincoln Association (which made available its extensive file on the case); Miss Norma Cuthbert, Henry E. Huntington Library and Art Gallery; Mr. William H. Townsend, Lexington, Ky., and Dr. Louis A. Warren, Lincoln National Life Foundation, Fort Wayne, Ind.

Lincoln's legal career and aspects of the Armstrong case have been treated by William H. Herndon and Jesse W. Weik: *Abraham Lincoln: The True Story of a Great Life* (2 vols., New York, 1892), II, 26–8; by Frederick T. Hill: *Lincoln the Lawyer* (New York, 1906); by Albert A. Woldman: *Lawyer Lincoln* (Boston and New York, 1936); by William E. Barton: *The Life of Abraham Lincoln* (Boston and New York, 1928), I, 494–607; by Carl Sandburg: *Abraham Lincoln: The Prairie Years* (New York, 1929), pp. 342–5; and by William H. Townsend: "Lincoln's Defense of Duff Armstrong," American Bar Association *Journal,* XI (1925), 81–4, as well as in his *Lincoln the Litigant* (Boston and New York, 1925). Ida Tarbell: *The Life of Abraham Lincoln* (New York, 1906), II, 65, includes the account of William A. Douglas, one of the witnesses. J. N. Gridley: "Lincoln's Defense of Duff Armstrong," Illinois State Historical Society *Journal,* III, 24–44, quotes an interview of a Mrs. DeSchweer with Duff's brother, A. P. Armstrong, in 1909, as well as a statement of John T. Brady, the last survivor of the jury. James L. King: "Lincoln's Skill as a Lawyer," *North American Review*, Vol. CLXVI (1898), 186–95, quotes an account by a spectator at the trial, Judge Abram Bergen, who also recounted the trial in an address delivered before the Kansas State Bar Association in 1897.

The false-almanac story was perpetuated in printed form by Ward H. Lamon, *The Life of Abraham Lincoln* (Boston, 1872), pp. 328 ff. In later American editions of *Ram on Facts* the index contains a reference: "Lincoln, President Abraham, how he procured an acquittal by fraud"; and the evidence pro and con is compactly summarized in "Lincoln Lore," Lincoln National Life Foundation *Bulletin*, August 6, 1935. The reference to the doctored almanac in the County Mayo case has been unearthed by Eston E. Ericson, in Illinois State Historical Society *Journal*, XXXI (1938), 105–6.

For Lincoln's Springfield, his most notable law partnership, and his law-office finances, see Paul M. Angle: *Lincoln, 1854–1861* (Springfield, 1939), and *Here I Have Lived: A History of Lincoln's Springfield, 1821–65* (New Brunswick, N.J., 1950); David Donald: *Lincoln's Herndon* (New York, 1948); and Harry E. Pratt: *The Personal Finances of Abraham Lincoln* (Springfield, 1943), pp. 50–4.

Many people have erroneously assumed that Edward Eggleston's account of the almanac trial in *The Graysons* (1888) was fact rather than fiction. Among those who went overboard in publishing a completely untrue account of the case, even to the extent of getting the names of the principals wrong, was Judge J. W. Donavan: *Modern Jury Trials* (5th ed., New York, 1924), pp. 702 ff. But Eggleston never attempted to verify his story. "To have investigated the accuracy of my version of the anecdote," he asserted, "would have been, indeed, to fly in the face and eyes of Providence, for popular tradition is itself an artist roughhewing a story to the novelist's hands."

An ambrotype of Lincoln taken by A. M. Byers on the

day of the Armstrong trial has caught a youthful and
tender look, which contrasts with the more mature and
dignified photograph taken after his debates with Douglas.
See R. R. Wilson: *Lincoln in Portraiture* (New York, 1935),
p. 39.

VIII. The Fate of the Flagrant Adulterer

With a few exceptions, there is a lacuna in the Sickles
Papers in the New York Public Library from 1857 to 1861.
Among the exceptions are the original of the anonymous
letter to Dan Sickles, dated February 24, 1859, which set
off the conflagration, and several communications endorsing
Sickles's reconciliation with Teresa. But by far the greater
part of the Sickles Collection relates to his post-Civil War
activities. A contemporary report of the trial was issued
by Robert M. de Witt, a New York publisher, in 1859;
and Graham's opening to the jury was published by
W. A. Townsend & Co. of the same city. A somewhat condensed version appears in *American State Trials*, edited by
John D. Lawson (St. Louis, 1919), XII, 494–762. Stanton's
argument on the instructions to the jury was reprinted in
William L. Snyder's *Great Speeches by Great Lawyers*
(New York, 1881). The New York and Washington press
gave the trial very full coverage, thoroughly exploiting its
sensational aspects, as did *Harper's* and *Leslie's* weeklies.
A recent version of the Kay-Sickles triangle has been presented by Edgcumb Pinchon in his lively biography *Dan
Sickles* (New York, 1945). Stanton's role in the trial is
referred to by F. A. Flower: *Edwin McMasters Stanton*
(Akron, Ohio, 1905). Mr. John F. Roche, of Fordham University, made helpful suggestions regarding the Sickles
papers.

IX. The Treason Trial of John Brown

Brown's trial was contemporaneously reported in a pamphlet: *Life, Trial, and Execution of Captain John Brown* (New York, 1859). Cf. also "Testimonies of Capt. John Brown at Harper's Ferry," *Anti-Slavery Tracts*, No. 7, n.s. (New York, 1860). The best newspaper coverage of the trial was provided by James Gordon Bennett's *New York Herald*. The official trial papers are in the courthouse at Charlestown. Other manuscripts furnishing background data include the Dreer Collection in the Historical Society of Pennsylvania, containing letters and official documents written by and sent to the Virginia authorities at the time of the raid, and the Thomas Wentworth Higginson Collection in the Boston Public Library.

Oswald Garrison Villard, whose monumental biography of John Brown (Boston and New York, 1910; New York, 1943) embodies enormous research on the subject, gathered, in the course of his investigation, a valuable collection of letters and papers relating to Brown, his career, and the trial, including research notes prepared for him by Katherine Mayo. These have now been deposited in the manuscript division of the Columbia University Library, and have proved especially helpful to me. James Redpath (Boston, 1860) and Franklin B. Sanborn, editor of John Brown's letters (Boston, 1885), both contributed to a sympathetic portrait of their hero.

Numerous legal critiques of the trial have been written. Among them may be mentioned General Marcus J. Wright: "The Trial of John Brown, Its Impartiality and Decorum Vindicated," *Southern Historical Society Papers*, XVI, 357–66; "The Trial and Execution of John Brown," *American Historical Association Papers*, IV (1890), 437–52; B. C. Washington: "The Trial of John Brown," in *Green Bag* (April 1899); George F. Caskie in *American Law Review* (May 1910), pp. 405–25; and Daniel C. Draper in *West*

Virginia History (January 1940), pp. 87–103. Documentary background for Botts's plea of insanity is found in James C. Malin's scholarly and objective study: *John Brown and the Legend of Fifty-Six* (Philadelphia, 1942). "The Mason Report," the results of the Congressional investigation of the Harper's Ferry raid, will be found in *U.S. Senate Reports, 36 Cong., 1 Sess.*, No. 278.

For suggestions on fugitive-slave cases preceding the Brown affair I am indebted to Dr. Leonard W. Levy and to Mr. Julius Yanuck, both of Columbia University.

X. Ordeal by Jury

All investigators of the Haymarket incident owe Henry David a profound debt for his brilliant analysis of the evidence in the case, which he takes apart in his *The History of the Haymarket Affair* (New York, 1936). The case is reported in *August Spies et al.* v. *The People of the State of Illinois, Abstract of Record* (2 vols., Chicago, 1887), and in condensed version in *American State Trials*, ed. by John D. Lawson, Vol. XII (St. Louis, 1919). The oral arguments of Black and Zeisler on appeal before the Illinois Supreme Court were published in Chicago in 1887, as were the briefs on the law and the facts for defendants in error. Numerous biographical sketches of the defendants appeared contemporaneously with the trial. Spies's own autobiography also reproduced his speech in court (Chicago, 1887). One of the defense attorneys, Sigismund Zeisler, published his reminiscences about the case in 1927. Numerous publicists, including Samuel P. McConnell and M. M. Trumbull, addressed themselves to an examination of the fairness of the trial. Altgeld's role is discussed in Waldo E. Browne's biography of the Governor (New York, 1924), and his own controversial pardon paper was published in Springfield in 1896. As might be expected, the Chicago and New York press gave the case detailed coverage.

XI. The Case of the Morphine Murder

The trial record has been published as *The Trial of Carlyle Harris, Taken from the Official Stenographer's Minutes* (New York, 1892). For the appeal, see Court of Appeals, State of New York, *The People of the State of New York against Carlyle W. Harris* (New York, 1892), and 136 N.Y. 423 (1893). Of all the New York papers, the *World* had the best coverage, from the beginning to the end of the case, 1891–3. I have preferred Francis Wellman's own record of his riposte to Dr. Wood, which he has reproduced in his classic: *The Art of Cross-Examination* (rev. ed., New York, 1924), at pp. 283–6, and referred to in his *Gentlemen of the Jury: Reminiscences of Thirty Years at the Bar* (New York, 1924). Aspects of the case have also been considered by Edmund L. Pearson: *Murder at Smutty Nose* (New York, 1925), chap. vii, and by Edward H. Smith: *Famous American Poison Mysteries* (London, 1927). The relation of Howe & Hummel to the case is alluded to by Richard H. Rovere in his fascinating study of these arch-shysters (New York, 1947). An entirely different version of the case from my own was written by Carlyle's mother, Mrs. Frances McCready Harris (Hope Ledyard): *The Judicial Murder of Carlyle Harris* (New York, 1893). Recollections of the case are found in Algernon Blackwood: *Episodes before Thirty* (New York, 1924).

XII. The Triangle Fire Case

Excellent coverage of the fire and trial will be found in the New York press, particularly in the *Call* and the *Jewish Daily Forward*. The role of the Fire Department in the disaster is sketched by Lowell M. Limpus: *History of the New York Fire Department* (New York, 1940), pp. 305 ff. Aron Steuer has treated his father's role at the trial in *Max D. Steuer, Trial Lawyer* (New York, 1950), pp. 83–110, a prettified version of the trial which I am unable to accept. Other treatments of the effects of the disaster will be found in Lewis Lorwin: *The Women's Garment Workers* (New York, 1924), Melech Epstein: *Jewish Labor in the U.S.A.* (New York, 1940), Benjamin Stolberg: *Tailor's Progress* (New York, 1944), and Maximilian Hurwitz: *The Workmen's Circle* (New York, 1936). On the extent of perjury in criminal trials, see Arthur Train: *From the District Attorney's Office* (New York, 1939), Basil H. Pollitt: "Defeat of Justice," *Florida Law Journal* (April 1949); Harry Hibschman: "You Do Solemnly Swear!" *Journal of Criminal Law*, XXIV (1934), 901–13.

XIII. The Clergyman, the Choir Singer, and the Pigwoman

In addition to the voluminous trial record, the case was extensively covered in the *New York Times,* the New York *World*, and the Philadelphia *Public Ledger,* and deplorably exploited by the New York *Daily Mirror*. Damon Runyon's daily coverage of the trial was reprinted in *Trials and Other Tribulations* (Philadelphia, 1947). The role of the newspapers in the case was treated by Carl E. B. Roberts: *The New World of Crime* (London, 1933) and by Alexander Woollcott: *Long, Long Ago* (New York, 1943).

XIV. The Case of Alger Hiss

The Congressional investigation is reported in *Hearings before the Committee on Un-American Activities: House of Representatives, 80 Cong., 2 Sess.* (Washington, D.C., 1948). The present analysis is based directly on a reading of the multivolume trial record, including the government and defense exhibits, the briefs on appeal, on petition for rehearing, and for a writ of certiorari. The initial stages of the Hiss case have been treated by Ralph Toledano and Victor Lasky: *Seeds of Treason* (New York, 1950). A more dispassionate and analytical account of the trials has been written by Alistair Cooke: *A Generation on Trial: U.S.A. v. Alger Hiss* (New York, 1950). The most dependable newspaper coverage was provided by John Chabot Smith in the *New York Herald Tribune,* by Alistair Cooke in the *Manchester Guardian,* and by Thomas O'Neill in the *Baltimore Sun.* Much of the remaining coverage was slipshod and slanted. Among the more provocative articles on the case are those by Diana Trilling in *Partisan Review* (1950), by Fred Rodell in the *Progressive* (April 1952), and comments in the form of a book review by Professor Charles Alan Wright in 35 *Minnesota Law Review* (1951), pp. 228–37. Julian Wadleigh's sensational confession story appeared in the New York *Post,* and Elizabeth Bentley told "all" in *McCall's* (1951). Whittaker Chambers's own story: *Witness* (New York, 1952) contains a wealth of absorbing details relating to the author's underground activities, but fails to clarify certain discrepancies in his testimony. See symposium in *Saturday Review* (May 24, 1952). Affidavits filed by the defense subsequent to the second trial indicate that Chambers had left the CP and secured work as translator for the Oxford University Press at least by early March 1938, though some Baltimore documents that he produced run to as late as April 1 of that year (Defense Notice of Hearing of Motion for New Trial, with Supplemental Affidavits, 1952).

A NOTE ON THE TYPE

THIS BOOK *was set on the Linotype in a face known by the style "Modern No. 21." The "modern" part does not mean modern in terms of* A.D. *1952. It indicates that Number 21 is a great-great-grandchild of faces that were* modern *in 1800—new as compared with the eighteenth-century types that preceded them, such as Caslon.*

The book was composed, printed, and bound by The Plimpton Press, Norwood, Massachusetts. The typography and binding design are by W. A. Dwiggins.